# ACADEMIC FREEDOM AND THE LAW

*Academic Freedom and the Law: A Comparative Study* provides a critical analysis of the law relating to academic freedom in three major jurisdictions: the United Kingdom, Germany and the United States. The book outlines the various claims that may be made to academic freedom by individual university teachers and by universities and other higher education institutions, and it examines the justifications that have been put forward for these claims. Three separate chapters deal with the legal principles of academic freedom in the United Kingdom, Germany and the United States. A further chapter is devoted to the restrictions on freedom of research that may be imposed by the regulation of clinical trials, by intellectual property laws and by the terms of contracts between researchers and the companies sponsoring medical and other research. The book also examines the impact of recent terrorism laws on the teaching and research freedom of academics, and it discusses their freedom to speak about general political and social topics unrelated to their work.

This is the first comparative study of a subject of fundamental importance to all academics and others working in universities. It emphasises the importance of academic freedom while pointing out that, on occasion, exaggerated claims have been made to its exercise.

D1610465

# Academic Freedom and the Law

## A Comparative Study

Eric Barendt

·H A R T·
PUBLISHING

**OXFORD AND PORTLAND, OREGON**
2010

Published in the United Kingdom by Hart Publishing Ltd
16C Worcester Place Oxford OX1 2JW
Tel: +44 (0)1865 517530
Fax: +44 (0)1865 510710
Email: *mail@hartpub.co.uk*
http://www.hartpub.co.uk

Published in North America (US and Canada) by
Hart Publishing
c/o International Specialized Book Services
920 NE 58th Avenue, Suite 300
Portland, OR 97213-3786
USA
Tel: +1 (503) 287-3093 or toll-free: (800) 944-6190
Fax: +1 (503) 280-8832
Email: *orders@isbs.com*
http://www.isbs.com

© Eric Barendt 2010

British Library Cataloguing in Publication Data
Data Available

ISBN: 978-1-84113- 694-3

Typeset by Compuscript Ltd, Shannon
Printed and bound in Great Britain by
CPI Antony Rowe, Chippenham and Eastbourne

# *Preface*

It is unlikely that university professors and lecturers spend much of their working lives actively thinking about academic freedom. But they generally assume it is fundamental; they consider exercise of the freedom essential for serious academic work, distinguishing university employment from work in business, industry and the civil service. In England academic freedom has largely been taken for granted. Lawyers in this country have shown little interest in the subject, perhaps because it has lacked until recently a clear legal dimension. So it has hardly been discussed in English periodical literature, and I could find only one book, *The Concept of Academic Freedom* by Kevin McGuinness, that contains any extensive discussion of this area of law in the United Kingdom. In contrast, there is a rich literature in the United States, Germany and, to some extent, other jurisdictions. So this book has been written to fill a major gap in English legal writing.

It is particularly important now to fill this gap, since in the last few years scholars and scientists have become increasingly concerned with what they perceive to be growing threats to their academic freedom. These threats come from a number of sources. Medical researchers argue that drugs companies or other sponsors impose restraints on the freedom to publish research findings so the sponsors can protect their intellectual property rights or their commercial reputation. Social scientists sometimes find troubling the restrictions imposed by ethics committees or by data protection laws, while criminologists and drugs advisers have complained of the restraints imposed by the governments for which they work. More generally, many academics consider that their freedom to teach and research is increasingly circumscribed, in particular by the demands of government to show that their work is socially relevant and economically productive and by the requirements of the 'managerial' university, which often sees itself as a business rather than a community of independent scholars.

This book deals with all these issues from a legal perspective, though not always at the level of detail that would be required by a practising lawyer. My intention has been to discuss academic freedom questions in general terms, exploring how they have arisen and how they have sometimes been resolved in decided court cases. It discusses the legal principles and court decisions in three major jurisdictions—the United Kingdom, Germany and the United States—for it is only through comparative law that we can begin sensibly to consider how problems arising in one system are of more than local interest and how they might best be resolved. The opening chapters of the book discuss some theoretical questions, which pundits on academic freedom ignore or treat cursorily: what is academic freedom, how does it relate to freedom of speech, and how can the freedom be justified? It is only when these questions have been answered, at least provisionally, that we can assess how seriously academic freedom is threatened by, say, legal restrictions on the conduct of research or by recent anti-terrorism laws.

This book does not attempt to answer the critical practical question regarding how much academic freedom has been lost in the last few decades in the United Kingdom, let alone in other jurisdictions. Giving a precise answer to that question would require prolonged empirical work over two or three years. What this book does show is that there are real *threats* to its exercise emanating from the sources referred to earlier in this Preface, and they are of concern to a number of scientists and scholars. And my impression based on several interviews and on my experience as a member of the Council for Academic Freedom and Academic Standards (CAFAS) is that these threats are now significant, particularly in the post-92 universities, where the managerial culture is most prevalent. University professors and lecturers should take academic freedom seriously, not to safeguard their own prerogatives but to assert the values of cultural independence and the search for truth with which the freedom is associated. (See the arguments in chapter three.)

My own interest in this subject began in 2005 when I was finishing the revision of my earlier book, *Freedom of Speech*. In particular I was intrigued by the relationship of freedom of speech and academic freedom: what does the latter add to freedom of speech (or expression), a fundamental human right that can be claimed by everyone, whether or not they work in a university or other higher education institution? I was also interested in the extent to which academic freedom should be regarded as an institutional freedom, similar to press or broadcasting freedom, a right that could be claimed by universities rather than by the individual professors and researchers who work in them. (These complex issues are explored throughout the book but particularly in chapter two.) Another personal note is that I was exercising my own academic freedom when I decided to do the research for and to write this book: my chair has been in Media Law, but nobody at UCL thought it wrong for me to spend the best part of five years on this project rather than on writing more articles on libel law or broadcasting regulation. UCL respected academic freedom!

I have endeavoured to take note of recent important legal and other developments in the United Kingdom up to the beginning of May 2010. Comments on the chapters dealing with German and US law (chapters five and six) confirm that they presented an accurate account of the law in those countries towards the end of 2009; I am confident that the exposition of legal principles in those jurisdictions remains sound at the time of writing this Preface.

I owe an enormous debt to the large number of people who have helped me at various stages in the course of writing this book. I am grateful to David Bentley, David Erdos, Hector McQueen, Gillian Morris, David Palfreyman and David Rabban, all of whom read two or more chapters, and to Aubrey Blumsohn, Bill Cornish, Thomas Groβ and Alex Weedon, who commented on particular chapters or sections. David Coleman, Roger Gair, David Healy, Paul Heywood, Sean Matthews, Nancy Olivieri and Rod Thornton all commented on aspects of the text of particular concern to them. I could not have written chapter ten without the provision of material by Chris Brand and without the help of others, in particular Halla Beloff, Vincent Egan and Hector McQueen. I would also like to thank David Erdos for encouraging me to explore the implications of data protection law for academic freedom, and Tim Hope, Sean Matthews, Dario Milo, Nancy Olivieri, David Palfreyman, Justine Pila and Michael Robertson for supplying me with material. I benefited at early stages of this work from conversations with Professor Malcolm Grant, Provost of UCL, and with the late Professor John Griffith, the founder of the Council for Academic Freedom and Democracy (the predecessor of CAFAS) and the most intrepid defender of academic freedom from the 1960s. Nicholas Cropp, a law graduate from UCL, provided invaluable research assistance in the summer of 2005; I am also grateful to Daniel Greineder for his work on German law in 2006.

The research involved two trips outside the United Kingdom. I am grateful to Professor Hans-Heinrich Trute, Dean of the Law Department at the University of Hamburg, for inviting me to spend the month of October 2008 to work on German law. I took the opportunity to discuss the German concept of scientific freedom, *Wissenschaftsfreiheit*, with Professor Trute, his colleagues and research assistants. Professor James Weinstein invited me to a workshop and panel discussion at Arizona State University, Phoenix, in March 2009, where aspects of academic freedom and the freedom to raise unorthodox ideas in universities were treated to vigorous debate. While in Phoenix, I benefited enormously from talking to a number of American scholars, in particular Professor Robert Post, former Counsel to the American Association of University Professors and now Dean of Yale Law School, and Professor James Moeser, Chancellor Emeritus of the University of North Carolina at Chapel Hill.

I would like to thank the Leverhulme Trust for the award of a Research Fellowship for the academic year 2008–09, and UCL for granting me study leave that year from normal teaching and administrative duties. Without the Fellowship and study leave, I would never have had the time to do the necessary research for this book, let alone to write it. Finally, I am grateful to Richard Hart and his colleagues for their patience in waiting for delivery of the manuscript and for their prompt production of the book, and to Lisa Gourd for her skilful editing of the text.

As always, my greatest debt is to my wife, Sheila, without whose encouragement and support I could never have completed this book.

Eric Barendt
May 2010

# Table of Contents

# Notes on Abbreviations

The German abbreviations used in the notes may be unfamiliar, so a list is appended here. The second group of abbreviations are of leading law reviews.

| | |
|---|---|
| BVerfGE | *Entscheidungen des Bundesverfassungsgerichts* (Decisions of the German Constitutional Court) |
| BVerwGE | *Entscheidungen des Bundesverwaltungsgerichts* (Decisions of the German Administrative Court) |
| BGBl | *Bundesgesetzblatt* (Federal Statute Gazette) |
| FS | *Festschrift* (Commemorative essays) |

| | |
|---|---|
| AöR | Archiv des öffentlichen Rechts |
| DÖV | Die Öffentliche Verwaltung |
| DVBl | Deutsches Verwaltungsblatt |
| JZ | Juristenzeitung |
| NJW | Neue Juristische Wochenschrift |
| NVwZ | Neue Zeitschrift für Verwaltungsrecht |
| NVwZ-RR | Neue Zeitschrift für Verwaltungsrecht-Rechtsprechungsreport |
| VVDStRL | Veröffentlichungen der Vereinigung der Deutschen Staatsrechtslehrer |

# Table of Cases

## Germany

## United Kingdom

## United States

## Other Jurisdictions

### Australia

### Canada

### European Court of Human Rights

### Hong Kong

## New Zealand

## South Africa

# Table of Legislation

## Germany

## United Kingdom

## European Union

## Hong Kong

## Japan

## New Zealand

## Portugal

## South Africa

## Spain

# 1

# *Introduction*

## I. THE PUZZLE OF ACADEMIC FREEDOM

GORDON CHILDE, A distinguished archaeologist and for a short period Prime Minister of New South Wales, once wrote, 'It is rather easy to talk rot about "academic freedom" and if the phrase is to remain a useful slogan it must be used with caution and reserve.'[1] Sir Peter Swinnerton-Dyer, giving evidence to the Nolan Committee on Standards in Public Life, seems to have been equally sceptical about academic freedom, referring to it as 'one of those motherhood phrases which is imported into arguments where it actually has no relevant place whatsoever…'[2] Yet academic freedom is highly prized by the vast majority of academics and by university vice-chancellors and presidents. The Minister of State who was responsible from 2005 to 2008 for higher education in England, Bill Rammell MP, regarded it as a fundamental principle of higher education, pointing to its incorporation in UK legislation governing universities.[3] In the United States claims to academic freedom by university professors have been

---

[1] Letter of 21 May 1952 to National Council of Civil Liberties, accepting invitation to chair a small committee examining the state of academic freedom in the United Kingdom, available in the papers of the Council for Academic Freedom and Democracy (CAFD) held in the archives of Hull University. On the CAFD, see below ch 4, s II(D).

[2] (1996, Cm 3270) para 93. The Nolan Committee itself was less hesitant, stating that the true importance of academic freedom should not be underestimated, if it is properly defined (ibid, para 97). Sir Peter Swinnerton-Dyer, a mathematician, was the last Chairman of the University Grants Committee from 1983, and the first Chief Executive of the Universities Funding Council, which replaced it in 1989. See below ch 4, s III(B).

[3] HC Debates, vol 458, col 239WH (20 March 2007). For the UK Education Reform Act 1988, s 202, see below ch 2, s III(A) and ch 4, s III.

vigorously asserted since the early years of the twentieth century, while Brennan J, delivering a Supreme Court opinion in 1967, wrote that the freedom is 'a special concern of the First Amendment'.[4] Moreover, academic freedom is guaranteed by explicit provisions in many constitutions, notably the German Basic Law and the Constitutions of Spain, Portugal, Japan, and South Africa, and is now one of the rights covered by the European Union Charter of Fundamental Rights.[5] It must therefore be taken seriously both as an idea and as a matter of legal and constitutional right.

Professors typically argue that academic freedom gives them rights to determine for themselves the topics of their research, their research methodologies and the manner in which they teach their subjects.[6] They may further claim that they have freedom to choose what they teach, irrespective of the requirements of their departments or directions issued by their deans or heads of department. They may also assert wide rights to contribute to public discussion on a range of issues, including educational policy, and to criticise the administration of the universities that employ them. How far they actually enjoy these rights is the subject of this book, which explores the legal protection of academic freedom in the United Kingdom, Germany and the United States. When academics make claims of this kind, they are asserting rights that are rarely, if ever, enjoyed by other employees. Most employees, apart from some highly skilled professionals such as doctors and lawyers, are not similarly free to determine how they work and are certainly not entitled to choose the area of their work or to make public comment on the conduct of their employers. So university professors and lecturers appear to claim work-related rights that put them in a position of privilege relative

---

[4] *Keyishian v Board of Regents of New York State University* 385 US 589, 603 (1967), discussed below in ch 6, s III(A).

[5] Art 13 reads: 'The arts and scientific research shall be free of constraint. Academic freedom shall be respected.' For comparative surveys of the legal protection of academic freedom in European states, see M Fehling, 'Commentary on Article 5,3' in R Dolzer, C Waldhoff and K Graßhof (eds), *Bonner Kommentar* (Heidelberg, CF Müller, 2004) paras 293–96; P Häberle, 'Die Freiheit der Wissenschaften im Verfassungsstaat' (1985) 110 *AöR* 329; and T Groß, *Die Autonomie der Wissenschaft im europäischen Rechtsvergleich* (Baden-Baden, Nomos, 1992).

[6] Often the term 'professors' is used in this book as a shorthand term for all members of a university's academic staff; it is not used to suggest that professors enjoy more academic freedom than lecturers, readers or research fellows.

to other employees. That is why academic freedom is so puzzling: what could justify such a privileged position?

This puzzle is particularly acute when we consider whether academic freedom confers special rights on academics to speak freely in public about, say, educational policy and to criticise the universities that employ them. For freedom of speech is a basic constitutional or human right that in principle we should all equally enjoy. It would surely be odd if academic staff could claim in effect a wider freedom than other employees to speak without constraint on matters connected with their employment. Yet this is what many university professors claim as an essential aspect of their academic freedom. Indeed, on one view, to be discussed in the next chapter,[7] academic freedom really means an unrestricted freedom for academic staff to put forward their views on any topic of public concern, no matter how offensive they are to the community and irrespective of any limits imposed by academic institutions.[8] Chapter two of this book explains why that view is too simple. But academic freedom is often treated as conferring some special freedom for university professors to engage in public debate on matters outside their expertise, when comparable speech by other employees is not permitted by their employers. This freedom of extramural speech is one of the most complex areas of academic freedom law; it is fully discussed in chapter nine, as well as being explored in the chapters dealing with the law in particular jurisdictions.

Obviously the puzzle would be solved if persuasive arguments can be made for affording academics some special freedom. These arguments are explored in chapter three. Historically, the justifications for academic freedom have been connected with the role of universities in providing a special place for reflection, inquiry and discussion, unconstrained by the requirements of the state and other authorities, religious or secular. An important argument for academic freedom is that it would be inconsistent with the role of universities to place limits on what their academic staff can teach and research;[9] indeed, it is this freedom that distinguishes a university from the research department of a government agency or of a commercial company where the employer

---

[7] See below ch 2, s II.

[8] Statement of Academic Freedom issued by UK Academics for Academic Freedom in December 2006.

[9] See below ch 3, s III(A).

is entitled to direct the inquiries of its staff. The freedom is termed 'academic freedom' rather than 'intellectual freedom', precisely because there is a close, perhaps even an essential, link between the liberties of professors and lecturers and the functions of the *university* that employs them. This does not, however, apply in Germany, where the rights of university professors and researchers are based on the constitutional right to scientific freedom (*Wissenschaftsfreiheit*), which can be claimed by anyone engaged in serious scholarly research and teaching.[10]

The link between academic freedom, as it is generally understood in the United Kingdom and the United States, and the role of universities gives rise to its own difficulties. If it is the special role of the university that gives rise to the liberties claimed by its academic staff, it would seem to follow that the academic head of a department, almost always a professor him or herself, could claim academic freedom when directing colleagues what they should teach or even which topics they should research. Further, a university itself may assert academic freedom when it decides to close down a department that attracts few students or from which, in its view, little good research emanates. (More controversially, as recent episodes in the United Kingdom have shown,[11] universities may concentrate on the practical scientific subjects favoured by the government and then, to save expenditure, shut down a small arts department that lacks this merit; that sort of decision is certainly taken in the exercise of the university's autonomy but would be harder to relate to a genuine academic freedom claim.) Conflicts between individual and institutional claims to academic freedom are discussed in general terms in chapter two and in the context of particular legal systems in later chapters.[12] They represent one of the most intractable issues in this area of law. In this respect, academic freedom is particularly puzzling. For when we are talking about freedom of speech or rights to privacy, we are clear that we are referring for the most part to the entitlement of *individuals*, even though (increasingly often in the United States)

---

[10] See below ch 5, ss I and III(B).

[11] In 2010, a number of universities, notably King's College London and the University of Sussex, announced cuts in humanities departments to cope with reductions in their funding. See *Times Higher Education,* 11 Feb 2010, 10; and 4 March 2010, 8.

[12] In particular, see ch 2, s V; ch 5, s IV(D); ch 6, s IV; and ch 8, s II(D).

corporations may lay claim to them.[13] We are less sure about this when we speak about academic freedom, an entitlement that is claimed in roughly equal measure by both universities and their academic staff.

There are then a number of theoretical difficulties within the idea of academic freedom. Conflicting claims to it may be made both by individuals and by the institutions which employ them. Partly because of these conflicts, it is difficult to define academic freedom in a sentence or two, or to be sure who can successfully assert a right to exercise the freedom. At the root of these difficulties is the question: how can academic freedom be justified, granted that it appears to confer special freedoms or rights on certain individuals and institutions? If that question can be answered, then we might be able to resolve some issues of principle; in particular, we might have a clearer idea of what academic freedom means, what its scope is and who can make legitimate claims to its exercise in particular circumstances.

## II. A VULNERABLE FREEDOM

Even if we can resolve these theoretical difficulties, academic freedom seems to be particularly fragile. Certainly, it is more vulnerable than the civil liberties or fundamental rights to which everyone is entitled, for example, freedoms of conscience and religion, freedom of speech, freedom from arbitrary arrest and detention, and fair trial rights. However persuasive the case for academic freedom may be, it is unlikely to enjoy widespread popular support. For many people, university life, with its traditional long vacations and relatively relaxed formal working schedules, is a legitimate object for satire and contempt.[14] It is easy, and now fashionable, to be critical of professional entitlements which give some people—university professors and other teachers—employment freedoms and privileges that others do not enjoy. Further, as Gordon

---

[13] For the freedom of speech of corporations, see E Barendt, *Freedom of Speech* (Oxford, Oxford University Press, 2007) ch 3, s 3(ii).

[14] Gordon Graham has argued that popular campus novels, such as Malcolm Bradbury's *The History Man* and David Lodge's *Changing Places* and *Small World* play a part in exposing universities to ridicule: *The Institution of Intellectual Values* (Exeter, Imprint Academic, 2005) 23–26.

Childe rightly said,[15] inflated claims to academic freedom do the idea
little service and leave it open to ridicule.

With the increasing numbers of students attending them, universities
may, however, now enjoy the respect of the general public—probably
more than individual academics do. But it is very doubtful whether
that respect means there is popular support for the idea of academic
freedom, whether that is understood in terms of university independence from government or of the teaching and research freedoms
of individual academics. What is clear is that the role of universities
has changed enormously over the last fifty years or so, in line with
the requirements imposed on them by governments and the popular
expectations that have been encouraged by these demands.[16] In the
United Kingdom, there are many more universities than there used to
be in the 1950s, and they are required to teach many more students.[17]
Universities are expected to contribute to the economic well-being
of the country and to be responsive to national needs.[18] Links with
employers to ensure that graduates are able to meet their requirements
are encouraged. Higher education institutions have a responsibility to
increase the public's understanding of complex decisions,[19] presumably
because that task should not be left to the media, politicians and political parties. Academics may be required to point to the economic or
social impact of their research when it is assessed for university funding
or for financial support from research councils.[20]

British universities therefore no longer provide ivory towers, dedi-
cated to the exchange of ideas and the teaching only of what is

[15] See above n 1.

[16] For a general survey of the changing role of universities in Britain in the
context of higher education politics, see R Stevens, *University to Uni*, revised edn
(London, Politico's, 2005).

[17] In 2008 there were 166 higher education institutions in the United Kingdom,
116 of which were characterised as universities (see the Universities UK website).
It is estimated that there are about 1,960,000 students.

[18] See the Report of the National Committee of Inquiry into Higher Education
under the chairmanship of Ron Dearing (1997), esp ch 1. Lord Dearing (1930–
2009) was a distinguished civil servant and chairman and chief executive of the
Post Office.

[19] Ibid, para 5.39.

[20] See below ch 4, s IV(E). The extent to which 'impact' will be taken into
account in funding arrangements under the new Research Excellence Framework
was not determined at the moment of writing.

intellectually, as distinct from practically or socially, significant. The vision of the university outlined by John Henry Newman in his classic work *The Idea of a University Defined and Illustrated*[21] was no longer shared by the mid-twentieth century, for Newman considered that universities existed essentially to teach universal knowledge rather than to conduct research. But the view that knowledge is a good in itself, fundamental to Newman's argument, may not be universally accepted now,[22] for universities are expected to conduct research that produces socially useful dividends and to equip students with knowledge they can use in their future employment. Moreover, universities find it difficult to resist these changes—even assuming that they want to—because, at least in Europe, they are more or less entirely dependent on public financing, which is ultimately made available by the government.

Academic freedom is clearly vulnerable in this climate. Universities cannot just teach and research what they and their academic staff consider worthy of study, but must bear in mind the needs of business, industry and the wider society in which they are established.[23] Arrangements for staff development and changes to the methods of governing universities have considerable implications for academic freedom.[24] The Dearing Committee, which carried out a major inquiry into higher education in 1997, insisted that ultimately a single body should have responsibility for decisions within a university, and it should have a majority of lay, that is, non-academic members[25]—a requirement that Oxford and Cambridge academics continue to resist, to some extent because it would be incompatible in their view with academic freedom.[26] The Dearing Committee considered that academic freedom confers responsibilities as well as rights; further, individuals and universities share a duty of accountability for their work and for the proper use of their resources. Dearing and other Committees in the United

---

[21]  Ed with introduction by IT Ker (Oxford, Clarendon Press, 1976). Originally given as lectures in 1852, Newman's discourses on the functions of the university were originally published in 1873.

[22]  See Graham (above n 14) 80–98.

[23]  For a discussion of these questions in Germany, see D Grimm, *Wissenschaftsfreiheit vor neuen Grenzen?* (Wallstein, Göttingen, 2007).

[24]  See below ch 2, s III(C) for claims by academics to control or participate in the taking of academic decisions.

[25]  Above n 18, paras 15.42–15.49.

[26]  See below ch 4, s V(C) and (D).

Kingdom from the 1970s have emphasised the importance of high standards of professional management to ensure these responsibilities are met.[27] Comparable concerns have influenced the moves in Germany to the 'managed' university, as distinct from the traditional model, in which university professors took all the significant decisions.[28]

In addition to the constant and increasing constraints arising from political pressure and from the changing expectations of universities, academic freedom seems to be particularly vulnerable during periods of social tension. Academic freedom in the United States had been strongly protected as a matter of university culture from the 1920s,[29] but that did not shield it from significant threats during the McCarthy period of the early 1950s.[30] Professors were frequently hounded for suspected membership of the Communist party or for sympathy for its objectives; they were required to take loyalty oaths and attend Congressional committee inquiries, and some were dismissed for failure to comply with these requirements. There may be similar dangers now arising from the panic induced by 9/11 and the bombings in London in July 2005; for instance, new anti-terrorism laws which proscribe the possession of material likely to be useful to someone committing or preparing an act of terrorism might be applied to bona fide researchers investigating extremist organisations.[31] Robert O'Neil, a leading American academic freedom scholar, has concluded that the reaction in the United States to 9/11 has not, hitherto at least, posed the same dangers for academic freedom as the hysteria engendered by McCarthyism.[32] The point to note, however, is that the freedom, like, of course, more fundamental liberties, may be even more liable than usual to legal and other constraints during periods of social anxiety.

Quite apart from these constraints, academic freedom may also be vulnerable to private pressures. These can arise principally from

---

[27] Further discussed below in ch 4, ss III and IV.

[28] See below ch 5, s VI.

[29] See below ch 6, s II.

[30] R O'Neil, *Academic Freedom in the Wired World* (Cambridge, MA, Harvard University Press, 2008) esp 23–25, 61–63 and 90–99.

[31] See the UK Terrorism Act 2000, s 58, discussed below in ch 8, s II(A).

[32] O'Neil, *Academic Freedom in the Wired World* (above n 30) ch 4; and R O'Neil, 'Academic Freedom in the Post-September 11 Era: An Old Game with New Rules' in E Gerstmann and MJ Streb (eds), *Academic Freedom and the Dawn of a New Century* (Stanford, Stanford University Press, 2006) esp 50–60.

two particular sources. Institutes or professorships may be endowed by companies or associations, which may expect the academics they finance to pursue research compatible with their own commercial or political objectives. The acceptance of such endowments by a university might compromise the freedom of its academic staff freely to choose the subjects of their research, the way in which they teach, or how they speak outside the campus. For example, the subscribers who financed a Chair of Modern Greek and Byzantine History, Language and Literature at King's College, London were exasperated when Arnold Toynbee, the first holder of the Chair, wrote press articles drawing attention to the atrocities committed by the Greek army in Asia Minor in the early 1920s; largely as a result of their pressure, Toynbee resigned in 1924.[33]

A second and now much more important type of constraint is that imposed by pharmaceutical and other companies when they commission and finance research in university laboratories or in partnership with university scientists; typically, contractual provisions prevent university researchers from publishing their findings without prior submission to the funding company for its approval or until a certain period has elapsed to enable a patent application to be filed. Alternatively, researchers may be denied access to data that would enable them to substantiate the findings that the company would like the research to establish. These restrictions are enforceable under contract law and through actions for breach of confidence; arguably, they amount to significant legal constraints on the exercise of academic freedom.[34] They have not received the same degree of scrutiny by courts and commentators, as have the limits imposed by government; that may be because traditionally constitutional and other fundamental rights are more fully protected against state action than they are against interference by private parties.[35] But Robert O'Neil has identified them as posing 'the gravest of new threats to the integrity and independence of research'.[36]

---

[33] R Clogg, *Politics and the Academy* (London, Frank Cass in association with the Centre of Contemporary Greek Studies, King's College London, 1986). See below ch 4, s II(C).
[34] See below ch 7, s IV for a full discussion of these issues.
[35] In the United States and Canada, constitutional rights are guaranteed only against the state or government, so it is hardly surprising that in those jurisdictions the restraints imposed by drugs companies cannot be challenged easily in the courts.
[36] O'Neil, *Academic Freedom in the Wired World* (above n 30) 274.

The particular episodes discussed in chapter seven of this book bring out the serious implications of these restraints, particularly for medical research.

## III. THE SCOPE OF THE BOOK

It may be helpful to explain how these topics are treated in this book. Chapters two and three are devoted respectively to two general theoretical questions: what is academic freedom and how can academic freedom be justified? These are questions of political philosophy as much as they are of law. It is now familiar jurisprudence that legal analysis, particularly of constititutional issues, cannot be sharply distinguished from the arguments of moral and political philosophy. A court can decide a controversial academic freedom claim, just as it can do justice to comparable free speech arguments,[37] only once it has formed a view about the proper scope of these claims in the light of their overall justification. (Courts are, of course, bound also to take account of relevant statutes and case law precedents when determining the scope of academic freedom, as they are when considering the application of other rights and freedoms.) So chapters two and three are concerned with arguments of political principle, though some reference, particularly in chapter two, is made to legal sources to show how these principles are reflected in legislation and in court opinions. Decisions of the courts give more precision to abstract claims to academic freedom, as well as exploring their implications for the resolution of concrete disputes.

There is no simple definition of academic freedom. But a number of distinctive academic freedom claims can be identified. They are most often made by individual professors and other university teachers; other institutional claims may be made by universities themselves. These different claims and the conflicts between them are discussed in chapter two. It is better to explore these various understandings of academic freedom before we consider in chapter three whether it is possible to justify it, whether it assumes the form of an individual or of an institutional claim. As we have seen already, academic freedom is a puzzle, for it appears to give privileges to a particular professional group and—or perhaps alternatively—to the institutions that employ

---

[37] See Barendt (above n 13) ch 1, esp 2–6.

them. So good arguments must be found to justify it, particularly to allow its extension to cover 'extramural speech', which appears to allow professors wider rights to freedom of expression than those enjoyed by other employees.[38]

The following three chapters (four through six) discuss the treatment of academic freedom in three jurisdictions: the United Kingdom, Germany and the United States of America. It was in Germany that the idea of academic freedom (now guaranteed by the Basic Law in its provision for *Wissenschaftsfreiheit*[39]) was first given theoretical formulation early in the nineteenth century by Wilhelm von Humboldt[40] and then given legal content to provide university professors (and students) with protection from government direction. Professors at German (and other European) universities are state officials (*Beamte*); in the absence of academic freedom they could be directed in the same way as other civil servants. The German principle is not only important and distinctive in itself;[41] it also influenced thinking on academic freedom in the United States towards the end of the nineteenth century.[42] Academic freedom in the United States, however, soon developed in different directions, particularly in its recognition for a wide freedom for university professors to speak freely on issues of public concern outside their expertise: the so-called 'freedom of extramural expression'.[43] Moreover, the US Supreme Court has formulated in the last fifty years a constitutional

---

[38] See below ch 3, s IV and ch 9.

[39] In the nineteenth century the more usual terms were *Lehrfreiheit* (freedom to teach) and *Lernfreiheit* (the freedom of students to choose their courses).

[40] Wilhelm von Humboldt (1767–1835) was a distinguished philosopher, linguist and diplomat; he was appointed Minister of Education in 1809 to reform the Prussian education system and established the Friedrich-Wilhelms University in Berlin (now Humboldt University) along liberal lines.

[41] See below ch 5.

[42] For a short account of this influence, see WP Metzger, *Academic Freedom in the Age of the University* (New York, Columbia University Press, 1961) ch 3. Metzger points as evidence to the foundation of Johns Hopkins University in 1876 as a research university on the German model and to the fact that over half of the signatories to the first Report in 1915 of the American Association of University Professors on Academic Freedom had studied in Germany.

[43] JR Searle has taken this distinction further: JR Searle, 'Two Concepts of Academic Freedom' in EL Pincoffs (ed), *The Concept of Academic Freedom* (Austin, University of Texas Press, 1972) 86–97. He argues that the US has adopted a General Theory of academic freedom under which professors and students enjoy the same rights to freedom of expression and association as they enjoy as citizens,

academic freedom under the First Amendment guarantee of freedom of speech, which protects the institutional freedom of universities to take decisions free from challenge.[44] Academic freedom as a legal topic has been extensively discussed in both Germany and in United States, and there is a rich case law in both countries.

In the United Kingdom academic freedom has largely been protected until the last twenty five years or so as a matter of convention and practice, which was almost invariably honoured within universities, and between them and government. Moreover, after some confrontations with the Crown towards the end of the seventeenth century, the old universities of Oxford and Cambridge and their colleges have enjoyed substantial independence from government control. A tradition of university autonomy was established from which other universities founded in the nineteenth and early twentieth centuries generally benefited.[45] Put shortly, academic freedom could be and probably was taken for granted. It was only in 1988 with the abolition of academic tenure that a legal right to academic freedom was formulated.[46] There is virtually no case law on academic freedom in the United Kingdom to compare with the rich US and German jurisprudence, and relatively little legal commentary on the topic, as distinct from discussion of the principle in political science or education journals. But academic freedom issues have been discussed in a few controversial episodes in British universities in the last fifty years. Some of these (occasionally bitter) disputes are discussed in chapter four and in other chapters.[47]

Chapters seven through nine are concerned with three special contexts where academic freedom deserves separate and fuller treatment. The first is the imposition of various restrictions on the freedom of researchers, for example, to conduct clinical trials or to publish their research findings. The former freedom is limited by regulations intended to safeguard the welfare of members of the public participating in these trials, but publication freedom can be constrained in a variety of ways: by intellectual property laws; by the terms of government research

---

in contrast to a Special Theory (found in Germany) that ties academic freedom to the role of universities. See below ch 3, s II.

[44] See below ch 6, s III.
[45] See below ch 4, s II.
[46] Education Reform Act 1988, s 202 (fully discussed below in ch 4, s III).
[47] See in particular ch 4, ss II(D) and IV(C)–(E); ch 9, s III(B); and ch 10.

contracts or of contracts with pharmaceutical or other companies financing medical research; or by data protection laws. Chapter seven examines how far academic freedom arguments can be used in the legal systems considered in this book to challenge these various restraints. Chapter eight is concerned with the protection of academic freedom in the present climate of fear of terrorism, when legislation may inhibit the freedom of researchers to examine, let alone publish material that might be of use to a prospective terrorist.

As already indicated,[48] one of the greatest areas of academic freedom controversy concerns the freedom of extramural expression—the freedom claimed by university professors to speak outside their own disciplines and expertise on matters of public concern. A university will often argue that it is entitled to discipline a member of its staff for bringing it into disrepute, if he or she publishes particularly controversial or unacceptable opinions, say, on the intelligence of different ethnic groups or on the Holocaust. On one view, academics in this context are really claiming to exercise broad free speech rights, rather than their academic freedom. Chapter nine discusses this question, as well as the complex case law in this area. Many of the cases come from the United States, where they may raise conflicts between individual and institutional academic freedom, but there have been a few interesting episodes in the United Kingdom, where the scope of extramural expression has been at issue. The final chapter, chapter ten, discusses one of these episodes in detail.

In the United States and, to a much lesser extent, in other jurisdictions,[49] academic freedom has sometimes been claimed by high school teachers and students. Indeed, cases involving these claims have on occasion been extensively discussed in litigation where academic freedom has been asserted by university professors—without much attention being paid to the distinction between schools and universities.[50]

---

[48] See above p 3.

[49] One interesting Canadian case is *Morin v Board of Trustees of Regional Administrative Unit No 3* (2002) 213 DLR (4th) 17, in which the majority of the Supreme Court of Prince Edward Island upheld the free expression right of a high school teacher to show a film about religious fundamentalism to his class against the objection of the school board; the dissent took the view that the teacher was not entitled to claim academic freedom and freedom of expression in this context.

[50] See, for example, the extensive discussion in *Urofsky v Gilmore* 216 F3d 401 (4th Cir, 2000), on which see below ch 6, s IV(C), of *Boring v The Buncombe County*

Schools are not institutions of higher education, so the argument for extending academic freedom to them and to school students is weak. The justifications for academic freedom discussed at some length in chapter three of this book simply do not apply at all in the school context, or apply only very weakly. So this book does not discuss the possible extension of academic freedom to cover claims by school teachers and students. It should, however, be pointed out that in Germany it would be possible for a school teacher, and even conceivably a school student, to assert *Wissenschaftsfreiheit* (scientific rather than academic freedom).[51] For that right can be claimed by anyone engaged in serious scholarly research and study; it is not confined to academic staff working in universities or other higher education institutions. But it has rarely been claimed outside the context of higher education.

*Board of Education* 136 F 3d 364 (4th Cir, 1998) where the Fourth Circuit Court of Appeals, 7–6, rejected the free speech and academic freedom claim of a high school teacher to determine the curriculum.

[51] See below ch 5, ss I and III(B).

# 2

## *What Is Academic Freedom?*


### I. INTRODUCTION

LORD ROBBINS, WHO had much to say about the subject, found a simple definition of academic freedom far from easy.[1] Edmund Pincoffs, the editor of a distinguished collection of essays by American lawyers and philosophers on the topic, also took this view: there is 'no clear and widely accepted definition or justification of academic freedom and no settled account of the way in which claims of violation may be assessed'.[2] Admittedly, there are similar uncertainties with regard to the definition of well-established constitutional freedoms such as freedom of speech and the right to personal privacy. The scope of those rights remains controversial even today: to what extent, for example, does freedom of speech confer rights on commercial advertisers; and do politicians and celebrities enjoy privacy rights when they are photographed in public? Yet these difficult questions do not cast doubt on the coherence of claims that there are rights to freedom of speech or to personal privacy and that they should generally be protected. In the case of these claims the strong moral and political arguments for their recognition have been widely accepted, while the decisions of constitutional and other courts have largely defined their scope. Consequently, it has become virtually impossible to

---

[1] Lord Robbins, 'Of Academic Freedom', British Academy lecture given on 6 July 1966 (Oxford, Oxford University Press, 1966) 2. Lionel Robbins (1898–1984) was a distinguished economist and head of the Economics Department at the London School of Economics; he was the chairman of a committee set up to consider the reform of higher education in the United Kingdom in 1962. See below n 26.

[2] EL Pincoffs, 'Introduction' in EL Pincoffs (ed), *The Concept of Academic Freedom* (Austin, University of Texas Press, 1975) vii.

question their coherence, though of course there may still be argument about their application to particular circumstances.

Academic freedom seems to be different from these established rights. Doubts are expressed not only in respect of borderline claims, as with freedom of speech or personal privacy, but with regard to its central meaning. Sceptics challenge the coherence of academic freedom even in core areas, such as, for example, the claim of university professors and lecturers to teach their courses as they think appropriate, rather than as directed by their heads of department. The scope of freedom of research—for many university staff the most crucial aspect of academic freedom—is far from settled.[3] Further, it is unclear how far academic freedom allows professors and lecturers to criticise openly the administrations of their universities or confers on them rights to participate in university governance.[4]

There are understandable reasons for these doubts and difficulties. In the first place, there is relatively little case law, even in the United States, on the scope and meaning of academic freedom, compared to the rich jurisprudence on well-established constitutional and human rights to be found now in many jurisdictions. In the United Kingdom a handful of statutory provisions recognise academic freedom, but its meaning has not been clarified by the courts.[5] As a result, it is difficult to point to an established legal tradition or jurisprudence which gives a clear meaning to the idea of academic freedom. Secondly, although there are some powerful arguments to justify the freedom,[6] they run counter to the prevailing (political) view that the primary role of universities is to contribute to national economic prosperity and social welfare. This view reinforces scepticism about the coherence of any claims to academic freedom. Associated with this perspective is the argument that academic freedom appears to confer special privileges or immunities on individual professors as well as on the institutions that employ them. As pointed out in chapter one, this feature makes academic freedom a puzzle, which is particularly troublesome in modern liberal societies where institutional and professional privileges have become suspect.

---

[3]  This will be discussed below in ch 7.
[4]  See further below s III(C).
[5]  See below ch 4, esp ss III(C) and IV(D).
[6]  These arguments are discussed below in ch 3.

It is not particularly helpful to attempt a single definition of academic freedom; it is too complex an idea to allow even for the framing of a provisional definition in one or two sentences. Rather, it is better to set out the different types of claims that may be made to academic freedom; each of these claims is at least partly recognised in the three legal systems considered in this book. These claims are supported by the different political and moral arguments discussed in the next chapter. They may conflict with one another, a matter which has posed considerable problems, particularly for courts in the United States.[7] But before we consider the variety of academic freedom claims, something should be said about the argument that academic freedom is really nothing more or less than the right of all academics to speak and write freely as they choose.

## II. ACADEMIC FREEDOM DISTINGUISHED FROM FREEDOM OF SPEECH

The view that academic freedom is essentially an unfettered freedom for academics to speak and write without restraint is a popular one in the United Kingdom. A statement issued by the UK Academics for Academic Freedom at the end of 2006 called for a new legal definition of the freedom, which would recognise as a fundamental principle the unrestricted liberty of academics, both inside and outside the classroom, to put forward controversial and unpopular opinions, however offensive these ideas might be.[8] Though criticised by some commentators, the statement enjoyed considerable support; within a few weeks, more than 225 academics had added their names to the campaign website.[9] There is clearly a close link between freedom of speech (or expression) and academic freedom. As will be seen in chapter three, a classic argument for the former—Mill's famous argument from truth—also underpins one important justification for academic freedom. The same provision of the German Basic Law, Article 5, covers both the freedom to express opinions (*Meinungsfreiheit*) and scientific (or academic)

---

[7] For a general discussion of these conflicts, see below s V.
[8] Http://www.afaf.org.uk/ (accessed 2 August 2010).
[9] *Times Higher Educational Supplement (THES)*, 12 January 2007, 1.

freedom (*Wissenschaftsfreiheit*),[10] while the the American Association of
University Professors Statement of Principles on Academic Freedom
and Tenure refers to, among other things, the freedom of teachers in
the classroom to discuss their subject and their right to 'speak or write
as citizens … free from institutional censorship or discipline'.[11]

Despite these close links between the freedoms, the argument that
academic freedom amounts to an unrestricted freedom of speech for
university teachers is fundamentally misconceived. A claim that academics enjoy the same freedom of speech as other citizens is true but
unhelpful. It does not ascribe any significance to a claim of *academic
freedom* as a distinctive right or freedom. Perhaps the claim should be
understood as asserting that academics enjoy wider rights to freedom
of speech than those enjoyed by other people, and that university
employers should respect these rights as a matter of law. It might be
claimed, for example, that literature teachers should have immunity
from general obscenity laws, whenever they discuss hardcore pornography in class, or that an art lecturer should be completely free to put
on an exhibition displaying sexually explicit work, even though in other
contexts prosecutions under obscenity laws might be brought in respect
of comparable publications or displays. Professors may also assert a
freedom to criticise their university in public—what in the United States
is termed freedom of 'intramural expression'.[12] Insofar as these claims
are to the recognition of wider free speech rights than those enjoyed
by employees in, say, business or industry, they certainly amount to
the assertion of distinctive rights. How far they should be recognised
as *aspects* of academic freedom remains one of the most difficult issues
concerning the scope of that freedom.

The claim that university teachers should enjoy *some* special free
speech rights that are wider or more generous than those to which
other employees are entitled is certainly coherent, though of course
arguments must be adduced to show why they should enjoy them.
What is indefensible is the claim that academic freedom simply means
unlimited free speech rights, as the statement of the UK academics

---

[10] See below ch 5, s III(C) for the relationship between scientific freedom and
freedom of expression in German law.
[11] AAUP Statement of 1940, points (b) and (c) on Academic Freedom. See also
below ch 6, s II.
[12] See below ch 6, ss II(C) and IV(B).

issued at the end of 2006 appears to suggest. Equally implausible is the claim that university teachers should enjoy unrestricted freedom of speech, whether or not that is identified as a discrete right to academic freedom.[13] It is far from clear why they should enjoy unlimited free speech rights or wider rights to freedom of expression than those to which other citizens are entitled. None of the arguments for freedom of speech clearly indicates that academics should be able to speak freely when that liberty is denied other people.[14] The arguments that freedom of speech is an essential aspect of or means to individual self-development apply equally to everyone, irrespective whether they work in universities or not. The argument from democracy does not privilege academic speech or writing; rather, it is essentially an egalitarian argument, contending that *all* citizens have equal rights to contribute to public discourse. Perhaps Mill's argument from truth has greater resonance for discussion in university seminars and academic publication than it has to general political debate.[15] But it hardly justifies a claim that academics are more entitled to say what they like—outside the university classroom—than other citizens.

Quite apart from this fundamental objection of principle, there are other reasons why the simple equation of academic freedom with unlimited freedom of speech must be rejected. Within the classroom the freedom of even the most distinguished professor to say what he or she likes is limited by constraints that are perfectly compatible with academic freedom. A mathematics professor does have not academic freedom to devote part of his course to a study of the modern novel or to discussion of the government's foreign policy, whatever the merits in other contexts of what he or she has to say on these matters. While lecturers on the law of torts have some discretion in determining the contents of courses, deciding whether, for example, to cover economic torts or defamation law, they would surely not be free to exclude reference to the law of negligence or to spend most of a course

---

[13] Ch 9 below discusses whether the freedom of academic staff to discuss political and social issues outside their fields of competence should be treated as an aspect of academic freedom.

[14] For the arguments for freedom of speech, see F Schauer, *Free Speech: A Philosophical Enquiry* (Cambridge, Cambridge University Press, 1982).

[15] Mill's truth argument as a justification for a general intellectual freedom or for a special scholarly freedom is discussed below in ch 3, ss II and III(A).

discussing leading cases on property or contract law. Moreover, a professor does not have academic freedom gratuitously to use racist or sexually explicit language in class, particularly if he appreciates that it is offensive to some of the students.[16] Away from campus, academics may have much more freedom to say or write what they like. There are no constraints of relevance; a university physicist is, for example, as free as anyone else to write letters to a newspaper doubting the Holocaust, but he or she has that right under general freedom of speech (or expression), not as a matter of academic freedom.[17]

The point is that academic speech—whether in the classroom, at conferences or in publications—is subject to *quality* controls, for which there are no equivalent constraints in public discourse. Everyone is free, at least in principle, to contribute to public discourse, whether they produce a structured argument in polished language or instead produce a string of indecent epithets. As Justice Harlan said when the US Supreme Court protected the free speech right of a protester to wear the slogan 'Fuck the Draft' on his jacket in a courthouse corridor, 'it is often true that one man's vulgarity is another's lyric'.[18] This relativism does not apply to the speech and writings of university professors and lecturers. Peer review generally determines whether an academic paper will be published in a journal or presented at a conference, while the overall quality of a professor's teaching may be subject to faculty review, perhaps after student evaluation. Publications are reviewed and assessed when academics apply for an appointment, for tenure (in the United States and other countries where that system of permanent appointment has been kept) or for promotion. Peer review does not infringe academic freedom; rather it is designed to ensure that its exercise complies with the appropriate professional standards.[19] In short, academic speech, unlike general political or public discourse, is essentially subject to quality controls on the basis of general professional standards of accuracy and coherence, as well as the specific requirement for

---

[16]   See the US cases discussed below in ch 6 s IV.

[17]   For further discussion, see below ch 9, s II.

[18]   *Cohen v California* 403 US 15, 25 (1971).

[19]   See M Finkin and R Post, *For the Common Good* (Newhaven, Yale University Press, 2009) 59–61; D Rabban, 'Does Academic Freedom Limit Faculty Autonomy?' (1988) 66 *Texas Law Review* 1405, 1410–12; and D Schatz, 'Is Peer Review Overrated?' (1996) 79 *Monist* 536.

publication in the better journals that it makes an original contribution to knowledge.

A further (and rather obvious) reason for distinguishing academic freedom from freedom of speech is that many forms of academic activity involve conduct rather than speech, or only tangentially involve the latter. The institution and equipment of a university department or laboratory, scientific experiments, social science surveys, the organisation of conferences and research teams are all activities which might be regarded as covered by a right to academic freedom. Instinctively, we would regard a government-imposed ban on conducting research through interviews and surveys on the effectiveness of, say, government policies for schools, as an interference with academic freedom, but the ban would only marginally limit the freedom of speech to discuss and criticise those policies. This point suggests it is surely better to treat academic freedom as conferring distinct claims that may overlap with claims to freedom of speech—most clearly in the case of freedom of publication and the freedom to choose the subject of a course of lectures—but that also assert the right to conduct academic activities without interference.

Academic freedom also has much in common with the freedoms claimed by doctors, lawyers and others to determine how they fulfil their vocation and discharge their responsibilities. Like the members of these other professions, academics claim the right to set their own standards and to apply them to their colleagues when, for example, they consider appointments and promotions. It is therefore a professional freedom rather than a set of individual rights.[20] Academics claim rights to participate in the formulation of important academic decisions or to be represented on university councils as aspects of academic freedom.[21] In Germany, courts and commentators have emphasised that *Wissenschaftsfreiheit* (scientific freedom) has an institutional and procedural dimension, so that, for example, professors must be able to determine themselves how research is evaluated. Academic freedom has an organisational dimension.[22] It is not to be equated with freedom of speech. Moreover, in some contexts the speech of academics is more

---

[20] R Post. 'The Structure of Academic Freedom' in B Doumani (ed), *Academic Freedom after September 11* (New York, Zone Books, 2006) 61, 64.

[21] Lord Robbins (above n 1) 5.

[22] See below ch 5.

circumscribed than that of other people, for their lectures and scholarly publications must satisfy professional standards.[23]

### III. THE VARIETIES OF ACADEMIC FREEDOM CLAIMS

A number of different claims to academic freedom may be made, or put another way, academic freedom may cover a variety of distinct rights. The New Zealand Education Act 1989,[24] for example, sets out five freedoms: the freedom of academic staff and students to put forward ideas and state unpopular opinions; the freedom of academic staff and students to engage in research; the freedom of an institution and its staff to regulate the subject matter of courses taught there; the freedom of an institution and its staff to teach and assess students; and the freedom of an institution through its chief executive to appoint its own staff. It is possible, however, to identify two principal varieties or types of academic freedom claim. This section discusses them, as well as a third type of claim, which can be regarded as separate from these other two.

The two principal claims are those made by individual professors and lecturers (and perhaps students) to scholarly academic freedom, and those of universities and other academic institutions to institutional autonomy or academic freedom. These are clearly distinct claims, which may conflict with each other.[25] They differ not only with regard to the character of the claimant—individual or institution—but also with regard to the body against which the claim is made, which might be the state, some branch of government or the university itself. The third, less

---

[23] W van Alstyne, 'The Specific Theory of Academic Freedom and the General Issue of Civil Liberty' in Pincoffs (ed), *The Concept of Academic Freedom* (above n 2) 75–76 points out that academics are less circumscribed than commercial employees are by the requirements of their employers but more constrained by professional ethical standards.

[24] S 161(2). It should be noted that the first two freedoms extend to students as well as to staff, a principle that is not explicitly recognised in the comparable UK provision discussed below and in ch 4; further, under the NZ statute, institutions are required, in exercising their academic freedom, to act consistently with the need for the maintenance of ethical standards and to permit public scrutiny in that context, and to act consistently with the need for accountability and the proper use of the resources allocated to them: s 161(3).

[25] See below s V and also ch 6, s IV for US case law on the conflict.

clearly distinctive claim is that of individual academics to participate in university government, which might be recognised to ensure the effective protection of individual scholarly freedom and therefore treated as an aspect of that freedom.

## A. The Rights of Individual Scholars

Academic freedom may in the first place be regarded as an individual liberty for professors, lecturers and other academic staff in universities and other higher education institutions. That is how it has been treated in the United Kingdom, particularly in the last fifty or sixty years. One example is the discussion of academic freedom in the Report of the Committee chaired by Lord Robbins on the reform of higher education.[26] The freedom, in the Committee's view, involved the freedom of individual scholars and scientists to publish; the freedom to teach according to a teacher's own concept of fact and truth; and the 'freedom to pursue what personal studies or researches are congenial'.[27] These freedoms were, however, not absolute; their exercise could be made subject to the performance of allotted duties, for professors had no right to refuse to discharge them. The Robbins Report admitted that academic freedom could be abused, but it was less dangerous to run that risk than to attempt to eliminate it by a general restriction on individual liberties. The most important statutory provision in the United Kingdom on academic freedom reflects this individualist perspective. When tenure was in effect abolished by the Education Reform Act 1988, a provision was put in the measure to safeguard academic freedom. In drawing up the new model statutes for universities, Commissioners were to have regard for the need to

> ensure that academic staff have freedom within the law to question and test received wisdom, and to put forward new ideas and controversial or unpopular opinions, without placing themselves in jeopardy of losing the jobs or privileges they may have at their institutions.[28]

---

[26] Committee on Higher Education, 'Higher Education' ('Robbins Report') (Cm 2154, 1963) ch XVI, 'Academic Freedom and its Scope'.

[27] Ibid, para 705.

[28] S 202. For detailed discussion of the background to this provision and its implications for academic freedom in British universities, see below ch 4, ss III–IV.

In its Second Report on Standards in Public Life, the Nolan Committee also took the view that the right of individuals to pursue lines of research and publication that may be unpopular is fundamental to the success of universities. The freedom had also been extended to create a 'tradition of freedom of speech within a university', an important check on impropriety within its administration.[29]

A similar perspective has been taken in other jurisdictions. In the United States, the 1940 Statement of the American Association of University Professors (AAUP) emphasised the freedoms of individual professors and other teachers: full freedom to conduct research and publish results; freedom of discussion within the classroom; and freedom of extramural expression, that is, the freedom of academics as citizens to speak or write without institutional censorship.[30] The AAUP formulated a *professional* freedom, which universities should respect in their dealings with individual scholars and which could be incorporated in the terms of academic employment contracts. It was not directly enforceable as a legal right.[31] We will see later in this chapter, and more fully in chapter six, that in the United States the Supreme Court (and to some extent other courts) have taken a different perspective on academic freedom as a *constitutional* right, viewing it primarily, perhaps solely, as the freedom of academic institutions. But some court decisions have protected the freedoms of individual university teachers,[32] while as a matter of convention and practice within universities, academic freedom and tenure are regarded as significant liberties for individual teachers.

In contrast, in Germany the comparable constitutional freedom is clearly to be treated as a matter of individual right. The Basic Law guarantees *Wissenschaftsfreiheit* (literally, 'scientific freedom') in the third paragraph of Article 5: art and science, research and teaching shall be free. The first paragraph of this Article safeguards the right of everyone to express and communicate their opinions, freedom of the press and freedom of reporting by broadcasts and films; the provision

---

[29] Committee on Standards in Public Life, 'Second Report on Standards in Public Life' (Cm 3270, 1996) para 97, further discussed below in ch 4, s IV(A).

[30] For further discussion of this Statement and the earlier 1915 Declaration, see below ch 6, s II.

[31] See below ch 6, s II(D).

[32] See below ch 6, s IV(B).

is furthermore contained in the part of the Law guaranteeing Basic Rights. So the clear implication is that scientific or academic freedom confers individual rights. In the leading *Hochschulurteil* (university judgement), the Constitutional Court shared this view of the constitutional freedom.[33] Further, it emphasised that the freedom can be enjoyed by everyone engaged in serious scholarly activity, whether they work in universities, other institutes or independently.[34] Indeed, it is possible that only individual rights are conferred by Article 5(3).[35] We will see in chapter five how the courts in Germany have interpreted this provision to require the state to promote scientific freedom and afford professors significant participation rights in university governance; the freedom has a wider scope than the core freedoms of teaching and research.

Claims to individual academic freedom may be made against a variety of bodies, just as threats to its exercise may come from a number of sources. Most obviously the government by law or administrative direction might attempt to control what professors can teach or research, though in the liberal democracies considered in this book this type of direct constraint is fortunately unknown. But academic freedom claims are commonly made that government or a funding or research council has withdrawn resources from or failed adequately to support a research programme, though courts, even in Germany, have rarely been sympathetic to this assertion of positive academic freedom rights.[36] But dangers to individual academic freedom may also be posed by universities themselves, albeit they may have been acting under government direction or reacting to pressure from private sponsors and funding organisations. If a university disciplines a professor because of something he or she has published or said during the course of his or her work, the claim lies against the university. Thus in the United Kingdom academic freedom—incorporated in university statutes—must be taken into account by a higher education institution if it contemplates disciplining a member of its academic staff.[37] In the United States the first statement of academic freedom drafted by the

---

[33] The *Hochschulurteil* is reported in BVerfGE 35, 79 (1973).
[34] Ibid, 112. For discussion of this important point, see below ch 5, ss I and III(B).
[35] See below ch 5, s IV(A).
[36] For further discussion in the context of Germany, see below ch 5, s IV(D).
[37] See below ch 4, s IV(B).

AAUP in 1915 was formulated in response to what it considered the indifference, sometimes even hostility, to its values of university administrators and trustees.[38] Insofar then as academic freedom confers some rights on individual academics, it follows that universities as well as the state and public agencies must respect them. This must be borne in mind when we consider now the second variety of claim: the freedom of universities to institutional autonomy.

## B. Institutional Autonomy

A second, quite different claim to academic freedom may be made by universities and other academic institutions themselves: a right to institutional autonomy. This freedom may be explicitly conferred by the constitution, as by the Basic Law of Hong Kong, which provides that '[e]ducational institutions of all kinds may retain their autonomy and enjoy academic freedom.'[39] In the United Kingdom institutional autonomy has traditionally been associated with the colleges of Oxford and Cambridge universities, many of which have substantial endowments and have therefore enjoyed some financial independence from the state. Even today, Oxford and Cambridge have retained a distinct sense of institutional independence, insisting in particular that academic self-rule is necessary to protect that independence and the academic freedom with which it is associated.[40]

A tradition of university autonomy was recognised when the new civic universities were established in the nineteenth and twentieth centuries; moreover, the arrangements for university financing through the University Grants Committee, with a majority of academics among its members, were designed to protect this independence from government

---

[38] WP Metzger, 'Academic Freedom in Delocalized Academic Institutions' in WP Metzger, et al (eds), *Dimensions of Academic Freedom* (Chicago, University of Illinois Press, 1969) 2–14 points out that the 1915 AAUP document said nothing about the relations of the academy to the state; violations of academic freedom were committed within the university.

[39] Art 137. It has been held that academic freedom under this provision extends to members of university faculties: *Secretary of Justice v Commission of Inquiry, Re Hong Kong Institute of Education* [2009] 4 HKLRD 11, Court of First Instance.

[40] Discussed further below in ch 3, s V and ch 4, s V.

as universities became increasingly dependent on public funding.[41] The Robbins Report in 1963 recognised the dangers to institutional freedom arising from the increasing material dependence on the state. It recognised nonetheless some key constituents of this freedom that should not and need not be eroded: the freedom of universities to make their own appointments; their freedom to devise their own degree courses and monitor standards; and the freedom to select their own students. Robbins even considered that this last freedom entitled universities not to cooperate with government policy on growth and to stipulate their own entrance standards.[42] Moreover, it was for universities themselves to determine the appropriate balance between teaching and research for their own institutions. Considerable institutional autonomy was not incompatible with selective public financing.

Many of these elements of institutional academic freedom in the United Kingdom have been considerably weakened in the last three or four decades, as governments of both political parties have put increasing emphasis on the responsibilities of universities to contribute to national economic and social progress and on their accountability to the public.[43] The almost total reliance of universities in the United Kingdom on state funding makes it difficult for them to assert their independence. Nevertheless, a degree of institutional autonomy is still officially recognised. It was accepted by the Nolan Committee in its 2nd Report on Standards in Public Life, which carefully distinguished it from the freedom of individual academics. An even more striking acknowledgement of institutional academic freedom in the United Kingdom is to be found in the Higher Education Act 2004,[44] which requires the Director of Fair Access, in performing his duty,[45] to protect academic freedom, including the freedom of higher education institutions to determine the contents of particular courses and how

---

[41]  See below ch 4, s II(B).

[42]  Robbins Report (above n 26) paras 711–16.

[43]  For a survey of this development up to 2000, see G Zellick's Atkin lecture, 'Universities and the Law: The Erosion of Institutional Autonomy' (London, University of London Press, 2001); and more generally, R Stevens, *University to Uni: The Politics of Higher Education in England since 1944*, 2nd edn (London, Politico's, 2005).

[44]  S 32(2).

[45]  The Director of Fair Access has the responsibility to ensure universities take steps to increase applications from students in under-represented groups.

they are taught, and to determine admissions criteria and their application. But the scope of institutional autonomy is limited. UK universities
are not free, for example, to set their own fees or disregard directions
from the Higher Education Funding Councils without jeopardising
their funding.

In the United States the classic statement of the institutional autonomy
and freedom of universities was given by Frankfurter J in his concurring
judgement to the Supreme Court ruling in *Sweezy v New Hampshire*.[46]
Expressing concern about the dangers of government intrusion, he
referred to a protest by South African universities against the apartheid
regime's attempts in the 1950s to impose on them a racially restrictive admissions policy. Frankfurter J cited with approval the protest's
emphasis on the fundamental freedom of a university to 'determine for
itself on academic grounds (i) who may teach, (ii) what may be taught,
(iii) how it shall be taught, and (iv) who may be admitted to study'.[47]
The principles formulated in *Sweezy* have been cited frequently in later
Supreme Court decisions[48] and have led to the development of a theory
of institutional academic freedom for universities that is guaranteed by
the First Amendment.[49]

Frankfurter J's argument linked the institutional autonomy of universities to individual academic freedom.[50] Without some guarantee of
their independence, universities would be unable to ensure that their
academic staffs enjoyed full academic freedom to teach and research
as they choose. If government can control universities, for example,
requiring them not to employ radical philosophy or history lecturers
or to teach a prescribed curriculum, then individual academic freedom would be indirectly endangered. These arguments suggest that

---

[46]   354 US 234 (1957).
[47]   Ibid, 263, quoting the Conference of Representatives of the Universities of
Cape Town and the University of Witwatersrand, the Open Universities of South
Africa, 10–12.
[48]   For example, see *Regents of the University of California v Bakke* 438 US 265, 312
(1978); *Widmar v Vincent* 454 US 263, 278 (1981); and *Grutter v Bollinger* 539 US 306,
329–30 (2003).
[49]   For discussion of these developments and the relevant cases, see below ch
6, s III.
[50]   Indeed, the academic freedom claim was made by an individual professor
that the state of New Hampshire was infringing that freedom by requiring him to
disclose to it the contents of his lecture at a state university.

the institutional autonomy of universities should be recognised as an academic freedom claim because it promotes the unrestricted exercise of individual scholarly freedom.[51] Historically, however, the case for the institutional autonomy of universities has had relatively little to do with securing the academic freedom of professors and lecturers. It has rested on quite different arguments: respect for the liberties of privately established institutions to be conducted according to the wishes of their founders[52] and a general preference for decentralised decision-taking and institutional pluralism.[53] Indeed, the institutional autonomy of universities and academic freedom can be regarded as entirely separate ideas.[54] It is only relatively recently that the link has been made between individual scholarly academic freedom and the independence from state control of universities and colleges. But it has now been widely accepted, so universities may claim indiscriminately their traditional independence or autonomy, or alternatively an institutional academic freedom.

Frankfurter J assumed in his judgement in *Sweezy*[55] that institutional academic freedom reinforces individual scholarly freedom. Indeed, as explained in the previous paragraph, that is the reason why the entitlement of universities to independence from the state may be recognised as a claim to institutional academic freedom. But in some circumstances, individual and institutional claims to the freedom may conflict.

A university might decide, as sometimes happens now in the United Kingdom, no longer to teach chemistry[56] and to redeploy so far as possible members of the chemistry faculty; or to close a philosophy faculty and require its members to teach basic philosophy courses for, say, medical and law students. If those decisions were to meet academic freedom objections from concerned professors and lecturers,

---

[51] See further below ch 3, s IV.

[52] See M Finkin, 'On "Institutional" Academic Freedom' (1982) 61 *Texas Law Rev* 817, 829–40.

[53] See GC Moodie, 'On Justifying the Different Claims to Academic Freedom' (1996) 34 *Minerva* 129, 147–49.

[54] Finkin (above n 52) 818.

[55] Above n 46.

[56] About 30 chemistry departments have been closed n the last decade, including those at Queen Mary, University of London, King's College London and the University of Exeter: see http://www.rsc.org/ScienceAndTechnology/Policy/Bulletins/Issue1/FutureUKChemDep.asp (accessed 19 April 2010).

they could be defended with the argument that the university itself has autonomy to determine what subjects to teach. This is one respect in which institutional claims to academic freedom give rise to difficulties; they may be asserted not to promote but rather to defeat the individual claims of professors and lecturers. These conflicts have given rise to a body of complex and often inconsistent case law in the United States[57] and also occasioned some difficulties in Germany.[58] The case law is discussed in detail in later chapters, but there is a short general discussion of this difficult topic below in section V.

One aspect of institutional academic freedom that might give rise to additional difficulties is that universities are generally public institutions. At least that is the position in Europe, including the United Kingdom. (In contrast, many of the most significant universities in the United States are private institutions, which are as entitled to assert constitutional rights as ordinary individuals.) In Europe universities are almost entirely financed by public grants and are subject to increasing direction with regard to research and teaching priorities from various agencies. At first it might seem odd that a public institution could claim academic freedom to challenge—perhaps even in the courts—the validity of state directions that constrain its autonomy. (It would be even odder if a particular faculty within a university used academic freedom arguments to question the decisions of the central university authority.[59]) In fact there is nothing unusual in ascribing rights to public institutions or bodies. Public broadcasters such as the BBC may assert rights to freedom of speech and broadcasting freedom.[60] Public universities should equally be able to claim academic freedom. These claims have been recognised to an extent in the United States,[61] though one commentator on academic freedom has argued that regulation by the state

---

[57]   Discussed below ch 6, s IV.

[58]   See below ch 5, s IV(D).

[59]   MG Yudof, 'Three Faces of Academic Freedom' (1987) 32 *Loyola Law Rev* 831, 854–57 raises this possibility.

[60]   This is not established for the BBC by any clear authority, but as a matter of principle the BBC should surely be entitled to challenge a government ban on the transmission of a programme: see H Fenwick and G Phillipson, *Media Freedom under the Human Rights Act* (Oxford, Oxford University Press, 2007) 115. A public broadcaster in Germany is entitled to challenge a restriction on its broadcasting freedom: see, for example, BVerfGE 31, 314, 322; BVerfGE 59, 231, 254.

[61]   See the cases cited above in n 48.

of their freedom might be upheld when comparable restrictions on private universities such as Harvard or Stanford would be invalidated as infringing the institutional academic freedom guaranteed by the First Amendment.[62]

Claims to institutional academic freedom rights might also be considered problematic in another way. It may be unclear to which person or body within the institution they should be ascribed: the President or Vice-Chancellor; the Board of Regents or University Council; or the Dean or Head of Department. In practice, of course, the allocation of responsibility for decision-taking within a university is determined by its Charter, statutes or regulations. The President or Vice-Chancellor normally has final authority to take executive decisions, but it is usual for academic questions to be determined by a complex network of university committees, with a university teaching committee or Academic Board having the last word in all but the most controversial circumstances.[63] Within a particular faculty or department, the Dean or Head of Department has authority over academic matters, though that would probably not extend to disciplining an individual professor or lecturer who claimed academic freedom (or other) rights against a decision concerning, say, the subject he or she is required to teach or the manner in which it is to be taught. Serious disciplinary decisions are usually taken by the Vice-Chancellor or President, typically after full consideration of the issues by a special committee or tribunal.[64]

The ascription of academic freedom within a university has something in common with questions that may be asked about rights within newspapers and other media organisations: can press or broadcasting freedom be claimed by individual journalists, editors or the owners

---

[62] DM Rabban, 'A Functional Analysis of "Individual" and "Institutional" Academic Freedom under the First Amendment' (1990) 53 *Law and Contemporary Problems* 229, 266–80.

[63] For a discussion of the academic freedom aspects of university governance in the US, see J Areen, 'Government as Educator: A New Understanding of First Amendment Protection of Academic Freedom and Governance' (2009) 97 *Georgetown Law Journal* 945.

[64] For the United Kingdom, see below ch 4, s IV(B) and also ch 10, where the procedures leading to the dismissal by Edinburgh University of Chris Brand are explained.

of media corporations?[65] In that context it seems right to ascribe the freedom to the person best placed to assert the values of freedom of expression with which press freedom is closely associated—usually the editor, rather than the owner whose interest is often primarily commercial. So institutional academic freedom—for example, the freedoms to appoint faculty and select students—is best ascribed to individuals with academic experience or to committees on which academics enjoy significant representation. This perspective is commonly reflected in the arrangements for university governance whereby decisions of this kind are taken by academics themselves. It plays an important part in the arguments for the third type of academic freedom claim: the claim to academic self-rule.[66] But however these problems of university governance are resolved, there is no doubt that the claims made by universities to institutional autonomy or academic freedom have been accepted, at least in the United Kingdom and United States; indeed, in the latter, as already mentioned, they frequently trump the competing claims made by professors to exercise individual scholarly freedom.[67]

## C. The Rights of Academics to Self-Rule or to Participate in Academic Government

A distinct third claim to academic freedom has sometimes been identified: the right of academic staff to self-rule or at least to participate in the taking of decisions of the university, particularly academic decisions—distinguished from, say, decisions concerning investments or the development or management of university property.[68] Often, however, it is treated as falling under the first variety of claim: the claim to individual scholarly freedom. That at least is how Lord Robbins regarded it.[69] For it is arguably linked to or an aspect of the fundamental scholarly freedoms asserted by professors and lecturers. Unless

---

[65] For discussion of this question, see E Barendt, *Freedom of Speech* (Oxford, Oxford University Press, 2007) 441–44.

[66] See below ch 3, s V.

[67] See below ch 6.

[68] Claims to 'academic rule' are treated as a distinct type of academic freedom claim by Moodie (above n 53) 143–46.

[69] See his British Academy lecture (above n 1) 5.

academic staff are strongly represented on the governing bodies of universities, they cannot, it is said, protect these freedoms effectively, as they will become subject to direction on academic matters by university administrators and ultimately by University Councils, which are often composed (almost) entirely of laymen—businessmen, ex-ambassadors and others with no significant experience of academic work. On that perspective, this is not really a distinct claim but rather falls under the first heading.

Despite that argument, there is something to be said for treating this claim to academic freedom separately from the others. First, it is not clear that scholarly freedom does require self-rule or strong participation rights for academics.[70] Only in the older universities of Oxford and Cambridge do UK academics enjoy a clear majority on the university councils; though they have strongly fought to maintain that position, to some extent on academic freedom grounds, it would be difficult to conclude that this degree of self-rule is inextricably bound up with the claims to scholarly freedom.[71] As will be explained in the next chapter, the argument for academic self-rule or participation is also an argument regarding the desirability of professional self-regulation, comparable to the claims made by doctors, lawyers and members of other professions to set their own professional standards and to regulate compliance with them.

Further, this variety of academic freedom claim differs from the typical claims made under the first heading of scholarly freedom in that it entails the recognition of positive rights for which university statutes must make provision.[72] The scholarly freedom considered earlier in this section usually involves negative liberties to research and teach as the individual academic chooses, free from interference by the state or by university authorities. (It may sometimes lead to (moral or political) claims that a state has, for example, a duty to provide adequate resources for research or to fund a particular research institute; the argument then is for the recognition of positive academic freedom rights, though it

---

[70] See Moodie (above n 53) 143.

[71] Further discussed below in ch 4, s V(C).

[72] For the distinction between positive and negative rights in the context of freedom of speech, see Barendt (above n 65) 100–16.

is virtually unknown for these to be accepted as a matter of law.[73]) But a claim that academics must be strongly represented on university councils and other decision-making bodies or that a university must listen to a particular professional association before it takes academic decisions amounts to the assertion of positive rights. So the German Constitutional Court recognised in the *Hochschulurteil* that the Basic Law confers some positive rights in this context, notably the right of professors to be properly represented in bodies taking academic decisions.[74] That decision reflects the general approach to basic rights in German constitutional law; they are not only negative liberties against state intervention but may also impose duties on the state to ensure their effective protection. In contrast, US courts have not recognised positive participation rights under academic freedom, an approach consistent with their general reluctance to recognise freedom of speech and other constitutional rights as more than bare liberties. Thus, in *Minnesota State Board for Community Colleges v Knight*[75] the Supreme Court refused to recognise a constitutional right under the First Amendment for faculty to participate in academic decision-taking.

On balance, therefore, it seems better to treat the claim to participation rights as a distinctive academic freedom claim, although the point may be of largely theoretical interest. However it is characterised, it is a claim against university authorities that they are organised in such a way as to afford an adequate voice for individual academics. It is important to note, however, that this claim, like the claim to individual scholarly freedom to which it is closely linked, may be opposed by assertions of institutional academic freedom. For an institution may claim that its prerogative to determine the arrangements for its own governance would be undermined by the recognition of participation rights, which might, in its view, endanger its capacity to take decisions, including academic decisions, quickly and effectively. This is another instance of conflict between individual and institutional academic freedom claims, a topic discussed below in section V.

---

[73] For the treatment of positive academic freedom claims in Germany, see below ch 5, s IV(D).

[74] BVerfGE 35, 79 (1973), discussed below in ch 5, s IV(A).

[75] 465 US 271 (1984). See further below ch 6, s III(C).

## IV. ACADEMIC OR INTELLECTUAL FREEDOM?

So far this chapter has explored the scope of *academic* freedom, rather than of a general *intellectual* freedom, which might be claimed by anyone engaged in scholarly or scientific work, whether or not he or she is employed in a university or other institution of higher education. The United Kingdom, the United States and most other countries where a comparable freedom is constitutionally guaranteed recognise academic freedom, not the more general right; in Germany, however, the Basic Law protects the freedom of scientific research and teaching, even though the law in practice is overwhelmingly concerned with the application of this freedom in the university context.[76] Something should therefore be said about the force of the adjective 'academic' when claims to this freedom are made. The use of this term is perhaps a little unfortunate, because in modern discourse it is all too commonly used as a synonym for one of its meanings: impractical, or of only theoretical interest.[77] But of course in this context it bears a different meaning: relating to an academy or to a community of scholars. In its turn, that meaning gives rise to an ambiguity. Academic freedom might refer to the freedom, or rights and privileges, of *members* of that community (or of the community itself) or alternatively refer to the *activities* characteristically conducted within it.[78]

The point has already been made that academic freedom is problematic, just because it appears at first glance to confer privileges on a particular group.[79] But it does not confer on academics legal privileges and immunities merely because of their status, as the law in the United Kingdom has done with regard to the Crown. It confers on them special freedoms, say, to determine what and how they teach, free from direction by university authorities, because of the high value placed on their particular activities. This is reflected in the key UK statutory provision on academic freedom, which refers to the freedom of 'academic staff … to question and test received wisdom, and to put forward new

[76]  Basic Law, Art 5(3), discussed below in ch 5.
[77]  There is an eloquent essay by Charles Morgan on this regrettable development: 'The Word "Academic"' in C Morgan, *The Writer and his World* (London, Macmillan, 1960) 55.
[78]  Moodie (above n 53) 132–34.
[79]  See above ch 1, s I.

ideas'.[80] The provision confers a right on *academic* staff—not all university staff—when they discharge their particular responsibilities of teaching, research and associated activities. It would be impossible to justify a broader freedom for them simply on the basis of their status as university professors. An analogy may be drawn with the privileges claimed by members of parliaments or other legislative assemblies. Parliamentary privileges are conferred to enable them to exercise their functions, in particular to conduct political debate and to represent their constituents, without fear of sanction; they are not given in simple recognition of their status.[81]

Academic freedom may mean that university professors and lecturers enjoy a freedom that is not shared by other employees—whether in public or private service—or even by other university staff such as administrators and secretaries. Challenges can be made to the wisdom of this position. It can be argued that other employees should have similar rights to determine how they do their work and to freedom of expression.[82] For example, health service employees may, at least in the United Kingdom, be disciplined if they publish material critical of the administration of their hospitals or of government health policy in general; but arguably they should be as free to publish material on such matters, on which they are likely to have real knowledge or expertise, as are professors exercising academic freedom. The case for academic freedom—discussed in the next chapter—is that it is the particular *responsibility* of members of a university faculty to engage in critical enquiry and publish their conclusions, and that extends to a freedom to draw the attention of the public to any maladministration of their university—the freedom of intramural speech, to use the American term.[83] But that is not the function of other employees, even when their speech on a particular topic raises matters of real public concern. When that is the case, an employee might be able to raise the general right to

---

[80]  Education Reform Act 1988, s 202(2)(a).

[81]  The AAUP Declaration of 1915 compared the freedom of university professors with the immunity of judges from interference by the executive; both are necessary to ensure the independence required for their role: see Finkin and Post (above n 19) 165.

[82]  RF Ladenson, 'Is Academic Freedom Necessary?' (1986) 5 *Law and Philosophy* 59.

[83]  See below ch 4, s IV for UK law and ch 6, s IV(B) for US law.

freedom of speech or expression either under the constitution or under a statute such as a law protecting 'whistle-blowing' at work.[84] But that is not the same as a claim made by university professors to exercise academic freedom in these circumstances.

There are troubling questions about the scope of *academic* freedom: should it cover only university professors and lecturers, or might it extend to research assistants, laboratory technicians, library staff or, perhaps in some circumstances, members of an administrative staff? It may be unclear whether probationary teachers are entitled to the same degree of protection as those who have been granted tenure or permanent positions. There are also difficult issues whether academic freedom should extend to academic staff working at academic agencies or research institutes rather than at universities.[85] On one view, they should not be entitled to full academic freedom of research, since there can surely be nothing wrong in the authorities at a specialist institute, whether that of government or of a pharmaceutical or other indus-trial company, determining what it wants to research and directing its employees how to set about it.[86] Insofar as the arguments for academic freedom are based on the special role of universities as places for the free exchange of ideas, they do not apply with the same force to academics working in research institutes. Similar questions arise with regard to university students; in principle, they should be entitled to claim academic freedom, at least to discuss controversial ideas in semi-nars, and research students should be free, in consultation with their supervisors, to determine the topics for their research and how they

[84] In the United States public employees have been entitled to speak as citizens on matters of public concern: see *Pickering v Board of Education* 391 US 563 (1968). For further discussion of academic freedom in the United States in relation to employee rights, see below ch 6, s IV(A).

[85] In 2008 there was controversy when the Director of the Higher Education Academy was suspended after writing a letter to the *Times Higher Education* critical of a student survey administered by the Higher Education Funding Council for England. See *Times Higher Education*, 29 May and 7 August 2008. The Academy is a public agency, owned and financed by UK universities; the question is whether the same principles of academic freedom apply to its staff as apply to that of the universities themselves.

[86] For these arguments in the context of the right to scientific freedom in Germany, see below ch 5, s VII.

conduct it. But in the United Kingdom the statutory right to academic freedom does not cover students.[87]

In short, academic freedom is not identical to intellectual freedom or to freedom of the mind, although it is closely linked to these broader freedoms. Intellectual freedom is a right to which we are all entitled, wherever we work. Like freedom of speech or expression, it is a general right belonging to all citizens. That is how it is treated in Germany, where everyone engaged in serious scholarly or scientific work may claim scientific freedom (*Wissenschaftsfreiheit*) under the Basic Law. On this approach the questions discussed in the preceding paragraphs become less troublesome. Students, laboratory technicians and researchers working at specialist institutes are all entitled to exercise *Wissenschaftsfreiheit*, though the scope of that freedom may be narrower than it is for university professors. Academic freedom as it is understood in the United Kingdom and the United States is, in contrast, a special right to which only those engaged in teaching and research at universities and other comparable institutions are entitled.

## V. CONFLICTS BETWEEN ACADEMIC FREEDOM CLAIMS

Institutional and individual claims to academic freedom may conflict with each other. In addition to conflicts about the subjects an individual is required to teach, a lecturer may argue that academic freedom is infringed if the university directs him or her to change the mark or grade assigned to a student or orders him or her not to discuss current political disputes or matters of religious faith in the context of a modern history course. Against these arguments, the university may claim its own institutional academic freedom to determine grading policy or to impose limits on the scope of what may legitimately be discussed in a university class. Further, the claims asserted by academics to participate in university government may be resisted by the institution's claim to determine how it governs itself; it might reject the argument that it should cede to its academic employees a right to be involved in the taking of major policy decisions, whether or not they concern academic matters.

---

[87] See below ch 8, s II(D) for the implications of this point for an episode at Nottingham University.

US courts have resolved these conflicts in a number of cases that are considered in chapter six.[88] The concern here is to discuss a few points of general importance. First, comparisons may be drawn between these conflicts and the conflict between individual free speech rights and press freedom when, say, an editor invokes the latter to refuse to publish a reply to a personal attack in a newspaper. Newspaper editors may bolster their legal claim to press freedom with the argument that this freedom is essential to ensure freedom of political debate and effective freedom of speech. Similarly, universities may claim institutional academic freedom to enable them to safeguard the individual liberties of the professors and lecturers whose employment and facilities they provide. Indeed, the university argument is in one respect stronger than that made by the institutional media. We can easily conceive of freedom of speech for individuals without the involvement of the mass media, whether we have in mind the speech of the lonely orator or leafleteer, or now communication on the internet. In contrast, academic freedom, as distinct from general intellectual freedom of the mind, cannot easily be divorced from a perception of the particular role of universities.[89]

But that does not mean that the institutional freedom should necessarily be regarded as paramount, so that it always trumps a conflicting individual claim. The strength of the competing claims should be evaluated, in the last analysis by courts when they are asked to interpret academic freedom provisions in a constitution or statute. How should the strength of an individual's assertion of academic freedom be weighed in relation to the institution's rival claim that it is exercising the same freedom when it disciplines a member of its staff? There is no simple answer to this question. On the one hand, academic freedom has usually been treated primarily as the right of *individual* scholars to pursue the truth and to exercise their independent academic judgement on, say, the appropriate materials for teaching and their chosen subject of research. Certainly, if academic freedom is a fundamental human right, then the claims of individual teachers and researchers should prevail over those competing claims made by an institution that appear to infringe that human right. But it is very doubtful whether a human rights case can be

---

[88] For the complex US jurisprudence, see ch 6, s IV.
[89] See the arguments below in ch 3.

made for academic freedom, as distinct from a broad intellectual and artistic freedom that can be claimed by everyone.[90]

From an historical perspective, academic freedom has most often been asserted by individual professors and other university teachers: in Germany against the state bureaucracy; in the United States against university administrators, which have often been indifferent to academic values and the disinterested search for truth. History should not, of course, determine how contemporary conflicts are to be resolved. But preferring institutional claims in cases of conflict would be to recognise the authority of the university administration over the freedom of the individual scholar, the very situation that the early claims to academic freedom, at least in the United States at the beginning of the twentieth century, were designed to correct.[91] Nevertheless, that solution would be acceptable, if a university is genuinely asserting a claim to academic freedom, for example, that it has come after careful consideration to a different judgement of the intellectual merits of, say, the contents of a course than the individual teacher and it is entitled to implement its own academic view. Further, the institutional claim would be a strong one if the decision had been taken by a faculty or university committee in which academics themselves exercised a decisive voice, for it would then represent a scholarly judgement.

However, as has been pointed out, claims to institutional autonomy have traditionally been made for reasons unrelated to academic freedom as it is now understood; rather, they have been made in order to protect a general independence from state control. A university might be defending its property or other interests under the guise of academic freedom. In a well-known American case Princeton University attempted unsuccessfully to defend the exclusion from its campus of a distributor of literature for the US Labor party, on the ground that it had an academic freedom right to determine how its property was used.[92] The argument was a thin one and was rightly rejected by the New Jersey Supreme Court, for the university was really defending a broad immunity from state control, including control by the courts, over how it used its property. In fact, the arguments justifying academic freedom—the values of openness of inquiry and the search for truth—pointed to allowing the

---

[90]  See below ch 3, s II.
[91]  See Finkin (above n 52) 851–54.
[92]  *State v Schmid* 423 A 2d 615 (NJ, 1980).

Labor party to present its case on campus, rather than excluding it.[93] In this case, it was right to prefer the individual claim to freedom of speech over the negligible academic freedom claim.

One aspect of this conflict is that courts are reluctant to uphold challenges to decisions by universities and associated bodies. This reluctance has been shown by the courts in England in applications for judicial review; the courts would prefer not to substitute their judgement for that of an academic body, whether it was deciding how to assess the quality of a department's or institute's research[94] or whether it was deciding how to classify a student in her final examinations.[95] As Sedley LJ said in the *University of Lincolnshire* case, 'there are issues of academic or pastoral judgment which the university is equipped to consider in breadth and in depth, but on which any judgment of the courts would be jejeune and inappropriate.'[96] The same principle has been articulated by the US Supreme Court and by other courts when considering challenges to university decisions. In *Regents of University of Michigan v Ewing*,[97] when rejecting the challenge brought by a medical student dismissed from his programme of study for failing a crucial examination, Stevens J for the Court said that judges should show great respect for faculty judgement when considering whether to review a genuinely academic decision. It is difficult for judges to formulate appropriate standards by which to assess such a decision, and further, they were reluctant 'to trench on the prerogatives of state and local educational institutions and our responsibility to safeguard their academic freedom'.[98] These principles have been applied to allow universities to take race into account when admitting students to a law faculty; the courts have given what O'Connor J, in the Supreme Court's judgement in *Grutter*, called

---

[93] Under UK law, a university could not exclude the distribution of this type of literature on campus: see Education Act (No 2) 1986, s 43, discussed below in ch 9, s III(A).

[94] *R v Higher Education Funding Council, ex parte Institute of Dental Surgery* [1994] 1 WLR 242, DC.

[95] *Clark v University of Lincolnshire and Humberside* [2000] 3 All ER 752, CA.

[96] Ibid, 756.

[97] 474 US 214 (1985). (See also *Board of Curators of University of Missouri v Horowitz* 435 US 78, 89–90 (1978).)

[98] Ibid, 226.

'a degree of deference to a university's academic decisions, within constitutionally prescribed limits'.[99]

There are perhaps two arguments here, which should be kept distinct. The first is that courts should hesitate to uphold challenges to university decisions, particularly on academic issues, because they lack the competence to review such decisions. As a US court put it when declining to interfere with a university direction to a professor to stop interjecting his religious belief into his university classes, 'federal judges should not be ersatz deans or educators.'[100] The second is that it would be wrong in principle to interfere with the decisions of universities because that would trespass on their prerogatives, in particular their academic freedom. The first argument is broadly acceptable, though courts are surely as competent to review academic decisions as they are the conduct of doctors, lawyers, architects and other professionals or the decisions of, say, planning or environmental protection authorities. Judicial review in many contexts should be exercised with caution; there is perhaps nothing special about academic decisions on this point.

The second argument is much more problematic. As formulated by Stevens J in the Court opinion in *Ewing*, it might on one view equate the prerogatives of universities and their academic freedom.[101] In *Piarowski v Illinois Community College*,[102] a leading case on the conflict between individual and institutional academic freedom, Judge Posner pointed out that the term 'academic freedom' is equivocal: it is used to 'denote the freedom of the academy to pursue its ends without interference from government' as well as the freedom of individual professors to pursue their ends without university interference.[103] This judgement in effect conflated university autonomy and academic freedom, assuming in effect that a college takes all its decisions in the exercise of its academic

[99]   *Grutter* (above n 48) 329. This case is discussed further below in ch 6, s III(B).

[100]   Floyd R Gibson, Senior Circuit Judge in *Bishop v Aronov* 926 F 2d 1066, 1074–75 (11th Cir 1991).

[101]   But Areen (above n 63) 978–79 has pointed out Stevens J's emphasis that the decision to dismiss the students was taken by the faculty.

[102]   759 F2d 625 (7th Cir 1985). The Circuit Court of Appeals upheld the right of the university to require the chair of its Art Department to remove sexually explicit and racially offensive artworks from his gallery, which adjoined a mall near the entrance to the campus, to a less frequented site.

[103]   Ibid, 629.

freedom. That assumption is surely unfounded. A university takes many decisions—most obviously on the use of its investments and the acquisition of property—that have nothing to do with academic freedom. Others, such as a decision to merge with another university or to close a department, may be taken for a mixture of general financial and academic reasons. The second argument for judicial restraint or deference in this context is therefore convincing only insofar as it is clear that the court is called on to review a university's *academic* decisions.

Nevertheless, some commentators have welcomed the US courts' recognition of a broad institutional autonomy anchored in the First Amendment guarantee of freedom of speech.[104] Fred Schauer, for example, has argued that an institutional account of the First Amendment 'provides the foundation for the best explanation, description, and justification for a right to academic freedom'; that account emphasises the value of independence for institutions like universities, libraries and media corporations, which have the role of fostering public debate.[105] In his view a desirable consequence of the institutional account in this context is that it precludes the recognition of individual academic freedom rights; they would limit the academic autonomy of the university itself.[106] The objection to this resolution of the conflict between individual and institutional academic freedom is that it provides no safeguard against the abuse by universities of their autonomy. On this perspective courts are bound to respect university autonomy, even when their decisions infringe the academic freedom interests of professors and lecturers. The academic freedom of individuals becomes merely a matter of practice or convention, not a right that may be enforced against the universities themselves.

This difficulty would be removed if the law were to provide academic staff with a strong voice in the taking of university decisions affecting their freedom. Provisions of this kind would afford individu-

[104] In addition to Schauer's articles cited below in n 105, see JP Byrne, 'Academic Freedom: A "Special Concern of the First Amendment"' (1989) 99 *Yale Law Journal* 251; and P Horwitz, 'Universities as First Amendment Institutions: Some Easy Answers and Hard Questions' (2007) 54 *UCLA Law Review* 1497.

[105] F Schauer, 'Is there a Right to Academic Freedom?' (2006) 77 *University of Colorado Law Review* 907, 920. See also F Schauer, 'Towards an Institutional First Amendment' (2005) 89 *Minnesota Law Review* 1256 for his general argument for an institutional understanding of freedom of speech.

[106] Schauer, 'Is there a Right to Academic Freedom?' (ibid) 919 and 921–22.

als a safeguard against university decisions inimical to their academic freedom taken under the guise of an institutional exercise of that same freedom. A claim to adequate participation rights is of course the third kind of academic freedom claim identified in this chapter.[107] Its recognition would itself acknowledge that professors and other teachers may make legitimate claims to academic freedom.

Further, universities, it may be argued, should enjoy full decisional autonomy in the context of academic decisions only insofar as they can reasonably claim to be exercising that autonomy to promote the values of academic freedom, including that of individual professors.[108] Their decisions would not be entitled to immunity from judicial review if they were challenged on the ground that they infringed the academic freedom of a member of academic staff. Courts should not hesitate to intervene if the institutional claim that it was exercising its own academic freedom is meretricious, as would be the case if it were to dismiss a professor because, say, it disapproved of his research topics or resented his criticism of university administration. In this context, it is surely important which person or body within the university effectively took the decision. A Head of Department, Dean or Faculty Committee could make a more plausible claim to exercise academic freedom than a University President, Council or Board of Regents. The former are themselves academics, competent to take decisions about course syllabi, methods of teaching, appointments or promotions, while University Councils are typically not academic bodies. In any case, a University Council is much less likely to attach weight to academic freedom, given that it is expected to take into account a range of financial and political factors when taking decisions.

There is then no single answer to the resolution of conflicts between institutional and individual claims to academic freedom. It would be wrong to allow the former automatically to trump the latter, because it would be too easy for a university to dress up a decision taken for political reasons or for reasons of administrative convenience as an exercise of its academic freedom. Moreover, it is facile to equate a claim to institutional autonomy with academic freedom. Equally, individual

---

[107] See above s III(C).

[108] See Areen (above n 63) 996: 'Courts should defer to a decision made by an institution of higher education if the institution can show that it was made on academic grounds.'

professors and researchers cannot intelligibly claim a right to academic freedom that necessarily outweighs the freedom enjoyed by a faculty committee or by a university board predominantly composed of other professors and academics who are themselves entitled to exercise that freedom. Universities do appropriately make claims to academic freedom that should sometimes be respected, even when they infringe the interests of individual scholars.

## VI. ACADEMIC FREEDOM AS A CONSTITUTIONAL VALUE

It is often assumed that academic freedom is a *right* which may be claimed by individual scholars or universities. Indeed, that assumption underlies much of the discussion in this chapter distinguishing the different claims which may be made to the freedom and how conflicts between them might be resolved. The assumption is understandable, particularly in view of the close association between academic freedom and freedom of speech, which is generally treated as a constitutional or statutory right for individuals. But this is not the only perspective on academic freedom. The freedom not only gives academic staff distinctive liberties but also imposes on them duties and responsibilities; professors and researchers are, for example, professionally bound to do research, to publish their findings and to bring out their research in their teaching. Academic freedom may also be regarded, and treated in law, as a *fundamental value* of constitutional dimension. On that understanding of the freedom, it shapes the interpretation of laws and regulations outlining the functions and powers of universities and governing their procedures. Academic freedom on this perspective is not only a right asserted by individual professors and researchers but also a legal principle influencing all aspects of the organisation of universities and research institutes.

The German Constitutional Court has taken this approach when interpreting the guarantee of *Wissenschaftsfreiheit* provided by Article 5(3) of the Basic Law. In the *Hochschulurteil* (university judgement) the Court explained that the freedom not only is a defensive right against state interference but reflects a value of constitutional significance. It governs the interpretation of any law concerning universities. This understanding of academic freedom carries two main implications. First, the state has a duty to facilitate research through the provision of adequate human, financial and organisational resources. Scientific research is now dependent on financial resources that only the state can provide. Secondly, it must ensure that universities are organised so that academic freedom is protected. Academic freedom as a value extends the scope of the individual rights conferred by Article 5(3) to embrace participation rights—the argument discussed above in section III(C).[109] The scope of these participation rights has been clarified by the Court in a number of subsequent decisions, most recently in a case examining their implications for the evaluation of professors' teaching and research in the allocation of financial resources.[110] *Wissenschaftsfreiheit* has therefore an organisational and procedural dimension, in addition to its protection of individual scholarly and scientific freedom.

It would be wrong, however, to conclude from this perspective that academic (or scientific) freedom necessarily *limits* the powers that legislation confers on universities (or other education agencies). In some circumstances academic freedom might be interpreted to give universities wider discretion when they take decisions or to reinforce an argument for exemption from generally applicable laws. In Germany, for example, universities have used academic freedom to support an entitlement to enter into fixed term contracts with research assistants and language teachers in order to promote efficiency and the appointment of new blood personnel; the practice has survived a constitutional challenge brought on the basis that it infringes freedom of association.[111] The US Supreme Court has invoked academic freedom to uphold the adoption by universities of affirmative action programmes, in derogation from the Equal Protection Clause of the Constitution, to ensure racially diverse student bodies.[112] One interpretation of these US judgements is that universities have a freedom to choose the composition of their student body as an aspect of their First Amendment *right* to institutional academic freedom.[113] But a better understanding of them is that they treat

[109]   BVerfGE 35, 79, 115–16 (1973).
[110]   BverfGE 111, 333 (2004). For discussion of this case and other decisions of the Constitutional Court, see below ch 5, ss IV(B) and VI.
[111]   BVerfGE 94, 268 (1996)
[112]   See the opinion of Powell J in *UC v Bakke* (above n 48) 311–12; and O'Connor J for the Court in *Grutter* (above n 48) 329–30.
[113]   JP Byrne, 'Constitutional Academic Freedom after *Grutter*: Getting Real about the "Four Freedoms" of a University' (2006) 77 *University of Colorado Law Review* 929.

academic freedom as a fundamental value, justifying only the conclusion that universities have a compelling interest in the diversity of student bodies in derogation from a strict interpretation of non-discrimination laws; these decisions need not be read as supporting a right to institutional academic freedom under the First Amendment.[114]

It is also possible to see this understanding of academic freedom at work in other jurisdictions. In *McKinney v Board of Governors of the University of Guelph and the Attorney-General for Ontario*[115] the appellants—professors and a librarian—challenged their compulsory retirement at age 65, on the ground that the retirement policy infringed the equality clause of the Canadian Charter of Rights. The Canadian Supreme Court by a 5–2 majority dismissed their appeal. The principal reason was that universities did not form part of the government and so were not required to comply with Charter rights;[116] indeed, the academic freedom of universities and their staff reinforced other arguments that they should not be treated as part of government for the purpose of Charter compliance. The Court went on, however, to consider the appellants' argument on the alternative footing that universities were bound by the Charter. The majority found that the mandatory retirement policies could be justified as necessary to enhance the ability of universities to maintain standards of excellence through faculty renewal and to preserve academic freedom. Without mandatory retirement, universities would have to reconsider academic tenure, which in Canada, as in the United States, is regarded as an integral aspect of academic freedom. Otherwise, universities might be compelled to keep in employment professors who have ceased to conduct serious research or teach efficiently as they become older. In the majority's view, if mandatory retirement went, universities would inevitably change the system of tenure with consequent dangers for the academic freedom of all university staff. (This particular argument is not very persuasive. In the United States, as the Canadian Court admitted, mandatory retirement for academics

---

[114] See RH Hiers, 'Institutional Academic Freedom, A Constitutional Misconception: Did *Grutter v Bollinger* Perpetuate the Confusion?' (2003) 30 *Journal of College and University Law* 531. These conflicting interpretations of the Supreme Court judgements are considered further below in ch 6, s III(D).

[115] [1990] 3 SCR 229. See also *Dickason v University of Alberta* [1992] 2 SCR 1103, where the same arguments were considered.

[116] Only the legislature and governments of Canada and the Provinces are bound by the Charter under s 32 of the Constitution Act 1982.

has gone without affecting the tenure system. In the United Kingdom academic freedom has survived the removal of tenure by the Education Reform Act 1988.[117]) The important point is that the Canadian Supreme Court treated academic freedom (and tenure) as an important social and educational value, in this case advancing the autonomy of universities to determine their appropriate retirement policies.

Another example of this treatment is provided by a recent case from South Africa involving a defamation action between two professors of sociology.[118] The appellant brought the action in respect of an email sent by the respondent to people on the distribution lists of academic sociological associations, which accused the appellant of directing colleagues at the university where he was a professor and Executive Director not to talk to the media about impending industrial action at the university; the respondent stated that the appellant's own email to university staff represented the 'corporatisation' of academia and did enormous harm to the university's environment as an 'oasis of liberty with regards to thought, research and teaching'.[119] The Court upheld the respondent's defence of fair comment. Froneman J pointed out that freedom of speech, which includes academic freedom under the South African Constitution,[120] is particularly important in university and academic life. These freedoms protect 'unfettered debate on issues surrounding the autonomy of a university and the roles that managerial and academic staff ... should play in that regard'.[121] The value of academic freedom persuaded the Court to uphold the application of the common law defence. The Court of Appeal in England might have had this sort of argument in mind when it held recently that a science commentator was entitled to rely on the defence of fair comment when he criticised claims made by the British Chiropractic Association for the treatments offered by its members;[122] it would be incompatible with the value of academic freedom—more precisely, in this case, the freedom

---

[117] Discussed below in ch 4, s III(C).

[118] *Chetty v Adesina* (High Court of South Africa, Eastern Cape Division, 22 November 2007).

[119] Ibid, para 3, where the respondent's email is set out.

[120] S 16(1)(d).

[121] *Chetty* (above n 118) para 11.

[122] *British Chiropractic Association v Singh* [2010] EWCA 350.

of opinion of scientific commentators—to require the defendant to prove the truth of his criticisms.

Two important features of this understanding of academic freedom should be emphasised. First, it does not prevent a court upholding the freedom as an individual or institutional *right* when that decision is appropriate. That is the position in Germany, where it is clear that *Wissenschaftsfreiheit* is in the first place a defensive or negative liberty right for individual professors and other scholars.[123] The point is that this status does not exhaust the freedom's significance. It is also a fundamental constitutional value, which must shape the interpretation and application of other laws. Secondly, understanding academic freedom in this way should assist the resolution of conflicting claims to the freedom. Courts can ask which party to the litigation has the stronger claim in the light of the values associated with academic freedom. It is these values that make persuasive the case for its recognition as a right to which claims may legitimately be made. What these values are is explored in the next chapter.

---

[123] BVerfGE 35, 112.

# 3

# *Justifying Academic Freedom*

## I. INTRODUCTION

AS I EXPLAINED in the preceding chapter, academic freedom means that university professors and other academic staff have privileges that are not usually enjoyed by other employees, irrespective whether they work in public or private employment.[1] University professors and lecturers, for example, are relatively free to determine how they work; in particular they are free, within limits, to decide what and how they teach and to choose the areas in which they research. They are generally entitled to criticise the management of their universities in public and to participate in their governance and administration, at least insofar as academic matters are concerned.[2] At a more mundane level, at least at the older or research-oriented universities, they are free to organise their time, for example, by spending a day or so a week in the library or laboratory, or at home studying or writing. These special freedoms must be justified. Otherwise, academic freedom appears to give academic staff at universities unwarranted privileges. This chapter explores the arguments that can be put forward to justify academic freedom.

No comparable justification is required, however, if academic freedom at universities is an aspect of a general right to intellectual or scientific freedom, as it is in Germany. The right to scientific freedom (*Wissenschaftsfreiheit*) conferred by Article 5(3) of the Basic Law may be asserted by anyone engaged in serious scholarly activity, whether he or she is working at a university or a research institute, in industry,

---

[1] Above ch 2, s IV.
[2] Ibid, s III(C); see also below ch 4, s IV(A) and (C) for UK law, and below ch 6, s IV for US law.

or wholly independently.[3] In that event, there is no need to justify privileged freedoms for university professors, say, to conduct and publish research, for in theory everyone enjoys the same rights. However, what does need to be explained is any special protection given to intellectual or scientific freedom—including the freedom to conduct research and teaching—that goes further than the guarantee extended to general freedom of expression and media freedom. This question will be discussed below in section II.

Academic freedom in the sense in which it is understood in the United Kingdom, the United States (and other legal systems where it is strongly protected) is integrally connected to the special role of universities. Traditionally, universities have been regarded as having, in the words of a distinguished American commentator, '... a distinctive task. It is the methodical discovery and teaching of truths about serious and important things.'[4] Professors, lecturers and researchers enable universities to discharge these special responsibilities, it is argued, only if they enjoy the academic freedom to discover and transmit knowledge of the truths of their discipline.[5] Governments—or for that matter university authorities themselves—that compel scholars to teach in particular ways or to conduct research on trivial topics are denying the distinctive tasks of the academy. On this perspective, academic freedom is not only, not even primarily, a professorial entitlement or privilege but imposes on university academic staff special responsibilities and obligations.

The argument in the preceding paragraph is developed below in section III. It usually takes the form of a consequentialist argument: without academic freedom, professors would be unable to carry out their responsibility to discover and transmit truth, and society would be much the poorer as a result. The difficulty with this type of argument is that it is vulnerable to the contention that overall it would in fact be better for society if academics were employed, say, to conduct research on topics identified by the government—or by some agency on its behalf—as important for public welfare or perhaps to teach exclusively subjects that are useful to students' prospective employers.

---

[3] BVerfGE 35, 79, 112; BVerfGE 90, 1. See above ch 2, s IV and below ch 5, ss I and III(B).

[4] E Shils, 'The Academic Ethic' (1983) 20 *Minerva* 3.

[5] Ibid, 6.

Because of the shortcomings of consequentialist arguments, some commentators have identified deontological arguments as better suited to justify academic freedom. On these arguments, it is inherent in the role of universities and scholars that they pursue the truth and advance knowledge, irrespective of the implications of their research, at least as assessed by the government or by authorities acting for it. In short, commitment to the pursuit of truth is an absolute duty for academics, just as it is the most fundamental duty of doctors to save life and safeguard health. On deontological arguments we might speak of academic freedom as a *right* that all scholars may assert against government or against their universities, not just as a freedom, or obligation, to be exercised by them for the public benefit.

On one view the distinction between consequentialist and deontological arguments in this context should not be exaggerated. It may not always be easy to characterise an argument for academic freedom—for example, the emphasis on the importance of the pursuit of truth—as belonging exclusively to one or other type of argument.[6] It might be suggested that academic freedom is valuable because it enables scholars to discover and communicate truths to the benefit of the public—a consequentialist argument, which nevertheless relies on non-consequentialist assumptions or preconceptions about the value of truth. Or it could be said that academics have a moral right to academic freedom irrespective of the consequences, as the discovery of truth is inherent in or integral to their calling. This looks like a deontological argument. But if one asks why the discovery of truth is so crucial to the academic profession, it is difficult to avoid deploying consequentialist arguments, such as the point that professors have a special responsibility to report to the public their scientific findings and conclusions. The case for academic freedom can therefore be framed in terms of either consequentialist or deontological arguments, though each type of contention may rely on the other at various stages.

Nevertheless, the debate about the types of argument used to justify academic freedom is surely not entirely a matter of abstract philosophy. Consequentialist arguments seem more vulnerable to changing perceptions of truth—truth is not a matter for objective research and

---

[6] AO Rorty, 'Dilemmas of Academic and Intellectual Freedom' in EL Pincoffs (ed), *The Concept of Academic Freedom* (Austin, University of Texas Press, 1975) 98–102.

discovery but is socially determined or to be found only in the practise of a particular profession.[7] Moreover, consequentialist arguments for academic freedom may not be sufficiently robust to meet the case, ever more frequently made by governments of all political persuasions, that it is for them, on behalf of the public that funds universities, to determine the priorities for academic research and teaching. Universities and the individual scholars who work in them must now make a stronger case for academic freedom, a case that relies on fundamental liberal values, in addition to the vulnerable arguments of public welfare and benefit.[8]

What is clear is that different arguments can be made to justify the varieties of academic freedom claim that were identified in chapter two of this book. Claims to university autonomy and independence—institutional academic freedom—do not rest entirely on the arguments that are made in justification of individual scholarly freedom. Equally, other arguments can be found to support the case for the third type of academic freedom claim discussed in the previous chapter—the claim that academics are entitled to participate in the governance of their universities.[9] Though there is some overlap in the arguments used to justify each type of academic freedom claim, they are sufficiently distinct to merit separate treatment in this chapter: section III lays out the case for scholarly freedom; section IV discusses the case for institutional autonomy; and section V examines the case for academic participation in university governance. Before that, we consider the arguments for a general right to intellectual or scientific freedom.

## II. THE CASE FOR INTELLECTUAL AND SCIENTIFIC FREEDOM

If intellectual, artistic and scientific freedom is a right to be enjoyed by everyone, as it is in Germany,[10] then its justifications are very similar to those that support comparable human rights and civil liberties, notably freedom of expression (or speech) and freedom of religion and

---

[7] See further below s III(A).
[8] See below ss III(B) and IV.
[9] Above ch 2, s III(C).
[10] See below ch 5.

conscience. It should, however, be remembered that scientific freedom, like academic freedom, is often exercised through *activities*—the conduct of experiments and surveys—and not merely by speech; it may, for instance, involve medical experiments on animals or the participation of members of the public, as in clinical trials.[11] Consequently, it is even harder to regard the exercise of scientific freedom as self-regarding than it is to treat speech in this way.[12] Nor is it easy to justify the freedom in terms of the arguments from self-development or self-fulfilment, which are often deployed in support of free expression rights.[13] Finally, it is far from obvious that a broad freedom of scientific research can be justified on the most familiar argument for freedom of speech and expression: its role in ensuring a lively and participatory democracy. Certainly, without scientific freedom liberal democracies would be much the poorer in spirit, culture and general welfare; but we could imagine a society in which full freedom of political expression were allowed but which nevertheless tightly regulated the arts and scientific research, though not the exercise of a general intellectual freedom, say, to give public lectures on political philosophy.

But these are minor reservations about the coherence of the case for a general intellectual and scientific freedom. There are at least two powerful arguments for its recognition as an important liberty. The first is the argument from truth: knowledge of the truth is a self-evident good to which many people (not only in universities and colleges) devote their lives. Moreover, the discovery of new truths about the physical and social sciences is, as John Stuart Mill argued,[14] important for human progress and political development. 'Truth' and 'the advance of knowledge' are the key ideas in any theory of intellectual or scientific freedom, and also of academic freedom, which may be regarded as a

---

[11] See below ch 7, s II for discussion of freedom of research in the context of clinical trials.

[12] As Fred Schauer has pointed out, speech is not a self-regarding act, though it is sometimes considered to be: F Schauer, *Free Speech: A Philosophical Inquiry* (Cambridge, Cambridge University Press, 1982) 10–12.

[13] Ibid, ch 4. MG Yudof has doubted whether a personal autonomy argument could justify the narrower right to academic freedom recognised in the United States: MG Yudof, 'Three Faces of Academic Freedom' (1987) 32 *Loyola Law Review* 831.

[14] JS Mill, 'Of the Liberty of Thought and Discussion' in JS Mill, *On Liberty and Other Essays* (Oxford, Oxford University Press, 1991).

special case of this broader freedom.[15] Indeed, one theory of academic freedom has been couched in terms of the general desirability of intellectual freedom, the exercise of which might be modified for university professors to take account of their special responsibilities.[16] The argument from truth is of course one of the principal justifications for freedom of speech and expression. But Mill's argument perhaps applies more easily to intellectual debate—in university seminars and at public lectures and meetings held in literary and scientific societies—than it does to public discourse and debate in the mass media and on the political hustings. It justifies liberty of discussion and liberty to search for truth in any environment, where it can safely be assumed that speaker and audience are committed to its discovery.[17]

The second argument is also one that is frequently made in the context of freedom of speech:[18] we should particularly distrust government when it attempts to censor or restrict freedom of intellectual inquiry and publication. And we should also distrust other authorities that apply sanctions to those whose work they disapprove: a Church, an Imam or other religious community or leader. The suppression of Galileo's work by the Papacy in the seventeenth century and the prohibitions on teaching the principles of evolution in US public schools illustrate this danger.[19] For governments and other bodies are as likely to intervene when teaching or research threatens their authority as when political speech challenges their decisions. This is evidenced by the cases in the United States during the 1950s and 1960s when state authorities attempted to ensure that universities did not employ Communist or other radical professors.[20] Sometimes the pressure to dismiss professors with unpopular views comes instead from the general public and the

---

[15] See the arguments of RM Dworkin, considered below in s III.

[16] JR Searle, 'Two Concepts of Academic Freedom' in Pincoffs (ed) (above n 6) 92–93.

[17] See B Williams, *Truth and Truthfulness* (Princeton University Press, 2002) 213–19, pointing out that university research is conducted in a regulated environment, not an open marketplace of ideas.

[18] Schauer (above n 12) 80–86.

[19] In *Epperson v Arkansas* 393 US 97 (1968) the Supreme Court invalidated a state law proscribing the teaching of evolution on the ground that it infringed both religion clauses of the First Amendment; by giving effect to fundamentalist principles the law established religion and prohibited its free exercise.

[20] See below ch 6, s III(A).

media, which attempt to enlist university authorities in support of their cause.[21] But the same point applies in these circumstances. Intellectual (and academic) freedom is necessary to ensure that the government, or the public, cannot suppress research and publications that it finds disturbing or challenging.

In Germany *Wissenschaftsfreiheit*, perhaps most accurately translated as 'scientific freedom', enjoys stronger protection than the freedom to express opinions and the press and broadcasting freedom, which are also guaranteed by Article 5 of the Basic Law.[22] While the exercise of these other freedoms may be restricted by general laws, Article 5(3) of the Basic Law provides more or less absolute protection for artistic and scientific freedom. (However, these freedoms may be restricted to protect other constitutional values, notably the inalienable right to human dignity.[23]) What justifies this stronger protection for artistic and scientific freedom, including freedom of research and teaching freedom? The reason may lie in the importance of truth; the search for truth cannot occasion the damage or harms that legislation may legitimately prevent.[24] While freedom of political expression might in some circumstances properly be restricted to, say, protect members of racial or religious communities against serious offence, artistic or scientific freedom should trump these concerns—provided it is clear that the work in question is a serious work of art or scholarship. A professor should perhaps be freer to advocate Marxist or other revolutionary ideas in university seminars than a street orator to put forward comparable views before a mob; the point is that the former can be more easily treated as a serious contribution to the search for political truth.

As far as the position in Germany is concerned, it is also relevant that scientific freedom (including freedom of research) is guaranteed by the provision in the Basic Law that covers *Kunstfreiheit* (artistic freedom), namely Article 5(3). As the German Constitutional Court said in the leading *Mephisto* case,[25] *Kunstfreiheit* protects the freedom of artists to determine for themselves how to portray reality, without any state

---

[21] See the Toynbee and Laski episodes in the United Kingdom, discussed below in ch 4, s II(C).
[22] See below ch 5, s III(C).
[23] Ibid, s IV(C).
[24] D Grimm, *Wissenschaftsfreiheit vor neuen Grenzen?* (Göttingen, Wallstein, 2007) 22.
[25] BVerfGE 30, 173, 190–91.

interference with their processes and decisions. Artists must be allowed the fullest degree of autonomy, for the Nazi period showed what happens when they become dependent on state approval. The same principles were inevitably applied in the leading scientific (or academic) freedom decision, when the Court held that this freedom could not be limited by general laws but only to safeguard other constitutional values.[26] Scientific freedom is entitled to the same more or less absolute protection as artistic freedom. Both must be regarded as hallmarks of a civilised nation under the obligation to defend a system of open and free scholarly inquiry.

### III. THE CASE FOR SCHOLARLY FREEDOM

This section is concerned with the arguments for *individual* rights of scholars and scientists to academic freedom (the freedom identified in section III(A) of the preceding chapter). We need arguments that justify the freedom of university professors, lecturers and researchers, for example, to teach a subject as they think appropriate by choosing the materials for discussion in class and to conduct research on topics that they consider important and by the methods that they think most fruitful for the inquiry. As explained earlier,[27] two types of argument can be made to justify these freedoms.

### A. Consequentialist Arguments

These arguments assert that academic freedom is necessary to enable university professors and teachers to advance human knowledge through conducting research, publishing their findings and communicating them to students in lectures and seminars. As the 1915 Declaration of the American Association of University Professors (AAUP) put it, an unlimited freedom to pursue inquiry and publish its results is '[t]he first condition of progress'.[28] Without the assurance of such freedom,

---

[26] *Hochschulurteil*, BVerfGE 35, 79, discussed in detail below in ch 5, s IV(A).

[27] Above s I.

[28] See the extracts from the 1915 Declaration in M Finkin and R Post, *For the Common Good* (Newhaven, Yale University Press, 2009) 167.

professors would be inhibited in their research and teaching, and students would lack confidence in the quality of the education provided at universities. Further, university academics would be less able to provide expert advice to the community on scientific, economic and social issues. In addition to freedom from government restrictions, these arguments justify freedom from direction by university trustees, governing bodies and administrators, all of whom are much less qualified than academic staff to determine how topics should be taught and which subjects should be researched. It does not, however, justify an absolute freedom for individual professors and researchers; their work is constrained by the professional standards of the particular academic community within which they work. To use a standard example, a university history teacher is not free to deny the Holocaust in class or in writing, for that would be incompatible with the standards of the academic profession to which he or she belongs.[29]

Some features of this argument are worth noting. First, it is almost always connected with the special or distinctive role of universities and other places of higher education in liberal societies; the function of universities is to discover truth and to advance knowledge on important matters.[30] The argument does not justify similar academic freedom for people providing specialist training in business or other place of employment; they do not work in institutions that have as their central mission the discovery of truth and the acquisition of new knowledge.[31] Of course, universities (or some of them) might lose their distinctive role of challenging received wisdom; states might set up or encourage universities to conduct research in and teach particular subjects, just as the Catholic Church and other religious bodies have required the universities they finance and support to communicate their views as the truth. But generally universities in modern liberal societies remain free to teach and conduct research on material they consider important, even though many aspects of their autonomy have been increasingly circumscribed;

---

[29] But a professor of engineering or physics might have freedom of expression to deny the Holocaust, for his or her speech to that effect would be unrelated to his or her academic work: see below ch 9, s II.

[30] See the remarks of Edward Shils quoted above n 4.

[31] See the argument of W van Alstyne, 'Reply to Comments' in Pincoffs (ed) (above n 6) 128–29.

the academic freedom of individual scholars and scientists is linked to that distinctive role and the autonomy it entails.

Equally, it can be argued that other people, for example, writers, press and broadcasting journalists are concerned to discover truth and advance our knowledge about (typically) social and political questions. That argument can legitimately be deployed in support of the general intellectual freedom, which was discussed above in section II—a fundamental right that anyone engaged in serious scholarly or scientific research could claim. But it does not, without further argument, support the extension of *academic freedom* to cover writers working outside universities. For it is not the responsibility of book publishers or the institutional media to pursue truth and advance knowledge on all important topics, as distinct perhaps from providing a platform for the exchange of political ideas and information. But that role is safeguarded by the right to freedom of speech (or expression) and the related freedom of the press and other media, not by academic freedom.

Secondly, consequentialist arguments for academic freedom necessarily claim that the freedom is vital to the discovery of truth. Mill's argument for liberty of discussion is relevant at this point. He argued that without the freedom to challenge accepted truths ('received wisdom'[32]), we might perpetuate error and fail to discover better ways of living. Further, we would never have any justification for acting on our beliefs by using them as a basis for social policy and legislation. Our beliefs might simply be misconceived, so in the absence of any challenge to them we would be acting on an assumption of infallibility. Against Mill, sceptics may contend that at least in some circumstances, open discussion and inquiry does not lead to the discovery of truth; even the most carefully conducted research may lead to erroneous conclusions. Alternatively, and more often, they may say that some truths are too dangerous to live with in comfort, for example, the claims of a few university academics that some racial groups are genetically less intelligent than others and that this difference should be reflected in educational and other social policies. In a context such as this it can be argued that university authorities or the government need not recognise

---

[32] The UK Education Reform Act 1988, s 202 refers to the freedom of academic staff to question and test 'received wisdom'. See below ch 4, s III(C).

academic freedom, for its exercise is too dangerous.[33] In summary, there are, and ought to be, it may be said, some orthodoxies that cannot be challenged—either in society generally or at universities.

These sceptical arguments do not amount to a decisive rebuttal of the consequentialist case for academic freedom. They support only the more modest conclusion that professors do not have an unqualified entitlement, say, to teach whatever they like and publish whatever comes into their heads; in some instances it is appropriate to limit the exercise of academic freedom, in order to ensure that research is conducted responsibly or that professors do not use their seminars to provide outlets for, say, terrorist or racist propaganda.[34] But proponents of academic freedom do not argue for unqualified entitlements for university professors but rather for the freedom to conduct research and teach on the basis of the standards set by the profession. Moreover, the freedom entails responsibilities, for example, to conduct research carefully and to publish findings that can be substantiated by evidence and argument. Conscientious discharge of these and other academic responsibilities remove the sting of the case made by the sceptics: knowledge is almost always advanced by free and open inquiry, and we have no reason to fear the consequences of its publication, provided it is released with the usual academic caveats and caution.

It may be more difficult to meet the challenge of philosophical arguments that deny objective truth altogether and take the postmodern view that truth or reality is socially constructed rather than determined or discovered by rational inquiry and argument. A leading truth sceptic, Richard Rorty, has argued that academic freedom can only be defended by socio-political arguments—by pointing, for instance, to the role that universities play in ensuring the accountability of democratic government—not by resort to misconceived epistemological arguments from 'truth'.[35] But if that is the case, it becomes impossible to meet the political argument that research and teaching in universities should be geared to public demands, not to the dispassionate search by academics for 'truths' that may not exist. The awkward question is whether academic

---

[33] For further discussion of this argument in the context of particular episodes, see below ch 9, s III(B) and ch 10.

[34] See below ch 8, s II for discussion of the impact of UK terrorism laws on the exercise of academic freedom.

[35] 'Does Academic Freedom have Philosophical Presuppositions?' in L Menand (ed), *The Future of Academic Freedom* (Chicago, University of Chicago Press, 1996) 27.

freedom can be justified once we abandon the view that objective, or at least better, truths can be discovered by research undertaken in universities by professionals committed to and trained for this work.[36] But the coherence of academic freedom does not depend on any particular theory of truth, and certainly not the 'correspondence theory'—the view that what is true corresponds to an objective reality existing out there in a metaphysical world. John Dewey, a leading American philosopher of pragmatism, considered that truth was essentially pragmatic, that is what worked effectively and removed difficulties. But he was at the same time one of the most prominent early defenders of academic freedom in the United States and the first President of the AAUP when it was established in 1915: '[t]he university function is the truth function'.[37]

Another criticism of the consequentialist or instrumental argument for academic freedom—that its exercise in the long term serves the discovery of truth—is that it is simply not sufficiently eloquent to justify the 'emotional power that many of us feel academic freedom has'—and that it must have if it is to resist utilitarian arguments for restrictions on its exercise.[38] It is too easy, on the instrumental argument, for a university authority or the government to justify limits on the funding of certain types of research on the basis that it is likely to be socially dangerous or divisive. For that reason, Ronald Dworkin has argued that we need to establish more powerful arguments for academic freedom to be couched in terms of its distinctive role in promoting a culture of intellectual independence (see below s III(B)). That is best regarded as a non-consequentialist argument for academic freedom, a perspective that views it as an intrinsic good rather than as serving important goals—the search for truth and social progress.

## B. Non-consequentialist or Deontological Arguments

A number of non-consequentialist arguments have been made for academic freedom. Thomas Scanlon, for example, has argued that it would be irrational for a state to establish universities to search for and reveal

---

[36] See TL Haskell, 'Justifying the Rights of Academic Freedom' in Menand (ed) (ibid) 73. See also Williams (above n 17) 7–9.

[37] J Dewey, 'Academic Freedom' (1902) 23 *Educational Review* 3.

[38] RM Dworkin, 'We Need a New Interpretation of Academic Freedom' in Menand (ed) (above n 35) 187.

the truth and then deny the people who work in them the capacity or freedom to advance knowledge and disseminate their findings. It would in short simply be inconsistent with the institution of free universities to limit the freedom of their academic staff.[39] Whatever its merits, this argument is confined to freedom of research and does not address other aspects of academic freedom, notably teaching freedom. Nor does it justify a strong right for individual academics to choose their own topics of research, let alone a right to its financial support.[40] The point is that on Scanlon's argument, the individual academic freedom of professors is parasitic or dependent on the special research mission of the universities or other institutions for which they work—just as it is on the consequentialist arguments considered earlier in this section.

Another deontological argument is that it would be unjust to deny professors academic freedom when they are under an obligation to find out and communicate the truth. Professional ethical standards require university professors to undertake careful and objective research and to impart their knowledge to their students, and they are also required do this work by the terms of their appointment and contracts of employment. It would therefore be unfair to inhibit them from discharging their responsibilities by circumscribing their freedom. There is therefore a moral right to academic freedom.[41] This argument is broader than Scanlon's in that it justifies academic teaching freedom, but like that of Scanlon, it links academic freedom to the special responsibilities of professors working in institutions devoted to free inquiry and teaching. It would be difficult to apply it to, say, a researcher working on a special project for a government research institute or a teacher at a Catholic university or seminary required to teach church doctrine to the students.

Dworkin has made a much bolder deontological argument for academic freedom. In his view, the freedom 'represents and reinforces the ideals of ethical individualism', which requires all individuals to

---

[39] T Scanlon, 'Academic Freedom and the Control of Research' in Pincoffs (ed) (above n 6) 239–42.

[40] See JJ Thomson, 'Academic Freedom and Research' in Pincoffs (ed) (above n 6) 255.

[41] HE Jones, 'Academic Freedom as a Moral Right' in Pincoffs (ed) (above n 6) 37.

determine for themselves what sort of life they want to live.[42] Academic freedom, like freedom of speech and freedom of belief, is an aspect of the culture of independence from the state. Universities have a special responsibility to promote that culture by providing a forum in which ideas can be freely exchanged and discussed and by training both scholars and students alike to cultivate the attitudes that enable individualism to grow.

Dworkin's thesis is attractive, largely because it places academic freedom within a broader libertarian context. However, his ethical individualism argument surely justifies an artistic and intellectual freedom that everyone engaged in serious creative or scientific work should be entitled to claim.[43] There is no reason to confine it to those conducting research and teaching in universities. Academic staff working in universities and colleges may well be entitled to claim special freedoms on this argument because of the particular responsibilities of these institutions for ethical individualism; teaching is a core activity in universities, though it would also be appropriate to recognise comparable freedoms for artists and writers who give instruction and training outside a university environment. An analogy might be drawn at this point with the arguments for press freedom. The best argument for press (and broadcasting) freedom is that these institutions promote, or should promote, vigorous public debate and serve the other values of freedom of speech (or expression).[44] Press freedom is not primarily protected in the interests of newspaper corporations but rather because the institutions that exercise it are well placed to foster free speech and therefore have special responsibilities to promote its values. Similarly, academic freedom in universities should be guaranteed and protected because it promotes the values of intellectual independence and freedom from cultural conformity.

## IV. THE CASE FOR INSTITUTIONAL AUTONOMY

Two distinct lines of argument can be used to justify the institutional autonomy of universities—institutional academic freedom. As far as

---

[42] Dworkin (above n 38) 190.

[43] See the arguments above in s II.

[44] See E Barendt, *Freedom of Speech* (Oxford, Oxford University Press, 2007) ch XII.

continental Europe is concerned, the first argument builds on the early history of mediaeval universities, which could call on the protection of the Papacy to defend their liberties and privileges against interference from the local sovereign.[45] In England, academic institutional autonomy can be traced back at least to the struggles of Oxford and Cambridge colleges in the late seventeenth century to assert their independence from the Stuart monarchs.[46] Universities have acted as a check on the power of the Crown or, in earlier times, on that of the Church, and in practice they have often played a prominent part in resisting authoritarian government. This first argument is similar in principle to those for the separation of powers and for federalism, or the devolution of power to provincial and regional authorities: centralised power in a single state authority is undesirable. University autonomy ensures a degree of pluralism and checks and balances in the framing and application of education (and perhaps other) policy.[47]

In the United States the argument from pluralism has been reinforced by the legal claim that states should respect charters setting up private colleges and that any attempt to assume control over these institutions would amount to an interference with contract contrary to Article 1, section 10 of the US Constitution.[48] This claim was upheld by the Supreme Court in its famous decision in *Trustees of Dartmouth College v Woodward*;[49] Marshall CJ for the Court ruled that it would violate the understandings on which its founders had established Dartmouth College to allow the state of New Hampshire to assume control of its Board of Trustees. The Court based its decision on the constitutional obligation of states to respect contracts rather than on the particular importance of institutional autonomy for education. This is an important point. The college's constitutional independence had to be respected, whether or not its

[45] J Thorens, 'Liberties, Freedom and Autonomy: A Few Reflections on Academia's Estate' (2006) 19 *Higher Education Policy* 87, 92–94.

[46] For these struggles, see below ch 4, s II(A).

[47] GC Moodie, 'On Justifying the Different Claims to Academic Freedom' (1996) 34 *Minerva* 129, 147–49.

[48] Art 1, s 10(1) provides: 'No State shall … pass any Bill of Attainder, ex post facto Law, or Law impairing the Obligation of Contracts …'

[49] *Trustees of Dartmouth College v Woodward* 17 US (4 Wheat) 518 (1819), discussed by M Finkin, 'On "Institutional" Academic Freedom' (1982) 61 *Texas Law Review* 817, 831–33.

decisions usually supported the scholarly freedom of its academic staff and promoted the values of academic freedom.[50]

These arguments for institutional autonomy for universities and colleges suffer from a number of drawbacks. First, in the form considered in the last paragraph, they are applicable only to private colleges that continue to be substantially financed by endowments and not by state finance. On the other hand, the general argument for institutional pluralism applies to all universities, whether are public or private, and however they are funded. This argument will be attractive to advocates of limited government who doubt the ability of politicians to take detailed decisions about education policy, for example, concerning the subjects which it is most important for universities to teach and conduct research on. But many will find the pluralism argument unpersuasive. Why should not a democratically elected government, which provides most of the finance for university teaching and research, determine—at least if it acts through expert research councils and other bodies—in broad terms how resources are allocated and whether, say, certain disciplines are considered more worthy of support than others? The argument from pluralism should certainly not be ignored, but its claims are unlikely to be accepted by the general public, which rightly expects the government—whether central or regional—to account for public expenditure.

Another point is that the pluralism argument appears to justify a generous institutional autonomy, the exercise of which may have little connection with the values of academic or intellectual freedom. It would support, for example, a claim by a university to set whatever fees it considered appropriate for its students—in order perhaps to pay higher salaries for its most prestigious professors, to support links with universities overseas or to finance its other projects. Such an entitlement would go beyond the scope of the institutional freedom usually claimed for universities—the freedom to select students, to appoint academic staff and to determine what courses are taught.[51] That does not of course amount to a decisive argument against that entitlement; the point is simply that the broad pluralism argument for institutional

---

[50] Ibid, 839–40.
[51] See above ch 2, s III(B).

autonomy justifies wider institutional freedoms than those usually recognised in this context.

A more significant reservation is that the case from pluralism might also be used to justify an institutional autonomy to take decisions inimical to the exercise by academic staff of their own scholarly freedom. A university might decide, for instance, to stop teaching philosophy or theology because it thinks these disciplines are useless and attract less financial support than more practical subjects; it might then require professors in these fields to provide service courses for, say, medical or engineering students ('medical ethics for doctors') or leave the university altogether. Or a department might require specialists in Roman or Anglo-Saxon history to teach popular courses on twentieth-century history and encourage them to undertake research on topics of obvious relevance to modern social and economic needs. On the pluralist argument for university autonomy, it is hard to deny an institutional entitlement to take decisions of this kind, but they would inevitably conflict with the claims of individual members of academic staff that their scholarly freedom has been infringed. It is hard to see how these conflicting claims could be resolved, for they would rest on entirely different arguments of principle.[52]

It is more usual now to defend institutional academic freedom with a second line of argument: institutional autonomy supports the academic freedom of individual scholars.[53] Without such autonomy, universities, it is claimed, would be unable to defend the academic freedom of staff from interference by governments and their agencies. It is no longer possible to explain institutional autonomy in terms of the traditional privileges of universities to be (relatively) immune from central government control. The only socially acceptable justification is that universities have a distinctive mission to promote the discovery of truth and to advance knowledge to the benefit of the public, and that mission requires them to safeguard academic freedom.[54] They can only do that if they are autonomous.

---

[52] For a general discussion of conflicting institutional and individual claims to academic freedom, see above ch 2, s V.

[53] Moodie (above n 47) 147–49; Thorens (above n 45) 95–96; and Finkin (above n 49) 829–30.

[54] Thorens (above n 45) 96.

It has been pointed out, however, that institutional autonomy may not guarantee individual academic freedom.[55] It does not always safeguard it against interference from (senior) colleagues in the department, while academic institutions themselves, as explained in the preceding paragraphs, may take decisions inimical to the exercise by individual scholars of their academic freedom. So institutional autonomy is not a sufficient condition for scholarly freedom. Nor perhaps is it necessary. The independence of British universities has been substantially limited in the last thirty years, so that now only lip-service may be paid to their autonomy.[56] But individual academics, at least at the older universities, still enjoy a great deal of academic freedom to determine what and how they teach and the topics on which they research. Nor is there any evidence that individual scholars and scientists at private US universities such as Harvard, Yale and Stanford enjoy greater academic freedom than their colleagues at the public state universities governed by politically appointed Boards of Trustees.[57] It is far from clear, therefore, that effective institutional independence is necessary for the effective exercise of individual academic freedom.

Nevertheless, it can hardly be denied that there is a link between institutional autonomy and individual academic freedom. An authoritarian government that exercises tight control on all aspects of university governance by, say, dictating what courses are taught would have no reason to tolerate individual academic freedom and would not allow it in practice. Free universities are much more likely to allow and indeed encourage their staff to exercise academic freedom, because they appreciate its essential role in discharging their responsibility to teach students to think for themselves and to advance knowledge. The strongest single argument for the institutional autonomy of universities lies in its link with individual scholarly freedom. It is reinforced by the general argument from institutional pluralism, but on its own that argument does not provide a coherent, let alone a widely accepted, justification for the independence of universities and colleges. It justifies too strong

[55] M Tight, 'So What is Academic Freedom?' in M Tight (ed), *Academic Freedom and Responsibility* (Milton Keynes, Open University Press, 1988) 123–24.
[56] See below ch 4, s V.
[57] Indeed, it is easier for academics at state universities to claim academic freedom (and freedom of speech) as constitutional rights: see below ch 6, s IV.

a freedom for them; it would allow them to ignore or even suppress the individual freedom of scholars and scientists.

Two conclusions follow from the discussion in the last few paragraphs. First, the case for institutional autonomy is largely dependent on the arguments for scholarly freedom considered in the previous section of this chapter. (If the latter arguments are considered unconvincing, the case for university independence rests entirely on the general argument from pluralism, which many find unpersuasive at a time when government is expected to determine the main lines of educational policy.) These arguments justify both the academic freedom of individual scholars and scientists[58] and, albeit indirectly, the autonomy of those institutions where they work. It does not follow, however, that the particular claims of an individual professor or researcher should necessarily be preferred over those of the institution whenever they conflict. For both claims are ultimately justified by reference to the special role and responsibilities of universities to foster a culture of intellectual and moral independence and to advance knowledge for the benefit of all. On that perspective, it is surely right to allow a university rather than individual scholars to determine what degree courses are offered,[59] though the latter should be free to determine the syllabus for those courses and what is covered in particular lectures and seminars.

The second conclusion is that university autonomy is valuable and to be protected only insofar as it promotes the exercise of academic freedom and its values. It is not an absolute independence or total immunity from general laws, as it might be on the basis of the pluralism argument, but rather a conditional freedom, recognised because it is linked to the exercise of scholarly freedom. This point is important, for it should enable an easier resolution of disputes between a university on the one hand and a member of its academic staff or an academic visitor on the other. Suppose a university disciplines one of its sociology professors or excludes a visiting professor from speaking to its students on campus because its governing body considers his or her views unpalatable (though within the law) or their expression harmful to the standing of the university with the government. Of course, a university enjoying

---

[58] Some of these arguments also justify a broader intellectual freedom that can be claimed by anyone: see above s II.

[59] How this decision should be taken within a university is another matter: see below s V.

(more or less) unlimited autonomy on the basis of the argument from pluralism would be entitled to take these measures. But it is unlikely that they could be defended as promoting or being compatible with scholarly freedom, so in these circumstances the claim of the individual professor against the university's decision should be upheld. University decisions should be respected against the claims of an individual member of academic staff only when they respect the values of academic freedom; it may also be relevant whether they were taken by a body on which academics themselves were appropriately represented.

## V. THE CASE FOR ACADEMIC SELF-RULE

A third type of academic freedom claim was identified in chapter two: the claim by academics to participate in the governance and administration of their universities. It is better to treat this as a separate claim,[60] distinct from the scholarly freedom of individual academics, largely because it entails the assertion of positive rights to be represented on university councils or to exercise a decisive voice in the taking of some decisions—the hiring and promotion of academic staff, the approval of new courses or (more controversially) major decisions such as those to stop teaching a particular subject or to shut down a department. It is a little artificial to regard these positive rights as natural extensions of the *negative* liberty to teach and conduct research as one wishes, free from the direction of the university management.

Three arguments justify a degree of academic self-rule or at least participation in university governance. First, there are general arguments for professional self-regulation, which apply as much to academics as they do to, say, lawyers, doctors and architects. Self-regulation reflects the traditions of and dignity attached to a particular profession, the members of which are more likely to respect the decisions of professional bodies than those imposed on them by external authorities. Moreover, the drafting of codes of conduct and their application to particular cases are best left to members of the profession, who have the capacity and experience to determine when, say, one of their colleagues has failed to meet professional standards. Coupled with these general points is the argument from professional competence. Only professors

---

[60] See above ch 2, s III(C).

and lecturers are qualified to determine academic appointments and promotions, the allocation of research grants, the suitability of new courses or the restructuring of existing ones. These arguments are widely respected by universities, where it is usual for, say, appointments and promotions to be taken by committees composed exclusively of academics.[61] Managers and accountants take no part in these decisions, nor should they.

The third argument for a degree of academic self-rule, in particular for recognising the decisive voice of professors and lecturers in decisions on appointments, promotions, etc is that their involvement safeguards scholarly freedom.[62] A body of laypeople, particularly if they are politically appointed, or university managers might decline to appoint or promote an applicant with radical or unorthodox views, in disregard of intellectual ability, while (it is assumed) academics would make a dispassionate assessment of the quality of the applicant's publications. It was for these reasons that the German Constitutional Court insisted on appropriate procedures to safeguard scientific freedom in the evaluation of research and emphasised that, on the facts of the case before it, the criteria for this evaluation were drawn up by the Senate, on which professors enjoyed majority representation.[63] This argument is similar to the most persuasive case for the institutional autonomy of universities: it promotes scholarly freedom. Indeed, it safeguards this freedom against any arrangements that a university with unlimited autonomy might make to endanger its exercise. A university should not have complete freedom to determine its own governance structure; in particular, it should allow academics a decisive voice in taking academic decisions.

At the universities of Oxford and Cambridge full academic self-government has been considered necessary to safeguard scholarly freedom, so that academics still form a majority on the governing

---

[61] For governance arrangements in the context of academic freedom, see below ch 4, s V(C) for the United Kingdom; ch 5, s VI for Germany; and ch 6, s II(C) for the United States.

[62] For this defence of academic self rule in an American context, see J Areen, 'Government as Educator: A New Understanding of First Amendment Protection of Academic Freedom and Governance' (2009) 97 *Georgetown Law Review* 945, 958, commending the principles formulated in the 1915 Declaration by the AAUP.

[63] BVerfGE 111, 333, discussed below in ch 5, s VI.

councils. That is not the position in other UK universities.[64] So we could conclude either that academic freedom is imperfectly safeguarded in most UK universities or that the case for academic self-rule can be exaggerated. It may not be a *necessary* safeguard, even if it is very desirable. Graeme Moodie concluded in his survey of the arguments, 'scholars only invite ridicule, or being ignored, when they seem to suggest that every issue that directly affect them is a proper sphere for academic rule.'[65] The arguments for academic self-rule do not mean that professors should take every decision that affects their welfare or even exercise a decisive voice in this context. Financial and development decisions, even those concerning the allocation of resources, are almost certainly best left to bodies in which laypeople form a majority, though it is important that academics are well represented on them. However, these arguments do justify the conclusion that academic decisions are taken by scholars; to that extent the case for academic self-rule is well made.

## VI. CONCLUSIONS

This chapter has considered a wide range of arguments, so it may be useful to summarise its principal conclusions. The first is that the arguments for scholarly academic freedom are powerful and convincing. The case is not only that without this freedom, scientists and other academics would be less able to advance knowledge by discovering new truths about the world and that as a result society as a whole would be the poorer—though that is surely a strong argument. It is that universities and their academic staff have a responsibility to foster a culture of independence in which individuals are free to think for themselves and lead, so far as possible, lives of their own choosing. These arguments in fact justify a freedom of artistic and intellectual inquiry and work that can be claimed by everyone, whether they work in universities or independently; but universities and their staff are particularly well placed to construct an environment in which this culture of independence flourishes.

---

[64] See below ch 4, s V.
[65] Moodie (above n 47) 146.

Secondly, there are a number of good arguments for the institutional autonomy of universities and colleges—institutional academic freedom—and for academic self-rule. But the most persuasive justification for these claims to academic freedom is that they encourage an environment and provide structures and procedures in which scholarly freedom flourishes. Other arguments, notably the case for decentralised decision-taking by independent universities, are also pertinent. But they are less attractive because they can be used to defend decisions curtailing individual academic freedom; in any event they are less generally acceptable in modern political circumstances when governments are held accountable for the allocation of public resources.

Some readers may be disappointed that this account has not brought out a single, or simpler, justification for academic freedom that supports equally all the varieties of claim that may be made to its exercise. They should not be disappointed. There are no simple explanations for why we value some basic civil liberties, though we know from experience how essential they are. For example, it is hard to find a single justification for freedom of speech. A number of explanations for that freedom have been provided, one of which may work well for some types of free speech claim (for example, freedom of political speech), while another might better show why other types of speech—the arts or sexually explicit speech—should be free from government restriction.[66] There is no reason to expect things to be more straightforward in the case of academic freedom. Other readers may not be persuaded that the case for academic freedom has been made by any of these arguments. Perhaps we should not rely exclusively on the abstract arguments made in this chapter. If we are sceptical of the purely intellectual case for academic freedom, we should examine other, historical arguments. We should look at the experience of societies that have denied the freedom in all of its forms and ask whether more fruitful research has been conducted in their universities and whether their citizens have led richer and happier lives.[67]

---

[66] For general discussion of the justifications for freedom of speech, see Schauer (above n 12) chs 2–6.

[67] For a survey of societies where academic freedom is denied, see J Connelly (ed), *Universities under Dictatorship* (University Park, Pennsylvania State University Press, 2005).

# 4

## *Academic Freedom in the United Kingdom*

### I. INTRODUCTION

T HERE IS RELATIVELY little law on academic freedom in the United Kingdom. Indeed, until recently it was entirely a matter of convention and practice. That was certainly the case insofar as it was understood as the institutional autonomy of universities; their freedom to govern themselves had in effect been recognised politically after the unsuccessful attempt of the Crown to exercise control over colleges in Oxford and Cambridge at the end of the seventeenth century (see below section II). The individual academic freedom of professors and other university teachers was largely protected through the system of tenure, initially the privilege of Fellows of the Oxford and Cambridge colleges, subsequently recognised as a right of academic staff at many, though not all, universities. It went without saying that they could teach and research what they liked, with minimal direction from Senior Tutors or Heads of Department. University teachers have also been relatively free to speak and write openly on matters of political and social controversy, whether or not these publications fall within their area of specialisation. In effect they enjoyed (as they still do) considerable freedom of extramural speech—to use the American term—though occasionally the exercise of this freedom gave rise to sharp controversy.[1] But these controversies did not lead to litigation. Writing in 1963, Lord Chorley, then Honorary General Secretary of the Association of University Teachers (AUT), remarked he was unaware of any case in which the term 'academic freedom' had been used by a

---

[1] See below s II(C).

judge; the freedom of universities and their staff was protected by a complex mixture of understandings and general practice.[2]

Now academic freedom is protected by law. As an *individual* freedom it is guaranteed for members of academic staff (at the universities established before 1992) by the Education Reform Act 1988 (ERA) in order to provide a safeguard against the possibility of arbitrary dismissal, which arose when their tenure was abolished by this legislation (see below section III). Moreover, there is some statutory recognition of *institutional* academic freedom, while court judgements declining to uphold challenges to university decisions recognise in effect their freedom to take academic decisions without interference (see below section V for institutional academic freedom in the United Kingdom). However, despite these legal developments, there is hardly any case law on academic freedom in the United Kingdom, in marked contrast to the position in Germany and the United States, where the scope and application of the freedom has been the subject of considerable litigation.[3]

There are a number of possible explanations for this striking dearth of case law on academic freedom in the United Kingdom. One is that universities prefer, for understandable financial reasons, to settle claims brought by any academics they have suspended or dismissed, rather than contest them before employment tribunals or the courts (see below s IV). Insofar as that happens, these bodies have little opportunity to clarify the scope of individual academic freedom or to resolve conflicts between the claims to academic freedom of individuals and the universities. A more attractive albeit too complacent an explanation is that universities in the United Kingdom show such respect for the individual academic freedom of their staff that the latter rarely have any cause for complaint. These explanations are of course quite compatible with each other.

A third explanation for the absence of judicial authority in this area is that there is no *constitutional* guarantee of academic or scientific

---

[2] Lord Chorley, 'Academic Freedom in the United Kingdom' (1963) 28 *Law and Contemporary Problems* 647, 649. Robert Chorley (1895–1978) was Cassell Professor of Commercial and Industrial Law at LSE and was elevated to the peerage in 1945. His view of the state of academic freedom has been criticised as complacent: see S Wallace, *War and the Image of Germany: British Academics 1914–1918* (Edinburgh, John Donald, 1988) 166.

[3] For Germany, see below ch 5; for the United States, see below ch 6.

freedom in the United Kingdom. As a result, legal arguments that might be the basis of a challenge in other jurisdictions cannot be made in the courts in England and Scotland. An individual professor in the United Kingdom cannot, for example, argue that the academic freedom provision in the ERA must be interpreted in a particular way in order to comply with his constitutional right to academic freedom. Nor is it open to a UK university to question the legality of any funding or other executive decision, let alone the terms of legislation, on the grounds of incompatibility with its own institutional freedom or autonomy. These arguments can at least be made in Germany and the United States, albeit in practice with limited success.[4] Admittedly, under the Human Rights Act 1998 individual university teachers in the United Kingdom are entitled to the European Convention right to freedom of expression, which they might invoke when they exercise their freedom of extramural speech. But this freedom (which is more fully considered in chapter nine) does not lie at the heart of academic freedom or of the broader *Wissenschaftsfreiheit* (scientific or intellectual freedom) recognised by the Basic Law of Germany;[5] moreover, freedom of expression is a right enjoyed by everyone, not solely academic or university staff.[6] The range of academic freedom arguments that can be made before UK courts is therefore considerably more limited than in jurisdictions such as Germany, Spain and South Africa, where the freedom is explicitly guaranteed by the constitutions. That provides a further explanation why there is so little judicial discussion of the freedom in the United Kingdom.

There is therefore much less legal analysis in this than in the following chapters outlining academic freedom law in Germany and the United States. Section II provides an historical account of the understanding of the freedom before the enactment of the Education Reform Act 1988. That legislation is discussed in section III; the enactment is of fundamental importance, for not only did it formulate the entitlement of

[4] There are some doubts whether individual university teachers, as distinct from the universities themselves, enjoy *constitutional* academic freedom rights in the United States (see below ch 6, s IV), but professors at state universities may certainly rely on First Amendment rights to freedom of speech.
[5] Ch 5, s III explains the broad constitutional right to scientific freedom recognised in Germany.
[6] See above ch 2, s II for the relationship of academic freedom to freedom of speech (or expression).

individual university teachers to academic freedom, but it significantly curtailed university autonomy as it had been traditionally understood and respected. Sections IV and V are concerned respectively with the subsequent treatment of the individual and with institutional freedoms, before section VI draws a few conclusions about the present state of academic freedom in the United Kingdom.

## II. AN HISTORICAL ACCOUNT OF ACADEMIC FREEDOM IN THE UNITED KINGDOM

### A. The Early History before 1919

The recurring conflicts between the Crown and the universities of Oxford and Cambridge—until the early nineteenth century the only universities in England—provide one of the most important themes of the early history of academic freedom in the United Kingdom.[7] Both Charles II and James II attempted to control appointments at colleges of these universities. The former succeeded in securing the dismissal of John Locke from a Studentship at Christ Church in 1684 against the wishes of its Dean,[8] while James II managed eventually to impose a President on Magdalen College, Oxford, in 1688.[9] He had also forced a Catholic Master on Sidney Sussex College, Cambridge. Religious conflicts lay at the root of these disputes. But when the colleges claimed their entitlement to determine the composition of their Fellowships and to appoint their own Masters or Presidents, they were primarily asserting their institutional independence from royal control. That independence might be used in the service of religious liberty, at least against Catholic monarchs, but it would be wrong to equate this autonomy with academic freedom as the concept is generally understood now.

---

[7] For a very short history of UK universities, see G Graham, *The Institution of Academic Values* (Exeter, Imprint Academic, 2005) 7–26. RO Berdahl, *British Universities and the State* (Cambridge, Cambridge University Press, 1959) chs 2 and 3 provide a fuller account, to which this section of the chapter is much indebted.

[8] For accounts of this early academic freedom episode, see HR Fox Bourne, *The Life of John Locke: Volume I* (London, Henry S King and Co, 1876) 481–88; and M Cranston, *John Locke: A Biography* (London, Longmans, 1957) 246–48.

[9] LWB Brockliss (ed), *A History of Magdalen College, Oxford* (2008) 180–85.

The independence of Oxford and Cambridge did not face any significant challenge in the eighteenth and early nineteenth centuries until two Royal Commissions were appointed to consider their reform in 1850.[10] The incapacity of Dissenters under college statutes to become students at the universities was the primary reason for disquiet, but there were also significant complaints against the quality of teaching and conservative degree courses—more familiar complaints to modern readers. The establishment of the Commissions was strongly opposed by the universities, which viewed them as a clear threat to their traditional independence. The Oxford Commissioners, however, concluded that public policy required steps to promote the efficiency of the university; Oxford was not an aggregate of purely private interests but was 'eminently national'.[11] Subsequent legislation to implement some of the Commissioners' recommendations and to abolish religious tests for Fellows and students indicated that there was no constitutional convention against state regulation of the universities.[12] University autonomy in the United Kingdom has never meant absolute immunity from such regulation.

Another development worth noting is the beginning of regular state funding in 1889 when a Treasury Minute set up a small ad hoc committee to advise on the allocation of £15,000 granted by the government to support university colleges.[13] The committee established the principle that grants should be allocated for five-year periods to enable universities to plan ahead—the origin of the quinquennial grants system, which prevailed until 1977. The first permanent Advisory Committee for the distribution of grants was constituted in 1906; it observed that universities and colleges should have more freedom than schools to

---

[10] Berdahl (above n 7) 30–34.

[11] Report of the Oxford University Commissioners (1852) 3.

[12] For example, Oxford University Act 1854, Cambridge University Act 1856, Universities (Scotland) Act 1858 and Universities Tests Act 1871. This last measure removed the disqualification of Dissenters from becoming student or teaching members of the universities.

[13] By 1889, in addition to Oxford, Cambridge and the Scottish universities, there were universities in London and Durham and university colleges in Wales and a number of cities in England, including Manchester, Bristol, Birmingham and Liverpool.

determine how they spend the sums allocated to them.[14] The principle was gradually established that public financing should not entail interference by the state with university autonomy.

## B. The University Grants Committee and University Autonomy

The University Grants Committee (UGC) was constituted in 1919 to advise the government on university needs and the grants that should be made to meet them.[15] It was placed under the Treasury rather than the Board of Education—then the government department responsible for education policy—largely to ensure its independence from government.[16] Consequently, it did not have to compete against schools for an adequate share of the total education budget. Both at its inception and generally throughout its existence, the UGC was composed predominantly of academics.[17] In 1946 new terms of reference required it to prepare plans for university development that were adequate for national needs.[18]

A full treatment of the work of the UGC falls outside the scope of this book.[19] It is important here to emphasise the care taken to ensure that state financing through the UGC did not intrude on university autonomy or academic freedom. First, the Treasury itself resisted attempts by the Public Accounts Committee (PAC) of the House of Commons to place the Committee under statutory authority; in its view such a step would have had worrying implications for the academic freedom of the universities.[20] This anxiety was almost certainly

---

[14]   See the Report of the University Grants Committee for 1957–62, Cmnd 2267, paras 523–30 for the history of university funding.

[15]   E Hutchinson, 'The Origins of the University Grants Committee' (1975) 13 *Minerva* 583.

[16]   Berdahl (above n 7) 57–62.

[17]   Compare the composition of the Higher Education Funding Council for England (HEFCE), discussed below in s V.

[18]   Berdahl (above n 7) 76.

[19]   For further discussion of the UGC, see Berdahl (above n 7) chs 8 and 9; and J Carswell, *Government and Universities in Britain: 1960–1980* (Cambridge, Cambridge University Press, 1985) esp 10–15 and ch 7.

[20]   Berdahl (above n 7) 118–21.

needless,[21] but it is important to note that it was felt. Secondly, for a number of years the UGC resisted scrutiny by the Comptroller and Auditor General and the PAC of its own books and records, as well as those of the universities. It worried that the PAC might make comments that could lead to parliamentary pressure for greater government control over universities and impel the UGC itself to exercise closer supervision over use of the grants it had allocated them.[22] When eventually the government accepted a PAC recommendation that the Comptroller and Auditor General should have access to these records, the Secretary of State for Education and Science assured the House of Commons that this check need not infringe university academic freedom.[23] The UGC itself commented a little delphically that a distinction should be drawn in this context between the intellectual freedom of individual academics and university autonomy.[24] The implication was that Parliamentary scrutiny might have repercussions for the latter, without endangering individual academic freedom.

A third point is that the UGC decided in 1952 to discontinue the practice of earmarked grants, which had been developed after the end of the Second World War when the government wanted to encourage the expansion of particular subjects.[25] Though the Committee did not share the criticism that such grants necessarily restricted university freedom, it preferred to allocate block grants over which universities, at least in principle, could exercise full control.[26] More generally, the UGC saw its role as balancing the increasing need for central planning of university teaching and research with the maintenance of academic freedom. In its Report for 1967–72 it emphasised that the government had never attempted to influence how much money was allocated to individual universities or to attach conditions to UGC grants. The UGC's own freedom enabled it to guarantee university independence.[27]

---

[21] A comparison may be made with the equally weak claim that it would endanger the independence of the BBC to constitute it by statute rather than by Royal Charter: see E Barendt, *Broadcasting Law* (Oxford, Oxford University Press, 1995) 67.
[22] UGC Report for 1962–67, Cmnd 3820, para 595.
[23] Hansard HC vol 751 cols 750–51 (26 July 1967).
[24] UGC Report for 1962–67 (above n 22) para 594.
[25] UGC Report for 1947–52, Cmd 8875, paras 95–99.
[26] See Berdahl (above n 7) 148–51.
[27] UGC Report for 1967–72, Cmnd 5728, para 181.

The government assumed much greater control over university policy during the 1970s, determining, for example, overall student numbers and the balance between arts and science, undergraduate and graduate students.[28] Correspondingly, the UGC lost influence; in 1977 the principle of the quinquennial grant was abandoned. During a period of economic decline, it was no longer possible politically to insulate universities from public expenditure constraints. In 1985, the Conservative government initiated a review of the UGC to examine its constitutional position and responsibilities within the context of the increasing requirement for universities to respond cost-effectively to national needs.[29]

## C. Individual Academic Freedom before the 1960s

The discussion so far has concerned institutional autonomy. This freedom is quite different, as was explained in chapter two, from the academic freedom of individual professors and lecturers. Indeed, there need be no connection between them; the independence of a university is neither a necessary nor a sufficient condition of the freedom of its academic staff to teach and conduct research.[30] The general assumption in the United Kingdom that independent universities are much more likely than state directed institutions to protect individual academic freedom is almost certainly justified; but it is not a necessary truth. Universities may claim the autonomy to limit the teaching, and perhaps even the research, freedom of their academic staff—the cases of conflicting claims to academic freedom discussed earlier in this book.[31]

It was sometimes assumed that academic staff at UK universities enjoyed academic freedom by virtue of their tenure before its abolition by the ERA 1988.[32] Under tenured employment, professors could not lose their jobs except for 'good cause', which was usually defined

---

[28] M Shattock, *The UGC and the Management of British Universities* (London, Society for Research into Higher Education and Open University Press, 1994) 12–19.

[29] See further below s III(A).

[30] See M Tight, 'So What is Academic Freedom?' in M Tight (ed), *Academic Freedom and Responsibility* (Milton Keynes, Open University Press, 1988) 126–28.

[31] See above ch 2, s V.

[32] See M Tight, 'Academic Freedom Re-examined' (1985) *Higher Education Review* 7, 19–20.

narrowly by the university statutes to cover such matters as criminal conduct, gross immorality or serious dereliction of duty. A university could not dismiss a professor simply because he or she failed to publish anything or because of poor-quality lectures, let alone because the university wanted to close a department or could not afford to keep the professor on the payroll.[33] Fellows of Oxford and Cambridge colleges certainly enjoyed tenure under their college statutes, and this privilege seems generally to have been extended to professors at the civic universities that were established in England and Wales in the nineteenth and twentieth centuries. It was only under pressure from the newly formed Association of University Teachers (AUT) that tenure was apparently extended in 1921 to readers and lecturers once the initial probationary period of their employment had passed satisfactorily.[34] In fact the position was more complex than this account suggests, for periods of probationary employment might be extended or lecturers employed under fixed term contracts.[35] Even the position of long-established tenured university lecturers was less secure than they had envisaged, as emerged from *Page v Hull University Visitor* in 1992.[36] The House of Lords, affirming the view of the Court of Appeal on the point, dismissed a philosophy lecturer's claim that Hull University was not entitled to terminate his employment on the ground of redundancy. Its statutes ('Subject to the terms of his appointment no member of the teaching … staff of the university … shall be removed from office save [for good cause]…) were to be read as allowing immediate termination of employment of teaching staff for 'good cause' and on three months' notice on other grounds, including redundancy.

---

[33] In *Pearce v University of Aston in Birmingham (No 2)* [1991] 2 All ER 469, Sir Nicholas Browne-Wilkinson V-C, on behalf of the Visitor, held that the University could not under its statutes dismiss its academic staff for redundancy; the contract of employment could be ended only for good cause.

[34] H Perkin, *Key Profession: The History of the Association of University Teachers* (London, Routledge and Kegan Paul, 1969) 81–85.

[35] S Court, 'Academic Tenure and Employment in the UK' (1998) 41 *Sociological Perspectives* 767.

[36] [1993] AC AC 682. The main point in the appeal to the House of Lords was whether the courts were entitled to intervene with a University Visitor's decision on the ground of error of law. By 3–2, it held that the courts could not intervene on this ground: see HWR Wade, 'Visitors and Error of Law' (1993) 109 *Law Quarterly Review* 155. For the abolition of the Visitor's jurisdiction, see s. III(D) below.

Even though the legal protection afforded university staff by the system of tenure might not have been as strong as they thought, professors and lecturers probably assumed that it safeguarded their academic freedom. Anxiety about dangers to this freedom was rarely expressed, at least in the pages of the journals of the AUT. It was only at the end of 1934 that its Council passed a Resolution affirming:

> [T]he public expression of opinion, within the limits of the law, on controversial matters is in no way incompatible with the position and responsibilities of a university teacher, it being understood that such expression of opinion is personal and does not commit the Institution to which he belongs.[37]

An Editorial Note in the AUT *Universities Review* stated that academic freedom had not been, nor was it likely to be, threatened by anyone.[38] In contrast, the *Review* expressed increasing concern at the loss of academic freedom in Germany and in other countries that had been annexed by the Nazi regime.

Whatever the general position, a few prominent episodes show that academic freedom could come under threat during this period. Bertrand Russell was dismissed from a non-tenured lectureship at Trinity College, Cambridge, after his conviction for expressing statements likely to prejudice recruitment to the armed forces during the First World War.[39] Another affair concerned Arnold Toynbee, the first holder of the Koraes Chair of Modern Greek and Byzantine History, Languages and Literature at King's College London (KCL).[40] The bulk of the endowment for the Chair was raised by the Greek community in London, which formed a subscribers' committee; under the terms of the endowment—apparently not disclosed to Toynbee when he accepted appointment in 1919—the holder of the Chair was required to inform

---

[37] (1934) 7 *Universities Review* 107–8.

[38] (1935) 8 *Universities Review* 2–3.

[39] See Wallace (above n 2) 150–56; and A Ryan, *Bertrand Russell* (London, Penguin, 1988) 61–62. A number of academics of German origin were compelled to resign during the First World War because of widespread hostility to them: Wallace (above n 2) ch 9.

[40] R Clogg, *Politics and the Academy: Arnold Toynbee and the Koraes Chair* (London, Frank Cass and King's College, London, 1986) contains a full account of this fascinating episode, including in an Appendix a reprint of Toynbee's letter to *The Times* of 3 Jan 1924.

subscribers about his teaching and research programme at the start of
the academic year and to submit a full report on his work every three
years. Toynbee angered the subscribers with a number of articles in the
*Manchester Guardian* in 1921 that were highly critical of the conduct of
Greek forces in Asia Minor (now Turkey). They also complained of his
failure to report to them on his work. The Principal of KCL, Sir Ernest
Barker, and initially the Senate of the University of London deprecated
the attempt by the subscribers to put pressure on Toynbee; on the
other hand, some members of the Senate, including Lord Justice Atkin,
and academic colleagues at KCL thought that Toynbee's articles went
beyond the limits of acceptable freedom of speech and endangered
the continued financing of the Chair. Not wishing to embarrass the
University further, Toynbee resigned in January 1924 but made it clear
in a letter to *The Times* that as a professor he should enjoy full freedom
to state his views on Greek–Turkish relations; moreover, he would not
have accepted appointment had he been aware of the obligations to
report regularly to the subscribers' committee.

A later episode also involved a controversy excited by the extramural speech of a distinguished London professor. Harold Laski, the
Professor of Political Science at the London School of Economics,
wrote a regular column in the *Daily Herald* in support of socialism.[41]
In a lecture in Moscow in 1934 he argued that in the absence of radical reform, class war and revolution in Britain was likely. His remarks
led to questions in Parliament and a fierce attack in a letter to the *Daily
Telegraph* by the London University MP, Sir Ernest Graham-Little, who
urged the LSE to take disciplinary action against Laski. This attack
prompted a letter to *The Times* by five LSE professors, defending
Laski's right to express his political views in exercise of his academic
freedom. The LSE Director, the distinguished social reformer William
Beveridge, and a Committee of its Court of Governors concluded that
Laski's newspaper articles damaged the reputation of the LSE; he had
infringed a Resolution passed in 1932 by LSE professors calling on

---

[41] For accounts of the Laski affair, see J Harris, *William Beveridge* (Oxford,
Oxford University Press, 1977) 290–303; and R Dahrendorf, *A History of the London
School of Economics and Political Science 1895–1995* (Oxford, Oxford University Press,
1995) 278–82. Dahrendorf, Director of the LSE 1974–84, considers it wrong to
extend academic freedom to cover the extramural speech at issue in the Laski affair
(283–85).

teachers to pay proper regard to the reputation of the School when expressing their views. Laski agreed to stop writing a regular column for the *Daily Herald*, but it is surely important to note that no formal disciplinary proceedings were taken against him.

The Toynbee and Laski affairs shared two features. Both involved for the most part extramural speech or writing rather than the teaching or research of the Professors. Indeed, on a narrow view of its scope there was no interference with academic freedom in either case, save for the requirement imposed on the holder of the Koraes Chair to report regularly to the subscribers about his work, outlining his programme of lectures and seminars at the start of each academic year. That obligation would make it easy for them to put pressure on the holder to teach particular topics or perhaps to teach them in a particular way. Secondly, both episodes show that academic freedom can be threatened initially by pressure from outside parties rather than from the state or the university: in the first case, from the subscribers who endowed the Chair and might discontinue its funding; in the Laski case from the conservative MP and from other right-wing groups and newspapers who loathed Laski's politics. In each case pressure was put on the university to take action against a teacher whose conduct offended these parties—in the Toynbee case successfully, to some extent because elements in London University agreed with the criticism of his newspaper articles.

## D. Academic Freedom in the 1960s and 1970s

A full account of academic freedom should mention a few events in the 1960s and the 1970s. First, the Report on Higher Education under the chairmanship of Lord Robbins emphasised its importance at both the individual and the institutional levels. While recognising that the individual freedom could be abused by university teachers, it considered that this danger was much less than that attendant on attempts to restrict their liberty. But individual academic freedom did not give university staff a right to refuse necessary administrative duties.[42] The increasing financial dependence of universities on the state created

---

[42] Committee on Higher Education, 'Higher Education' ('Robbins Report') (Cm 2154, 1963) paras 705–6. See above ch 2, s III(A) and (B).

difficulties for their institutional freedom, but the Robbins Report was able to formulate its essential constituents easily enough: university control over appointments, curricula and standards, and the admission of students; the freedom to determine the balance between teaching and research; and generally, the direction of development.[43] With academics constituting a majority of its members, and through its block grant system, the UGC was, the Report concluded, a valuable safeguard of the institutional freedom.[44]

Questions about the scope of academic freedom arose during the prolonged and bitter disputes at the London School of Economics from 1967 through 1969.[45] In the summer of 1968 during a lull in a period of student unrest, gates were erected inside the LSE buildings to control the access and movement of possible demonstrators.[46] On the evening of 24 January 1969 a motion was passed at an emergency meeting of the student union to take down the gates; some of them were removed immediately with the use of chisels, crowbars and a sledgehammer. The Director promptly closed the school, which did not reopen until 19 February.[47] Both sides in the dispute claimed to be defending academic freedom. Some members of the academic staff considered that student protest, in particular the interruption of lectures, infringed their freedom to teach and that of non-protesting students to learn. Radical students much less plausibly invoked academic freedom in defence of their boycott and picketing of lectures. That argument is very thin, for it equates academic freedom with a general liberty of action; moreover, it wholly ignores the interests of those who wanted to give or attend lectures and other classes.

The most important discussion of academic freedom arose in the context of the dismissal of two lecturers for expressing their encouragement of or support for the removal of the gates by force. No fewer than 43 members of the LSE teaching staff considered the lecturers' dismissal

---

[43] Ibid, paras 707–24.

[44] Ibid, paras 725–32.

[45] A full account of them is provided by Dahrendorf (above n 41) 443–75; and from a student perspective by C Crouch, *The Student Revolt* (London, Bodley Head, 1970).

[46] Dahrendorf (above n 41) 464–65.

[47] See (1969) 7 *Minerva* 812–22 for a detailed history of the events in the first six months of 1969.

for the expression of their views infringed academic freedom.[48] One of the lecturers, Robin Blackburn, appealed to an Appellate Tribunal, chaired by Desmond Ackner, QC, subsequently a Law Lord.[49] Blackburn argued that he was exercising his academic freedom of opinion when he expressed support for the taking down of the gates, both at a public meeting held on the evening of January 24 and in a BBC television interview a few days later. The Tribunal rejected this argument.[50] In its view, academics did not enjoy freedom to say whatever they wanted, irrespective of the consequences. Blackburn had expressed his views in a dangerous situation, at a time when further damage to the LSE was likely—though, as the Tribunal admitted, no violence resulted from his speeches. It concluded that 'academic freedom is fundamentally the same freedom that all citizens enjoy and which they can enjoy only so long as law, order and civilised standards are respected.'[51] The LSE was entitled to dismiss Blackburn for misconduct in expressing support for the violent conduct of the students in removing the gates in a way that indicated a general support for and encouragement of violence in comparable circumstances.

Both Blackburn's argument and the Tribunal decision appear to have treated academic freedom as equivalent to the freedom of speech of university staff—a common misapprehension.[52] Arguably the case had nothing to do with Blackburn's real academic freedom to teach and research sociology as he wished. On the other hand, it was much less clearly a case of extramural speech than the earlier episodes involving Toynbee and Laski. Blackburn was expressing views about the administration of the LSE and the appropriateness of student conduct rather than about general political matters. In a sense, therefore, the expression was linked to his employment. Had he expressed his opinion more moderately, it might have been legitimately regarded as an exercise of the freedom of university staff to express their views

[48]  Ibid, 817.

[49]  The other members of the Tribunal were two distinguished but conservative-minded legal academics: Professor GW Keeton (UCL) and Professor HWR Wade (then St John's College, Oxford and later Professor of Law at Cambridge). The Tribunal was constituted by the Standing Committee of the Governors of LSE in consultation with the Vice-Chancellor of London University.

[50]  The Tribunal decision is reported in (1970) 8 *Minerva* 100.

[51]  Ibid, para 36.

[52]  See above ch 2, s II.

on issues of academic administration—intramural speech, to use the American term.[53] The Tribunal rightly held that the public support by an academic of violence as a means of university reform is outside the scope of academic freedom. But its general statement that the freedom is 'fundamentally the same freedom that all citizens enjoy' is questionable; in some circumstances academic freedom may confer wider rights of speech and conduct than those enjoyed by other employees.[54]

The events at the LSE and Blackburn's dismissal led to the formation of the Council for Academic Freedom and Democracy (CAFD) in July 1970, to resist what its founders regarded as encroachments on academic freedom and to campaign for the democratisation of universities and other colleges, which it considered a necessary condition for full academic freedom.[55] John Griffith, Ralph Miliband and John Westergaard, all LSE academics, were among the founding members; Griffith, the Professor of Public Law and a leading critic of the LSE administration during the Troubles, was particularly prominent.[56] CAFD Reports provide an invaluable source for historians of academic freedom in the 1970s and early 1980s, as well as for reflection on questions of principle that are still important.

CAFD argued that academic competence should be the only criterion for appointment to a university post; it was illegitimate for appointing committees to take into account a candidate's political opinions or conduct. Even the expression of racist or fascist views should not disqualify someone from appointment.[57] The Council was also particularly concerned about attempts to control the contents of lecturers' courses or to remove them from teaching particular topics because of their perceived political bias.[58]

---

[53] See below ch 6, s IV(B) for intramural expression in the United States.

[54] See the arguments above in ch 2, s IV and ch 3, s III.

[55] Annual Report of CAFD for 1970–71, available in the Archives of Hull University.

[56] It should be noted that Dahrendorf (above n 41) 454–55 pays tribute to Griffith's devotion to and 'indispensable contribution to the sanity of LSE'.

[57] Annual Report of CAFD for 1972–73 (Hull University Archives).

[58] See the CAFD Report in 1972, *The Craig Affair*, on the removal of David Craig, a lecturer in the English Department at Lancaster University, from teaching modern literature courses, apparently for the inclusion of political content in these courses and for intemperate criticism of his head of Department and other university authorities. The dispute between Craig and the University was eventually settled: Annual Report of CAFD for 1971–72, 6.

The Report of CAFD on the decision of Birmingham University not to appoint Richard Atkinson to a lectureship in the Sociology Department raised a number of interesting issues.[59] Atkinson, who had been an active radical student at LSE during the troubles in the late 1960s, was turned down by the University Appointments Committee after the Departmental Committee, by a 5–4 majority, had recommended his appointment. It is unclear whether Atkinson's left-wing political beliefs played any part in the decision. He was not appointed, it seems, because the Appointments Committee doubted whether he would collaborate constructively with his colleagues. In CAFD's view that was not only an inappropriate criterion but was harmful to the life of a university, which should be willing to 'explore ideas in a free atmosphere of unrestricted argument and discussion'.[60] The CAFD Report was also critical of aspects of the appointments procedure; the University Appointments Committee did not contain an expert sociologist able to assess Atkinson's academic ability, nor apparently did it consider referring the matter back to the Departmental Committee when it formed a different view of his suitability for appointment. Finally, it refused to tell CAFD what the reasons for its decision were.

It is possible to have some sympathy with the CAFD Report without agreeing with its conclusion that it was illegitimate for the university to take any factors other than academic competence into account when deciding whether to confirm Atkinson's appointment. It is surely reasonable for a university to take into account such matters as whether an applicant is likely to work well with colleagues with whom he or she might be asked to share teaching or supervisory responsibilities, or discharge necessary administrative duties responsibly. That is quite different from taking into consideration the applicant's political beliefs or activity. The problem is that it is difficult to devise appointments criteria or procedures that allow an appointments committee to take the former range of factors into account but preclude the consideration of other irrelevant arguments. There is no legal obligation on a university to give

---

[59] CAFD, 'The Atkinson Affair: Findings of the Commission of Inquiry established in February 1971' (available in Hull University Archives). See also A Arblaster, *Academic Freedom* (Harmondsworth, Penguin, 1974) 113–16. Arblaster himself was a prominent member of CAFD.

[60] Ibid, para 58.

detailed reasons for its decision to appoint or reject someone for a post,[61] and there are moreover powerful arguments why it would generally be undesirable to require them to do so. There are in the first place arguments of institutional autonomy and freedom, which would be inhibited by a general duty to give reasons in these cases. Secondly, the provision of reasons would in all probability give rise to more controversy than it would remove, quite apart from occasioning embarrassment and distress to unsuccessful candidates for chairs and lectureships.

Sadly by the early 1980s it was clear that CAFD had begun to run out of steam. Its annual reports chronicle a declining membership and branch activity. The concerns that had brought it into being may have been less widely felt as students, and perhaps also academics, became less radical, even rather conservative. With Griffith's retirement in 1983, it became less active; but another organisation, the Council for Academic Freedom and Academic Standards (CAFAS), has taken over its role from 1994. Through publicity and pressure on university authorities, it provides support for individual university teachers whose academic freedom has been infringed.

## III. THE EDUCATION REFORM ACT 1988

### A. The Background to Statutory University Reform

The climate of opinion concerning university governance changed considerably during the 1980s, as higher education colleges faced financial cuts under the Conservative government of Margaret Thatcher. The system of tenure was regarded as an obstacle to reform, since it was difficult for universities to retrench by making professors and lecturers redundant. Two reports in particular should be mentioned as prefacing the reforms to university financing and staffing made by the Education Reform Act 1988. The Committee of Vice-Chancellors and Principals (CVCP) itself commissioned a committee under the chairmanship of Sir Alex Jarratt to enquire into the efficiency of university governance.[62]

---

[61] See further below s V for judicial review of university decisions.

[62] Jarratt was Chief Executive of Reed International and Chancellor of Birmingham University. Among the other members was Sir Peter Swinnerton-Dyer, then Chairman of the UGC.

It made a number of recommendations, in particular encouraging an enhanced role for Vice-Chancellors as academic leaders and chief executives of universities and the general development of management skills on the part of senior academics.[63] Part of the Jarratt Report appeared sceptical of the value of Senates or Academic Boards, where professors and other members of academic staff meet to determine academic issues; the division of effective roles between the Senate and the Council (or Court in Scotland), in which generally laypeople (non-university members) form the majority, had no parallels in industry or public authorities.[64] Its overall approach was summarised in a sentence from the Report, much criticised by academic commentators: 'in our view universities are first and foremost corporate enterprises to which subsidiary units and individual academics are responsible and accountable.'[65]

Another recommendation of the Jarratt Report was that an inquiry should be conducted into the role and structure of the UGC. A review of the Committee under the chairmanship of Lord Croham proposed that it should be reconstituted as a University Grants Council, with broadly equal numbers of academic and non-academic members.[66] While the new UGC should have clear powers to attach conditions to university grants and to earmark them for particular purposes, the government itself should play no part in the distribution of university grants and should not even give guidance on their allocation.[67] The Croham Committee considered university autonomy and academic freedom to be distinct though related concepts; in its view, individual academic freedom was not threatened by the decisions of a national funding body that dealt with universities as institutions.[68]

[63] Report of the Steering Committee for Efficiency Studies in Universities ('The Jarratt Report'), March 1985.

[64] Ibid, para 2.2.

[65] Ibid, para 3.41, on which see M Kogan. 'Managerialism in Higher Education' in D Lawton (ed), *The Education Reform Act: Choice and Control* (London, Hodder and Staughton, 1989); and J Griffith, 'The Education Reform Act: Abolishing Independent Status of the Universities' (1990) 2 *Education and the Law* 97.

[66] Croham Committee, 'Review of the University Grants Committee' (Cm 81, 1987) Rec 1 and para 2.37.

[67] Ibid, Recs 18 and 21; and paras 5.8–5.9.

[68] Ibid, para 2.10.

## B. The Replacement of the UGC by the Universities Funding Council

The Education Reform Act 1988 (ERA) departed from the recommendations of the Croham Committee on UGC reform. The UGC was replaced by a Universities Funding Council, while a new Polytechnics and Colleges Funding Council was established for the funding of the polytechnics and other colleges transferred from local authority to national control in 1988. (These Councils have themselves been replaced by three Funding Councils, covering respectively the entire public university systems in England, Wales and Scotand.[69]) The new Council was to be composed of 15 members appointed by the Secretary of State for Education and Science, of whom between six and nine were to have had experience or be currently engaged in higher education.[70] The Secretary of State was (and is under the legislation now in force)[71] required to have regard to the desirability of appointing members with experience in industry, business or the professions. The Councils were given power to make grants to universities, subject to the terms and conditions they thought appropriate.[72]

The departure from the Croham recommendations came in the powers conferred on the Secretary of State with regard to the allocation of funds by the Councils. When making grants, the Councils had to comply with any directions given them by the Secretary of State;[73] he could impose conditions on the grants he gave the Councils for them to allocate to universities, though these conditions could not relate to the allocations of grants to any particular institution.[74] The government therefore gained explicit power to direct the allocation of funds to ensure, say, greater provision for particular subjects, the study of which it considered economically important. This marks an intrusion

---

[69] By the Further and Higher Education Act 1992 (FHEA) and the Further and Higher Education (Scotland) Act 1992, which abolished the binary division between the universities and polytechnics. The latter became part of the university sector and are consequently known as post-1992 universities. See R Stevens, *University to Uni* (London, Politico's, 2005) 50–52.

[70] ERA, s 131.

[71] FHEA, s 62.

[72] ERA, s 131(6).

[73] Ibid, s 134(8).

[74] Ibid, s 134(6)–(7).

on the autonomy of the universities to determine what they teach, an independence that had been jealously guarded by the former UGC, on which, by convention, academics themselves constituted a majority of members.

## C. The Abolition of Tenure and the Provision for Academic Freedom

One of the principal aims of the ERA, insofar as it concerned higher education, was to enable universities to make staff redundant when, for example, they decided for reasons of economy to close or reduce the size of a department.[75] University Commissioners were appointed to ensure that university statutes included provisions enabling them to dismiss any member of academic staff for redundancy or for good cause.[76] To respect existing tenure rights, however, the new redundancy provisions were not to apply to a member of academic staff unless he or she was appointed or promoted on or after 20 November 1987 (the date when the Bill was published).[77] The odd result was that universities were more free to dispense with the services of new or more ambitious members of their staff while senior members, content with their present status, kept their tenure.

With tenure removed, there was anxiety that individual academic freedom might be threatened. Despite government opposition, Lord Jenkins of Hillhead, Chancellor of Oxford University, successfully moved an Amendment to the Bill in the House of Lords to ensure the freedom was safeguarded.[78] The Lord Chancellor, Lord Mackay, the only speaker in the debate to defend the government's opposition, argued

[75] See G Zellick, 'British Universities and the Education Reform Act 1988' (1989) *Public Law* 513, 516–18. For a judicial criticism of the new emphasis on 'managerial interests', see Dillon LJ in *Pearce v University of Aston in Birmingham* [1991] 2 All ER 461, 463.

[76] ERA, s 203(1)(a)–(b). Five Commissioners could be appointed under ERA, Sch 11; their functions ended in 1996 when their powers were no longer renewed by statutory instrument.

[77] Nevertheless, a university has been entitled to make academic staff redundant, even if appointed before this date, if the terms of their appointment allowed this: see *Page v University of Hull Visitor* (above n 36).

[78] Hansard HL vol 497 cols 444–62 (19 May 1988).

that academic freedom was too imprecise to protect by statute.[79] Other speakers pointed to the unanimous support given the Amendment by the CVCP; it was also argued that the academic freedom clause was necessary not only to protect staff against unfair dismissal but to preserve the atmosphere of free inquiry in universities and to ensure there was no undue pressure on junior staff.[80]

The academic freedom clause provides that, in exercising their functions (of modifying statutes), the University Commissioners must have regard for, among other factors, the need

> to ensure that academic staff have freedom within the law to question and test received wisdom, and to put forward new ideas and controversial or unpopular opinions, without placing themselves in jeopardy of losing their jobs or privileges they may have at their institutions…[81]

A number of points should be made about the provision. It applies only to *academic staff* at the universities defined by the section as 'qualifying institutions'.[82] That means it covers broadly academics only at the universities funded by the Universities Funding Council (or the former UGC) but not the polytechnics, which were subsequently brought into the university sector in 1992. In other words, it covers only what are known as the pre-1992 universities. (But academic freedom is sometimes conferred on staff at the post-1992 universities by their instruments of government.[83]) The term 'academic staff' is not defined in the Act, though it might include staff, such as senior administrative or library staff, whose terms or contracts of employment are in the Commissioners' view similar to those of academic staff.[84]

The academic freedom recognised by the provision seems largely to be the right to teach and research ('to question and test received wisdom') free from direction—the traditional individual freedoms for professors and other university teachers identified by the Robbins Report,

---

[79] Ibid, cols 453–55.
[80] Ibid, cols 457–58 (Lord Peston).
[81] ERA, s 202(2)(a).
[82] Ibid, s 202(3).
[83] See below s IV(B).
[84] ERA, s 203(4). Probationary lecturers are not regarded as 'academic staff' for the purposes of dismissal procedures (*D v Queen's Universith of Belfast* [1997] ELR 431), so it is doubtful whether they would enjoy the protection of the academic freedom clause.

the American Association of University Professors and German law as central to any idea of academic freedom.[85] On the other hand, the next limb of the clause ('to put forward new ideas and controversial or unpopular opinions') suggests that extramural speech might also be covered; the freedom is not explicitly limited to the communication of ideas in lectures and seminars. Moreover, if it covers, as it clearly must, a publication freedom, it would be difficult to defend drawing a distinction between academic and popular publication; an historian, for instance, might claim academic freedom when he or she writes an article for a weekly review or Sunday newspaper, at least if the article is related to his or her expertise. The freedom might even cover the publication of an article outside an academic's expertise, although it is better to treat that as an exercise of the general freedom of speech or expression, which academics enjoy equally with other citizens.[86]

Two points are, however, very clear. First, the freedom is one 'within the law'. A university lecturer has no academic freedom under the UK statute to infringe the criminal law by, for instance, inciting racial hatred in the course of a seminar discussion; by publishing hardcore pornography contrary to obscenity laws; or by downloading images of child or extreme pornography. Of course, it may be hard to determine whether a speech or publication is illegal. In principle universities should give lecturers the benefit of the doubt and not discipline (let alone dismiss) them unless they are confident a criminal prosecution would succeed; in practice universities may not meet that standard. The point is that academic freedom gives university lecturers no immunity from the general law, even when they are engaged in teaching or research. The second point is even clearer. The UK statute recognises a freedom for *academic staff*, not, as German constitutional law does, a scientific freedom that may be enjoyed by everyone engaged in serious intellectual enquiry.[87]

There is no indication that the UK academic freedom clause confers on academic staff any more than a liberty to teach and research, and perhaps speak freely, without risk of interference or sanction by their university employers. In other words, it does not confer any positive rights on professors and researchers to claim, say, adequate facilities, funding or other support for their work; a professor could not, for

---

[85] See above ch 2, s III(A).
[86] For further discussion, see below s IV; and below ch 9, s II.
[87] See below ch 5, s I.

example, use the statute to make a claim that academic freedom was infringed if research leave was denied by the university or its library stopped subscribing to essential journals. Such claims might in theory be made, as will be seen, in Germany, where the Constitutional Court has held that the state must make basic provision for university professors to enable them to do their work—though they have not succeeded in practice.[88] On the other hand, there is no reason why the academic freedom clause could not be understood as reflecting a general legal principle that could be employed to interpret legislation or to develop the common law.

Two examples show how this might be done. An academic sued in defamation could invoke the provision in some circumstances to strengthen a fair comment or other defence; the courts, it could be argued, should be particularly solicitous of a lecturer's freedom to comment on another's work, because such comment would be an exercise of academic freedom.[89] Secondly, a statutory provision that might impinge on the freedom—for example, a provision in race relations or anti-terrorism legislation—should be interpreted not to curtail exercise of the freedom recognised by the ERA, unless that is its plain and inescapable meaning.[90] The clause might in these ways have legal significance beyond those circumstances where a university directly jeopardises exercise of academic freedom.

## D. Removal of the Jurisdiction of University Visitors

Until the passage of the ERA all disputes relating to a university's internal affairs, including those concerning the employment of academic staff, were determined by the university or college's Visitor, often the King (or Queen) or the Lord President of the Privy Council, who would appoint a senior judge to hear the dispute on their behalf.[91]

[88]  Below ch 5, s IV(A) and (D).

[89]  See the South African case referred to above in ch 2, s VI.

[90]  This point is developed below in ch 8, s II (anti-terrorism legislation) and in ch 9, s III (race relations legislation). Other legislation should be interpreted broadly to protect academic freedom: see the whistleblower provisions discussed below in s IV(D).

[91]  There is a rich literature on University Visitors, including JW Bridge, 'Keeping Peace in the Universities: The Role of the Visitor' (1970) 86 *Law Quarterly Review*

A university lecturer could not complain to the ordinary courts or to an employment tribunal if he or she were dismissed; the Visitor's jurisdiction was exclusive, though judicial review was available to challenge a decision where this jurisdiction had plainly been exceeded or abused.[92] The 1988 Act removed the Visitor's jurisdiction over disputes concerning members of academic staff with regard to appointment, employment 'or the termination of … appointment or employment'.[93]

The Visitor's authority was regarded as anomalous, insulating universities and academic staff from usual legal procedures. Arguably, it conferred a privilege on a professor or lecturer who had been dismissed or wished to pursue an employment grievance, since the Visitor might provide less formal and expensive redress than a court or tribunal.[94] The consequence of these procedural reforms is that university staff have lost these procedural privileges. As the Court of Appeal confirmed in *Pearce v University of Aston in Birmingham*,[95] they must now resort to the ordinary courts or an employment tribunal if they wish to make claims of breach of contract or unfair dismissal.[96]

## IV. INDIVIDUAL ACADEMIC FREEDOM AFTER 1988

### A. General Principles

Individual academic freedom and institutional autonomy have both been considered by official committees in the last twenty years. The Nolan Committee on Standards in Public Life was concerned with

---

531; PM Smith, 'The Exclusive Jurisdiction of the University Visitor' (1981) 97 *Law Quarterly Review* 610; and GL Peiris, 'Visitatorial Jurisdiction: The Changing Outlook on an Exclusive Regime' (1987) 16 *Anglo-American Law Review* 376.

[92] *Thomas v University of Bradford* [1987] AC 795 is the leading modern case.

[93] ERA, s 206(1). Later legislation has further abolished Visitor jurisdiction in relation to all staff disputes (as well as student complaints): see Higher Education Act 2004, ss 20 (student complaints) and 46 (staff disputes).

[94] *Patel v Bradford University Senate* [1978] 3 All ER 841, 852 per Megarry V-C.

[95] [1991] 2 All ER 461.

[96] The Visitor had jurisdiction when an employment dispute was referred to him before a 'relevant date': ERA, s 206(2). The dispute in the *Pearce* case was duly referred to the Visitor, who decided the University had wrongly dismissed the lecturers for redundancy (above n 33). See PH Pettit, 'Academic Tenure and the Education Reform Act 1988' (1991) 54 *Modern Law Review* 137.

university independence and accountability in the context of its review of the standards of conduct to be expected of local public bodies.[97] But almost in an aside the Report stressed the importance of individual academic freedom to the success of academic institutions. '*By extension* [the freedom] has created a tradition of freedom of speech within a university which is an important check on impropriety' (emphasis added).[98] In other words, the right of academics to speak openly about maladministration on the part of university authorities provides a valuable safeguard against their misuse of public funds; the right should be recognised as an aspect of academic freedom, even though it does not form part of that freedom in the stricter or narrower understanding of that term, under which it would be confined to an academic's freedom to teach and research. The extension is significant. This wide academic freedom of speech has been at the heart of many of the most significant disputes between academic staff and their university employers.[99]

The Committee of Inquiry under the chairmanship of Ron Dearing was the most important review of national university policy since the Robbins Report in 1963.[100] The Dearing Committee's treatment of individual academic freedom was hardly extensive, perhaps indicating the relatively low value attached to it in comparison at least with the emphasis the Committee placed on the social and economic responsibilities of universities and their staff. In the Committee's view, the importance of academic freedom could be assumed, but it should be 'managed responsibly' both by individual academics and by institutions.[101] Academics, according to the Committee, are accountable for their work and are stewards of the public resources that fund it. Dearing concluded that though some evidence suggested the scope of individual academic freedom had contracted as a result of the pressure for greater accountability, it was still alive.[102] He endorsed the principle established by the Nolan Committee that there was no room generally for confidentiality clauses in university employment contracts; academic

[97] Committee on Standards in Public Life (the 'Nolan Committee'), 'Second Report' (Cm 3270, 1996).
[98] Ibid, para 97.
[99] See below s IV(C) and also below ch 9.
[100] National Committee of Inquiry into Higher Education, *Higher Education in the Learning Society: Report of the National Committee*, 1997.
[101] Ibid, para 15.14.
[102] Ibid, paras 15.61–63.

staff should be free to report to an appropriate authority their concerns over the maladministration of resources by universities, though that represents perhaps a dilution of a broad academic freedom to speak openly about matters of academic administration and standards.[103]


## B. University Statutes and Articles of Government

Under the ERA the University Commissioners were in effect required to ensure that university statutes protected academic freedom. They drew up a Model Statute, the terms of which reflected that Act's requirements with regard to university discipline, dismissal and grievance procedures, redundancy arrangements and academic freedom. Universities base their own statutes on the terms of the Model Statute, a revision of which by a Universities working party in 2001–02 was approved by the Privy Council in March 2003. It requires universities to apply their own statutes to give effect to the principle of academic freedom, as defined by the ERA; the new Model Statute further provides that when the meaning of academic freedom is at issue in redundancy, dismissal or grievance procedures, regard should be paid to provisions in a United Nations Educational, Scientific and Cultural Organization (UNESCO) Recommendation of 1997.[104] Under these provisions, the right of academic staff to express freely their views about the institution or system within which they work and the freedom to participate in representative academic bodies are included within the definition of academic freedom.[105]

The statutes of the older pre-1992 universities have adopted the terms of the Model Statute, sometimes with minor variations. The new post-1992 universities (usually former polytechnics) are not bound by the provisions of the ERA, but their Articles of Government typically incorporate academic freedom provisions.[106] The effect of all these

[103] Ibid, para 15.67, endorsing the recommendations of the Nolan Committee (above n 97) paras 98–101.

[104] Model Statute, cl 2.

[105] UNESCO Recommendation concerning the Status of Higher-Education Teaching Personnel of 11 November 1997, Art 27.

[106] For example, Art 9.1 of the Articles of Government of the University of Bedfordshire requires its Governors to have regard to academic freedom as defined in ERA, s 202 when they make rules with regard to the conduct of staff.

provisions is that internal tribunals set up to consider the discipline or dismissal of a member of the academic staff, or the Vice-Chancellor or Principal of a university taking the final decision in these proceedings, must consider academic freedom before determining whether suspension, dismissal or other sanction is appropriate. The freedom should also be considered when an academic invokes a grievance procedure to complain about, say, bullying or discriminatory conduct on the part of a senior member of staff or Head of Department. But generally the issue will arise in the interpretation of 'good cause' for dismissal or removal of a member of the academic staff, in particular in determining whether his or her conduct was 'of an immoral, scandalous, or disgraceful nature incompatible' with employment duties.[107] Suppose, to take a hypothetical case, a university were to consider the dismissal of a lecturer for frequent use of racist language in lectures, which offended students. Its disciplinary bodies must pay regard to academic freedom: a sociology lecturer, for example, could argue that he or she was exercising that freedom when this language was used in seminar discussions to illustrate, say, the causes of racial tensions. It is in this sort of context that the academic freedom provisions of the ERA clearly should be enforced.

## C. The Davies Report on Swansea University

Academic freedom issues were fully considered by Sir Michael Davies, a former High Court judge, in his Report on a long-running and bitter controversy between the University College of Swansea and four lecturers, three of them attached to the Department of Philosophy.[108] They had all expressed in public strong criticism of the administration of and standards at a Centre for the Study of Philosophy and Health Care that was attached to the Philosophy Department; their criticism extended, it was alleged, to serious denigration of a colleague, disruption of meetings and breaches of confidentiality. One of the critics reluctantly accepted

---

[107] See the term of the Statutes of Oxford University of 2003, Statute XII, s 5(1)(b). For a general discussion of dismissals in universities, see R Lewis, 'Disciplinary Dismissals and Redundancies in Higher and Further Education' (1995) 7 *Education and the Law* 211.
[108] *The Davies Report* (Bristol, Thoemmes Press, 1994).

voluntary redundancy, with a clause in her severance agreement binding her not to publish comment on the university or criticise it, whether publicly or privately.[109] Two others were suspended; an inquiry recommended that the university authorities consider the dismissal of one of them. Four inquiries into the conduct of the critics and their grievances against the university authorities had failed to resolve the dispute, so Swansea University referred it to the Visitor, the Queen; Sir Michael Davies acted on her behalf.

The Davies Report noted that academic freedom could be invoked on both sides of the controversy. The critics asserted a right to make honest criticism of their colleagues and academic standards within the Department; a colleague who had been denigrated for advising a firm of solicitors on a controversial matter asserted academic freedom to do this work without harassment. The Head of the Philosophy Department and other university authorities could claim a freedom from unreasonable challenge.[110] Sir Michael's conclusions were striking. He emphasised that universities are not commercial companies but academic institutions. While academic staff did not have complete licence under the academic freedom recognised by the ERA, in drawing the line between the legitimate exercise of academic freedom and its abuse, 'the fact that it is a line to be drawn in an adult academic world and not in a commercial jungle is of profound importance.'[111] Though some of the critics' comments had been annoying and gone too far, they had substantial ground for criticising the university authorities. Consequently, it was right to lift the suspension (or extended leave) of two of the lecturers, while the third, who had taken 'voluntary' redundancy, was to be reinstated. Sir Michael declined to impose formal restraints on the lecturers, but they were to be reminded of their obligations under their employment contracts.[112]

The Davies Report is perhaps the clearest statement how academic freedom gives university lecturers greater freedom than the staff of commercial companies to criticise their employers' conduct. The lecturers' arguments, supported by the Association of University Teachers,

---

[109] Sir Michael wondered whether this complete gag could be legally enforced and doubted whether it was appropriate (ibid, 79).

[110] Ibid, 66.

[111] Ibid, 114.

[112] Ibid, 116.

were accepted. Its findings in effect gave university 'whistleblowers' who publicise their complaints about academic standards more freedom than they would enjoy under the Public Interest Disclosure Act 1998.[113] But Sir Michael's conclusions are of course not binding on courts or employment tribunals.


## D. Other Academic Freedom Cases

Courts and tribunals have had little occasion to interpret or apply the academic freedom provision of the ERA. For understandable reasons universities prefer to settle disputes with lecturers who might invoke it.[114] They may agree terms for a controversial lecturer's early retirement, thereby saving the difficulty of initiating proceedings to dismiss him or her. Or they may subsequently settle a claim for unfair dismissal or breach of contract before the case comes before the employment tribunal or court. These courses were taken by the universities concerned in the widely publicised Frank Ellis and Chris Brand affairs, which involved extramural speech and are discussed in chapters nine and ten respectively.

Even if academic freedom were raised before a court or employment tribunal, it is not clear that it would be prepared to question a university decision to dismiss a lecturer on the grounds of academic incompetence. As will be explained shortly, judges are reluctant to uphold challenges to university decisions taken on academic grounds. In a leading case, Sedley J (as he then was) said that fairness did not require reasons to be given for purely academic decisions—though they were not beyond challenge if, say, irrelevant factors had been taken into account in assessing someone's work.[115] However, this statement was qualified by Sedley J himself in a later case in which Gillian Evans challenged the university's refusal to promote her to a personal readership: reasons might be required when academic decisions, though not clearly wrong,

---

[113] See below s IV(D).

[114] For a short discussion of 'disciplining' of academic employees, see D Palfreyman, 'A Note on the Misconduct of Academics in UK HEIs' (2005) 17 *Education and the Law* 155.

[115] *R v Higher Education Funding Council, ex p Institute of Dental Surgery* [1994] 1 WLR 242, 261, DC.

were important to an individual.[116] Under that approach, a university would surely be required to produce reasons for decisions taken on academic grounds to dismiss (or not promote) a lecturer, particularly insofar as the decision might have impinged on the lecturer's own individual academic freedom. But there is no authority on the point. Indeed, the only mention of academic freedom in a recent English case occurred when Lightman J approved a consent order under which a university agreed not to publish derogatory comments about the work of an author it had declined to publish: the order was not to be construed to muzzle the academic freedom of expression of individual scholars to criticise the work.[117]

Academic freedom arguments may, however, underlie the recent decision of the Court of Appeal in *Paul Buckland v Bournemouth Higher Education Corporation*.[118] In that case, the court upheld a claim of constructive unfair dismissal brought by a professor when his students' examination papers were re-marked without his consent, after his grades had been accepted by the examination board. In legal terms the decision to re-mark the papers destroyed the relationship of trust and confidence between the university and the professor. Arguably, the decision amounted to a fundamental breach of contract because it infringed the professor's academic freedom to assess his own students, but no reference was made to the concept in the judgements.

Academic freedom could be invoked to strengthen a university whistleblower's argument that disclosure—to either a university employer or, in some cases, more widely—of a criminal offence or some other failure to comply with legal obligations is a 'protected disclosure', so it would be unfair to dismiss the lecturer for making it.[119] The scope of

---

[116]   *R v University of Cambridge, ex p Evans* [1998] ELR 515, 523, DC. The application for leave was granted, but proceedings were stayed to enable Cambridge to revise its promotion procedures. (Judicial review proceedings in a later application were dismissed on the ground that the appropriate remedy was a private law action for breach of contract: *R (on the Application of Evans) v University of Cambridge* [2003] ELR 8, DC.)

[117]   *Malcolm v Chancellor, Masters and Scholars of University of Oxford* [2002] ELR 277.

[118]   [2010] EWCA Civ 121. For comparable US cases on academic freedom and the re-grading of student examinations, see below ch 6, s IV(B).

[119]   Public Interest Disclosure Act 1998, amending the Employment Rights Act 1996. The provisions were invoked by an academic in *Darnton v University of Surrey* [2003] IRLR 133, on which see D Farrington and D Palfreyman, *The Law of Higher Education* (Oxford, Oxford University Press, 2006) para 12.40.

the protection conferred by these provisions should be interpreted to take account of the academic freedom of university staff to draw attention to any maladministration on the part of their employers, including, it is suggested, the lowering of academic standards by a higher education institution, its failure to follow correct procedures when making appointments or promotions, or an arbitrary decision on the part of a Principal or Head of Department to stop the teaching of a particular course. Any of these could be regarded as 'a miscarriage of justice' under the 'protected disclosure' provisions, if they are interpreted in the light of the academic freedom recognised by the Nolan Committee. The Higher Education Funding Council for England (HEFCE) has encouraged universities to draw up 'whistle-blowing' protocols and issued guidance on their provisions to safeguard the freedom of academic staff to raise their concerns about university governance, financial malpractice and abuse of procedures.[120] However, a recent House of Common Committee[121] has noted that academic whistleblowers are inadequately protected by the existing legal provisions—though that conclusion would not be warranted if they were generously interpreted.

The leading court decision on academic freedom in this context comes from New Zealand.[122] Rigg, a Senior Lecturer in German at Waikato University, alleged in an article in a student newspaper that inadequate supervision of a University biology laboratory had probably resulted in student deaths from cancer and further that the University had concealed the matter to safeguard its reputation. After the rejection of these allegations by an independent public committee, the University Council resolved to dismiss Rigg on the ground that he had made wholly unfounded public allegations about the University in a manner incompatible with his position as a Senior Lecturer. Accepting the Report of two Commissaries,[123] the Visitor confirmed the Council's decision. The Commissaries heard a great deal of expert evidence on academic freedom of speech, including reports from the UK AUT and

---

[120] Guidance of HEFCE for members of university governing bodies, 2001: 01/20, Annex K.

[121] 11th Report of the Innovation, Universities, Science and Skills Committee, 'Students and Universities' HC (2008–09) 170-1, paras 231–35.

[122] *Rigg v University of Waikato* [1984] 1 NZLR 149.

[123] Sir Clifford Richmond, a former judge, and Professor KJ Keith, a distinguished public law scholar.

the American Association of University Professors. It rejected Rigg's argument that academics had special rights to freedom of expression apart from *academic* freedom of expression; that freedom could be justified by 'the need for academics, whether teachers or students, to feel free to pursue the search for knowledge and learning and truth without fear of institutional disciplinary action' to compel agreement with the views of the university authority.[124] Even assuming that Rigg could exercise this academic freedom of expression outside his field of expertise, he did not enjoy uninhibited licence to say whatever he liked. The Report accepted there were ample grounds to view his article as irresponsible. In particular, there was no basis at all for the allegation that the University had deliberately concealed the incidence of cancer to protect its reputation.[125]

The Report rightly distinguished this case from those concerning extramural speech.[126] Rigg's article concerned the administration of the university, not political, economic or general public affairs regarding which he enjoyed the same freedom of speech as everyone else. It was appropriate for the Commissaries to consider the scope of the right to criticise the University authorities, an aspect of academic freedom in the United Kingdom recognised, for example, by the Nolan Committee. The difficulty was that there was no basis for the extravagant allegations of a cover-up, although it would almost certainly have been legitimate for Rigg to have expressed concern in public about the incidence of cancer and its apparent link to the University's biology laboratory.

## E. Academic Freedom and Official Quality Controls

The claim that official quality controls over research inhibit academic freedom should be considered at this point. The requirements of the UK Research Assessment Exercise (RAE), first introduced in the 1980s as the basis for the allocation of recurrent university research grants, may have had repercussions on the exercise by university staff of their academic freedom. Scholars may have come under pressure to publish

---

[124] *Rigg v University of Waikato* (above n 122) 207.
[125] Ibid, 205.
[126] Ibid, 208.

the results of their research before they consider that appropriate or to abandon long-term projects in order to write articles to satisfy their obligation to produce four pieces of written work within the research assessment period.[127] Equally, requirements to show the social and economic impact of research as a condition of research council funding may divert scientists and social scientists from pure research to more practical, applied research topics, for which it is easier to provide evidence of public benefit.[128]

Requirements of this kind certainly constrain individual academic freedom, if that is understood as entailing an *effective* right for academics to choose the topics of their research and the time of its publication entirely immune from pressures from their university departments or financial considerations.[129] But academic freedom has never been understood in the United Kingdom to confer a right to public funding or to financial provision for research; the freedom confers only a liberty against interference from the state or the university.[130] Moreover, the pressures applied by the RAE do not prescribe or proscribe research topics; nor does the system favour particular perspectives. It would of course be different if research were assessed by government officials or agents, for that control would clearly inhibit the freedom of academics to challenge orthodox ideas and to put forward radical alternatives to traditional wisdom. But the RAE (and the allocation of funds by research councils) is conducted through peer review, under which academics assess the quality of their colleagues' work and research profiles. In principle, this system, whatever its weaknesses, should allow for a rich variety of perspectives and safeguard academic freedom as that has been understood in the United Kingdom.

---

[127] For a sustained critique of the RAE from this perspective, see D Gillies, *How should Research be Organised?* (London, College Publications, 2008) chs 1–5.

[128] In February 2009, 20 scientists wrote a letter protesting against the research councils' requirement for applicants to provide statements about the financial and other impact of their research proposals: *Times Higher Education,* 12 February 2009, 32. See also J Ladyman, 'Against Impact', 294 *Oxford Magazine,* Eighth Week MT 2009, 4.

[129] For example, see the arguments in C Russell, *Academic Freedom* (London, Routledge, 1993) 74–81.

[130] See above s III(C). Compare the position in Germany, where the Constitutional Court has formulated a right to some basic provision for academic work: below ch 5, s IV(A) and (D).

Nevertheless, there is a serious argument that current funding arrangements, as well as systems of peer review, might inhibit, even if they do not directly restrict, the effective exercise of academic freedom, particularly if that confers some expectation of financial and other support for radical innovative ideas.[131] How far these expectations are legitimate raises large policy issues, among them the desirability (and practicability) of more research funding from private industry and research foundations to supplement state provision; these matters are outside the scope of this book. Arguably, the RAE, as it has been conducted, has applied opaque and vague standards ('international excellence', 'national standing'), encouraged the production of a mass of little read material and produced on occasion arbitrary results. In short, it may have served genuine intellectual values badly.[132] But that does not mean that official funding arrangements infringe academic freedom, as that freedom is generally understood in the United Kingdom.

## V. INSTITUTIONAL ACADEMIC FREEDOM AFTER 1988

### A. Statutory Provisions

There has been much less emphasis on institutional academic freedom or autonomy in the last twenty years than there used to be when the UGC had responsibility for the allocation of university grants. The University Funding Council has been replaced by separate councils for England, Wales and Scotland. The Higher Education Funding Council for England (HEFCE) consists of between 12 and 15 members; in appointing its members the Secretary of State must have regard to the desirability of including both persons with experience of higher

[131] Gillies (above n 127) is particularly critical of the ability of contemporaneous peer review to spot innovative work of real brilliance. The work of Frege and Copernicus was poorly regarded by their contemporaries, while Wittgenstein would not have published enough work during his lifetime to satisfy the requirements of the RAE. See also S Braben, *Scientific Freedom: The Elixir of Civilisation* (Hoboken, New Jersey, Wiley-Science, 2008).

[132] For these criticisms from different perspectives, see J Griffith, *Research Assessment: As Strange a Maze as E'er Men Trod* (CAFAS Report No 4, 1995); Graham (above n 7) 98–110, Gillies (above n 127) ch 5; and R Briggs, 'Contribution Review and Research Monitoring', 240 *Oxford Magazine,* Eighth Week TT 2005, 24–28.

education and those currently engaged in its provision, as well as the importance of including those with industrial, commercial or professional experience.[133]

Statutory provisions have extended the grant-making powers of the Higher Education Funding Councils and also given the government minister responsible for higher education (at the time of writing the Secretary of State for Business, Innovation and Skills) greater authority to issue directions and to make grants to HEFCE subject to conditions, which it must then impose on the universities.[134] The government determines funding priorities, whereas they used to be decided by the UGC, on which academics formed a majority of the members.[135] For example, in his allocation of grants for 2009–10, the Secretary of State, John Denham, MP, required HEFCE to promote the STEM subjects (science, technology, engineering and mathematics), 'since these are subjects that employers consistently tell us they will need in the long term'.[136] (The government has also identified Islamic studies as a strategically important subject, while modern foreign languages and quantitative social science, among others, have been deemed strategically important and vulnerable by an advisory group of HEFCE.[137])

Nevertheless, universities continue to be regarded in theory as independent, autonomous institutions, which are free to make their own decisions.[138] The principle is reflected in the important statutory provision, precluding the Secretary of State from framing conditions in his grants to HEFCE by reference to particular courses of study, research programmes or the criteria for the selection and promotion of academic staff.[139] There is therefore a statutory limit on the extent to which the government can intrude on university decisions. But it is now free to impose conditions that apply to every

---

[133] FHEA 1992, s 62. Nine of the 15 members of the Board at the time of writing are or have been heads of universities or other higher education institutions.

[134] See FHEA 1992, ss 65–68 and HEA 2004, s 23. For details, see Farrington and Palfreyman (above n 119) paras 3.16–3.33

[135] Above s II(B).

[136] Public Letter of 21 January 2009 from the Secretary of State to HEFCE, para 7.

[137] HEFCE 2008/38.

[138] Ibid, para 7.

[139] FHEA 1992, s 68(3).

institution—or every institution falling within a class specified in the terms and conditions; universities must comply with these conditions to be eligible for financial support.[140] Arguably, university autonomy in the United Kingdom has gradually been eroded in the last decade or so, as the government has increasingly relied on universities to make a significant contribution to national prosperity and to train their students to do work of social and economic benefit. Evidence from the Vice-Chancellor of Oxford University to a recent House of Commons Committee indicated that university autonomy had declined from earlier periods:[141] the Committee itself thought it was time for HEFCE, universities and student bodies to agree a concordat to define the areas over which universities retained autonomy, with a definition of academic freedom, and those areas where it is legitimate for government to intervene.[142]

There is one explicit reference in a statute to the 'academic freedom' of institutions. The Higher Education Act 2004 instituted a Director of Fair Access to Higher Education, whose role is to ensure that universities take measures to increase applications by students from groups under-represented in higher education; in the absence of approved measures universities are unable to charge higher tuition fees. There was some anxiety that these arrangements would infringe the traditional freedom of universities to select their own students, so the Director is required to protect 'academic freedom, including the freedom of institutions' to determine the contents of their courses and how they are taught, and to fix and apply the criteria for the admission of students.[143] It should be noted that the requirement is designed only to protect university freedom against the Director; it does not spell out any right for universities to dictate to their lecturers how to teach particular courses.[144] This provision should not perhaps be taken too seriously, for the Access Director is also required to take into account any guidance given by the Secretary of State; guidance has encouraged the Director to challenge

---

[140]   Ibid, s 68(2).

[141]   11th Report of the Innovation, Universities, Science and Skills Committee (above n 121) 170-II, Q 175.

[142]   Ibid, 170-I, para 242.

[143]   HEA 2004, s 32(2).

[144]   This point has been raised in the context of teaching terrorism courses: see below ch 8, s II(D).

university selection policies.[145] But it is better perhaps to pay lip-service to academic freedom than to ignore it altogether.

## B. The Courts and University Decisions

In 1993 the Institute of Dental Surgery challenged a Higher Education Funding Council decision that had formally ranked the Institute's research at Level 2 in the RAE.[146] There was no right to appeal this assessment, and the chief executive of the funding council declined to give reasons for it, on the ground that disclosure would undermine the whole nature of the assessment process.[147] The Divisional Court, in a judgement given by Sedley J, dismissed the Institute's application for judicial review. It held that fairness did not require reasons to be given when there was no evidence to suggest that the challenged decision was other than 'an informed exercise of academic judgment'.[148] Sedley LJ (as he had now become) explained this principle in a later case: a university is equipped to consider in depth issues of academic or pastoral judgement (about students), on which a court ruling would be inappropriate.[149] Courts should not intervene to correct the marks or class of degree assigned a student or the assessment by an academic panel of the quality of an institute's research. The principle has been applied by the courts on a number of subsequent occasions.[150] It does not mean that courts never interfere with academic decisions; they may intervene on general principles of administrative law if it is shown that a university has failed to observe the principles of natural justice or its

---

[145] Farrington and Palfreyman (above n 119) paras 3.59–60; and T Birtwhistle, 'Academic Freedom and Complacency: The Possible Effects of "Good Men Do Nothing"' (2004) 16 *Education and the Law* 203.

[146] The assessment of the Institute's research was done by a specialist panel for clinical dentistry.

[147] *Ex p Institute of Dental Surgery* (above n 115) 242, 250.

[148] Ibid, 261.

[149] *Clark v University of Lincolnshire and Humberside* [2000] 3 All ER 752, 756, CA

[150] *R v Cranfield University, ex p Bashir* [1999] ELR 317 322, CA|; *R v University of Cambridge, ex p Persaud*, DC [2001] ELR 64 (but see the decision of the Court of Appeal, upholding the challenge on procedural grounds: [2001] ELR 480); *Higham v University of Plymouth* [2005] ELR 547, DC; *Van Mellaert v Oxford University* [2006] ELR 617, Gray J.

own procedural rules or if it has broken the terms of its contract with its students.[151]

The implication of these decisions is that universities and other bodies such as funding councils enjoy unfettered discretion to make purely academic judgments. This is tantamount in effect to institutional autonomy or academic freedom, albeit a freedom that is not explicitly conferred by legal text but rather recognised by courts when they decline to intervene in disputes concerning the exercise of academic judgment. There are, as will be seen in later chapters, equivalent principles in Germany and the United States; courts in these jurisdictions are also reluctant to interfere with university decisions, thereby implicitly recognising an institutional autonomy.[152] Interestingly, Sedley J has suggested that reasons may be required when an academic decision of a university is important to an *individual*, for example, when an application for promotion is rejected.[153] In these circumstances, the de facto institutional freedom recognised by the courts might have to give way to the interests of university staff, including perhaps their academic freedom.

## C. University Governance

One type of academic freedom claim is that the academics who teach and conduct research at universities should govern them; it can be argued that this is essential for the protection of their individual scholarly freedom.[154] Academic self-rule still obtains at Oxford and Cambridge Universities, as well as at their constituent colleges. But it is not the case with the other pre-1992 universities in the United Kingdom, where the governing bodies and executives are Councils (or in Scotland, the Courts) with a majority of lay, that is, non-academic members. Councils have a minority representation of academic members, elected usually by members of the Academic Board or Senate, the body that takes decisions on academic matters, subject sometimes to formal approval or ratification by the Council.[155] The new post-92

---

[151] See *Clark* (above n 149) 756; and the decision of the Court of Appeal in *Persaud* (ibid).
[152] See in particular ch 5, s VI(C) and ch 6, s IV(D).
[153] *Evans* (above n 116) at 523.
[154] See above ch 2, s III(C) and ch 3, s V.
[155] See Farrington and Palfreyman (above n 119) paras 5.29–5.38.

universities—higher education corporations—are governed by Boards of Governors, the composition of which is prescribed by their Instruments of Government, which are in turn issued by the Privy Council under statutory authority.[156]

Governance by Councils on which academics have only minority representation has long been accepted as a general principle for universities other than Oxford and Cambridge. In the 1980s the Jarratt Committee concluded that universities need strong leadership by bodies that are aware of the needs of business and industry, and it has become increasingly difficult to make the argument for academic self-rule.[157] The Dearing Committee recommended that all Councils should have a majority of lay members and for reasons of efficiency should consist of no more than 25 members. In this context, the governance arrangements of Oxford and Cambridge may appear increasingly anomalous. The Lambert Review of Business–University Collaboration recommended changes in these structures, so that government and the public can have greater confidence in their management.[158] But the Review contained no specific proposals for change. In December 2006, Oxford rejected the Vice-Chancellor's plans to give the University Council a majority of lay members; HEFCE itself has pressed for reform along these lines, but its calls have so far been rejected by both Oxford and Cambridge.[159]

One important institutional development should be noted: the foundation of a private university at Buckingham in 1973. Its establishment was attributable to concern, felt particularly by conservative academics, at the increasing financial dependence of universities on the state.[160] At the University's foundation, Lord Hailsham, a former Secretary of State for Education and Science, admitted that the receipt

[156] ERA, s 124A(3). See ibid, paras 5.39–5.49.

[157] See above s III(A).

[158] HM Treasury, December 2003, paras 7.45–7.50. See Stevens (above n 69) 133–34 for Richard Lambert's interim report, which was very critical of the governance structures of Oxford and Cambridge.

[159] *Times Higher Education Supplement*, 23 November 2007, 6–7. For a reply to the argument that charities law requires a majority of lay, non-academic trustees, see N Bamforth, 'University Governance and Legal Argument' (2005) 239 *Oxford Magazine*, Fourth Week TT, 3.

[160] See Lord Beloff, the first Vice-Chancellor of Buckingham, 'British Universities and the State' (1994) 32 *Minerva* 188.

of state moneys on the modern scale inevitably curtailed universities' academic independence.[161] The University of Buckingham takes no public money from the government or HEFCE and is not obliged to submit to review of its teaching standards by the Quality Assurance Agency (QAA).[162] There are now three other private providers of university education with degree awarding powers, including the College of Law.[163]

An interesting legal question is whether academic freedom entails a right to establish a private university with a legitimate expectation that its degrees will be recognised.[164] There is of course no authority on the point, though it might conceivably arise in practice if, say, the degrees awarded by a private college were refused recognition for reasons of hostility to these institutions or to their courses.[165] In principle the freedom should entail this right,[166] just as press freedom means a right to establish a newspaper or printing press, free from state licence. The analogy with the press is, however, imperfect. While it would be incompatible with press freedom to apply quality controls before a newspaper can lawfully be published, some protection against the award of bogus degrees by 'degree mills' is appropriate; that can only be provided by an official agency with the role of ensuring that degree courses meet basic minimum standards. Subject to control over its general standards, the right to establish a private university with power to award degrees should be recognised. In enabling an alternative to government funded universities, the right affords some safeguard against the possible abuse by government of its increasing powers to regulate higher education; the right may also safeguard individual academic freedom, in that (maverick or idiosyncratic) lecturers denied appointment (or promotion)

---

[161]  J Pemberton and J Pemberton, *The University College at Buckingham* (Buckingham, Buckingham Press, 1979) 39–41.

[162]  For QAA review, see Farrington and Palfreyman (above n 119) paras 3.68–3.77.

[163]  Universities UK Research Report, 'The Growth of Private and For-Profit Higher Education Providers in the UK' (2009) para 3.2.

[164]  See DJ Christie, 'The Power to Award Degrees' (1976) *Public Law* 358.

[165]  In fact the Council for National Academic Awards initially refused to validate Buckingham degrees because they could be obtained after only two years' study: see Christie (ibid) 394.

[166]  Commentators consider there is such an institutional right in Germany: see below ch 5, s VII.

at public universities would then have opportunities for employment in the private sector.

## D. The Debate over the Oxford Business School

The implications of institutional arrangements for academic independence and freedom were discussed at length in debates in 1997 over the governance of the Said Business School in Oxford. Questions were raised about the independence of the School, following the benefaction from Mr Said to the former School of Management Studies. There were understandable academic freedom objections to the original composition of the body of Trustees, on which the University only had minority representation. It was revised to provide for an equal number (four) of representatives of both the University and the benefactor, with two independent members to constitute a body of ten Trustees. The key point was that the Trustees had authority not to approve the appointment of the Director of the Business School, thus giving rise to the possibility that non-academics might veto an academic appointment. For many speakers in the debate held in Congregation in June 1997,[167] these arrangements did not endanger academic freedom; the university representatives would have to win over only one other Trustee to prevent any infringement of university independence. Professor Roy Goode, an academic lawyer of great distinction, pointed out that the Trustees' approval could not be unreasonably withheld.

On the other side, powerful arguments were made by two distinguished jurists, Ronald Dworkin and John Finnis. The former pointed out that the non-university Trustees could object to an appointment on academic grounds; this could not be regarded as unreasonable, even though all the university members thought their arguments were unsound. It was wrong to trust to the integrity of the benefactor and his representatives; that provided no guarantee that their successors would not differ on academic matters from the university view. The fundamental point in Dworkin's view was that the University was surrendering part of its independence 'to appoint the directors of our institutions ... to represent the values and convictions, the academic values and

---

[167] Supplement (2) to *University Gazette*, No 4442, 23 June 1997.

convictions that are ours', no matter how much those convictions may be considered wrong outside the university.[168] The only difficulty with this argument is that it proves too much; taken seriously, it would surely mean that no university in the United Kingdom, apart from Oxford and Cambridge, has ever enjoyed academic independence, for key decisions on their governance are regularly taken by Councils on which academic members may be outvoted.


## VI. CONCLUSIONS

In 2006 a survey of academics found that about 40 per cent of them considered their academic freedom was gradually being eroded; the increase in management controls and the pressure to publish exerted by the RAE were prominent among the explanations for this trend.[169] There has certainly been a marked change in university culture in the last thirty years. The institutional freedom and independence of universities have been substantially curtailed as the government and funding councils have been granted more extensive powers to determine research priorities. HEFCE does not appear nearly as concerned as the UGC was to protect institutional academic freedom;[170] its pressure on Oxford and Cambridge Universities to change their governance arrangements suggests it is more interested in what it perceives to be institutional efficiency—in the belief that the highest good is winning the confidence of business and industry. Moreover, HEFCE has recently suggested that in extreme circumstances, it should have authority to direct the governing body of a university to replace its Vice-Chancellor (or other head), when HEFCE lacks confidence in the Vice-Chancellor's ability to ensure adequate management and academic standards;[171] universities understandably feel that this proposal would mark a further erosion of their already limited institutional autonomy. In the view of one leading

---

[168] Ibid.

[169] *Times Higher Education Supplement*, 4 August 2006.

[170] See the criticisms of HEFCE by the University and College Union in its evidence to the House of Commons Education and Skills Select Committee, *Times Higher Education Supplement*, 26 January 2007, 3.

[171] 'Consultation on Changes to the Funding Agreement between HEFCE and Institutions', HEFCE 2009/46, esp paras 16 and 21, issued in the wake of HEFCE dissatisfaction with the management of London Metropolitan University.

commentator and writer on academic freedom, UK universities in the last two or three decades have experienced more harassment from their government than those in Germany and the United States.[172]

It is hardly surprising that the gradual decline in institutional auton- omy should lead to increased anxiety on the part of academic staff that their individual freedom is under threat, even though legally it is protected through the incorporation of the ERA academic freedom clause in university statutes and in articles of government. Although individual academic freedom is not necessarily safeguarded by the insti- tutional independence of universities, the loss of that independence is likely to lead to curtailment of the individual freedom. Pressures on universities to become more efficient, to cut costs and to be more responsive to government, public and student demands are inevitably passed on to their employees. The core academic freedoms to teach and to select research topics are perhaps as well respected now as they have ever been, at least at the older universities. But there are increas- ingly significant restrictions on the conduct of research in both the natural and social sciences.[173] While the Davies Report found that it is wrong to subject university staff to the constraints commonly applied in industry and business,[174] many academic staff, particularly in newer, post-92 universities, are apparently reluctant to criticise their Heads of Department, let alone their Vice-Chancellors or university admin- istrations, for fear that such remarks may jeopardise their promotion prospects or make them likely candidates for redundancy when their universities are compelled to make savings.[175]

HEFCE and the government may still regard university indepen- dence as a paramount principle, even though these references have something of a ritual quality. Academic freedom is apparently discussed from time to time at meetings of Universities UK, albeit in the context of other issues such as the maintenance of university standards and the control of terrorism. As this chapter has shown, UK universities should

---

[172] E Shils, 'The British Universities in Tribulation' (1994) 32 *Minerva* 200, 208.
[173] See below ch 7.
[174] See above s IV(C).
[175] See the quarterly bulletins of the Council for Academic Freedom and Standards, available at the CAFAS website, http://www.cafas.org.uk/index.htm (accessed 10 August 2010); and the article by Z Corbyn on academic freedom in *Times Higher Education*, 11 February 2010, 32–41 for evidence of these fears.

respect academic freedom in their dealings with their academic staff. The principle can be invoked in arguments before courts and tribunals, although there is regrettably little evidence how far this is done with success. It may be premature to share the gloomy assessment of Conrad Russell that the UK legal provision for academic freedom has 'become a bit like the pagan temple of Victory preserved in the Senate of Christian Rome: a sentimental reminder of departed glories'.[176] But regrettably it seems only a little premature.

---

[176]  Russell (above n 129) 109.

# 5

# *Academic Freedom in Germany*

## I. INTRODUCTION

THE KEY LEGAL provision in German law concerning academic freedom is quite simple. Article 5(3) of the Basic Law (or Constitution) provides:

> Art and science, research and teaching, shall be free. Freedom of teaching shall not absolve from loyalty to the constitution.[1]

In the absence of any explicit restriction, the freedoms of science and research appear to be absolute; in this respect they are more generously protected than the freedom of expression, which is also guaranteed by Article 5 of the Basic Law (*Grundgesetz*). Only teaching freedom (*Lehrfreiheit*) may be limited—by a broad obligation to respect the Constitution. But this appearance of simplicity is extremely deceptive. The German law of *Wissenschaftsfreiheit* (literally translated as 'scientific freedom') is in fact very complex. One explanation for this complexity may lie in its relatively long history, briefly surveyed below in section II of this chapter. The first constitutional provision concerning *Wissenschaftsfreiheit* can be found in the Imperial constitution of 1849, but its ideas can be traced back at least to the Enlightenment and to early nineteenth-century political thought.[2] Moreover, the writings of philosophers and sociologists have been as important as constitutional provisions and court decisions to the development of the distinctive German tradition of academic freedom.

---

[1] The translation is provided by the Press and Information Office of the Federal Government. The German text reads: 'Kunst und Wissenschaft, Forschung und Lehre sind frei. Die Freiheit der Lehre entbindet nicht von der Treue zur Verfassung.'

[2] H Zwirner, 'Zum Grundrecht der Wissenschaftsfreiheit' (1973) 98 *AöR* 313.

Other difficulties are more conventionally legal. The interpretation of Article 5(3) is far from straightforward: what is the relationship, for example, of the concepts of science (*Wissenschaft*), research *(Forschung)* and teaching *(Lehre)*? It should of course be pointed out that the German term *Wissenschaft* does not refer only to the natural sciences (physics, chemistry and biological or life sciences); it refers to all branches of scholarship and knowledge, so one can, for example, speak of the study of law as *Rechtswissenschaft*. General interpretative issues concerning the terms of Article 5(3) are discussed below in section III. That section also examines the relationship of freedom of expression and academic freedom in German law, though there is a further treatment of this topic in chapter nine dealing with the freedom of university staff to engage in extramural speech. Another question considered in this section is the extent to which academic freedom binds private persons and institutions, as well as the state itself and other public authorities.

Many of these questions of interpretation have been resolved, at least in principle, by decisions of the German Constitutional Court (Bundesv erfassungsgericht). In its seminal ruling in 1973 in the *Hochschulurteil* (university judgement),[3] the Court established the fundamental principles of academic freedom for modern Germany—principles that have been repeatedly confirmed in its later rulings, albeit with significant modifications. Among them is the key idea that scientific research and teaching is an autonomous sphere that must be free from state regulation. It is for researchers themselves to determine what they research and study, their research methods and how their findings are assessed and published.[4] Another important principle established by the *Hochschulurteil* is that *Wissenschaftsfreiheit* is not only a negative or defensive right (*Abwehrrecht*) for individual researchers and scholars against state intervention; it also constitutes an objective value of constitutional weight. Consequently, the state is under a constitutional duty to safeguard the value by making some provision for the effective exercise of academic freedom.[5] Further, as Hans-Heinrich Trute and Eberhard Schmidt-Aßmann, two leading commentators on *Wissenschaftsfreiheit*, have argued, there are significant organisational, institutional and procedural dimensions to

---

[3] BVerfGE 35, 79. The decision is universally referred to in German literature as the *Hochschulurteil*, so that term is used in this book.

[4] Ibid, 112–13.

[5] Ibid, 114–16.

the freedom; it should not be seen entirely as a matter for individual rights.[6] The principles formulated in the *Hochschulurteil* are discussed below in section IV. That section also examines the subsequent treatment of these principles and the limits that may be imposed on the exercise of *Wissenschaftsfreiheit* in the light of subsequent rulings of the Constitutional Court and, to some extent, of other courts.

It is clear from the *Hochschulurteil* that the freedom to research and study is a right to be enjoyed by anyone who is engaged in such activity.[7] It is not confined to the academic staff employed by universities and other places of higher education, though that case itself, like many others, involved questions of university organisation. For that reason the term 'scientific freedom' is generally used in this chapter; 'academic freedom' is too narrow a translation to capture the meaning of *Wissenschaftsfreiheit*. In this respect German law differs fundamentally from the legal right to academic freedom in the United Kingdom, which is conferred on the academic staff of universities.[8] (Comparisons with the United States are more difficult since, as will be seen in the following chapter, distinctions can be drawn there between the traditional professional freedoms enjoyed by university professors and the constitutional right to academic freedom under the First Amendment, which in principle may be claimed by everyone.) Indeed, some commentators have criticised the traditional accounts of *Wissenschaftsfreiheit* for their undue concentration on its implications for university academics.[9] In contrast, its significance for the research conducted outside universities has been relatively neglected, at least until recently.[10]

Nevertheless, the implications of *Wissenschaftsfreiheit* for universities and their staff remain of central importance. They are explored below

---

[6] See H-H Trute, *Die Forschung zwischen grundrechtlicher Freiheit und staatlicher Institutionalisierung* (Tübingen, JCB Mohr, 1994); E Schmidt-Aßmann, 'Die Wissenschaftsfreiheit nach Art 5, Abs 3 GG als Organisationsrecht' in *Festschrift für Werner Thieme* (Köln, Carl Heymans, 1993) 697.

[7] *Hochschulurteil* (above n 3) 112.

[8] See above ch 4, s III(C).

[9] Notably Trute (above n 6); see also M Schulte, 'Grund und Grenzen der Wissenschaftsfreiheit' (2006) 65 *VVDStLR* 110, 117–18.

[10] See CD Classen, *Wissenschaftsfreiheit außerhalb der Hochschule* (Tübingen, JCB Mohr, 1994) for a comprehensive study of academic freedom in research institutions other than universities, and T Groß and N Arnold, *Regelungstrukturen der ausseruniversitären Forschung* (Baden-Baden, Nomos, 2007) for a detailed examination of the legal organisation of four research institutes.

in sections V and VI. The former section is concerned with university legislation enacted by the states (*Länder),* in particular insofar as its terms have raised academic freedom issues. In the last twenty years or so, there have been significant reforms to the organisation of German universities, to some extent similar to the developments that have occurred in the United Kingdom and other European countries: the move towards the so-called 'managed university', with its central concerns to reduce costs, to streamline decision-taking and to meet international competition. The implementation of some of these reforms by state legislation might be considered incompatible with *Wissenschaftsfreiheit,* although the most recent ruling of the German Constitutional Court suggests that the Court is unlikely to interfere with these reforms.[11] In section VII there is a brief discussion of scientific freedom in research foundations and industry. The final section summarises the main themes of the chapter and assesses from a comparative perspective the significance of the German experience of academic freedom.

## II. THE HISTORY OF SCIENTIFIC FREEDOM IN GERMANY

The origins of the idea of scientific freedom in Germany can be traced back to the late eighteenth-century Enlightenment.[12] They are particularly associated with the principles formulated by the Prussian Minister of Education Wilhelm von Humboldt when he established a new public university in Berlin in 1809—a development encouraged by the King of Prussia in reaction to the poor state of university education in earlier periods. The Friedrich-Wilhelms University was based on the principles of the unity of science (which entailed bringing together different faculties within the same institution), the unity of research and teaching, and freedom of research and teaching.[13] However, Humboldt did not envisage that universities should be entirely free from state

---

[11] Decision of 26 October, 2004, BVerfGE 111, 333 (considered below in ss IV(B) and VI).

[12] An important text is Kant, 'An Answer to the Question: "What is Enlightenment?"' in which he quotes Horace, *Sapere aude* (Dare to be wise), reprinted in HS Reiss (ed), *Kant: Political Writings* (Cambridge, Cambridge University Press, 1991) 54.

[13] R Hendler, 'Die Universität im Zeichen von Ökonomisierung und Internationalisierung' (2006) 65 *VVDStRL* 238, 240–41. For a general history

regulation; they were not to be autonomous institutions, as, say, Oxford and Cambridge were. Indeed, he saw the state's overall responsibility for university administration as providing a guarantee for the freedom of research.[14] The state had the responsibility to ensure that professors researched and taught without interference from the churches and from other private institutions and groups. To that end governments themselves appointed professors, sometimes in disregard of a faculty's wishes, and even intervened on occasion to dismiss them for their political conduct.[15]

It was partly in reaction to these official measures that the Frankfurt Constitution of 1849 provided that 'science and its teaching are free'.[16] But the Constitution did not create any enforceable rights against the state. University professors remained state officials, subject to the same legal restrictions as other officials in respect of their conduct outside the lecture hall. Indeed, if anything the state was more active towards the end of the nineteenth century in the promotion and direction of research, to some extent through its support for the foundation of research institutions outside universities.[17]

The Weimar Constitution of 1919 guaranteed freedom of science and its teaching; it added the arts (*Kunst*) to the scope of the clause.[18] Interestingly, the second sentence of Article 142 required the state to protect the arts and science and to participate in their promotion, but this seems to have had little significance in practice.[19] The article was incorporated in the part of the Constitution concerned with education

of German universities, see D Fallon, *The German University* (Boulder, Colorado Associated University Press, 1980) esp 5–53.

[14] *Hochschulurteil* (above n 3) 117.

[15] The most famous example was the dismissal of seven professors, including the Grimm brothers, from Göttingen University in 1837 when they protested against the revocation by the King of a constitution for Hanover.

[16] S 152 of the *Paulskirche Verfassung*, so called because the Constituent Assembly met in St Paul's Church, Frankfurt. For a short account of the framing of this provision, see Zwirner (above n 2) 318–26; and M Fehling, 'Commentary on Article 5, 3' in R Dolzer, C Waldhoff and K Graßhof (eds), *Bonner Kommentar* (Heidelberg, CF Müller, 2004) paras 2–8.

[17] R von Bruch, 'A Slow Farewell to Humboldt?' in MG Ash (ed), *German Universities Past and Future* (Providence, Berghahn Books, 1997) ch 1.

[18] The first sentence of Art 142 reads: 'Die Kunst, die Wissenschaft und ihre Lehre sind frei.'

[19] Fehling (above n 16) para 11.

and schools, rather than that devoted to fundamental rights. The leading constitutionalist, Rudof Smend, placed importance on this point when he argued in 1927 that the provision protected the basic rights of German universities; it guaranteed an institutional rather than individual freedom. The core of the right was the freedom of universities to regulate their own activities, because of the high value placed by society and by the Constitution on their independence.[20] Smend's article was seminal, laying the ground for the view that academic freedom is an institutional right, at least as much as an individual one, and should perhaps trump the latter when they conflict. It was a widely shared perspective until the Constitutional Court in the *Hochschulurteil* case (re)established the primacy of the freedom as an individual right.[21]

After the Nazi period when universities were brought under comprehensive state control,[22] the final stage in the history of scientific freedom as a constitutional right was the drafting in 1948–49 of the provision in the Basic Law.[23] The initial draft repeated the terms of the first sentence of Article 142 of the Weimar Constitution, but it was later amended to include an explicit reference to research (*Forschung*). On the other hand, it was considered unnecessary to repeat the Weimar provision requiring the state to participate in the promotion of science, as the federation was given explicit legislative competence to promote scientific research.[24] Most of the debates in the Parliamentary Committee, in considering the initial draft of the scientific freedom clause, concerned its second sentence: the so-called *Treueklausel*, indicating in effect that lecturers are not free to preach disloyalty to fundamental principles of the Basic Law itself.

One final point is worth making. Originally, *Kunstfreiheit* and *Wissenschaftsfreiheit* were guaranteed, as they had been under the Weimar Constitution, by a separate article; it was only in order to simplify the text that they were finally incorporated in the same provision of the

---

[20] R Smend, 'Das Recht der freien Meinungsäußerung' (1928) 4 *VVDStRL* 44.

[21] See Zwirner (above n 2) 335–36; and P Freundlich, *Zur Interpretation des Grundrechts der Wissenschaftsfreiheit—Art, 5 III S 1 GG—unter besondere Berücksichtigung der Rechtsprechung des Bundesverassungsgerichts*, Dissertation (Göttingen, 1984) 21.

[22] M Grüttner, 'German Universities under the Swastika' in J Connelly and M Grüttner (eds), *Universities under Dictatorship* (University Park, Pennsylvania State University Press, 2005) 75.

[23] See Fehling (above n 16) paras 13–17.

[24] Art 74(1) No 13 GG.

Basic Law (Article 5), which guarantees freedom of expression and related freedoms, notably press and broadcasting freedom. Scientific freedom and freedom of the arts are, like freedom of expression, concerned with communication, so the decision to cover them in the same provision was understandable. Unfortunately, it lent some support to an argument—now discredited—that *Wissenschaftsfreiheit* covers only the freedom of expression of individual state employees.[25]

The legal history of academic freedom in Germany shows a remarkable consistency. Science and its teaching have been explicitly guaranteed for over a hundred and fifty years. As a cultural value it has been respected, at least in name, for even longer—since von Humboldt articulated its basic principles at the beginning of the nineteenth century. That perhaps explains why there was relatively little discussion about its meaning during the drafting of the Basic Law in 1948. What is important now is that scientific freedom is legally enforceable against the state, for the basic rights guaranteed by the *Grundgesetz* bind the legislature, the executive and the judiciary.[26]

### III. INTERPRETING *WISSENSCHAFTSFREIHEIT*

#### A. Relevant Provisions of the Basic Law

A few provisions of the Basic Law other than Article 5(3) should be mentioned, for they may overlap with its terms or be in some way relevant to the resolution of cases in which scientific freedom is at issue. The most important is undoubtedly Article 5(1), which guarantees freedom of expression of opinion and related freedoms, such as press and broadcasting freedom. A university lecturer (or other writer) may claim the protection of both Article 5(1) and Article 5(3), for example, in respect of his or her publications. The general view is that Article 5(3) is a lex specialis that should be applied in cases of possible overlap in preference to the more general freedom of expression clause.[27] This is clearly the right approach, for the exercise of *Wissenschaftsfreiheit*, unlike freedom of expression, may not be restricted by general laws, unless

---

[25] See below s III(C).
[26] Art 1(3) GG.
[27] Fehling (above n 16) para 267.

they are enacted to protect a fundamental constitutional value. But there are some nice questions about the relationship of these two provisions, which are considered later in this section.

Theology professors and faculties may also be able to rely on the terms of Article 4 (freedom of conscience, faith and creed). Of more general importance in this context is Article 12, which guarantees *Berufsfreiheit* (the freedom to choose an occupation, including a place of training). One view is that Article 5(3) is a lex specialis that governs, for example, the organisation of professional education, to which Article 12 might also apply.[28] On the other hand, the allocation of places at training schools is governed by Article 12.[29] Questions concerning the relationship of these provisions have most often arisen in the context of research institutes and foundations other than universities, where scientific freedom principles have been applied only relatively recently.[30]

Finally, Article 33 should be mentioned. This provision concerns the equal political status of all Germans, in particular their equal eligibility for public office, irrespective of their religious and philosophical denomination or persuasion (Article 33(2) and (3)). But under Article 33(4) and (5), employment in the public service is to be regulated by law with due regard to the traditional principles of the professional public service, for example, neutrality and moderation in dealing with members of the public.[31] University professors and other teachers are public employees, so in principle these constitutional provisions and the legislation enacted to regulate the civil service apply to them, but these rules must themselves be interpreted in the light of the freedoms guaranteed by Article 5(3).

## B. The Terms of Article 5(3)

Article 5(3) provides that the arts, science, research and teaching are free. The freedom of the arts (*Kunstfreiheit*) covers, among other things,

---

[28]  Ibid, para 270.

[29]  Ibid.

[30]  See below s VII.

[31]  For a short discussion of the relevant principles, see HD Jarass and B Pieroth (eds), *Kommentar zum Grundgesetz für die Bundesrepublik Deutschland*, 9th edn (Munich, CH Beck, 2007) paras 51–52 of commentary on Article 33.

satirical reviews and theatrical productions, parodies and street theatre;[32] it is not invoked in scientific freedom cases, though it would surely be relevant to, say, the resolution of a claim by a university lecturer teaching fine arts who wanted to mount a controversial exhibition against the wishes of the university president or the state government.[33] Rather, we are concerned with the protection of science, research and teaching. This raises some related questions of interpretation. First, what is the relationship of the three protected activities? Are they three entirely distinct and separate spheres or areas of protection, or must, for example, teaching be related to science or to research to qualify for protection? Secondly, how can or should the law define *Wissenschaft*—in some ways the most opaque or least clear of the concepts used in Article 5(3)?

Taking the last question first, it is wrong on one view for the law to define *Wissenschaft* or to circumscribe its scope, for that entails the imposition of limits by the courts—one of the three branches of government—on what should be an entirely autonomous activity. What amounts to scientific research and scholarship should be determined only by academics themselves; naturally they have formulated a number of tests by which these activities can be identified. Among them are such familiar criteria as the disinterested attempt to discover truth; the openness of all scientific investigation and research to testing and to contradiction by other scholars; the character of the methods used in the research; and perhaps the open publication of scholarship and research findings. But courts cannot avoid decisions in this area, for they—in Germany, ultimately the Constitutional Court—must determine the scope of *Wissenschaftsfreiheit* when scientists or scholars challenge some state or university regulation that, in their view, inhibits their freedom. The judicial interpretation of the freedom may of course run counter to the general scientific view; it does not invalidate the latter as a matter of science but must be authoritative as a matter of law.

In fact, the Bundesverfassungsgericht has adopted a broad definition, which it has applied consistently since its formulation in the seminal ruling in the *Hochschulureil* case: the freedom extends to all scientific activity

---

[32] For a brief discussion of the leading principles of *Kunstfreiheit*, see E Barendt, *Freedom of Speech* (Oxford, Oxford University Press, 2007) 62–63 and 229–30.

[33] See the US case *Piarowski v Illinois Community College District* 759 F 2d 625 (7th Cir, 1985) where on these facts the Court of Appeals applied academic freedom principles.

that on the basis of its content and form is to be seen as a serious, systematic endeavour to discover what is true.[34] The Court emphasised that the freedom was not wedded to any particular scientific theory. Its broad approach stemmed from the provisional character of all scientific discoveries. Clearly, this perspective gives rise to some interesting questions: would, or should, the courts in Germany be willing to treat research into or the teaching of complementary medicines, parapsychology or even astrology, as covered by *Wissenschaftsfreiheit*?[35]

Some clarification of the concept is provided by a later decision of the Constitutional Court.[36] The complainant to the Court had written and published a book arguing that the Second World War had been forced on Germany by its enemies. He challenged a decision, upheld by the Federal Administrative Court, listing his book as dangerous to young people, with consequent restrictions on its advertisement and distribution. The Bundesverfassungsgericht rejected the claim that the listing infringed the complainant's rights under Article 5(3), while upholding his claim under freedom of expression. In the Court's view the book was not covered by scientific freedom, for it did not amount to a serious attempt to ascertain the truth. It reflected only the prejudices and preconceptions of the writer and made no attempt to deal with the documentary and other evidence indicating that Hitler desired and bore responsibility for the war. The Court rejected the argument that a publication is covered by Article 5(3) merely because its writer regarded it as academic. The systematic exclusion of facts and sources that challenged an author's views indicated that a work was not an exercise of *Wissenschaftsfreiheit*.[37] The decision shows that courts must inevitably make some assessment of the character of a work for it to qualify as an exercise of the freedom, though the Court was careful to emphasise that it is not for them to determine its truth; scientific freedom protects minority views and heterodox, even wrong, research findings, provided they are reached in the course of a serious endeavour to discover the truth.

The *Hochschulurteil* also established that *Wissenschaft* is a generic term (*Oberbegriff*), which determines the meaning of the closely related terms 'research' and 'teaching'. The former of these covers all activity devoted

---

[34] *Hochschulurteil* (above n 3) 113.
[35] Freundlich (above n 21) 122ff raises questions of this kind.
[36] BVerfGE 90, 1.
[37] Ibid, 13.

to the discovery of new knowledge, conducted methodically and systematically, and with its conclusions open to examination.[38] It is not confined to pure research and scholarship conducted in universities but extends to applied and contract research undertaken by other institutions, including industry; the individual researchers may themselves have little or no choice regarding the research programme, but their work is covered by *Forschungsfreiheit*, provided they conduct it systematically and assess its results on the basis of rigorous and objective tests.[39] In practice, the meaning of freedom of research does not appear to have given rise to much difficulty.

The scope of teaching freedom (*Lehrfreiheit*) has given rise to more controversy, at least among commentators on scientific freedom. In the *Hochschulurteil* the Court indicated that teaching should be understood in conjunction with the other activities protected by Article 5(3). Freedom of teaching is guaranteed by this provision insofar as it is linked to scientific or scholarly research, and because it then itself encourages further research work.[40] The freedom protects a right to determine the contents of a course and how it is taught.[41] It is immaterial, however, whether the teaching is linked to the teacher's own research;[42] a lecturer is entitled to the protection of Article 5(3) even if his or her lectures are based on the scholarly or scientific work of others. Neither is there any need for an institutional link between teaching and research, so that only those who work for universities or other places of research enjoy teaching freedom. Ann-Katrin Kaufhold has recently argued that teaching freedom should be regarded as an independent basic right, justified in terms of its critical and cultural role, entirely independent of its function in communicating research findings; nevertheless, even in her view it must have some academic content to distinguish it from other types of communication or expression which are covered by Article 5(1) of the Basic Law.[43] On her argument teaching freedom would cover teaching of an advanced character in schools as well

[38] *Hochschulurteil* (above n 3) 113.
[39] For a general discussion of these issues, see Fehling (above n 16) paras 71–82; and see also Trute (above n 6) 99–107.
[40] *Hochschulurteil* (above n 3) 113–14.
[41] BVerfGE 93, 85, 97.
[42] Trute (above n 6) 128–30; Fehling (above n 16) para 83.
[43] A-K Kaufhold, *Die Lehrfreiheit—ein verlorenes Grundrecht?* (Berlin, Duncker and Humboldt, 2006) esp 108–38, 172–74 and 188–206. Her conclusions that *Wissenschaftsfreiheit* is a redundant concept and that the content of Art 5(3) is captured

as, say, a lecture given over the radio or on television. But the usual view is that the rights conferred by Article 5(3) do not extend to teaching in schools, even at higher levels.[44] In that context, Article 7 of the Basic Law, which is concerned with school education, is a *lex specialis*.

There is no explicit constitutional protection of a student's *Lernfreiheit* (freedom to learn), which might entail a freedom to choose courses and perhaps some freedom to determine when to attend lectures and when to take examinations. Traditionally, German university students have enjoyed a wide degree of freedom in these contexts. On one view this is not a matter of constitutional right;[45] at most, students' interests may be taken into account when teachers claim their own rights to teach, say, free from the interference that is caused by strikes and boycotts to the conduct of university lectures. On the other hand, in the *Hochschulurteil* the Court recognised that university students are not to be equated with pupils at school but should be treated at academic seminars as independent members of the university.[46] It might be inferred that they do have rights under Article 5(3), but the Court's judgement left open whether they enjoy any constitutional right to participate in academic government.[47] In a later case, however, the Court did suggest that insofar as they are ready and able to participate in academic study, they should enjoy the basic rights of Article 5(3).[48]

## C. *Wissenschaftsfreiheit* in Relation to Other Article 5 Freedoms

Scientific freedom is guaranteed by the same provision of the *Grundgesetz* that protects freedom of expression (*Meinungsfreiheit*), freedom of the press and freedom of reporting by broadcasting and films. But while those other freedoms may be limited under Article 5(2) by general laws, by statutes enacted to protect youth and by the right to respect for personal honour, there is no explicit restriction on the exercise of

by reference only to separate research and teaching freedom are heterodox and run counter to the decisions of the Constitutional Court.

[44] Fehling (above n 16) para 86.
[45] Kaufhold (above n 43) 201–5.
[46] *Hochschulurteil* (above n 3) 125.
[47] Ibid; see further below s IV.
[48] BVerfGE 55, 37, 67. See Fehling (above n 16) paras 96–102.

academic freedom, except for the provision that teaching should not preach disloyalty to basic constitutional values, the *Treuepflicht*. This difference makes it important to determine whether, say, the publications (or broadcasts) of a university professor or independent scholar are covered by *Wissenschaftsfreiheit*—in which case they appear to enjoy more or less absolute protection[49]—or whether they enjoy only the more limited protection granted by Article 5 to freedom of expression (or to broadcasting freedom).

In a classic article written before the *Hochschulurteil*, Gerd Roellecke argued that the right to scientific freedom conferred by Article 5(3) was a special case of the individual right to freedom of expression conferred by the first clause of the Article.[50] It ensured that all officials, including school teachers and the custodians of galleries and museums, as well as university professors, enjoyed the same freedom of speech as ordinary citizens. Written against the background of the general view at the time that Article 5(3) conferred institutional rights on universities,[51] Roellecke's article emphasised the individual, personal character of *Wissenschaftsfreiheit*. On the other hand, he thought it wrong to draw any implications from Article 5(3) for the organisation of universities; that would circumscribe legislative discretion, in effect privileging academic staff, whose speech might then enjoy greater protection than that of private citizens.

As will be explained shortly, the Constitutional Court in the *Hochschulurteil* did interpret Article 5(3) as carrying implications for the organisation of universities. *Wissenschaftsfreiheit* has an organisational dimension, as well as guaranteeing an individual right. It is wrong, as Roellecke himself subsequently admitted,[52] to treat it as recognising only an individual freedom, and only freedom of expression. A number of *activities*—the organisation of laboratories, the installation of equipment and the recruitment of research teams—are not directly

---

[49] In fact, as a result of an important decision of the Constitutional Court in 1978 (BVerfGE 47, 327) limits may be imposed on the exercise of scientific freedom if they can be related to a competing constitutional right or value: see below s IV(C).

[50] G Roellecke, 'Wissenschaftsfreiheit als institutionelle Garantie?' (1969) *JZ* 726. For a reply, see F-L Knemeyer, 'Garantie der Wissenschaftsfreiheit und Hochschulreform' (1969) *JZ* 780.

[51] See above s II.

[52] G Roellecke, 'Wissenschaftsfreiheit als Rechtfertigung von Relevanzansprüchen' in *Festschrift für Werner Thieme* (above n 6) 681, 696.

connected with freedom of expression but are clearly aspects of scientific (or 'academic') freedom. The simple equation of scientific or academic freedom with freedom of speech or expression, as has been argued elsewhere in this book,[53] ignores the multifaceted character of scientific and scholarly research, particularly in the natural sciences. Further, as the Constitutional Court has recognised, the publication of a book may fail to qualify for the protection of Article 5(3) because it makes no attempt to discover the truth, but it may be covered by the constitutional protection of freedom of expression.[54] Academic publications and discourse, depending on their context, are assessed by standards of relevance, coherence and integrity, which it would be quite wrong to apply to the regulation of political or public debate falling under freedom of expression.[55]

A writer may claim the protection of both *Wissenschaftsfreiheit* and *Meinungsfreiheit* (freedom of expression) in respect of a genuinely scholarly publication or the dissemination of his or her research. In practice, the writer would rely on the former, since it is not limited in the same way as freedom of expression, the exercise of which may be restricted by general laws, etc. There are then nice questions whether a university professor may claim scientific freedom in German law if he or she expresses political views or criticises the university administration, say, in the course of a radio interview or in a newspaper or general journal article. While he or she is surely covered by *Wissenschaftsfreiheit* if these views are expressed in the course of a faculty meeting or in an academic publication, it is less clear whether he or she can rely on the broader freedom when engaging in extramural speech outside the university campus. The German law on this topic is discussed below in chapter nine.

One further question can be usefully discussed here. Comparisons are frequently drawn in German writing between *Wissenschaftsfreiheit* and *Rundfunkfreiheit* (broadcasting freedom), a freedom that is guaranteed by the second sentence of Article 5(1) of the Basic Law. The Constitutional Court regards broadcasting freedom as an instrumental freedom (*dienende Freiheit*), protected to safeguard the free speech rights and interests of viewers and listeners, as well as those of the

---

[53]  See above ch 2, s II.
[54]  BVerfGE 90, 1, discussed above in s III(B).
[55]  Smend (above n 20) 71 recognised this distinction.

broadcasters themselves.[56] The freedom is moreover not primarily a negative freedom but requires the state to ensure that the broadcasting media are used to promote free speech values, notably an informed democracy and the exchange of a variety of views and opinion. Consequently, legislation can impose programme standards and require that programmes, particularly those of the public service broadcasters, are balanced and objective. The question is whether this provides an appropriate model for the interpretation and understanding of scientific freedom. Arguably, *Wissenschaftsfreiheit* serves similar, though not identical, social functions as those promoted by broadcasting freedom: the benefits of objective scientific research and scholarship, economic and political progress and the general attributes of a cultured society. These ends justify scientific freedom at least much as the protection of the individual interests of researchers and scholars.[57]

Nevertheless, the analogy has been rejected by commentators on German scientific freedom law.[58] They point out that there is a fundamental difference between the two freedoms. Unlike broadcasting freedom, *Wissenschaftsfreiheit* is treated by the Constitutional Court as primarily providing individual rights for everyone engaged in research or scholarship. There is no need for it to be conducted within an institution or organisation, a significant difference from the traditional model of broadcasting. As will be discussed shortly in the context of university governance structures, scientific freedom is also an organisational freedom; universities must be organised in such a way that the core of scientific freedom is not endangered. But it is the individual freedom that in principle is paramount. Moreover, there are no rules of scientific freedom equivalent to those that are standard in the context of broadcasting regulation. Broadcasters in Germany (and other European countries) are generally required to be balanced in their presentation of controversial political issues, while some of them must also transmit a range of original programmes of high quality. Scientific freedom

---

[56] See in particular the decision in the Third Television case, BVerfGE 57, 295, 320. For general discussion, see EM Barendt, *Broadcasting Law* (Oxford, Oxford University Press, 1995) ch 2.

[57] See above ch 3, s III.

[58] For example, Trute (above n 6) 283–89; Schmidt-Aßmann, 'Die Wissenschaftsfreiheit' (above n 6) 704–5; and K-H Ladeur, 'Die Wissenschaftsfreiheit der "entfesselten Hochschule"' (2005) *DÖV* 753, 757–58.

precludes the imposition of similar requirements on or by universities: lecturers are free to determine the contents of their courses and their methods of teaching. The principal constraints are imposed by the ideas implicit in *Wissenschaft* itself: research must be objective and its findings open to scrutiny, while teaching must be relevant to the syllabus and not merely reflect a lecturer's unchecked preconceptions and prejudices.

## D. Who is Bound to Respect Scientific Freedom?

The final general question of interpretation concerns who is bound to respect the freedom. A basic right such as *Wissenschaftsfreiheit* is protected as a defensive right (*Abwehrrecht*) against infringement by the state, including public bodies and authorities. That means that public, state-financed and organised universities not only are themselves the holders of some rights to scientific freedom[59] but are also bound to respect the right in the context of claims by individual professors and lecturers. Indeed, arguably individual professors, themselves public officials, are bound to respect the scientific and scholarly freedom of their colleagues.[60]

Harder questions concern the obligations of private foundations and institutions: private universities and research institutes, as well as companies that conduct or sponsor research. They are not directly bound by the rights set out in the Basic Law. But under well-developed constitutional principles formulated by the Constitutional Court in one of its important early decisions,[61] the basic rights constitute fundamental values that must be respected in all areas of law, including private law. Under this *Drittwirkung* principle, rights therefore have some indirect horizontal effect on private parties. These principles apply to scientific freedom, as they do to freedom of expression and other basic rights. Their implications are most important in the context of the research conducted outside universities by private foundations and companies and are therefore discussed below in section VII. These principles sharply distinguish the law in Germany from that in the United States,

---

[59] See below s IV(D).
[60] Fehling (above n 16) para 56.
[61] *Lüth,* BVerfGE 7, 198, 205, cited with a number of other decisions instantiating this principle by the Court in the *Hochschulurteil* (above n 3) 114.

where the constitutional principle of academic freedom, derived from the First Amendment, binds only state universities.[62]

## IV. *WISSENSCHAFTSFREIHEIT* IN UNIVERSITIES

Although *Wissenshaftsfreiheit* is a right enjoyed by everyone, whatever their position, it is in the university context that it has been most often asserted—and on occasion upheld. In an interesting but opaque early ruling,[63] the Bundesverfassungsgericht upheld the standing of universities themselves to challenge decisions affecting them but left it open whether they enjoyed independent constitutional rights under Article 5(3); it did however clearly recognise the rights of individual scholars. It gave much fuller consideration to the freedom in its *Hochschulurteil* in 1973. The Court's ruling in that case has been of seminal importance, laying down principles that have been followed for the last 35 years or so. However, as will be explained, subsequent decisions may to some extent have limited its significance. Also important is a later decision of the Court on a Hesse university statute, establishing that scientific freedom is not, as might appear from the text of Article 5(3), an absolute right (subject only to the *Treuepflicht*); it further formulated principles for balancing the freedom against other constitutional values. This section finally discusses court decisions that flesh out the rights which university professors and other academic staff enjoy under the principles formulated by the Constitutional Court in its jurisprudence.

## A. The *Hochschulurteil*

The background to this case, decided in May 1973, is provided by the significant changes to the organisation of German universities brought about by state laws in the early 1970s, after a period of student unrest and widespread public dissatisfaction with the previous structures. Under the earlier regime, often described as the *Ordinarienuniversität*, universities were largely controlled by full professors (*Ordinarien*), though the states ensured that their control met legislative requirements. The reforms

[62] See below ch 6, ss I and IV(A).
[63] BVerfGE 15, 256, on which see Freundlich (above n 21) 160–70.

of the 1970s were designed to give substantially more voice to other members of the academic staff and to representatives of the students and non-academic staff.[64] Under the new model of the *Gruppenuniversität*, employees were divided into groups—for example, professors and other fully qualified teachers (*Hochschullehrer*); teaching and research assistants (*wissenschaftliche Mitarbeiter*); and other non-academic staff. Each group was to be represented in the various governing bodies and committees of universities. The *Hochschulurteil* involved a challenge by about 400 professors and other teachers to a law in Lower Saxony that set up committees in which their representatives enjoyed between 30 per cent and 50 per cent of the membership but in which—with the exception of examination boards—they did not have a majority.

The Court first formulated the principle that *Wissenschaftsfreiheit* constitutes an individual right to be enjoyed by everyone against infringement by the state, and it then clarified the terms of Article 5(3): science, research and teaching.[65] But this provision established additionally, in the Court's view, a fundamental value (*Wertentscheidung*) applicable to all areas of law, which must therefore be interpreted and applied in accordance with the value of scientific freedom. Further, a state that saw itself as cultured had an obligation to safeguard and promote this value. Two principles followed. First, the state must provide adequate structures and financial support to ensure that scientific freedom flourishes, for without such provision independent research and teaching, particularly in the natural sciences, could not be conducted. Secondly, the state must shape its organisational measures so as to ensure so far as possible that the fundamental right to scientific and scholarly freedom remains inviolate. Under these principles, the individual rights of academic staff are strengthened by an entitlement to share in some basic support for their work and by a right to those organisational measures necessary to safeguard their freedom. The Court clearly saw these principles as a matter of constitutional right, not simply as desirable objectives.[66]

The Court made it clear that scientific freedom did not mandate any particular structure for universities. It further refrained from deciding

---

[64] For a survey of these developments, see Fallon (above n 13) 69–90; and K Künzel, 'The State and Higher Education in the Federal Republic of Germany' (1982) 17 *European Journal of Education* 243.

[65] See above s III(B).

[66] *Hochschulurteil* (above n 3) 114–16.

whether the Basic Law provided a constitutional right for German universities—the right asserted by Smend under the Weimar constitution.[67] It was unnecessary to answer that question, since state laws and some state constitutions clearly guaranteed their freedom. The Court recognised that universities now had to take account of a number of interests—those of all of their employees and their students—as well as their increasing responsibility to provide practical training. The states generally had wide discretion in framing university legislation. Nevertheless, Article 5(3) imposed some limits on how states organised their universities; an effective protection of *Wissenschaftsfreiheit* required organisational structures to ensure that professors and other academics could conduct their research and teaching responsibilities freely.[68]

The Court had no objection to the replacement of the traditional model by the *Gruppenuniversität* structure, nor to several features of the new structure, including the representation of academic assistants (*wissenschaftliche Mitarbeiter*) or of students on university committees. However, it insisted that university teachers were entitled to exercise a decisive voice on questions of university administration that directly concerned research, and a significant influence on teaching. That did not of course mean that individual professors and lecturers had a right to sit on the governing bodies of universities; that would be impracticable. Nor had their representatives a right to a majority vote over all university decisions. But they were entitled to that in respect of decisions concerning research.[69] Moreover, Article 5(3) (in conjunction with the equality principle guaranteed by Article 3 of the Basic Law) required that the representative group of university teachers should be properly composed of professors and other teachers of similar standing; otherwise their voice could be distorted by the inclusion within their group of, say, teachers who act under direction and are not concerned with research.[70] The Lower Saxony law did not satisfy these requirements in a number of respects; in particular, the group representing professors and other university teachers did not have a majority vote on research issues, and the law did not make any provision for tied votes in faculty

---

[67] See above s II.
[68] *Hochschulurteil* (above n 3) 120–24.
[69] Ibid, 128–33.
[70] Ibid, 134–35.

committees on teaching issues.[71] Further, the law failed to ensure that the representative group of university teachers was properly composed; it had grouped together all teachers with different qualifications and responsibilities, irrespective whether they acted independently or under direction.[72]

There was strong dissent from two members of the Court. While they agreed with the basic principles of the judgement, they thought the majority had usurped the role of the legislator when it prescribed these requirements for university governance. It was particularly wrong to construe Article 5(3) as providing university teachers with a permanent privileged position in these arrangements.[73] Certainly, the majority ruling is remarkable for its analysis both of the implications of *Wissenschaftsfreiheit* for university governance in general and of the particular functions of the various bodies and committees prescribed by the Lower Saxony law. But if scientific and scholarly freedom is taken to be more than a negative freedom and establishes, as all members of the Court agreed, a fundamental constitutional value, it will inevitably have repercussions for the organisation of universities, including the composition of their governing bodies and committees.

## B. Subsequent Decisions on University Organisation

In a number of later decisions the Constitutional Court upheld challenges to state laws on the basis of these principles.[74] In particular, it has ensured that fully qualified academic staff are not grouped with teaching assistants for the purpose of representation on university bodies. On the other hand, it rejected a challenge to provisions in a Baden-Württemberg law that allowed only higher ranked professors the right to vote for university Rectors and guaranteed them, but not lower ranked professors, places on university councils.[75] It also upheld the constitutionality of a provision in a North-Rhine Westphalia law

---

[71]  Ibid, 142–44.

[72]  Ibid, 139–40.

[73]  Ibid, 150.

[74]  BVerfGE 42, 242; BVerfGE 56, 192; BVerfGE 61, 210. See Freundlich (above n 21) for a discussion of the early post-*Hochschulurteil* decisions.

[75]  BVerfGE 54, 363.

giving professors only a 2/5 share of the vote in decisions of the *Konvent* (General Council).[76] The point was that the *Konvent* was not directly concerned with decisions concerning research or teaching; the fact that some of its decisions would inevitably have some impact on academic work was immaterial. The *Konvent* chose the Rector and Pro-Rectors of the universities, so the Court carefully considered the repercussions of this power for *Wissenschaftsfreiheit*. It did not infringe Article 5(3), since the Rector's authority did not extend to academic matters of research and teaching.

In many of these decisions the Court has emphasised the considerable discretion that state legislatures enjoy in framing the rules for university organisation; the only condition is that these rules must not infringe the core of scientific freedom. It has, for example, upheld laws strengthening the powers of the Deans of faculties in relation to those of the faculty acting collectively, and extending the Deans' term of office to four years.[77] The Court rejected the argument that scientific freedom under the Basic Law requires full observance of a principle of collegiality; it was compatible with Article 5(3) to allocate to an individual the responsibility to take decisions of a largely executive or technical character,[78] while a four-year term could be justified for reasons of efficiency and for the strengthening of the universities' powers of self-government. But the Court did examine the legislation to ensure that Deans could not legally interfere with teaching freedom.

The Court's reluctance to interfere with state legislation concerning the organisation of universities is shown most clearly in its decision in 2004 on a Brandenburg statute that imposed a measure of external institutional supervision over state universities and gave powers to university presidents to evaluate teaching and research.[79] This significant decision is considered when we discuss the significance of recent developments in the organisation of German universities for scientific freedom (below in section VI). At this stage, it may be noted that while the principles of the *Hochschulurteil* remain of paramount significance for any understand-

---

[76] BVerfGE 61, 260. See also BVerfG Decision of 7 May 2001, reported in *DVBl* 2001, 1137.

[77] BVerfGE 93, 85.

[78] Ibid, 96.

[79] BVerfGE 111, 333.

ing of this freedom in German law, their actual impact on the practical organisation of German universities may be declining.

## C. Balancing *Wissenschaftsfreiheit* with Other Values

In 1974 the state of Hesse amended its university law to require all university staff engaged in teaching and research to take into account the social consequences of their scientific discoveries. It also imposed on them an obligation to inform an appropriate faculty authority or a central university body, when it was clear that the irresponsible application of their research might pose a serious danger to health, life or social peace (*friedliche Zusammenleben der Menschen*).[80] This statute was challenged, on the ground that it inhibited the exercise of *Wissenschaftsfreiheit* and so infringed Article 5(3), which appears to confer unlimited protection on scientific freedom, save for the *Treuepflicht*. In rejecting the challenge,[81] the Court confirmed that this freedom could not be limited by an ordinary statute; the restrictions listed in Article 5(2) that can be imposed on the exercise of freedom of expression do not apply to freedom of the arts and sciences.[82] But it then applied to scientific freedom the principles it had formulated in its famous *Mephisto* ruling on *Kunstfreiheit*, also guaranteed by Article 5(3) of the Basic Law.[83] The exercise of these apparently unlimited rights may be restricted to protect other rights and values guaranteed by the Constitution itself. The courts must balance the importance of conflicting constitutional values, not in abstract but in the light of their importance in individual cases. This approach was justified on the ground that *Wissenschaftsfreiheit* is protected, at least partly, in the interests of society at large, and it is therefore right to limit its exercise when it imperils other significant social values.

The principal argument in support of the constitutional challenge in the Hesse case was that the obligation imposed by the statute was so imprecise that it would necessarily deter the conduct of innovative scientific research that might have unpredictable and conceivably

---

[80]　Hesse University Law of 11 Sept 1974, s 6.

[81]　BVerfGE 47, 327.

[82]　Freedom of expression may be limited by general laws, by statutory provisions to protect youth and by the right to respect for personal honour.

[83]　BVerfGE 30, 173.

dangerous social implications. The Court found that, properly and narrowly interpreted, the statutory obligations did not infringe freedom of scientific research. The obligation on researchers to take social consequences into account applied only to serious implications of their research for constitutionally guaranteed values. The duty to provide information to university authorities extended only to the possible misuse of research findings which a researcher could anticipate in the light of specialist knowledge. He or she was not expected to provide information about the unforeseeable abuse of his or her discoveries.[84] The Court conceded that even after this restrictive interpretation, the clause had a broad meaning. But that was acceptable. The obligation to take account of serious social consequences was not an onerous one and left much to the judgement of the researchers themselves.[85]

Though not free from criticism,[86] the approach taken by the Constitutional Court in the Hesse case does not appear to have given rise to great legal difficulties. The Basic Law protects a wide range of fundamental rights, for example, the right to human dignity (Article 1); the right to life, physical integrity (including health) and the development of personality (Article 2); the right to faith and conscience (Article 4); and the right to property (Article 14). Legislation promoting any of these rights may limit the exercise of freedom of science and research, if its protection can be regarded in the particular circumstances of the conflict as more important than the restrictions imposed on *Wissenschaftsfreiheit*. When balancing competing rights or values, there is no presumption in favour of scientific freedom.[87] On this basis laws restricting the use of human embryos for medical research, and perhaps those regulating stem cell research, would almost certainly be upheld, as they are enacted to protect the basic right to dignity, an inalienable right regarded as the most fundamental of the freedoms recognised by the Basic Law.[88] Data protection and other laws restricting access to personal information may limit freedom of research, as these laws promote

---

[84]  BVerfGE 47, 327, 381–83.

[85]  Ibid, 386.

[86]  See R Dreier, 'Forschungsbegrenzung als verfassunsrechtliches Problem' (1980) *DVBl* 471; and M Nettesheim, 'Grund und Grenzen der Wissenschaftsfreiheit (2005) *DVBl* 1072.

[87]  Fehling (above n 16) para 160.

[88]  But a Munich court has upheld a freedom to show preserved corpses for a medical exhibition open to the public; in these circumstances *Wissenschaftsfreiheit* did

the right to the development of the personality guaranteed by Article 2; freedom of research may, however, trump privacy concerns if the data are anonymised so they do not relate to identifiable individuals.[89]

One area of difficulty has been the relationship of freedom of research and teaching to the protection of animals used in medical experiments. *Wissenschaftsfreiheit* could not in principle be limited by legislation regulating the use of animals unless that law could be related to a constitutional right or value. It used to be unclear whether there was any constitutional basis for such legislation. However, the Federal Administrative Court accepted that teaching freedom might be limited by a federal law protecting animals, though in the particular case it rejected a zoology student's argument that she had a right under Article 4 (freedom of faith and conscience) not to participate in experiments on animals killed for that purpose.[90] The Court found that the experiments could be regarded as necessary for teaching purposes, as it had not been shown that other methods—the exhibition of films or computer simulations—would be equally effective for these purposes. It is now clear that *Wissenschaftsfreiheit* might be limited by laws protecting animals, as the Basic Law was amended in 2002 to impose a duty on the state to take appropriate measures to protect them, as well as the natural environment.[91]

The one specific limitation in Article 5(3) itself concerns the requirement imposed by its *Treueklausel* on those engaged in teaching not to depart from loyalty to the Constitution. The provision was clearly inspired by experiences under the Weimar Republic; university teachers should not exploit their positions to make propaganda against basic democratic values and to engage in violent political agitation.[92] Arguably, the *Treuklausel* has largely declaratory significance, for use of the lecture hall for pure propaganda should not and would not

not infringe human dignity: VGH Munich, Decision of 21 February 2003, *NJW* 2003, 1618.

[89] Fehling (above n 16) paras 171–72. The same principle applies in UK data protection law: see below ch 7, s VI.

[90] BVerwGE, 105, 73. See Fehling (above n 16) para 177.

[91] Art 20a GG.

[92] C Starck, 'Commentary on Article 5 GG' in H von Mangoldt, F Klein and C Starck (eds), *Kommentar zum Grundgesetz: Band I*, 5th edn (Munich, Vahlen, 2004) para 427.

be regarded as an exercise of *Wissenschaftsfreiheit* in the first place.[93] Moreover, scientific freedom does not absolve university teachers from their obligations under Article 33(5) of the Basic Law to observe the traditional principles of constitutional loyalty.[94] On the other hand, the abstract teaching of Marxist values and strong criticism of the existing Constitution is in principle covered by teaching freedom and does not violate the *Treuepflicht*.[95] A state may rely on the loyalty clause not to appoint to one of its universities a lecturer who had an active role as an official of the Communist party.[96]

## D. The Specific Rights of University Teachers

The *Hochschulurteil* outlined in very general terms the rights enjoyed by university teachers under Article 5(3). In addition to their freedom to teach and conduct research free from state interference, they also have a right to basic facilities to enable them to carry out their work.[97] Subsequent decisions of the courts have, however, generally rejected specific claims by university teachers under these principles. In an important decision four years after the *Hochschulurteil* the Federal Administrative Court rejected a claim by a physics professor that he had not been given adequate support to enable him to conduct his research.[98] The Court held that his needs should have been taken into account when resources were distributed, but the university was free to allocate them on the basis of its own assessment of its teachers' needs. It must not, however, act arbitrarily or treat applicants unequally. An administrative court in Baden-Württemberg followed these principles when it rejected a claim by a professor that the university should have allocated him research assistants.[99] The court added that it was

---

[93] See the judgement of the Administrative Court of Berlin of 1 June 1972, reported in *JZ* 1973, 209, 211.

[94] Decision of the Constitutional Court of 31 July 1981, *NJW* 1981, 2683.

[95] See BVerfGE 5, 98, 141–49; and Decision of Administrative Court of Berlin of 1 June 1972 (above n 93), with a critical note by JA Frowein.

[96] BVerwGE 52, 313.

[97] See above s IV(A).

[98] BVerwGE 52, 339.

[99] Decision of 29 January 1982, *DÖV* 1982, 367.

difficult for it to question university decisions assessing the appropriate provisions to satisfy academic needs.

Claims to the protection of teaching freedom have also been rejected. The Constitutional Court itself dismissed a challenge to a clause in a Bremen University law providing that short, minor disturbances resulting from reasonable student complaints did not amount to violations of student duties.[100] In principle, university teachers are entitled under Article 5(3) to some protection against disturbances that interfere with their freedom, but that right did not extend to the minor interruptions tolerated by the Bremen law, which itself had to be strictly interpreted in the interests of teaching freedom.[101] Of perhaps more general significance are rulings to the effect that teaching freedom does not give university teachers dispensation from obligations to teach at the level for which they are qualified, in this case applied technologies,[102] nor does it give them freedom to choose the size of the groups in which they teach and select their own students.[103] What *Lehrfreiheit* does confer is the right for lecturers to choose the contents of their courses and their teaching methods.

One explanation for the courts' reluctance to recognise strong individual rights to research and teaching is their recognition that other interests are implicated by these claims, and that the university is generally much better placed than a court to balance competing rights and interests. The scope of an individual's right to *Wissenschaftsfreiheit* may have to be balanced against the rights to the same freedom that may be asserted by other members of a university's academic staff, and perhaps against the interests of the university itself.[104] A university, whether private or public, may itself assert rights to freedom of science, research and teaching, against a state that attempts to interfere with these freedoms by, say, prescribing the research it

---

[100] BVerfGE 55, 37.

[101] Ibid, 73.

[102] BVerfGE 88, 129, 142–43.

[103] Decision of Administrative Court of Rhineland-Pfalz of 9 May 1997, *DVBl* 1997, 1242.

[104] See the decision of the Constitutional Court refusing to stop the Senate of a university in Dresden taking decisions until a full challenge to its composition had been heard. The Court said that *Wissenschaftsfreiheit* was for the benefit of the university as well as an entitlement of the professors requesting the order: Decision of 1 July 2003, *NVwZ-RR* 2003, 705.

may conduct or determining how its professors teach a particular subject.[105] Moreover, a court has recognised the procedural rights of a university to state its case under Article 5(3) before student courses are closed under a state law.[106] But does it follow that in German law a university might be able to claim the right to *Wissenschaftsfreiheit* against the competing claim to this freedom made by an individual professor or other lecturer?

The question has been answered by the Federal Administrative Court in an important ruling on the entitlement of a university to assess the research findings of one of its professors who worked in a biophysics institute.[107] It had been suggested that there were serious discrepancies in his published writing on the treatment of melanoma, which he had refused to put right. The Dean set up an ad hoc Commission to review the matter. It found against the professor and requested him to reconsider his research conclusions; the Commission's report was given wide circulation, though it did not have any legal force. The Federal Administrative Court upheld the professor's challenge, holding that the Commission's decisions infringed his freedom of research. It had not been wrong for the university to set up an inquiry to consider whether the professor's research fell altogether outside the boundaries of serious research or scholarship or whether it damaged other constitutional rights. But it was an infringement of his scientific freedom for the Commission to publish and circulate a report merely because it disagreed with the conclusions of his research. Strong disagreements with research findings must be resolved through academic discourse. In the course of its reasoning the Court found, contrary to the university's argument, that neither it nor the Faculty enjoyed an independent right under Article 5(3) on the basis of which it could review the professor's research. The university's responsibility was rather to defend his individual rights.[108] Moreover, the academic reputation of the university and its departments did not amount to a constitutionally protected value that

---

[105] See Fehling (above n 16) paras 124–26 on the basic rights of public universities.
[106] Decision of Berlin Constitutional Court of 22 October 1996 stopping the closure of courses at the Free and Humboldt Universities until their objections had been heard: *NVwZ* 1997, 790.
[107] BVerwGE 104, 304.
[108] Ibid, 309.

could justify an infringement of scientific freedom, particularly in the absence of clear proof of its abuse.

This decision has been criticised for failing to do justice to the organisational dimension of scientific freedom and to the responsibilities of universities to exercise some control over the quality of research emanating from them.[109] On the approach of the Administrative Court, which was upheld by the Constitutional Court,[110] a university acts unconstitutionally if it expresses public disapproval of poor research, unless it has established that without doubt the professor had gone beyond the limits of scientific freedom. The decision suggests that in cases of conflict between a university and a member of its academic staff, only the latter can rely on *Wissenschaftsfreiheit*; the university should defend the freedom of its professors. (However, the Constitutional Court, when declining to intervene, left open whether the university can also rely on Article 5(3) in this situation.) Whatever its merits, the spirit of this decision is inconsistent with recent developments in German law, which have strengthened the autonomy of universities themselves and which, in the view of some commentators, put at risk the traditional freedom of individual professors and other academics.[111]

## V. UNIVERSITY LEGISLATION

Under the *Grundgesetz*, education, including the organisation of universities, is the responsibility of the states (*Länder*) rather than the federal government and Parliament. The federation (*Bund*) does have a concurrent power to take legislative measures to promote research,[112] and it may enter into co-operative agreements with the states to promote projects of scientific research at universities.[113] But the organisation of public universities, whether they are general research universities or vocational training schools (*Fachhochschule*), is for the states. However, under a constitutional amendment of 1969, the federation was given

---

[109]  E Schmidt-Aßmann, 'Fehlverhalten in der Forschung—Reaktionen des Rechts' (1998) *NvWZ* 1225, 1233–34.

[110]  Decision of 8 August 2000, *NJW* 2000, 3635.

[111]  In particular, see M-E Geis, 'Das Selbstbestimmungsrecht der Universitäten' (2004) 37 *WissR* 2.

[112]  Art 74(1) No 13 GG.

[113]  Art 91b GG.

authority to introduce framework legislation for the general principles governing higher education, with which state legislation had to comply. This step reflected the greater involvement of the federal government over the previous decade in university matters, in particular their research; at that time it was considered that the *Länder* were too weak adequately to promote and develop higher education.

The first framework law for universities (*Hochschulrahmengesetz* (HRG)) was enacted in 1976. It was frequently amended to take account of changes in German higher education policy in the 1980s and 1990s, in particular to give the universities more independence from detailed state regulation of their internal organisation, to introduce evaluation of research and teaching (with student participation in the latter process) and to establish new structures for the academic profession, including the introduction of the rank of junior professor.[114] The framework law for the most part contained general provisions about the conduct of student courses and examinations, admissions to study at universities and the basic rules relating to the appointment of professors and their terms of employment. Professors, for example, could be transferred to other universities only with their consent, though they could be transferred to an equivalent position in another university without consent if their department was closed or merged with another.[115]

The framework law required states and universities to ensure that members of the latter enjoyed *Wissenschaftsfreiheit* under Article 5(3) of the Basic Law. Under the HRG teaching freedom included a lecturer's right to express opinions on scientific and cultural matters. University authorities were, however, permitted to take decisions with regard to the organisation of research and the development of research centres, provided they did not infringe freedom of research. They had similar authority with regard to the organisation of teaching.[116] The Law also recognised freedom of study (*Freiheit des Studiums*), including the right of students to choose which lectures and seminars they attended and to determine their areas of specialisation within the scope of their degree

---

[114] For a survey of these developments, see R Pritchard, 'Trends in the Restructuring of German Universities' (2006) 50 *Comparative Education Review* 90.

[115] HRG of 19 January 1999, *BGBl* I, S 18, art 50(2), discussed by U Hufeld, 'Rechtsfragen zur Schließung von Studiengängen und Fakultäten' (1997) *DÖV* 1025, 1031–32.

[116] Ibid, art 4.

courses. It also recognised their freedom to develop and express their own academic ideas.[117] Section 6 provided for the regular evaluation of universities' research and teaching and the publication of evaluation results, without prescribing how this was to be done: this was left to the discretion of the states. Another important principle was established by section 58 of the HRG: universities had a right to self-regulation, within the limits established by state laws, and they could, subject to state approval, formulate their own basic regulations.[118] But state laws, as we will see shortly, significantly circumscribe the practical freedom of universities to regulate themselves, so it is unclear whether this provision was much more than cosmetic.[119]

The organisational structures of universities have, however, been regulated by the laws of the 16 states. These laws are broadly similar in content, though they naturally vary in detail. Typically they begin by prescribing the legal status and responsibilities of universities, coupled with a statement of freedom of research, teaching and study, and by stating the basic rules about their financing. General provisions concerning evaluation and assessment of teaching and research follow. Separate parts of the laws invariably contain more detailed rules on, among other things, the following topics: admission of students to universities; student courses and examinations; the appointment and promotion of academic staff; and the organisation of the university, its principal bodies and its faculties. German universities are therefore subject to much greater regulation by these state laws than universities and colleges in the United Kingdom. A few aspects of state legislation will be discussed in the following section, when we examine the implications of the most significant recent developments for scientific freedom.

The guarantees of scientific freedom provided by the state laws generally follow the terms of the HRG. But the relevant Baden-Württemberg provision adds that all members of the university, including students, are bound to be honest and to observe the standards of good academic practice. There is a breach of these requirements when false information is disseminated intentionally or very carelessly or there

---

[117]   Ibid, art 4(4).
[118]   Ibid, art 58.
[119]   See T Groß, 'Das Selbstverwaltungsrecht der Universitäten—Zusätzliches zur Wissenschaftsfreiheit' (2006) *DVBl* 721.

is a significant interference with the research of other people.[120] Under the Brandenburg statute research and teaching freedom does not dispense academic staff from observing the rules required to ensure good relations between university members.[121]

Following constitutional reforms of 2006, the Bund no longer has authority to issue framework laws for higher education.[122] (Instead it has concurrent legislative power with the states over the registration and dissolution of universities and related matters.)[123] The Bund has also lost its concurrent legislative power with regard to the payment of public servants, including university staff. The states now have exclusive powers over the governance, organisation and financing of universities, the evaluation of teaching and research, and the appointment and payment of staff. This is a significant development; the *Länder* will be free to compete in the provision of the most favourable conditions and financial payments for university professors and researchers, a further step in the more competitive environment for university education established in Germany during the last decade of the twentieth century.

## VI. RECENT UNIVERSITY REFORMS AND
### *WISSENSCHAFTSFREIHEIT*

Under state laws the organisational structures of universities have undergone considerable changes in the last twenty years, which have been identified broadly as a move towards a more competitive model: the 'management university'.[124] Universities have to some extent been deregulated from state control and allowed greater autonomy, for example, with regard to financial and academic planning; they may now have freedom to appoint their own professors, without even the formality of

---

[120]  S 3(5) of Baden-Württemberg Law of 1 January 2005, GBl 2005, 1.

[121]  Brandenburg Law of 6 July 2004, GVBl 2004, 17, s 394.

[122]  See S Westerburg, 'Auswirkungen der Föderalismusreform auf die rechtlichen Rahmenbedingungen von Wissenschaft und Forschung' (2006) 39 *WissR* 358.

[123]  Art 74(1) No 33. For commentary, see Jarass and Pieroth (eds) (above n 31) on Art 74, paras 72–73.

[124]  See Schulte (above n 9) 125; and T Groß, 'Wissenschaftsadäquates Wissenschaftsrecht' (2002) 35 *WissR* 307, 310–12.

approval by the state government.[125] The intention has been to make universities more efficient, so that they can compete effectively both within Europe and internationally, and also make their administrations more accountable for the significant public resources allocated to them. Indeed, these goals imply greater autonomy for universities, so they can determine for themselves, for example, which departments should be strengthened, how they should be organised and in which areas new appointments should be made. Although these developments have been welcomed,[126] some legal scholars have drawn attention to the dangers they may pose for the *Wissenschaftsfreiheit* of individual scientists and scholars.[127] In particular, they are concerned about the move from a collegial system of university governance to one in which greater powers are concentrated in small committees or single individuals—the President or Rector—and about the authority now enjoyed by university councils (*Hochschulrat*), on which academics may have only minority representation. Further, there are concerns about the procedures for conducting the evaluation of research and teaching.

Before these particular issues are discussed, an outline should be given of the recent leading decision of the Constitutional Court on the Brandenburg University Law of 1999 (as amended in 2004).[128] It was concerned, among other matters, with the specific issues discussed later but also indicates the general approach that the Court now takes to *Wissenschaftsfreiheit*. Faculties and professors at two state universities challenged the law, principally on the grounds that the powers given to university Presidents to allocate funds to Faculties and to close them when appropriate, infringed scientific freedom, and that the authority conferred on the *Hochschulräte* infringed both this freedom and the independence of the universities themselves. The Court rejected the challenges while admitting the standing of university faculties to challenge these provisions, including those that enabled resources to be allocated in the light of the evaluation of research and teaching.

---

[125] S 13 of the Hamburg Law of 18 July 2001, HmbGVBl 2001, s 171; s 37 of the NorthRhine-Westphalia Law of 31 October 2006, GV NRW 2006, s 474.

[126] See Nettesheim (above n 86). Geis (above n 111) reports the wide support for these developments but proceeds to draw attention to their disadvantages.

[127] In addition to Geis (above n 111), see Ladeur (above n 58); Hendler (above n 13); and W-R Schenke, 'Neue Fragen an der Wissenschaftsfreiheit—Neue Hochulgesetze im Lichte des Art 5 III GG' (2005) *NVwZ* 1000.

[128] BVerfGE 111, 333.

While the Constitutional Court repeated the principles formulated thirty years previously in the *Hochschulurteil*, it pointed out that scientific freedom is not protected against regulations intended to promote the effective co-operation of individual professors with their colleagues. It also stressed that the rights enjoyed by professors to participate in the organisation of their universities are limited to involvement in those decisions that could endanger their own freedom to research and teach.[129] More controversially, it added that organisational rules could be challenged successfully only if it were shown that as a structure, or essentially, they created dangers for the exercise of these freedoms; it was not enough to allege that they might do so in a particular case. The Court laid particular emphasis on the wide discretion enjoyed by state legislators in framing organisational laws, for they were in a better position than individual academics to balance the competing interests and policies.[130] Further, there was a legitimate role for institutions external to the university to make a contribution to its governance, for they could counteract the dangers of too rigid an adherence to the existing arrangements for academic self-government.

On the basis of this approach, it is hardly surprising that the Court rejected the challenge on all the points brought before it. The judgement overall indicates a partial albeit significant retreat from the principles established in the *Hochschulurteil*, or at least a reluctance to develop them to review the constitutionality of significant reforms to university organisation. Great stress is placed on the discretion enjoyed by state parliaments, and the Court expressed some reserve about the capacity of academics themselves to come to appropriate judgements about university administration.

## A. The Strengthening of Central Management Powers

State laws now typically confer wide management powers on small executive committees that are composed of four or five members, with one member, generally known as the President, acting as the chairperson.[131]

---

[129] Ibid, 354.
[130] Ibid, 355. Ladeur (above n 58) 758–59 is particularly critical of these aspects of the Court's decision.
[131] See, for example, ss 20–21 of the Bavarian Law of 23 May 2006, BGVBl 2006, 245; ss 16–18 of the Baden-Württemberg Law of 1 January 2005 (above n 120).

These powers for the most part are concerned with the formation of structural and development plans, buildings, the implementation of budgets and other administrative matters that do not raise scientific freedom issues; but they also include authority to allocate the funds and other resources made available by the state and the selection of criteria for evaluating teaching and research—decisions that do have implications for academic activity and for the exercise of scientific freedom. Further, specific powers may also be given to the President of the university. Some commentators have therefore argued that the strengthening of central university authority is constitutionally challengeable, unless the academic community is able to control its exercise by, for example, an ability to recall the President if he or she abuses such power.[132]

This argument was considered by the Constitutional Court when it considered the challenge to the constitutionality of the Brandenburg University Law.[133] Section 65 conferred a wide range of powers on university Presidents, including the responsibility for establishing and closing faculties and central departments, for the co-ordination of their academic work and for the evaluation of their research. The Court had no objection to the strengthening of the powers of central university authorities at the expense of the traditional institutions of collegial government. The new arrangements, in its view, did not pose any structural danger for scientific freedom. The collegial bodies—the academic Senate—had rights under the law to supervise the discharge by Presidents of their responsibilities as well as the right to dismiss them. The Court also rejected a challenge to the Faculty Dean's authority over teaching duties.

## B. University Councils

Even more controversial than the strengthening of central university institutions has been the authority given by state laws to university councils (*Hochschulräte*). The composition of these bodies varies considerably from one state to another, but generally at least half their members must be leading figures from commerce, industry and the arts

---

[132] See, for example, Groß, 'Das Selbstverwaltungsrecht der Universitäten' (above n 119) 726–27; Hendler (above n 13) 250; and Schenke (above n 127) 1003–4.

[133] BVerfGE 111, 333, 356–58.

who work outside the university; under some laws, such external figures must form a majority of the council members or even form the entire membership.[134] Indeed, the councils were set up to enable outsiders, particularly those working in industry, to advise universities on their social and economic responsibilities. In the view of one commentator, they were modelled on Boards of Trustees, which govern universities in the United States.[135] There could be no constitutional objection to the formation of these councils, provided their role was purely advisory, but some state laws now confer on them decision-making powers. This is particularly clear in the case of the Baden-Württemberg council (*Aufsichtsrat*), which has authority to control or approve decisions on a wide range of topics relating not only to economic and development matters but also the institution of university departments and the description of the functions of new professorships.[136] The fact that under the state law this council must have a majority of outside members means that the institutional autonomy of public universities has been compromised, with perhaps unacceptable risks to the exercise of scientific freedom on the part of its professors and teachers.[137]

In the Brandenburg case, the Constitutional Court rejected a challenge to a provision in the state law that empowered the state *Hochschulrat* to nominate the President of a university.[138] The Senate—an academic body—had to approve the nomination (and also had power on a two-thirds majority vote to recall a President), so the Court did not consider there was any infringement of the universities' autonomy. More generally, it had no objection to the institution of independent university councils, which exercised some public control over universities. Indeed, they could help to secure the independence of scientific work from the state itself. The Court emphasised that the responsibilities of the *Hochschulrat* were overwhelmingly advisory, leaving open the possibility

---

[134] See, for example, s 20(3) of the Baden-Württemberg Law of 1 January 2005 (above n 120); and s 48 of Hesse Law of 3 November 1998, GVBl 1998, I S 431, 559. In Hesse all members of the Council may be external to the university, but it has only advisory functions.

[135] Groß, 'Das Selbstverwaltungsrecht der Universitäten' (above n 119) 727.

[136] S 20(1) of the Baden-Württemberg Law of 1 January 2005 (above n 120).

[137] A full critique of the Baden-Württemberg Law is to be found in Schenke (above n 127) esp 1005–6. See also Hendler (above n 13) 251–53; and Schulte (above n 9) 126–27.

[138] BVerfGE 111, 333, 363–64.

that it might uphold a challenge to the establishment of a council with significant executive powers.


## C. Evaluation of Teaching and Research

As already mentioned, state laws contain provisions for the evaluation of teaching and research. They sometimes include arrangements for external evaluation, as well as for internal review by the universities themselves, and provide for the participation of students in the regular assessment of the quality of teaching.[139] The legislation does not usually spell out the details of the procedures by which evaluation takes place but leaves them to be determined by the university itself in its decrees and regulations.

In the Brandenburg case, the professors and faculties argued that the broad discretion of the university Presidents to allocate departmental funds on the basis of the results of the evaluation procedures infringed their rights under Article 5(3) of the Basic Law. Though it rejected these arguments, it was this aspect of the challenge that caused the Constitutional Court most difficulty.[140] In its view the evaluation of teaching and research was not incompatible with *Wissenschaftsfreiheit*, nor was it unconstitutional to allocate departmental funds on the basis of the results of an evaluation process. But the procedures by which the evaluation was conducted must ensure that research and teaching are assessed appropriately, without infringing the constitutional requirements of scientific freedom. In the first place, that meant that academics themselves must be involved in establishing the appropriate criteria by which research and teaching are assessed. Secondly, account must be taken of the differences between academic disciplines; it would be wrong to assess long-term basic research by the criteria appropriate for short-term applied research. Nor would it be right to assess research entirely on the basis of whether it had attracted outside research funding.

The Court admitted that the Brandenburg University Law was more or less totally silent on the evaluation criteria, particularly with regard to the assessment of research. But it did not think that mattered at this

[139] For example, s 5 of the Baden-Württemberg Law (above n 120); Art 10 of the Bavarian Law (above n 131); and s 7 of the North Rhine-Westphalia Law of 31 October 2006, GV NRW, 2006, s 474.
[140] BVerfGE 111, 333, 358–62.

early stage, when evaluation procedures, both nationally and internationally, were in the course of development. It was legitimate to leave them to be determined by the universities themselves on the basis of a procedure that the law did outline. The crucial point for the Court, on its reading of the Brandenburg statute, was that the Senate—a body on which professors had a majority—had responsibility for determining the criteria for evaluating research. (It reached that conclusion by a generous interpretation of the provision enabling the Senate to determine the fundamental principles of teaching and research.) Moreover, the Court held that an additional constraint could be derived from the statutory guarantee of freedom of research; this principle was understood to require the states to make some basic provision for pure research that was unlikely to be supported commercially and could not be assessed by its immediate results. On this basis the Court dismissed the challenges to the provisions of the Brandenburg Law concerning the evaluation of scholarly activity.

The Court's decision and approach has been strongly criticised.[141] Arguably, it placed too much reliance on the use of organisational and procedural rules to safeguard the exercise of scientific freedom in this context. The Law should have made at least some provision for their content. Moreover, even if the Senate determined appropriate criteria for the evaluation of research, there was no guarantee that they would be appropriately applied in the allocation of departmental funds, so the procedural provisions were perhaps themselves inadequate to stop the use of these funds for the purpose of influencing the directions of academic research. Overall this aspect of the Court's ruling in this important case is the least satisfactory from the perspective of scientific and scholarly freedom.

## VII. SCIENTIFIC FREEDOM OUTSIDE STATE UNIVERSITIES

The discussion in the last three sections has been concerned exclusively with *Wissenschaftsfreiheit* in the public universities, in particular with the implications of the freedom for university organisation. But an account

---

[141] See the trenchant criticism of Ladeur (above n 58) 759–62; and also Hendler (above n 13) 256–58; and KF Gärditz, 'Hochschulmanagement und Wissenschaftsadäquanz' (2005) *NVwZ* 407, 408–9.

centred on these universities ignores the fact that an increasingly significant amount of research in Germany takes place outside them. In the first place, there are now a few successful private universities, until recently a negligible sector in the German university system.[142] Of more importance is the role of research foundations and institutes, which exist entirely outside the university system. They may be publicly financed and organised, such as the well-known Max Planck Institutes and the Leibniz Institutes, or be entirely private. Furthermore, industrial corporations often have research departments with very large budgets for applied scientific research. According to one commentator, about three-quarters of annual research expenditure by the Bund and the states in 2003 was allocated to private institutions, while two-thirds of research activity was conducted by industry.[143] So it is important to examine how the principles of scientific freedom apply to research foundations and to industrial research, where the traditional structures and ethos of state universities do not apply.

There are obvious differences between research in universities and that conducted in foundations and industry. Whether funded publicly or privately, research outside universities, particularly in industry, is geared to the discovery of results that can be exploited economically or that serve a particular social purpose, for example, a reduction in crime. Such research is much less likely to be pure or conducted disinterestedly, solely for the discovery of new scientific or scholarly truths. Secondly, it will be directed by a supervisor or research director rather than determined by an individual academic or by a team of departmental colleagues.[144] Of course, university research may share these features of industrial or public policy research, but the important point is that they are not characteristic of work in universities. Moreover, employment contracts between an industry or other foundation on the one hand and its researchers on the other may constrain how free the latter are to publish their findings or to engage in research work outside their employment. Conflicts may consequently arise between the interests of employers and their researchers, for which there is no equivalent in the university sector.

---

[142] K Künzel, 'Political Control and Funding' in Ash (ed) (above n 17) 189.
[143] Schulte (above n 9) 117.
[144] Classen (above n 10) 10–11 draws attention to these structural differences between research within and outside universities.

There are threshold questions regarding how far the legal principles of scientific freedom should apply to the activities of institutions that do not share the traditional ethos of state universities. After they have been considered, this section discusses the part these principles may play in the resolution of conflicts between employers and the researchers working in these institutions.[145] Unfortunately, there are relatively few court decisions relevant to these questions; the discussion is based almost entirely on the views of leading commentators.

## A. Constitutional Principles

One important point is of course that *Wissenschaftsfreiheit* is a right belonging to everyone; it is not confined to academics working within universities. Individual researchers working on their own or in industry or other foundations are as entitled to claim it as are university professors. Private institutions may also claim it. Under Article 19(3) of the Grundgesetz, basic rights also apply to domestic juristic persons to the extent that the nature of these rights permits. That means that private universities enjoy the protection of scientific freedom, which almost certainly confers a right to establish such a university, just as the right to press freedom confers rights to found a newspaper or journal.[146]

There is no difficulty in ascribing scientific freedom to public or private research foundations, where much pure, as well as applied or results-oriented, research is conducted, or to the researchers who work there. This was confirmed by a decision of the Constitutional Court in 1992,[147] when scientists and a Central Institute for Physical Chemistry challenged the dissolution of the German Democratic Republic's Sciences Academy following reunification of West and East Germany. The Court held that a public research institute could rely on Article 5(3) to challenge state decisions interfering with the conduct of their research, but scientific freedom did not give it a right to its continued existence.[148] Previously the Court had considered challenges to restrictions on the freedom of privately employed researchers under Article 12

---

[145] See also below ch 7, s IV(E).
[146] Fehling (above n 16) para 129.
[147] BVerfGE 85, 360.
[148] Ibid, 385.

of the Basic Law, guaranteeing the right to choose an occupation or profession (*Berufsfreiheit*),[149] but restrictions on the scope and methods of research within these institutions should now be examined in relation to Article 5(3). But it would be wrong to apply the principles of scientific freedom formulated in the context of universities in the same way to research institutes; the arrangements for the governance of these institutes, for example, should take account of their distinctive missions, which do not allow the same freedom for their researchers as universities do for their academic staff.[150]

The application of the principles of scientific freedom to industrial research raises more difficult questions. Arguably, it is wholly inappropriate to apply them to research when the topic is determined not for reasons of disinterested intellectual curiosity but for economic or perhaps political reasons, and when there are significant restraints on the freedom of the researchers to publish their findings, unless they are approved by their industrial employers. The more usual view, however, is that industrial researchers and their research departments can invoke *Wissenschaftsfreiheit* provided they enjoy some freedom to determine their research methods and, most importantly, are not constrained in the evaluation of their findings.[151] At the stage of evaluation, objectivity is crucial for the research to qualify for constitutional protection. On the other hand, decisions about the economic exploitation of research findings fall outside the scope of scientific freedom—but might be covered constitutionally by Article 14 of the Basic Law, guaranteeing property rights, including intellectual property rights.

There are also nice questions whether the sponsors or funders of research can claim scientific freedom; on one view they are entitled to the guarantee if their activity is closely integrated to research by, for example, participating in its evaluation and dissemination.[152] Similar uncertainty concerns the position of publishers. If their concern is solely economic, it would be hard to justify their protection under Article 5(3),[153] but that doubt does not apply to academic publishing houses, which should enjoy its protection. Without their involvement,

---

[149] BVerfGE 48, 376.
[150] See Groß and Arnold (above n 10) 158–63.
[151] See Classen (above n 10) 83–88; and Fehling (above n 16) para 136.
[152] Ibid, para 141.
[153] Ibid, para 144.

much scholarly and scientific writing would never be disseminated to the public.[154]

## B. Conflicts between Employers and Their Researchers

Both individual researchers and their employers—whether private or public foundations or the research departments of industrial corporations—may claim scientific freedom.[155] Neither of them has exclusive rights to the freedom. They could both assert these rights if the *state* infringed them, by, for example, proscribing without good reason a particular field of research.[156] But neither an individual researcher nor a *private* employer (whether an industry or a research foundation) could successfully claim *Wissenschaftsfreiheit* against the other party if there were, for instance, a dispute over the publication of research findings.[157]

One point is that neither individuals nor private institutions are directly bound by the basic rights provided by the *Grundgesetz*, though under the *Drittwirkung* principle these rights must be respected in disputes between private parties.[158] The other point is that employment contracts regulate the freedom of individual researchers, for example, to disclose the results of their research or to determine their research methodologies. The general view is that individual researchers waive or surrender their rights under Article 5(3) when they enter into employment contracts. Whether a researcher is free to publish his or her research findings or to engage in research outside his or her employment is determined by the terms of the contract and by private law, though constitutional values must be respected in their interpretation. An employer could not, for instance, insist on the publication of findings that its researchers consider unwarranted, let alone alter the substance of their reports, for that would wholly fail to respect the researchers' personality rights, as well as their scientific freedom.[159]

---

[154] See the decision of the Appeal Court of Köln upholding the rights under Art 5(3) of the publisher of an academic dissertation: *NJW* 1984, 1119.

[155] Classen (above n 10) 142ff ascribes the rights to industrial concerns, irrespective whether their research is conducted in a separate department.

[156] Fehling (above n 16) paras 138–39.

[157] Ibid, para 137. See also Classen (above n 10) 145–50.

[158] See above s III(D).

[159] Classen (above n 10) 160–68.

Different principles apply in the context of disputes between publicly organised and financed research foundations and their employees. The former are directly bound under the Basic Law to respect the scientific freedom of their research staff, whose position is similar to that of professors and other teachers at universities. Admittedly, in a research foundation the research programme is typically determined by a governing council, with state representatives among its members; staff are employed to implement that agenda and are not free, as in universities, to determine their own research programme.[160] But a public research foundation would infringe *Wissenschaftsfreiheit* if it totally prevented the freedom of its researchers to publish their findings, though it might be able to justify some limits on that freedom in the interests of other researchers or to delay publication of applied research findings while it explored the possibilities for its commercial exploitation or taking out patents.[161] The point is that publicly funded research institutions, like universities, have an ethical or social responsibility to publish their research findings, largely so the public can be satisfied that they are doing their work properly. That provides another reason why the position of public foundations is different from that of private corporations in this context.

## VIII. CONCLUSIONS

The German law of *Wissenschaftsfreiheit* is distinctive in a number of respects. First, it confers rights that can be enjoyed by anyone engaged in scientific or scholarly research or teaching. Unlike academic freedom in Britain and many other jurisdictions, it is not confined to professors and other teachers at universities. That is to be applauded. As Karl Jaspers remarked in *The Idea of the University*, it is arrogant to assume that 'the university is sole and proper place for an intellectual life'.[162] Secondly, under the *Hochschulurteil* duties were imposed on the state to allocate sufficient resources so that scientific freedom can

---

[160]  Ibid, 290–91. (See also Groß and Arnold (above n 10) 160–63.)

[161]  Ibid, 294–98. See also W Thieme.'Die Wissenschaftsfreiheit der nichtuniversitären Forschungseinrichtungen' (1994) *DÖV* 150.

[162]  K Jaspers, *Die Idee der Universität*, HAT Reiche and HF Vanderschmidt (trans), K Deutsch (ed) (London, Peter Owen, 1960) 88.

be effectively exercised within universities, while university teachers have a constitutional guarantee that they can safeguard their freedom through participation in university government. A third, related feature has been the development of organisational and procedural rules to ensure that *Wissenschaftsfreiheit* as a fundamental value is safeguarded; for example, universities may have a right to be heard before the state closes student courses,[163] while even in its cautious Brandenburg ruling the Constitutional Court required an academic body—the university Senate—to have responsibility for determining the criteria for the evaluation of teaching and research.[164]

Scientific freedom is therefore much more than a negative individual freedom—in that respect German law appears more sophisticated and developed than the comparable principles in the United Kingdom or in the United States. In contrast to academic freedom in those countries, *Wissenschaftsfreiheit* is, however, rarely invoked in cases involving the rights of university staff to speak on public issues outside the campus—the freedom of extramural speech—because in Germany these cases are regarded as falling under the separate right to freedom of expression (*Meinungsfreiheit*).[165] Courts and commentators take the view that scientific freedom is primarily an individual freedom that both states and universities must protect. Universities do not have a clear institutional right under the Basic Law to scientific freedom that can be asserted successfully against individual professors—another contrast with the constitutional position in the United States.[166]

The recent major reforms to the governance of universities have, however, posed difficult challenges for the traditional understanding of *Wissenchaftsfreiheit*. The freedom no longer guarantees effectively a system of collegial government in which professors exercise a decisive voice on all academic matters—the perspective taken by the Court in the *Hochschulurteil*. In its Brandenburg decision it declined an invitation to apply the principles in its earlier judgement to invalidate provisions that significantly strengthen the authority of central university institutions. Whatever the merits of the particular decision,

[163] See above s IV(D).
[164] See above s VI(C).
[165] See below ch 9, s II(C).
[166] BVerwGE 104, 304, discussed above in s IV(D). Compare the position in the United States, which is discussed below in ch 6, s IV.

the Court's approach in that case indicates that scientific freedom may now have relatively little impact on the structures of university government, even if the core of that freedom as a negative individual right for professors to research and teach as they choose remains largely unaffected.

# 6

## *Academic Freedom in the United States*

### I. TWO DEFINITIONS OF ACADEMIC FREEDOM

WALTER METZGER, THE most prominent historian of
academic freedom in the United States, has identified two
definitions of the freedom:[1] the professional definition
first formulated by the American Association of University Professors
(AAUP) in 1915[2] and the constitutional definition developed in a series
of Supreme Court decisions from the 1950s. The scope of the former
is relatively clear; it protects the professional freedom of professors
to research and teach and to speak freely, particularly about university
affairs. The freedom was formulated to safeguard professors against
interference from university administrators and Boards of Trustees,
particularly their attempts to dictate to academics the subjects of their
research or teaching methods. The scope of the constitutional freedom, rooted in the First Amendment guarantee of freedom of speech,
is in contrast much harder to outline. It has been said that, '[L]acking
definition or guiding principle, the doctrine floats in the law, picking
up decisions as a hull does barnacles.'[3] In particular, it is unclear how
far constitutional academic freedom protects individual scholars or
whether, as the majority of court decisions indicates, it safeguards
primarily—perhaps only—the institutional freedom of universities and
colleges.

---

[1] WP Metzger, 'Profession and Constitution: Two Definitions of Academic
Freedom in America' (1988) 66 *Texas Law Review* 1265.

[2] AAUP Declaration of Principles on Academic Freedom and Academic Tenure.
Substantial excerpts are printed as Appendix 1 in M Finkin and R Post, *For the
Common Good: Principles of American Academic Freedom* (New Haven, Yale University
Press, 2009).

[3] JP Byrne, 'Academic Freedom: A "Special Concern of the First Amendment"'
(1989) 99 *Yale Law Journal* 251, 253.

These different understandings of the freedom make academic freedom in the United States a much more complex subject than it is in the United Kingdom or Germany, where the freedom is based respectively on a statutory right (the UK Education Reform Act 1988) or a constitutional right (the German Basic Law). While it is relatively easy to outline the history and scope of the professional freedom formulated by the AAUP (section II below), it is much more difficult to evaluate the significance of this freedom in the context of the newer constitutional freedom (discussed in section III). Insofar as that freedom confers rights on academic institutions to take decisions that are immune from judicial control, the traditional professional freedom of individual professors may be less secure than it used to be. Conflicts between constitutional institutional and individual academic freedom claims are usually resolved in favour of the former (see section IV below).

A few introductory points bring out the complexity of the law in the United States. The professional freedom applies to both state and private universities. Under the principles formulated by the AAUP and overwhelmingly accepted by US universities, there is no difference between the academic freedom enjoyed by professors at, say, the University of California, a state university, and Stanford, a private university. On the other hand, the constitutional freedom can be asserted only against state authorities and universities. Professors at Stanford cannot claim that their university has interfered with constitutional academic freedom, or even with their freedom of speech, with which the former freedom is closely associated. The reason is that under the 'state action' doctrine, rights under the First Amendment, like other constitutional rights and freedoms, are directly protected against only interference by state (or public) authorities or institutions, not against infringement by private persons or bodies.[4] On the other hand, institutional academic freedom may be claimed by both private and state universities, though it is likely that the former enjoy greater freedom from control by state government.[5]

---

[4] For a short account of the doctrine, see E Barendt, 'State Action, Constitutional Rights and Private Actors' in D Oliver and J Fedtke (eds), *Human Rights and the Private Sphere* (London, Routledge-Cavendish, 2007) 399, 400–16.

[5] D Rabban, 'A Functional Analysis of "Individual" and "Institutional" Academic Freedom under the First Amendment' (1990) 53 *Law and Contemporary Problems* 227, 266–80.

These distinctions are important. In contrast to the position in the United Kingdom and Germany, there are a large number of academically significant and financially well-endowed private universities in the United States, for example, Harvard, Yale, Princeton, Columbia, the University of Chicago, Duke and Stanford. It would be odd if, as a result of the development of constitutional academic freedom, professors at these great universities enjoyed less academic freedom than their peers at, say, the University of Iowa or Nevada, though that seems to be the position, if we leave out of account the professional freedom enjoyed in practice by all professors.

A second point to emphasise is that the development of the constitutional academic freedom is comparatively recent. Indeed, the term 'academic freedom' hardly appeared in judicial decisions until it was mentioned in some Supreme Court rulings in the early 1950s.[6] Even now it is far from clear whether the freedom should be regarded as a constitutional *right*, as distinct from a value to be taken into account by courts when they interpret and apply, for instance, the principles of non-discrimination law.[7] While the long-established professional freedom safeguarded the rights of individual academics against interference from university authorities, the constitutional freedom was formulated during the McCarthy period to protect universities against state intervention that was designed to ensure that they did not employ Communists and other left-wing radicals.

The Court derived academic freedom from the First Amendment, though unlike freedom of speech and of the press, it is not explicitly covered by its terms. Of course academic freedom and freedom of speech may overlap, most obviously when a professor claims that he or she has a right to publish research findings or is entitled to criticise in public the administration of the university; both of those claims could be based on either freedom of speech or academic freedom. But we have seen that academic freedom should not be conflated with freedom of speech.[8] Academic speech is subject to professional

---

[6] See the Comment 'Academic Freedom and the Law' (1937) 46 *Yale Law Journal* 670. An exception was the notorious decision of Justice McGeehan revoking the appointment of Bertrand Russell as professor of philosophy at the City College of New York in 1940: *Kay v Board of Higher Education* 18 NYS (2d) 821 (Sup Ct 1940).

[7] See further below s III.

[8] Above ch 2, s II.

standards and to peer review, which it would be quite inappropriate to apply to regulate political speech, while academic freedom covers much more than the speech and publications of university professors. Indeed, the academic freedom recognised by the Supreme Court protects the right of universities to take fundamental decisions; it has in the words of one writer a 'governance dimension'.[9] Constitutional academic freedom in the United States rests, it may be thought, on uncertain foundations, though strong arguments can certainly be made that the values underlying the First Amendment—in particular the need for informed as well as vigorous public debate—justify its recognition.[10] But perhaps it is not surprising that US courts have found it difficult to shape a clear and consistent academic freedom jurisprudence in the absence of an explicit warrant in the text of the Constitution for its development.

The origins, scope and application of professional academic freedom are covered in the next section of this chapter. Section III outlines the evolution of the constitutional freedom in the decisions of the Supreme Court and examines the coherence of the institutional freedom that most of those decisions support. Conflicts between this institutional freedom and the constitutional academic freedom, or freedom of speech, claimed by individual professors are covered in section IV. The relationship between professional and constitutional academic freedom is discussed in section V. In some respects the content of the two freedoms appears to differ significantly, but in others they are broadly similar; in particular, recent attempts in some states to regulate academic teaching may infringe both the professional and the constitutional freedom (see below section V(B)). One or two aspects of US law are explored in greater depth in subsequent chapters. Constraints on freedom of research are examined in the next chapter, while the freedom of US professors to engage as citizens in extramural speech is given further treatment in chapter nine.

---

[9] J Areen, 'Government as Educator: A New Understanding of First Amendment Protection of Academic Freedom and Governance' (2009) 97 *Georgetown Law Review* 945, 947.

[10] See Rabban (above n 5) 229–32 and 241–43.

## II. THE PROFESSIONAL FREEDOM

## A. History and the 1915 AAUP Declaration

Some knowledge of the background to the AAUP Declaration on academic freedom is important for an appreciation of its significance. During the nineteenth century professors were treated in the same way as other employees of their universities: they could be dismissed summarily by the President, perhaps at the instigation of the Board of Trustees or other governing body. The faculty were not represented on these bodies, which also, at least in the early 1800s, often determined the curriculum and supervised teaching by academic staff.[11] Gradually, with the increasing emphasis on the importance of scientific research and the dispassionate search for truth, professors claimed greater freedom from university trustees; only scientifically competent academics could properly take intelligent decisions on the appointment and promotion of their colleagues.[12] The central ideas of academic freedom began to take root.

Another influence was the contemporary idea of academic freedom in Germany, to which American scientists and scholars became exposed when they studied in that country.[13] They were impressed by the importance attached to research in German universities; one consequence, for example, was the foundation of Johns Hopkins University in 1876 on the German model, to promote graduate studies and research. However, the principles of academic freedom in the United States soon developed along distinctive lines: while in Germany *Lehrfreiheit* (teaching freedom) was concerned exclusively with the freedom of professors in lecture halls, some American professors thought academic freedom also conferred a right to contribute to general social and political debate, though that might equally have been asserted under the free speech clause of the First Amendment. A qualified freedom of extramural speech has therefore been claimed as an aspect of academic freedom in

---

[11] WP Metzger, *Academic Freedom in the Age of the University* (New York, Columbia University Press, 1955) 29–33.

[12] Ibid, 89–92.

[13] Ibid, ch 3.

the United States, while in Germany that freedom is protected by the general freedom of expression provisions of the Constitution.[14]

One notorious episode should be mentioned to illustrate the position in the United States before the AAUP formulated the principles of academic freedom. In 1900 Edward Ross, an economics professor, was dismissed from Stanford University at the instigation of Mrs Leland Stanford, who had founded the University with her deceased husband. She disliked Ross's support for free silver and for the public control of essential utilities, as well as his opposition to the import of cheap labour from Asia. Though for several years the University President attempted to support Ross, whose teaching and research he regarded as impeccable, eventually he had to give way to the dictates of the founder (who exercised the full authority of a board of trustees until 1903).[15] These events led to the resignation of several professors, among them Arthur Lovejoy, an associate professor of philosophy and one of the principal framers of the 1915 Declaration.

The AAUP was established in 1915 following a conference convened by professors at Johns Hopkins University.[16] Its first President was the distinguished philosopher of pragmatism John Dewey. The Declaration of Principles on Academic Freedom and Tenure[17] was drafted by Committee A of the AAUP, which included Roscoe Pound from the Harvard Law School, in addition to a number of economics professors and social scientists. In a discursive fashion, the Declaration formulated a number of key principles. Academic institutions had three main functions: to promote inquiry and advance knowledge; to provide general instruction for students; and to develop experts for the use of the wider community. A university could perform these functions only if it observed academic freedom, which has three elements: freedom of inquiry and research; freedom of teaching; and freedom of extramural utterance and action.

---

[14] See further below ch 9, s II.
[15] For accounts of this episode, see Metzger, *Academic Freedom in the Age of the University* (above n 11) 162–68; and TL Haskell, 'Justifying the Rights of Academic Freedom in the Era of "Power/Knowledge"' in L Menand (ed), *The Future of Academic Freedom* (Chicago, University of Chicago Press, 1996) 43, 48–53.
[16] Metzger, *Academic Freedom in the Age of the University* (above n 11) ch 5.
[17] See above n 2.

The Declaration said little about the first element, which it considered to be well safeguarded. Teaching freedom was necessary to ensure the respect of students; they would have no confidence in professors who taught under instruction from their Heads of Department or Deans. Nor could society as a whole place any reliance on the work of scientists or scholars unless they enjoyed full freedom to publish the results of their research. On the other hand the Declaration was a little more hesitant about the freedom of extramural speech: professors should avoid hasty, intemperate and exaggerated statements, but as citizens they should be free to speak freely about political and social issues, whether or not they are expert on the particular topic.

The most important points made by the Declaration are that while academic freedom does not imply an entire absence of restraints, those restraints should be self-imposed and enforced by the academic profession itself.[18] That is why it is appropriate to describe the freedom as a 'professional freedom'. Appointments and promotions should be determined by academics—the system of peer review, under which it is also decided whether a scholar should be able to publish his or her research in the pages of a scientific journal. These matters should not be determined by university administrators or Boards of Trustees, let alone by general public opinion. For these reasons, it was wrong to treat academic staff as employees of the university who could be dismissed at will, as Ross had been from Stanford. Members of the faculties are appointees, with responsibilities to the general public that they must discharge subject only to the judgment of their profession. In the exercise of their teaching and other functions, professors should no more be subject to control by university authorities than are judges subject to Presidential control when they write their opinions.[19]

## B. The 1940 AAUP Statement of Principles

The Declaration of 1915 was a relatively lengthy document, which set out the case for academic freedom as much it formulated its principles. Moreover, it reflected the views of only an elite group of senior

---

[18] Finkin and Post (above n 2) 179.
[19] Ibid, 164–65.

professors and was not supported by the universities themselves.[20] In 1940 the AAUP reached agreement with the Association of American Colleges (the leading organisation for liberal arts colleges) on a Statement of Principles on Academic Freedom and Tenure, which has set the standard for the professional freedom in the last seventy years.[21] It sets out the following academic freedom principles:

(a) Teachers are entitled to full freedom in research and in the publication of the results, subject to the adequate performance of their other academic duties…

(b) Teachers are entitled to freedom in the classroom in discussing their subject, but they should be careful not to introduce into their teaching controversial matter which has no relation to their subject…

(c) College and university teachers are citizens, members of a learned profession, and officers of educational institutions. When they speak or write as citizens, they should be free from institutional censorship or discipline, but their special position in the community imposes special obligations… Hence they should at all times be accurate, should exercise appropriate restraint, should show respect for the opinions of others, and should make every effort to indicate that they are not speaking for the institution.[22]

The qualifications to every aspect of these freedoms reflect the compromise in the 1940 Statement between the different interests of professors and their universities. The significance of the set of qualifications concerning extramural speech in point (c) was, however, reduced by an Interpretive Comment issued in 1970, which stated that a faculty member's expression of opinion as a citizen should not amount to a ground for dismissal unless it clearly showed unfitness for his or her position. The Comment added that this would rarely be the case.[23]

The Statement was more precise than the 1915 Declaration with regard to tenure: it identified tenure as a means to the ends of academic freedom and of a sufficient degree of economic security to make the academic

---

[20] Metzger, *Academic Freedom in the Age of the University* (above n 11) 203 and 208–11 points out that initially the AAUP admitted only senior professors of high standing, and its Declaration was not supported by colleges and universities.

[21] For a comprehensive discussion, see WP Metzger, 'The 1940 Statement of Principles on Academic Freedom and Tenure' (1990) 53 *Law and Contemporary Problems* 3.

[22] Reprinted in Finkin and Post (above n 2) Appendix 2.

[23] Ibid.

profession attractive to able men and women. Tenure was regarded in the Statement as indispensable for the success of academic institutions. After their probationary period, teachers and researchers should enjoy permanent employment that can normally be ended only for adequate cause. However, under the Statement (filled out by some subsequent AAUP Recommended Institutional Regulations on Academic Freedom and Tenure), even tenured appointments may be terminated 'under extraordinary circumstances because of a demonstrably bona fide financial exigency', defined in the Regulations as a financial crisis that threatens the survival of the institution; and such appointments may also be terminated consequent to a bona fide formal discontinuance of a programme or department. In either case the institution should make every effort to place the faculty member in another suitable position.[24]

The protection of tenure as a necessary safeguard for the exercise of academic freedom contrasts sharply with the position in the United Kingdom, where the statutory freedom was conferred in 1988 to compensate for the removal of tenure for newly appointed or promoted members of academic staff.[25] Interestingly, tenure was abolished in the UK because it was thought that university departments could not declare tenured academic staff redundant; in the United States, tenure affords professors against dismissal by universities that disapprove of their teaching or research but has never provided them with a complete safeguard against redundancy.

## C. The Interpretation of Academic Freedom by Committee A

The principles of academic freedom formulated in the 1940 Statement have been interpreted and applied in reports of the AAUP Committee on Academic Freedom and Tenure, known as Committee A. When a faculty member complains that his or her freedom has been infringed by a university in breach of Statement principles, an investigation

---

[24] Regs 4(c) and (d) of the AAUP Recommended Institutional Regulations on Academic Freedom and Tenure, available from the AAUP website at http://www.aaup.org/ (last accessed 2 August 2010). The 1968 Regulations were considered by the DC Circuit Court of Appeals in *Browzin v Catholic University of America* 527 F 2d 843 (1975).

[25] See above ch 4, s III(C).

may be conducted by an ad hoc committee of two or three AAUP members, if earlier attempts to achieve a negotiated settlement have failed.[26] Committee A evaluates and may publish the ad hoc committee's findings; in this way a body of informal case law has developed on the meaning of the academic freedom principles set out in the Statement.[27]

Universities rarely impose limits on professors' freedom of research and publication, so this aspect of the Statement has produced relatively few reports. In their recent study of the interpretation of professional academic freedom, Matthew Finkin and Robert Post discuss the *University of Missouri* case (1929), in which professors were disciplined after questionnaires had been left in student mailboxes concerning the sexual attitudes and conduct of students.[28] The questionnaire had been prepared by a student and approved by the professors for use in conjunction with a course on family relationships. The University took the view that the research conducted through the questionnaire was unlikely to produce worthwhile results and that its distribution was likely to harm and offend students. But the AAUP report concluded that it was not for university administrators to decide the value of research, and further there was little or no evidence that students would be harmed by answering the questionnaire. It was clear that the university officials had been responding to public criticism of the project. Academic freedom, however, requires that the utility of research is assessed by professional judgment—sometimes through the system of peer review—and not by public opinion. Other constraints on freedom of research in the United States are considered in the next chapter.[29]

There has been more controversy about the meaning and scope of teaching freedom, largely because its exercise impinges on the interests of students (and their parents). The reservation in the 1940 Statement to the effect that teachers should not introduce into the classroom controversial matter irrelevant to the subject has itself been 'qualified' in the 1970 Interpretive Comments: the purpose of the reservation was not to discourage controversy but to emphasise that lecturers should avoid the persistent introduction of irrelevant material into their teaching.[30]

---

[26] For details of the procedure, see Finkin and Post (above n 2) 49–52.
[27] Committee A increasingly refers to its previous reports, so building up an informal system of precedent: see ibid, 211 n 52.
[28] Ibid, 62–69.
[29] See below ch 7, ss II and III.
[30] Finkin and Post (above n 2) Appendix 2.

So it would clearly be wrong for teachers to devote whole classes to discussion of their political or religious beliefs, but sometimes analogies can appropriately be drawn, for example, in an ancient history class, between the extension of the Roman Empire to Mesopotamia, and the United States and British invasion of Iraq two thousand years later.[31] In a number of cases, the AAUP has reported adversely when universities dismissed professors who offended students by drawing comparisons between historical and contemporary events or by indicating their support for particular politicians.[32] But it declined to support an Assistant Professor of history who devoted his foreign policy class the day after Martin Luther King's assassination to a speech about that event.[33] In its 2007 report 'Freedom in the Classroom' the AAUP emphasised that professors are bound by professional standards; they are not therefore obliged under any requirement of balance to present all points of view on a matter of political or social controversy. Nor need they refrain from challenging students' views on these matters. Indeed, one purpose of university teaching is to challenge student preconceptions.[34]

The 1940 Statement says nothing explicit about the rights of faculty members to participate in the governance of their universities. But they are described as 'officers of educational institutions', as well as citizens and members of a learned profession.[35] So it is reasonable to infer that professors have some rights to participate in university administration, to be consulted and to speak freely about the management, educational policies and academic standards of their universities.[36] Their right to engage in

[31] See the question posed by N Kristof, 'Et tu George?' in the *New York Times*, 23 January 2007, cited in AAUP, 'Freedom in the Classroom', AAUP Report (2007), available from AAUP website (above n 24).
[32] Finkin and Post (above n 2) 94–99, discussing the dismissals of Associate Professor of History Ralph Turner from the University of Pittsburgh for frequent recourse to contemporary parallels in his history teaching; and of Assistant Professor of Religion and Philosophy George Parker from Evansville College for introducing contemporary political issues, including the Henry Wallace Presidential campaign, into his classes.
[33] Ibid, 99–100.
[34] See the discussion of Academic Bills of Rights below in s V.
[35] Above n 22, cl 3.
[36] In *NLRB v Yeshiva University* 444 US 672 (1980) the Supreme Court held that as the faculty had absolute authority with regard to academic matters, they formed part of the university management and so were not entitled to collective bargaining rights.

intramural expression on university and academic matters should be distinguished from the more controversial freedom of academics to engage in extramural expression on general political and social topics (discussed in chapter nine).[37] Professors can contribute through their expertise and knowledge to the organisation and governance of an academic institution, to which they may well have been committed for much longer than the university President or administrative officials they are criticising. A Statement agreed between the AAUP, the American Council on Education and the Association of Governing Boards of Universities and Colleges in 1966 laid down some general principles concerning university governance, among them the prerogative of faculties to take primary responsibility for academic matters such as research, curriculum, the subject matter and methods of teaching, and faculty status. The President and governing body should normally concur with faculty judgements on these matters, unless they have compelling reasons to take a different view.[38]

## D. The Legal Status of AAUP Principles

William van Alstyne, a distinguished legal commentator on academic freedom and a former President and General Counsel of the AAUP, has described its 1940 Statement as 'very soft law'.[39] It is not directly enforced by the courts. But the Statement has been endorsed by a large number of educational associations and has been incorporated into many faculty handbooks. Its principles of academic freedom and tenure, and also the AAUP Recommended Institutional Regulations, are often adopted as terms of faculty members' contracts. Courts therefore refer to the AAUP academic freedom principles in actions for breach of contract[40] and in this way may enforce them indirectly. But Judge J Skelly Wright has doubted whether it would be appropriate to incorporate AAUP

---

[37] See Finkin and Post (above n 2) 113–14 for the distinction between intramural and extramural expression, which relates to the content of the speech, not the place where it is made.

[38] 1966 Statement on Government of Colleges and Universities, available from the AAUP website (above n 24) pt 5.

[39] W van Alstyne, 'Academic Freedom and the First Amendment in the Supreme Court of the United States: An Unhurried Historical Review' (1990) 53 *Law and Contemporary Problems* 79.

[40] See for example *Browzin* (above n 24); *Krotkoff v Goucher College* 585 F 2d 675 (1978).

investigatory reports as terms of a contract, since, unlike the Statement, they reflected only the views of the professors and could not be taken to represent the common position of universities and academic staff.[41]

Whatever the legal status of the 1940 Statement on Academic Freedom and Tenure and its investigatory reports, there can be little doubt that they have created a culture of respect for the freedom, at least among members of the university community. In 1963 a former President of Princeton wrote that at no time had its Board of Trustees acted to threaten the professional freedom of faculty members.[42] In recent years, however, state politicians and legislatures have occasionally attempted to interfere with academic freedom, because they have been concerned by what they perceive to be an undue liberal bias in university teaching: Bills have been introduced into state legislatures to ensure that teaching is 'balanced' and that student beliefs are respected. If implemented, these proposals would clearly infringe the freedom of professors to teach their subjects according to the appropriate professional standards and to challenge their students with new and controversial ideas. They might also be subject to constitutional challenge as violating the academic freedom protected by the First Amendment.[43] With regard to this aspect of teaching, the professional freedom asserted by the AAUP and the constitutional right may have much the same content. In other contexts, however, it is less clear how the emerging constitutional academic freedom right relates to the traditional professional freedom (see further section V below).

### III. CONSTITUTIONAL ACADEMIC FREEDOM IN THE SUPREME COURT

The Supreme Court has referred to constitutional academic freedom in a number of cases from the 1950s, though the freedom has significantly influenced its decision in only a few of them.[44] Although the principle has now frequently been articulated, its scope remains far from settled.

---

[41] *Browzin* (above n 24) 848 n 8.

[42] HW Dodds, 'Academic Freedom and the Academic President' (1963) 28 *Law and Contemporary Problems* 602.

[43] See below s V(B).

[44] For a recent analysis of the Supreme Court and other court decisions on academic freedom, see R O'Neil, *Academic Freedom in the Wired World* (Cambridge, MA, Harvard University Press, 2008) ch 3.

In particular, it is unclear whether it is correct to speak of a constitutional *right* to academic freedom based on the First Amendment. On an alternative interpretation of the Supreme Court jurisprudence, it might be more accurate to refer to academic freedom as a constitutional *value* that shapes the interpretation and application of other constitutional rights and of legislation (see section III(D) below).[45] It is also not entirely clear whether the constitutional freedom is concerned solely with the institutional autonomy of universities or whether it also protects, in some contexts, individual professors and teachers. While some decisions and judgements suggest the former interpretation is correct, others provide support for the recognition of individual academic freedom rights. Finally, the justification for basing academic freedom— whether institutional or individual—on the First Amendment should be explored. We will return to these difficult questions after discussing the principal decisions of the Supreme Court on the constitutional freedom.

## A. The Early Cases in the 1950s and 1960s

Although academic freedom provided the basis for a dissenting judgement of Douglas J in 1952,[46] it was not considered at length by the Court until 1957. In *Sweezy v New Hampshire* it reversed the contempt conviction of a Marxist economist who had refused to answer detailed questions put to him by the State Attorney General in the course of an investigation of subversion.[47] Sweezy, it should be noted, was at this time a scholarly journalist, though he had previously been an assistant professor at Harvard. Some of the questions related to the contents of a guest lecture Sweezy had given at the University of New Hampshire, a state university. The Court held that the state legislature had improperly

---

[45] For a general discussion of academic freedom as a constitutional value, see above ch 2, s VI.

[46] *Adler v Board of Education* 342 US 485, 508 (1952). Douglas J dissented from a Supreme Court decision rejecting a challenge by school teachers to a New York statute banning the employment in the public service of, inter alia, any person belonging to an organisation that supported the use of violence against the government. Douglas J argued that the statute violated freedom of speech because it inhibited academic freedom in classroom discussion.

[47] *Sweezy v New Hampshire* 354 US 234 (1957).

delegated its investigatory powers to the Attorney General, but Warren CJ in the Court's opinion explicitly referred to an invasion of Sweezy's liberties 'in the area of academic freedom and political expression'. The Chief Justice emphasised the importance of freedom within the university community and of free inquiry by both teachers and students.[48]

It was, however, the separate concurring opinion of Frankfurter J that first clearly established the principle of constitutional academic freedom. His judgement, in which Harlan J concurred, argued that political authorities should not intrude into the activities of universities, whose freedom should be as unfettered as possible in order to enable them to pursue open inquiry into intellectual and social problems. University freedom was for the good of society. Frankfurter J quoted extensively from a statement of South African scholars defending free universities from the racialist policies of the National Party government:

> It is the business of a university to provide that atmosphere which is most conducive to speculation, experiment and creation. It is an atmosphere in which there prevail 'the four essential freedoms' of a university—to determine for itself on academic grounds who may teach, what may be taught, how it shall be taught, and who may be admitted to study.[49]

This passage has been enormously influential; it has frequently been cited in later Supreme Court judgements and provides the foundation for the principle of a constitutional academic freedom that safeguards the autonomy of academic institutions, at least as much as it protects the individual rights of scientists and scholars.

There are, as has been pointed out,[50] some odd aspects to Frankfurter J's statement of the principle. It relied on extra-judicial sources and standards for its formulation. There was no reference to previous case law on the First Amendment, though that is perhaps hardly surprising because there was none on which he could have relied. The opinion suggested the case was concerned with university freedom, although Sweezy of course was the successful party; he was able to resist the demand of the Attorney General to hand over his lecture notes. In this context, it might be relevant that Sweezy himself was not an academic,

---

[48]  Ibid, 250.

[49]  Ibid, 263, quoting the Conference of Representatives of the University of Cape Town, the University of Witwatersrand and the Open Universities of South Africa (1957) 10–12.

[50]  Byrne, 'A "Special Concern of the First Amendment"' (above n 3) 290–93.

so might not have been able to claim any distinct individual academic freedom right. In any event, the AAUP did not intervene in the case.[51]

What does seem clear is that Frankfurter J linked university freedom to the values underlying the claims to academic freedom that may be made by individual researchers and scholars: the importance of open inquiry and the freedom to examine traditional ideas. It is therefore some authority for the recognition of a constitutional individual academic freedom. An institutional academic freedom is valuable only because it promotes freedom of research and teaching, not because universities should enjoy broad freedoms and immunities in respect of all their activities and decisions. This reading seems to be confirmed by a subsequent Court decision rejecting the argument that Congressional Committee inquiries into the political affiliations of a former university lecturer impinged on academic freedom.[52] The Court opinion, in which Frankfurter J joined, distinguished between permissible inquiries into an individual's links with the Communist party and inquiries into university teaching, which are covered by academic freedom. The implication is that this freedom protects the freedom of professors to teach and conduct research.

The last case in this group of early academic freedom decisions is *Keyishian v Board of Regents*.[53] The Court in a 5–4 ruling upheld a challenge by faculty members of a state university to a New York law that required the removal from public employment of anyone who had engaged in treasonable or seditious acts or utterances or had refused to sign a certificate concerning current or previous membership in the Communist party. The Court held that these provisions were too vague or overbroad; they might be understood, for example, to require the dismissal of a professor who had spoken sympathetically about Marxist principles in a politics lecture. But the case is best known for Brennan J's ringing endorsement of academic freedom:

> Our Nation is deeply committed to safeguarding academic freedom, which is of transcendent value to all of us and not merely to the teachers concerned. That freedom is therefore a special concern of the First Amendment, which does not tolerate laws that cast a pall of orthodoxy over the classroom... The classroom is peculiarly the 'marketplace of ideas'. The Nation's future

---

[51]  Ibid, 291 fn 150.
[52]  *Barenblatt v United States* 360 US 109 (1959).
[53]  385 US 589 (1967).

depends upon leaders trained through wide exposure to that robust exchange of ideas which discovers truth 'out of a multitude of tongues, [rather] than through any kind of authoritative selection'.[54]

Much of this is overblown rhetoric. In particular, it is nonsense to equate university teaching and classroom discussion with the 'marketplace of ideas' that characterises free political discourse; standards of relevance, coherence and civility, which do not constrain such discourse, can and should be applied to academic teaching. But Brennan J rightly brought out the importance of academic freedom for the education of future generations and the dangers of government attempts to impose constraints on what may be said in lectures and seminars. The decision safeguards the academic freedom, or freedom of academic speech, of individual professors, for they had mounted the challenge to the New York statute.

## B. The Recognition of Institutional Academic Freedom

A number of Court decisions and individual judgements from the late 1970s have recognised an institutional academic freedom that may go further than the freedom intimated by Frankfurter J in *Sweezy*. It was first formulated by Powell J in his opinion in *Regents for the University of California v Bakke*.[55] He held that universities, in pursuit of the educational benefits of diverse student bodies, are entitled to take account of race and national origins in admitting students, though they may not impose strict racial quotas. Though not 'a specifically enumerated right', academic freedom had long been regarded as a special concern of the First Amendment.[56] In Powell J's view, it followed that universities should be free to choose those students who will contribute most to the exchange of ideas. This freedom is a countervailing constitutional interest that could, as in this case, justify what would otherwise be an infringement of the proscription of racial discrimination under the Equal Protection Clause of the Fourteenth Amendment. It should,

---

[54] Ibid, 603.
[55] 438 US 265 (1978).
[56] Ibid, 312.

however, be pointed out that Powell J's opinion did not speak for the Court but represented only his own views.

A few years later in a separate concurring opinion,[57] Stevens J suggested that universities are entitled to distinguish between academically valuable and worthless speech in deciding which student organisations and societies to support. He did not dissent from the Court decision that it was unconstitutional for a state university to deny students use of campus facilities for religious worship and discussion but disagreed with its view that a university would have to show a compelling reason to justify discriminating between types of speech when taking decisions of this kind. That did not do justice to the freedom of universities, for example, to decide which courses to offer. Stevens J's judgement at one point referred to the 'academic freedom of public universities' and at another to the assessment of 'academicians', so it is not entirely clear whether he had an institutional or an individual academic freedom in mind. However, his opinion is generally understood as supporting an institutional right to academic freedom under the First Amendment.[58]

Of more importance is Stevens J's opinion for a unanimous Court in *Regents of University of Michigan v Ewing*.[59] The Court held that a student could not argue that his due process rights had been infringed when a state university denied him readmission to the Medical School after he had been dismissed following a bad failure in some examinations. Stevens J reasoned that courts should respect a medical faculty's professional judgment and should intervene only in exceptional cases, when, for example, it was clear that the faculty had been biased or had not exercised any real judgment on the matter. He expressed 'a reluctance to trench on the prerogatives of state and local educational institutions and our responsibility to safeguard their academic freedom'.[60] Interestingly, in a footnote he acknowledged that academic freedom entailed the

---

[57]    *Widmar v Vincent* 454 US 263, 278 (1981).

[58]    See Byrne, 'A "Special Concern of the First Amendment"' (above n 3) 316–17; and Finkin, 'On "Institutional" Academic Freedom' (1982) 61 *Texas Law Review* 817, 845.

[59]    474 US 214 (1985). See also *Board of Curators of University of Missouri v Horowitz* 435 US 78 (1978).

[60]    Ibid, 226.

free exchange of ideas between teachers and students and, 'somewhat inconsistently', the autonomy of the academy itself.[61]

The view that academic freedom gives universities decisional autonomy was supported in the concurring judgement of Souter J (with which Stevens and Breyer JJ agreed) in *Board of Regents of University of Wisconsin v Southworth*:[62] universities are permitted under the First Amendment to charge students mandatory fees to fund speech and activities by student associations. Students could not object to paying fees to support organisations whose speech they found objectionable, anymore than they could refuse to fund courses they disapproved of. These decisions show that constitutional academic freedom is concerned with more than freedom of speech and has an organisational dimension.[63]

Perhaps the clearest statement of an institutional academic freedom based on the First Amendment is in *Grutter v Bollinger*.[64] In that case the Court held that the Michigan Law School's affirmative action programme, which entailed having a significant number of students from underrepresented racial minorities, did not infringe the Equal Protection Clause prohibition of racial discrimination. In her opinion for the majority of the Court, O'Connor J said that 'universities occupy a special niche in our constitutional tradition'[65] and cited Powell J's opinion in *Bakke* invoking a constitutional dimension, based on the First Amendment, to educational autonomy. Courts should defer to the judgement of universities, in this case the decision of the Law School that admitting a 'critical mass' of underrepresented minority students was essential to realise the educational advantages of a diverse student body.[66] Arguably this decision establishes that academic freedom is a constitutional right that can be claimed by universities, whether they are private or state.[67] We will return to that question later in section III(D).

---

[61] Ibid, n 12.
[62] 529 US 217 (2000).
[63] See Areen (above n 9).
[64] 539 US 306 (2003).
[65] Ibid, 329.
[66] Ibid, 330.
[67] See JP Byrne, 'Constitutional Academic Freedom after *Grutter*: Getting Real about the "Four Freedoms" of a University' (2006) 77 *University of Colorado Law Review* 929.

## C. Decisions Rejecting Academic Freedom Claims

The decisions considered so far in this section have all upheld academic freedom arguments. However, claims to academic freedom have been rejected by the Supreme Court in a few cases. Of these the most important is *University of Pennsylvania v EEOC*.[68] The Court held unanimously in that case that academic freedom did not give a university a special privilege not to disclose 'peer review' materials to the Equal Employment Opportunity Commission (EEOC) when it was investigating an associate professor's charge of discrimination after she had been denied tenure. The AAUP, Harvard and Stanford all submitted amicus curiae briefs in favour of the academic freedom claim. But Blackmun J for the Court held that earlier academic freedom decisions could be distinguished, as they had involved attempts by states to control speech, in particular teaching, in universities. The claim in this case was to 'an expanded right of academic freedom to protect confidential peer review materials from disclosure'.[69] The privilege was too remote from the academic freedom right to choose who teaches at universities. There was no reason to believe that academics would report less candidly on a colleague who is being considered for tenure or promotion because of the risk that their views might be disclosed to the EEOC. The Court did not need to consider the Commission's alternative argument that its substantial interest in eradicating discrimination should trump the University's academic freedom rights under the First Amendment.

The Court ignored a possible academic freedom argument when in a brief per curiam ruling it upheld Ohio legislation requiring state universities to develop teaching workload standards for their professors, which would be exempt from collective bargaining arrangements.[70] Professors had no claim under the Equal Protection Clause of the Fourteenth Amendment; it was rational for the state to achieve its objective of increasing faculty time in the classroom through regulation of their workload outside collective bargaining. Stevens J in dissent considered that the statute might impinge on professors' academic freedom. In his view, they should have greater, not less, bargaining freedom

---

[68]    493 US 182 (1990).
[69]    Ibid, 199.
[70]    *Central State University of Ohio v AAUP* 526 US 124 (1999).

than other public employees, so it was unclear that there was a rational basis for the statute. Interestingly, he referred to the academic freedom of *individual* faculty members, which might be infringed by the standards introduced by the universities under state law.

In *Board of Regents v Roth*[71] the Court appears to have dismissed the argument that freedom of speech, or academic freedom, confers procedural rights on a non-tenured professor to a reasoned decision and a hearing when his one-year teaching contract was not renewed.[72] More clearly, a 6–3 majority of the Court in *Minnesota State Board for Community Colleges v Knight*[73] rejected the claim by members of a college faculty, not members of the faculty association, that their First Amendment rights were denied because under state law only representatives of the association had a right to participate in formal talks with university administrators. O'Connor J for the Court denied that faculty had a constitutional right to participate in policy-making at academic institutions,[74] but Brennan J dissenting considered that academic freedom was engaged. A direct ban imposed on a particular group from submitting its views to the university administration would certainly infringe academic freedom. The Court in these decisions has been unwilling to uphold procedural and organisational rights as essential aspects of individual academic freedom, though there is a good case in principle for their recognition.[75]

## D. The Coherence and Scope of the Constitutional Freedom

There are a number of difficult issues to explore. The first is whether the development of academic freedom rights on the basis of the First Amendment is warranted. This of course is not identical to the question

---

[71]  408 US 564, esp 574 n 14 (1972), on which see Rabban (above n 5) 298–99. The dissent of Douglas J clearly considered academic freedom did confer a right to a hearing and reasoned decision in these circumstances.

[72]  However, in *Perry v Sindermann* 408 US 593 (1972) the Court did recognise that academic freedom was engaged if the contract of a non-tenured professor was not renewed because the university disapproved of the professor's academic speech.

[73]  465 US 271 (1984). For discussion of the decision, see van Alstyne, 'Academic Freedom and the First Amendment in the Supreme Court' (above n 39) 143–45.

[74]  *Minnesota State Board for Community Colleges v Knight* (ibid) 288.

[75]  See above ch 2, s III(C) and ch 3, s V regarding academic self-rule.

whether there are good arguments or justifications for academic freedom. The case for academic freedom might be made—perhaps for the professional academic freedom advocated and defended by the AAUP—but a separate argument needs to be made for a First Amendment right to academic freedom. There are difficulties with any argument for an individual constitutional right to academic freedom that goes beyond the freedom of speech that all citizens clearly enjoy under the First Amendment, albeit only against infringement by state actors. Academic freedom of course overlaps with freedom of speech, particularly in the context of extramural freedom of expression, and in those circumstances there can be no objection to recognising a right to freedom of academic speech.[76]

But there are at least two reasons why we might hesitate to accept a distinct individual First Amendment right to academic freedom that goes beyond citizens' freedom of speech. First, it confers wider rights on university professors to, say, criticise their employers and to determine how they do their job.[77] Secondly, as mentioned earlier, because of the state action doctrine, a constitutional academic freedom is guaranteed only against infringement by the state and by public universities, not against similar infringement by private universities. That is true of course with regard to their freedom of speech. But the recognition of an individual First Amendment right to academic freedom would make this disparity of treatment even more clearly anomalous.

Despite these difficulties, an argument can be made for an individual academic freedom right on the basis of the First Amendment. Insofar as there is a public interest in the freedom of university professors and other researchers to pursue their inquiries, to publish their research findings and to teach, uninhibited by state or official direction, then the values underlying the First Amendment—the search for truth, informed and intelligent public debate, the intellectual development of both speakers and (student) audiences—suggest that academic freedom should be protected.[78] That freedom, however, may give both wider and narrower rights than the general freedom of speech that all citizens

---

[76] See below s IV(A) and ch 9.

[77] There is of course no equivalent difficulty to recognising a right to intellectual or scientific freedom that everyone enjoys, as is the case under the German Basic Law, Art 5(3). See above ch 5, s II.

[78] See Rabban (above n 5) 241–44.

enjoy in equal measure.[79] Professors should have wider rights than other employees to do their work free from their employers' directions, and they might also have freedom to speak openly about, say, their working conditions when other civil and public servants could be restrained by their employers from speaking on these matters. On the other hand, professors are bound to honour professional standards, particularly when they lecture and publish; an historian cannot deny the Holocaust or a biologist dismiss the theory of evolution, and then claim academic freedom if disciplined by the university. In this respect they enjoy less freedom than ordinary citizens, who should generally be free to express these views in public without jeopardising their employment.

Whatever the merits of these arguments for individual academic freedom, the Supreme Court appears to have formulated an *institutional* freedom, based on the First Amendment, for universities. At first sight, this seems just as difficult to justify as the case for an individual freedom: why should educational institutions, which are not explicitly identified in the text of the First Amendment (or for that matter by other provisions of the US Constitution) enjoy a constitutional freedom, the exercise of which may not be closely linked to any exercise of the freedom of speech, which is explicitly covered by the Amendment? In some contexts, institutional academic freedom or autonomy admittedly supports—indeed may be necessary to—the uninhibited exercise of individual academic freedom and freedom of speech, as Frankfurter J suggested in *Sweezy*. But that sort of argument proves too much. On that basis the Supreme Court would have to recognise rights to travel, rights to good quality broadcasting and to free public libraries, which are similarly related to the effective exercise of individual freedom of speech. There is another difficulty. The institutional academic freedom recognised by the Court in *Ewing*, and more clearly in *Grutter*, is only indirectly related to the First Amendment freedom of speech, even if that is understood to cover freedom of speech within university lecture halls and seminar rooms. Those rulings protected the freedom of universities to take decisions—about the admission and continued registration of students—which appear to have little connection with freedom of speech.

---

[79] Rabban (above n 5). See also W van Alstyne, 'The Specific Theory of Academic Freedom' in EL Pincoffs (ed), *The Concept of Academic Freedom* (Austin, University of Texas Press, 1975) 59, 75–77.

The First Amendment does of course explicitly protect one institutional freedom: freedom of the press, which is guaranteed because
of the special role the media have in fostering freedom of speech
through investigating and commenting on stories of public interest and
providing a platform for the exchange of views. It is certainly possible
to make an argument that the Amendment also protects others that are
equally linked to or associated with freedom of speech and its values.
Peter Byrne has, for example, argued that a constitutional academic
freedom builds on two legal sources: the reluctance of courts to question expert academic judgments, as instantiated for instance by the
Supreme Court ruling in *Ewing*, and the recognition of public university
autonomy in some state constitutions.[80] More generally, he has concluded that the preservation of academic values of free and open inquiry
and liberal education justify the constitutional right.[81] Attractive though
these points are, they are far from persuasive. They show perhaps that
a liberal constitution ought to protect academic freedom—as many
now do—but they do not convince that the US Constitution, properly
interpreted, does protect it.

A related question is the scope of the institutional right or freedom
that might be asserted by universities under the First Amendment. It
has been pointed out that historically university autonomy had little or
nothing to with academic freedom or freedom of speech but was linked
to respect for the property rights of the founders of the university. From
respect for these rights developed a commitment to institutional pluralism.[82] Pluralism considers desirable the devolution of authority from
central government to autonomous institutions, particularly to bodies
like universities, which have long experience in self-regulation.[83] Under
this principle universities could claim independence from regulation by
state government or by federal agencies, irrespective whether the claim
was related to academic freedom. A university might claim, for example,
that it is free to exclude visiting speakers from its campus because it is

---

[80]  Byrne, 'A "Special Concern of the First Amendment"' (above n 3) 320–31.

[81]  Ibid, 338.

[82]  See Finkin, 'On "Institutional" Academic Freedom' (above n 58) 829–33,
commenting on the Supreme Court decision in *Trustees of Dartmouth College v
Woodward* 17 US (4 Wheat) 518 (1819) in which it invalidated state legislation in
effect placing the college in the hands of state appointed trustees.

[83]  For fuller discussion, see above ch 3, s IV.

entitled to determine the use of its property,[84] or that it need not accommodate on its premises armed forces recruiting personnel because it is opposed to its graduates serving in the forces.[85] But it is hard to relate these broad claims to the scope of the First Amendment's guarantee of freedom of speech and of the press, and freedom of assembly.

Because of this difficulty, it has been argued that institutional academic freedom should be restricted to 'providing institutional autonomy for decisions on academic grounds concerning core intellectual interests in teaching and scholarship'.[86] It does not insulate universities from state regulation, such as planning and zoning laws, or from the application of taxation, general employment or antitrust laws. There is no reason, for example, why college football broadcasting contracts should be immune from antitrust regulation, since these agreements have nothing to do with the academic purposes of a university.[87] Nor, as mentioned earlier, do universities have any academic freedom privilege to withhold documents from a body investigating a charge of discrimination on the grounds of race or sex.[88] But outside the core areas of teaching and research the scope of this limited or conditional institutional freedom is clearly contestable; on one view, it should not have been extended in *Grutter* to protect a university's freedom to choose a 'critical mass' of students from underrepresented ethnic groups, a decision which is not directly related to the contents of university courses or teaching methods.[89]

Nevertheless, there is scholarly support for recognition of a broad institutional academic freedom, on the grounds that it makes sense of the general idea of academic freedom to ascribe it to the university as an institution, and that it provides an attractive understanding of the First Amendment.[90] The argument is that the values of freedom of

---

[84]  See *State v Schmid* 423 A2d 615 (1980), cert denied, 455 US 100 (1982).

[85]  *Rumsfeld v Forum for Academic and Institutional Rights* 547 US 47 (2006).

[86]  Byrne, 'Constitutional Academic Freedom after *Grutter*' (above n 67) 947.

[87]  In *NCAA v Board of Regents* 468 US 85 (1984) the Court held that a college agreement to restrict the number of television football matches violated the antitrust legislation.

[88]  *University of Pennsylvania v EEOC* (above n 68).

[89]  See the dissent of Thomas J in *Grutter* (above n 64) 362–64.

[90]  F Schauer, 'Is there a Right to Academic Freedom?' (2006) 77 *University of Colorado Law Review* 907, 920; and P Horwitz, 'Universities as First Amendment Institutions: Some Easy Answers and Hard Questions' (2007) 54 *UCLA Law Review* 1497.

speech guaranteed by the First Amendment—the search for truth and the dissemination of valuable information—are best served by allowing institutions such as universities, libraries and broadcasters freedom to take decisions without interference from government. But these same values have also been invoked in support of the case for the individual academic freedom right.[91] It is not clear why there is a stronger argument for invoking them to justify an institutional right. Quite apart from that point, there remain several difficulties to the case for institutional academic freedom, among them the questions which institutions should enjoy academic freedom and how conflicts between university administrators and faculty—either collectively or individual members of faculties or departments—should be resolved?[92]

One other problem should be discussed at this point. Is it now correct as a matter of US constitutional law to speak of an institutional *right* to academic freedom, or would it be better to make the more limited claim that academic freedom is a value which supports or strengthens a university's argument that it has not violated some other constitutional right, for example, when it takes decisions on the admission or dismissal of students? In *Ewing*, academic freedom was used to bolster the university's argument that it need not comply with due process when dismissing a student on educational grounds, and in *Grutter* the traditional autonomy of universities entitled it to choose a diverse student body, even though that entailed taking race into account in its admissions process, in derogation from strict adherence to the non-discrimination principles mandated by the Fourteenth Amendment. Arguably, in neither of these two significant decisions did the Court articulate a constitutional right, which it would have to do if it were to invalidate state or federal legislation infringing academic freedom.[93] It held only that the university decisions did not infringe the constitutional rights to due process (*Ewing*) or to non-discrimination on the grounds of race (*Grutter*). It is not clear that the Supreme Court would uphold as an exercise of academic freedom a university's decision to select

---

[91] See the text above at nn 78 and 79.

[92] See below s IV(B) for conflicts between institutional and individual claims to constitutional academic freedom.

[93] RH Hiers takes this view in 'Institutional Academic Freedom, a Constitutional Misconception: Did *Grutter v Bollinger* Perpetuate the Confusion?' (2004) 30 *Journal of College and University Law* 531.

students solely on the basis of intellectual merit, in violation of a state or federal law requiring it to choose a racially diverse student body.[94] But it would have to uphold such a decision if a broad institutional academic freedom is to be taken seriously as a constitutional right.

Whatever these reservations concerning the coherence and scope of an institutional First Amendment right to academic freedom, lower courts have had little difficulty in accepting it. Moreover, they have often held that it trumps the competing claims to constitutional academic freedom asserted by individual professors. These conflicts will be considered in the next section. But it is worth emphasising that these conflicts have not yet reached the Supreme Court, and further even that Court has perhaps not committed itself fully to the recognition of an institutional right to academic freedom.

## IV. CONFLICTS BETWEEN PROFESSORS AND UNIVERSITIES

### A. The Free Speech Rights of Employees

Academic staff are employed by their universities, even if they may also be regarded, as under the AAUP Statement of 1940, as officers of educational institutions.[95] So a claim by a university professor or researcher to academic freedom under the First Amendment has to be examined in the context of the constitutional law concerning employee free speech rights. Traditionally, employers, including the government, were free to discipline their staff for disruptive speech or for the communication of confidential information; freedom of speech rights did not extend to the workplace. However, in *Pickering v Board of Education* (1968) the Supreme Court drew a distinction between the speech of a public employee *as a citizen* on a matter of public concern on the one hand and his or her speech on a matter of purely personal interest on the other hand.[96] The former is covered by the First Amendment. With

---

[94] See Byrne, 'Constitutional Academic Freedom after *Grutter*' (above n 67) 937 n 39. While he understands *Grutter* to establish a constitutional right, he is equivocal regarding whether it could be invoked in these circumstances.

[95] See above s II(B).

[96] *Pickering v Board of Education* 391 US 563 (1968). The case concerned a school teacher's letter to a newspaper, which was critical of the budget management of a high school board.

regard to such speech, a balancing test should be applied to determine whether the employer's interest in promoting efficiency in providing the public service outweighs the employee's interest in communicating his or her views on public affairs. In contrast, public employees have no First Amendment right to express, say, their personal grievances against their employers,[97] while under the state action doctrine, private employees have no constitutional free speech rights against discipline by their employers, no matter what the subject of the speech.

This jurisprudence has some clear implications for the freedom of speech of university professors. As already explained, professors at state universities may have wider rights against their employers than, say, professors at Harvard, Princeton or Stanford. The right to speak freely on matters of public concern most obviously covers the extramural speech of professors when, for example, they publish in newspapers, appear on television or write blogs to comment on matters of current political debate. But it may also cover intramural speech, commenting on the administration of their universities or criticising the poor running of a department or research centre. University management, and even more clearly education policy, is a matter of public concern, to which professors and other academic staff can make particularly important contributions.[98] It is less obvious how the *Pickering* distinction should be applied to speech within lecture halls or seminar rooms. On one view, academic lectures do raise matters of public and not solely private concern. But courts have reached the opposite conclusion and have distinguished the decision in *Pickering*, which upheld the right of a school teacher to speak freely about matters of educational policy and management.[99] They have been reluctant to uphold individual free speech rights in the classroom against university employers.[100]

This reluctance has become even more marked following the recent decision of the Supreme Court in *Garcetti v Ceballos*.[101] The Court ruled 5–4

---

[97] The leading case concerning such speech is *Connick v Myers* 461 US 138 (1983).

[98] See the cases discussed below in s IV(B); and MW Finkin, 'Intramural Speech, Academic Freedom, and the First Amendment' (1988) 66 *Texas Law Review* 1325.

[99] For example, see *Clark v Holmes* 474 F2d 928 (1972); *Day v South Park Independent School District* 768 F2d 696 (1985); and *Keen v Penson* 970 F2d 252 (7th Cir 1992).

[100] See below s IV(C).

[101] 547 US 410 (2006).

that a public employee—in this case a district attorney who had publicly challenged the reliability of a police affidavit—was not speaking as a citizen when he made a statement pursuant to his official duties. This ruling significantly qualifies *Pickering*: it means that the First Amendment does not preclude managerial discipline for employee speech made in the course of discharging official responsibilities, even if it might otherwise be held to discuss a matter of public concern. On this basis, a professor would clearly be subject to discipline for making what his or her university employer regarded as inappropriate remarks in a lecture, as they would be made in the course of discharging his or her teaching responsibility. Significantly, Kennedy J for the Court said that the analysis might not apply in the same way to speech concerning scholarship or teaching, while Souter J in dissent hoped the majority ruling would not endanger the First Amendment protection of academic freedom.[102]

## B. Decisions Upholding Individual Academic Freedom

Quite apart from cases concerning extramural expression,[103] a few decisions have upheld individual academic freedom claims against universities, although it is almost always possible to point to other court rulings that on comparable facts protected an institution's conflicting academic freedom.[104] In *Cooper v Ross*,[105] a District Court ordered the reinstatement of an assistant professor who had not been reappointed because of his public support for communism and his membership of a radical political party. The judge was less sure whether academic freedom protected a lecturer's right to determine his teaching methodology, but the point did not have to be decided, as it seems the university had not objected to the professor's teaching of history classes from a Marxist perspective. The Ninth Circuit Court of Appeals has held it

---

[102] The AAUP has considered the implications of the decision in 'Protecting an Independent Faculty Voice: Academic Freedom after *Garcetti v Ceballos*' (2009), available through their website (above n 24).

[103] Considered further below in ch 9.

[104] For conflicts between individual and institutional rights, see Rabban (above n 5) esp 280–300; and O'Neil (above n 44) ch 8.

[105] 472 F Supp 802 (1979). See Metzger, 'Profession and Constitution' (above n 1) 1311; and Rabban (above n 5) 281 and 289.

was against the First Amendment to apply a vague sexual harassment policy to a professor who had required his literature students to define pornography and who on occasion used sexually explicit language in class.[106] In contrast, another Circuit Court held that a college was entitled to suspend a professor for using such language in the classroom when it was irrelevant to the subject matter of his course and for disseminating to the faculty and media his reply to student complaints of sexual harassment.[107] The court emphasised that a professor's academic freedom is not absolute and that account should be taken of the interests of the university and the students in an environment conducive to learning.

In one unusual case the court upheld a professor's claim that his academic freedom was infringed when he was ordered to change a student's grade, though it said there would be no difficulty if university officials themselves ultimately changed the grade.[108] Other courts have refused to follow or have distinguished this ruling.[109] In *Brown* the Court of Appeals for the Third Circuit ruled that grading was an aspect of professors' teaching duties, so their assignment fell under the university's freedom to determine how a course is taught,[110] an extremely broad understanding of institutional academic freedom.[111]

Courts used to uphold individual academic freedom claims under the First Amendment most often in the context of intramural expression: the right to criticise educational policy and university administration. In *Johnson v Lincoln University of Commonwealth System of Higher Education*[112] it was held that faculty members were entitled to raise their concerns about grade inflation and academic standards, as these matters were of general public concern, not just of interest to the particular department.

---

[106] *Cohen v San Bernadino Valley College* 92 F 3d 968 (9th Cir 1996), discussed by O'Neil (above n 44) 71–72. See also *Doe v University of Michigan* 721 F Supp (852 ED Mich 1989).

[107] *Bonnell v Lorenzo* 241 F3d 800 (6th Cir 2001). See O'Neil (above n 44) 72–74.

[108] *Parate v Isibor* 868 F2d 821 (6th Cir 1988).

[109] *Keen v Penson* 970 F2d 252 (7th Cir 1992); *Brown v Armenti* 247 F3d 69 (3rd Cir 2001).

[110] Ibid, 74–75.

[111] O'Neil (above n 44) 220–21.

[112] 776 F2d 443 (3d Cir 1985). Also see *Trotman v Board of Trustees of Lincoln University* 635 F2d 216 (3d Cir 1980).

Professors may also express disagreement with their university Presidents' policies without jeopardising their positions.[113] A university's argument that it is disruptive to retain a troublesome professor on the academic staff is only one factor to take into account when balancing its interest against that professor's First Amendment freedom of speech and academic freedom.

The standing of these decisions is very uncertain after the Supreme Court ruling in *Garcetti v Ceballos*.[114] For intramural speech in some circumstances might now be treated as made under a professor's official duties and so fall outside the principle established in *Pickering*.[115] In *Renken v Gregory*,[116] the Seventh Circuit Court of Appeals followed *Garcetti* when it held that a professor's criticism of the university's misuse of grant funds he had been awarded fell outside the First Amendment. He was speaking in this context as a faculty employee about an aspect of his service duties, not as a citizen. The irony is that the wider the responsibilities assumed by professors on matters of university administration, the more likely it is that courts will find that their speech concerning such matters is made in pursuance of their official duties and so falls outside the First Amendment.[117]

## C. Decisions Upholding Institutional Academic Freedom

With the exception of some of the cases mentioned in the preceding paragraphs, courts have upheld institutional claims when they conflict with claims to individual academic freedom rights. They have, however, often recognised that academic freedom may be asserted by both

---

[113] *Rampey v Allen* 501 F2d 1090 (10th Cir 1974).

[114] Above n 101.

[115] Above n 96.

[116] 541 F3d 769 (7th Cir 2008).

[117] See *Hong v Grant* 516 F Supp 2d 1158 (CD Cal 2007), where the District Court emphasised the wide range of the professor's administrative responsibilities when concluding that he could be disciplined for criticising university hiring decisions; and *Gorum v Sessons* 561 F 3d 179 (3rd Cir 2009), where it was held that a professor was speaking in pursuance of official duties and so liable to dismissal when he advised a football player faced with disciplinary charges and when he withdrew an invitation to the University President to speak at a fraternity meeting.

parties. In *Piarowski v Illinois Community College*, in a much quoted statement of principle, Judge Posner said:

> The term ['academic freedom'] is equivocal. It is used to denote both the freedom of the academy to pursue its ends without interference from the government ... and the freedom of the individual teacher (or in some versions— indeed in most cases—the student) to pursue his ends without interference from the academy; and these two freedoms are in conflict, as in this case.[118]

The court resolved the conflict in the university's favour. It did not infringe the First Amendment rights of the chairman of its Art Department when it required him to remove some sexually explicit and racially offensive works from a gallery near the entrance to the university campus to a less conspicuous site. A decision in his favour would have limited the university's freedom to manage its affairs and made it more difficult, in the court's view, for it to attract black and female students.

In a number of cases courts have rejected constitutional challenges by individual professors that their teaching contracts were not renewed because their universities objected to some aspect of their work.[119] A university is entitled to control the curriculum and to determine the materials that may be used to teach courses.[120] In particular, professors have no right to intrude their religious and ethical beliefs into classroom discussion, unless they are clearly germane to the subject,[121] and they cannot complain if, following student evaluations, the university decides that their teaching methods are inappropriate.[122] University classrooms are not open public forums where professors have absolute freedom to speak as they like.[123]

The strongest rejection of an individual claim came from the Fourth Circuit Court of Appeals when a full court in *Urofsky v Gilmore* upheld,

---

[118] 759 F2d 625, 629 (7th Cir 1985).

[119] *Clark v Holmes* 474 F2d 928 (1972); *Hetrick v Robert K Martin, President of E Kentucky University* 480 F2d 705 (1973); *Carley v Arizona Board of Regents* 737 P2d 1099 (Ariz App 1987); *Lovelace v Southeastern Massachusetts University* 793 F2d 419 (1st Cir 1986).

[120] *Edwards v California University of Pennsylvania* 156 F3d 488 (3rd Cir 1998).

[121] *Bishop v Aronov* 926 F2d 1066 (11th Cir 1991); *Piggee v Carl Sanburg College* 464 F3d 667 (7th Cir 2006).

[122] *Hetrick* (above n 119).

[123] See Floyd R Gibson, Circuit Judge in *Bishop v Aronov* (above n 121) 1074. Cf the dicta of Brennan J in the Supreme Court in *Keyishian* (above n 53).

8–4, the constitutionality of a Virginia law that restricted the access
of state employees to sexually explicit material on computers owned
or leased by the state.[124] Six professors at state universities challenged
the statute, arguing principally that the restriction inhibited their First
Amendment academic freedom right to conduct research.[125] According
to the majority judgement, any constitutional right to academic freedom
belongs to the university, not to individual scholars; the Supreme Court
has never recognised an individual right to academic freedom under the
First Amendment, only an institutional right. The Court had declined
to recognise an individual right in previous cases when it might have
done so.[126] Only Chief Judge Wilkinson, in a separate concurring judgement, seemed willing to recognise that the law restricted the freedom of
professors to research and write on topics that might entail reference to
sexually explicit material; he implicitly recognised a First Amendment
right of individual academic freedom. The statute, however, was valid
in his view because 'agency heads' could grant permission to access
such material. Universities allocated this task to Deans and Heads of
Department, themselves academics discharging administrative functions. Academic freedom was therefore safeguarded through the system
of university self-governance, a recognition of the institutional dimension to the freedom.[127] The decision is significant, because the court
majority rejected an individual academic freedom right grounded on
the First Amendment. Other decisions, which have been referred to in
these paragraphs, had generally held either that professors had such a
right but it was trumped on the facts by the institutional freedom, or
that the individual right did not cover the particular claim.

---

[124] 216 F3d 401 (4th Cir 2000).
[125] Their other argument that it inhibited the freedom of speech of all public
employees was also rejected, as access to sexually explicit material for the purposes
of their work did not involve speech of public concern.
[126] *Urofsky* (above n 124) 414–15, referring to the Supreme Court decisions in
*Epperson v Arkansas* 393 US 97 (1968) and *Edwards v Aguillard* 482 US 578 (1987)
involving respectively a ban on teaching evolution and a requirement to teach
creation science if evolution were taught in state schools. In both cases the statutes were held incompatible with the prohibition in the First Amendment of the
establishment of religion. They might have been held incompatible with the academic freedom of science teachers, if academic freedom extended to high schools:
see ch 1, s 3.
[127] *Urofsky* (above n 124) 432–33.

## D. The Scope of Institutional Freedom in Cases of Conflict

Courts are very reluctant to invalidate decisions taken by academic institutions, even if they appear, on one view of the matter, to constrain the professional freedom of professors and other academic staff. They are concerned that 'federal judges should not be ersatz deans and educators'.[128] This anxiety is nicely illustrated by the decision of the Seventh Circuit Court of Appeals in *Feldman v Ho*,[129] when it rejected a challenge by an assistant professor to the nonrenewal of his teaching contract after he accused a colleague of academic misconduct. Easterbrook J said that it must be for the university to decide whether a charge made by one scholar against another is sound; the dispute concerned the department's conduct of its core business of determining which teachers to keep and to promote. The university might come to wrong conclusions, but 'the only way to preserve academic freedom is to keep claims of academic error out of the legal maw.'[130]

This principle is coherent and eminently defensible when university decisions are taken by academics or by bodies on which academics are well represented. For a court to intervene then in litigation between an individual professor and his or her university would be to take sides in what can be characterised as a dispute between scholars. It is less obvious that courts should refrain from intervening when a decision impinging on individual academic freedom is taken by university administrators, particularly if their decision departs from the view formed by academic colleagues of the individual concerned.[131] In that event, a university's claim to immunity from judicial review on the basis of academic freedom is relatively weak. In *Brown v Trustees of Brown University*[132] the Circuit Court of Appeals upheld the claim of an associate professor that her university had discriminated against her on the basis of sex when she was denied tenure for insufficient publications. Her case was a strong one because the departmental tenure committee and the appointments committees of both the faculty and the university had all

---

[128]  Floyd Gibson J in *Bishop v Aronov* (above n 121) 1075.
[129]  171 F3d 494 (7th Cir 1999).
[130]  Ibid, 497.
[131]  See Areen (above n 9) 995–96.
[132]  891 F2d 337 (1st Cir 1989). See also *Smith v Losee* 485 F2d 334 (10th Cir 1973).

recommended granting tenure, taking the view that the quality of her published work compensated for its lack of quantity; the Provost, however, came to a different view, and tenure was denied by the President and the Trustees. The weight of academic opinion in this case was strongly in favour of the individual claim, and the university's academic freedom argument thin. Institutional academic freedom claims should also not be sustained if a university has denied tenure in breach of contract or after misrepresenting to the applicant what needs to be done to obtain it.[133] On the other hand, it is reasonable to uphold university decisions when tenure has been refused after expert academic opinion has been fully considered.[134]

Courts should also be willing to uphold an individual professor's claim against a university when it is clear that the latter's decision was significantly influenced by political or public pressure. In that event the university's claim to have exercised its own academic freedom is bogus. This point explains the decision in *Cooper v Ross*:[135] the university in that case was strongly pressed by members of the Arkansas state legislature not to reappoint the claimant because of his radical political views, so it was not really exercising its own academic freedom when it succumbed to that pressure. The point in short is that a university's claim to exercise institutional academic freedom should not be accepted if there is good evidence to suggest that it did not independently exercise academic judgment in reaching its decision. Moreover, it should be remembered universities may wrongly claim academic freedom when they are really acting to safeguard their property rights or their commercial interests.[136]

## V. THE RELATIONSHIP BETWEEN PROFESSIONAL AND CONSTITUTIONAL ACADEMIC FREEDOM

Two contrasting views can be taken of the relationship between professional and constitutional academic freedom. While admitting that the two freedoms have different origins and bases, van Alstyne considered

---

[133] *Craine v Trinity College* 791 A2d 518, 540 (Conn 2002).
[134] *Weinstock v Columbia University* 224F3d 33 (2nd Cir 2000).
[135] Above n 105.
[136] See above ch 2, s V.

the case law on their interpretation—the decisions of Committee A and the jurisprudence of the Supreme Court—overlapped; both the AAUP and the Court understandings of academic freedom were significantly influenced by the other's approach.[137] Arguably, one effect of the constitutionalisation of academic freedom might have been to give legal teeth to a professional right that previously had lacked bite when resisted by universities. The other, more persuasive view is that the two perspectives are fundamentally different. Metzger concluded that professional academic freedom requires universities to be neutral; they should not as institutions determine what is true or false but leave professors and other academic staff free to state the truths they have individually identified and wish to disseminate. The constitutional perspective, on the other hand, emphasises the autonomy of universities to determine such matters as what should be taught and how it should be taught, and for that reason it was 'seen by the organized profession as a lesser good and potentially as a serious threat'.[138]

There are, on this view, inevitably tensions between the professional understanding of the freedom and the courts' preference for institutional autonomy, which in litigation often trumps individual claims. This section explores important differences between the two understandings of academic freedom and then examines one context in which they might lead to the same conclusion: attempts by state legislatures to constrain the teaching freedom of university professors might infringe both their professional freedom and constitutional academic freedom.

## A. Differences between Professional and Constitutional Academic Freedom

The primary differences concern teaching freedom and the freedom of professors to participate in and criticise the governance of their universities. Professional academic freedom recognises that professors must be free to determine how they teach, provided they observe the scholarly standards of their particular disciplines and do not attempt to indoctrinate their students. Under the 1940 Statement they must not

---

[137] Van Alstyne, 'Academic Freedom and the First Amendment in the Supreme Court' (above n 39) 81–82.

[138] Metzger, 'Profession and Constitution' (above n 1) 1322.

introduce controversial matter gratuitously into classroom discussion but should be free to do this if it illuminates or is educationally relevant to the subject under discussion.[139] While some of the court decisions examined above in section IV(C) are compatible with these principles, others appear to allow individual professors little or no freedom to determine how they teach their subjects[140] and hold that it is for the university, not the professor, to choose the materials for discussion in class.[141] Certainly, the plain meaning of Frankfurter J's remarks in *Sweezy* is that the freedoms to determine the syllabus and how it is taught are essential aspects of an institutional freedom.

The professional and constitutional understandings of academic freedom also appear to take different views about the right of individual professors to participate in university governance and to engage in intramural expression. On the former understanding the faculty should take academic decisions, while university administrators must have powerful reasons to depart from them.[142] Decisions to discipline or dismiss faculty members, whether tenured or not, should be taken by academics only after the member has been given a hearing. As an aspect of these participatory and procedural freedoms, academics are free to criticise in public the conduct of university administrators. In contrast, the Supreme Court has declined to uphold due process rights for non-tenured professors whose teaching contracts have not been renewed[143] or to uphold a constitutional right to be consulted on matters of university governance and administration.[144] Equally, freedom of intramural expression has been significantly curtailed in a number of recent decisions following the Supreme Court ruling in *Garcetti v Ceballos*.[145] Unless that ruling is held inapplicable to university employment, academics will have no First Amendment right to criticise the university administration, particularly insofar as administrative matters fall within the academics' own official duties.[146]

---

[139] Finkin and Post (above n 2) 87–94.

[140] *Hetrick* (above n 119).

[141] *Edwards v California University of Pennsylvania* (above n 120); and *Brown v Armenti* (above n 109).

[142] See above s II(C).

[143] *Roth* (above n 71).

[144] *Minnesota State Board v Knight* (above n 73).

[145] S IV(A) and (C) above.

[146] See *Hong v Grant* (above n 117).

These points show that there are significant differences between the professional and constitutional freedoms. They reflect the fundamental distinction between the professional freedom's protection of individual members of the academic profession, provided they comply with the appropriate scholarly standards, and the guarantee of institutional autonomy under the First Amendment. The explanation for this divergence, of course, is that the former protects individual academics against interference with their professional freedom by university administrators, Presidents and governing boards, while the constitutional freedom has been developed to protect universities (and to a lesser extent their academic staff) against state interference. It is hardly surprising that courts have sometimes found it relatively difficult to uphold individual constitutional rights to academic freedom *against universities*, when in other contexts they have defended the institutional autonomy of the universities themselves. However, both individual professors and universities might be able to invoke academic freedom against interference by the state.

## B. Academic Bills of Rights

Attempts have been made during the last decade to introduce in Congress and state legislatures an Academic Bill of Rights (ABOR) to ensure that students are exposed in university teaching to a wide variety of diverse points of view and to safeguard the intellectual independence of both faculty and students.[147] These aims appear harmless, even laudable, on the surface. The model ABOR[148] refers to the principles of academic freedom formulated by the AAUP and to the Supreme Court decision in *Keyishian*.[149] The background to the introduction of these Bills was increasing disquiet among right-wing students and political conservatives regarding what they perceived to be the predominance of liberals among university professors and their bias in teaching courses, particularly on history, social and political sciences. So a clause in the model ABOR provides that '[c]urricula and reading lists

---

[147]   O'Neil (above n 44) ch 9.

[148]   Available at http://www.studentsforacademicfreedom.org/documents/1925/abor.html (accessed 5 August 2010).

[149]   Above n 53.

in the humanities and social sciences should reflect the uncertainty and unsettled character of all human knowledge in these areas by providing students with dissenting sources and viewpoints where appropriate.' Moreover, disciplines should welcome a diversity of approach and faculty have the responsibility to expose students to the spectrum of significant scholarly views. In the process of hiring and promoting faculty in the humanities and social sciences, decisions should be taken, inter alia, 'with a view toward fostering a plurality of methodologies and perspectives'. Some state Bills would have given students statutory rights to complain to university authorities if they considered that classroom teaching did not reflect the diversity of views on a topic, or would have required the university authorities themselves to report annually on the steps they had taken to comply with the requirements of the ABOR.

The AAUP has naturally opposed these measures, since they would in effect transfer the supervision of teaching away from the faculty to university administrators, and perhaps ultimately to the state legislature. Moreover, the ABOR requirements of balance and diversity could be understood as requiring professors to present a range of political perspectives on a particular topic, even if this was not warranted by scholarly standards.[150] The AAUP concluded that an Academic Bill of Rights would undermine the very academic freedom it purported to defend, because it would interfere with the judgment of university faculty with respect to teaching materials and methodology. The Association was anxious to defend the profession's ability to regulate itself.

In fact no Academic Bill of Rights has been enacted, although in two states (Missouri and South Dakota) measures were approved by the lower house of the legislature.[151] If one were enacted, it would be vulnerable, according to Byrne, to constitutional challenge as infringing the First Amendment rights of individual professors and universities to determine what is taught, free from legislative oversight: 'legislators would be providing rules for the conduct of core university functions ... and determining on academic grounds who may teach and what may be

---

[150] See the Statement of the AAUP on Academic Bill of Rights (2003) available at http://www.aaup.org/AAUP/comm/rep/A/abor.htm (accessed 15 August 2010).

[151] O'Neil (above n 44) 255–56.

taught.'[152] Moreover, an ABOR would be vague and too broad, grounds on which the Supreme Court has invalidated state laws for infringing academic freedom.[153] It has been doubted whether such a law could be challenged unless and until it were implemented by a university in such a way as to put academic freedom in danger.[154] At that stage, however, a conflict would arise between, on the one hand, a faculty or informal group of professors and, on the other, a university; a court might hesitate to interfere with a university's assessment that more intensive teaching regulation was justified to protect academic freedom.[155] The attraction of Byrne's argument is that it would join universities and professors in a challenge to an interference with academic freedom by the state for political purposes. If upheld by the courts, constitutional academic freedom would be at one with the professional understanding of the freedom.

## C. The Effective Protection of Academic Freedom

A final question is whether the academic freedom of individual professors and other teachers is now effectively protected, given that their recourse to the courts is often unsuccessful. Arguably, the relatively high volume of litigation—compared to that in the United Kingdom and Germany—suggests that universities frequently fail to observe the principles in the AAUP Statement; academics would have no need to resort to the courts if universities always complied with its principles or if the AAUP were able to intervene successfully on their behalf. Individual academics cannot rely on a constitutional academic freedom right, because courts are more likely to uphold the conflicting constitutional claims of the university or are at least reluctant to challenge university decisions taken on academic grounds.[156] Moreover, courts in the United States have not developed any principles comparable to those in German constitutional law, under which even private universities (and

---

[152] Byrne, 'Constitutional Academic Freedom after *Grutter*' (above n 67) at 943–44.

[153] *Keyishian v Board of Regents* (above n 53).

[154] O'Neil (above n 44) 257–60.

[155] See the cases discussed above in s IV(C).

[156] See *Ewing* (above n 59).

research institutes) may be bound to respect the fundamental values of academic freedom in their dealings with individual professors and researchers.[157]

The effective protection of professorial academic freedom in the United States rests ultimately on its acceptance by university boards, Presidents and other administrators, and its vigorous defence by bodies such as the AAUP. The Association may reinforce findings that a university has infringed a principle in the 1940 Statement through a formal censure, which may subsist for a number of years until the university administration changes its offending policy.[158] Professional associations and learned societies may refuse to accredit universities that consistently infringe academic freedom, though it has been suggested that they are not as vigorous in using this 'sanction' as they should be.[159] Collective bargaining to ensure that academic freedom is incorporated into academic staff contracts is also important.[160] Publicity and political pressure therefore play as vital a role in ensuring the effective protection of academic freedom in the United States as they do in other legal systems. And despite the wealth of litigation, they are just as important as decisions of the courts.

[157] See above ch 5, s III(D).
[158] Finkin and Post (above n 2) 50–51.
[159] O'Neil (above n 44) 277–78.
[160] Ibid, 35–36 and 40–41.

# 7

## *Restrictions on Freedom of Research*

### I. INTRODUCTION

ACADEMIC FREEDOM CLEARLY includes the freedom of research, understood broadly as the right of individual academics to choose the subject of their research and how they propose to study it—their research methodology. They also generally claim a freedom to determine themselves, albeit in consultation with colleagues and collaborators, when and where to publish the results of their research.[1] This aspect of freedom of research is valuable, since the premature publication of provisional research results, particularly if made in a low-ranking journal, might undermine the credibility of the final conclusions and lessen the opportunity of the professor or lecturer to enhance his or her academic reputation or standing; a delay in publication, on the other hand, might lose a scientist the opportunity to claim originality or novelty for his or her research findings (and so lose the chance of taking out a patent for any invention made in the course of the work).[2]

But research freedom is not absolute—even in German law, where scientific freedom is apparently guaranteed without exception in this context.[3] This chapter is concerned with the limits imposed on freedom of research by three different types of law. It discusses in section II the impact of laws requiring medical (and other types of) research involving human beings to obtain the approval of ethics committees or other boards before it can be conducted, or at least before government

---

[1] See the statement of principles by the Federal Court of Australia in its recent decision in *University of Western Australia v Gray* [2009] FCAFC 116. See below s III(B) for discussion of the decision.

[2] See below s III.

[3] See above ch 5, ss I and IV(B).

funding is made available. Section III is concerned with the complex relationship between intellectual property laws and freedom of research. On one view, copyright and patent laws, by conferring in effect monopoly rights on authors and patent owners to exploit their copyrighted works and inventions,[4] necessarily limit the freedom of research of scholars and scientists. On the other hand, intellectual property rights are themselves intended to reward creative work in the arts and sciences and so promote rather than discourage scholarship and scientific research. What is explored in this part of the chapter is the extent to which academic freedom itself has influenced the understanding and interpretation of intellectual property laws; perhaps it ought sometimes to be given greater weight in this process.

Section IV of the chapter examines the restraints on academic freedom, in particular on the right of medical researchers to publish their research findings as they consider appropriate, which may be imposed by the pharmaceutical or other companies sponsoring and financing their research. These constraints are imposed by terms of the contract under which companies commission and support the research; other contractual provisions may restrict the access of scientists to full research data, which they may need to substantiate their research findings. Further, a sponsoring company may draft articles with the use of 'ghost writers' and expect university researchers to add their names to add credibility to the research. These practices appear to undermine academic freedom, but it is unclear how far the freedom can be asserted legally to counter them. In contrast, it may be easier, at least in the United States, to challenge any publication constraints imposed by government departments when they commission university professors or university departments to undertake research on their behalf; this topic is considered in section V, which also discusses whether scientific advisers to the government may claim academic freedom when it finds the public expression of their views uncongenial. Section VI then briefly considers the implications of the UK Data Protection Act 1998 for freedom of research and publication.

This chapter does not provide an exhaustive treatment of the various restrictions on freedom of research. For example, the legal regimes

---

[4] Strictly speaking, copyright law does not confer monopoly rights, since it does not stop an author from independently producing an identical or similar work without copying the copyright work.

governing the use of animals and medical research on embryos and cloning are not discussed.[5] Their existence indicates, of course, that research freedom—like other aspects of academic freedom—is far from absolute. Another topic not covered at length is the restraints imposed by libel law. The prospect of a defamation action may inhibit the freedom of a scientist to comment critically on a drug, medical product or treatment, or a scholar to review critically the publications of other academics.[6] The 'chilling effect' of libel laws impinges therefore on publication freedom—an aspect of academic research freedom. Defences to libel actions, in particular the fair comment and privilege defences, should be interpreted liberally to protect the exercise of academic freedom, or more broadly the freedom of expression of university professors and other commentators on science and the arts.[7]

Nor is this chapter concerned with the variety of constraints on research that may be imposed through assessment procedures, such as that conducted in the United Kingdom by means of the Research Assessment Exercise, or by research councils when they require applicants for funding to state the economic or social impact of their proposed research.[8] These procedures and requirements may have an undesirable effect on the exercise of research freedom—in particular by discouraging long-term basic research—but they do not impose *legal* restrictions on the exercise of that freedom.

It may be helpful to make a few introductory remarks that are relevant to all of the topics considered in this chapter. Research freedom, like other aspects of academic freedom, is not identical to freedom of speech or expression. Publication of the results of research is of course

---

[5]  Research involving animal experiments is regulated in the United Kingdom by the Animals (Scientific Procedures) Act 1986.

[6]  A number of libel actions have been brought in England recently against scientists and doctors (see Second Report by the Media, Culture, and Sport Committee, 'Press Standards, Privacy and Libel' HC (2009–10) 362 [138]–[142]) while a criminal prosecution has been brought in France in respect of a book review in a law journal that, the claimant alleges, made a number of false and damaging allegations against her work: (2009) 20 *The European Journal of International Law* 967.

[7]  As in the recent decision of the Court of Appeal in *British Chiropractic Association v Singh* [2010] EWCA Civ 350, characterising an allegation that the claimant association knowingly promoted bogus treatments as an expression of opinion, not one of fact.

[8]  For discussion of these restraints in the United Kingdom, see above ch 4, s IV(E).

covered by freedom of speech, as well as constituting an aspect of research freedom. But many aspects of research, in particular medical and scientific research, only tangentially involve speech: eg, the institution and equipment of a laboratory; the conduct of experiments; the examination and analysis of body parts, blood or other samples; drug testing and brain scanning. Research is essentially an activity; only social science research, conducted by means of interviews and surveys, typically involves a lot of conversation or written communication.[9] These points are important; they suggest that restrictions on research may be open to constitutional challenge only insofar as academic (including research) freedom is a distinct constitutional right, separate from, albeit closely related to, freedom of speech. On the other hand, constraints on publication are clearly vulnerable to challenge as infringing freedom of speech (or expression) as well as any separate right to academic freedom.

The discussion hitherto has assumed that only two interests are involved in determining the legitimacy of restrictions on research freedom: those of research scientists (and their university departments) on the one hand, and the interest supporting a restriction on the other. That latter interest might be the dignity of individuals participating in medical research,[10] intellectual property rights of the author or inventor (who might of course be an academic or a university)[11] or the concern of a pharmaceutical or other company financing research to defend its commercial interests from the impact of any adverse publicity occasioned by an academic publication.[12] But a third interest is generally involved in these conflicts: the public interest in the openness of scientific procedures and in access to the results of academic research. It is indeed these interests or goals that provide a significant part of the case for academic and research freedom, and explain why it is inappropriate to regard the freedom as essentially a privilege for university professors and other researchers.[13]

---

[9] These points are made by J Weinstein, 'Institutional Review Boards and the Constitution' (2007) 101 *Northwestern University Law Review* 493, 494–95.

[10] Below s II.

[11] Below s III(B).

[12] Below s IV.

[13] See the discussion above in ch 3, s III.

This third interest is reflected in the traditional norms or principles of scientific research, identified by the American sociologist Robert Merton: 'universalism', in the sense that the truth of observations is determined by shared impersonal criteria; 'communism', meaning that research findings result from collaboration and are for everyone's benefit; 'disinterestedness'; and 'organised scepticism'.[14] It is through observing these principles that science produces 'certified knowledge' of public benefit. They entail a freedom to publish research findings; indeed, arguably, researchers are under a duty to disclose their findings, though it is a matter for their judgement when and where this is appropriate. To some extent, the intellectual property rights and other restrictions on publication freedom discussed in this chapter can be viewed as conflicting with these traditional norms.[15] The important point is that restrictions on research not only inhibit the freedom of scientists and other researchers but run counter to the fundamental norms and values of scientific research which benefit the general public.

## II. LICENSING AND ETHICS COMMITTEES

Quite apart from restrictions on embryo research and cloning,[16] medical research is subject to significant regulation, largely to ensure the safety and welfare of human participants in the research. In the United Kingdom the conduct of clinical trials involving the testing of drugs and other products on human participants is governed by the Medicines for Human Use (Clinical Trials) Regulations,[17] drafted to implement an EU Directive.[18] Such trials require the approval of both the Medicines and Health Care Products Regulatory Agency—responsible for the licensing of new drugs—and an ethics committee, which considers both

---

[14] R Merton, *The Sociology of Science: Theoretical and Empirical Investigations* (Chicago, University of Chicago Press, 1973).

[15] RS Eisenberg, 'Proprietary Rights and the Norms of Science in Biotechnology Research' (1987) 97 *Yale Law Journal* 177, 184. See also H Nowotny, 'The Changing Nature of Public Science' in H Nowotny et al (eds), *The Public Nature of Science under Assault: Politics, Markets, Science and the Law* (Berlin, Springer, 2005) 1.

[16] For this topic in UK law, see M Brazier and E Cave, *Medicine, Patients and the Law*, 4th edn (London, Penguin, 2007) 358–64.

[17] SI 2004/1031.

[18] Directive 2001/20/EC (Clinical Trials Directive).

ethical and medical aspects of the clinical trial, including such matters as the balance of risks and benefits, the suitability of the investigator and the facilities, and the procedures for obtaining the informed consent of the participants in the trial.[19] The Clinical Trials Regulations refer to the Declaration of Helsinki on Ethical Principles for Research involving Human Subjects, agreed by the World Medical Association; Article 5 of the Declaration lays down the principle that the well-being of human participants in research should take precedence over the interests of science and the public interest in new medical knowledge.

Ethics committees now play an important role in the licensing of clinical trials in many European jurisdictions.[20] In Germany their responsibility to ensure the effective protection of participants in drug and other medicinal products trials has been put on a statutory footing since 1994 by the Medicinal Products Act and by the Law on the Trade in Drugs (Arzneimittelgesetz (AMG)).[21] As in the United Kingdom, any proposal to conduct a clinical trial of a drug or other medicinal instrument and device must be referred to an ethics committee. A positive decision from such a committee is now necessary for a clinical drugs trial to proceed.[22] The majority of members of ethics committees are doctors and medical researchers, but they must have lawyers, and sometimes there are theologians or bioethicists. But it is apparently unusual for a layperson to sit as a member to represent the interests of the general public.[23]

There can be no constitutional objection to these requirements, provided the appointment, composition and responsibilities of ethics committees are set out with sufficient precision by statute.[24] For the German Constitutional Court in its decision on the Hesse University

---

[19] Clinical Trials Regulations, reg 15(5), discussed by Brazier and Cave (above n 16) para 16.5.

[20] For a comparative treatment of their responsibilities, see D Beyleveld, D Townend and J Wright (eds), *Research Ethics Committees, Data Protection and Medical Research in European Countries* (Aldershot, Ashgate, 2005).

[21] AMG, ss 40–42; and see M Kettner, 'Research Ethics Committees in Germany' in Beyleveld, Townend and Wright (eds) (ibid) 73–83.

[22] Under the version of the AMG in force before amendments in 2004, a trial can proceed, even in the absence of a positive assessment by an ethics committee, if it has not been forbidden by the competent authority within 60 days. That is still the position for trials of medical devices under the Medicinal Products Act.

[23] Kettner (above n 21) 74.

[24] C Starck, 'Commentary on Article 5 GG' in H von Mangoldt, F Klein and C Starck (eds), *Kommentar zum Grundgesetz*, 5th edn (Munich, Vahlen, 2005) para

law (discussed above in chapter 5) ruled that state legislation may impose limits on scientific and research freedom in order to safeguard human dignity and other constitutional rights and interests.[25] But the restrictions should be imposed by bodies that are constituted by and act under statute, rather than informally, since it is important that researchers appreciate the constraints under which they operate. Ethics committees should take the constitutional right guaranteed by Article 5(3) of the Basic Law into account when they consider applications to conduct clinical trials.[26] Arguably, the AMG and other legislation fail to set out sufficiently precise standards for ethics committees to apply when they assess research proposals; too much is left to their discretion. There is inadequate guarantee that their decisions will respect freedom of research.[27] Ethics committees should not be regarded solely as a system of professional self-regulation, for their decisions have an impact on the welfare of patients and the concerns of the general public. In that context it is probably wrong for doctors to constitute a majority of the membership. Certainly in German law, the principle of scientific freedom surely requires that the decisions of ethics committees are open to challenge in the courts.

While there can be little objection in principle to the requirements to obtain the approval of an ethics committee before conducting a clinical trial, the extension of these requirements to research in the social sciences and humanities is much more controversial. In the United Kingdom National Health Service (NHS) authorities require the approval of an ethics committee for any research involving interviews with or access to patients and other human participants. Under the Economic and Social Research Council (ESRC) Framework for Research Ethics 2010, funding will normally be given for research involving more than minimal risk to human participants, including data collection, only if it has

424; and M Fehling, 'Commentary on Article 5, 3' in R Dolzer, C Waldhoff and K Graßhof (eds), *Bonner Kommentar* (Heidelberg, CF Müller, 2004) para 165.

[25] Above ch 5, s IV(C), also discussing the limits that may properly be imposed to safeguard animal welfare.

[26] K Sobota, 'Die Ethikkommissionen: Ein Neues Institut des Verwaltungsrecht?' (1996) 121 AöR 229, 242 and 255.

[27] C Gramm, 'Ethikkommissionen: Sicherung oder Begrenzung der Wissenschaftsfreiheit?' (1999) 32 *Wissenschaftsrecht* 209 argues that the Ethics Commissions' discretion to consider broad ethical standards without statutory guidelines is constitutionally problematic.

been given prior ethical approval by an independent ethics committee organised by the applicant's university. Universities whose staff undertake any research of this kind must therefore set up such committees. A committee's primary role is to protect the dignity and welfare of people participating in the research, but it is also expected to have regard for the consequences of the proposed study.[28] It should take independent advice on the scholarly or scientific merits of a proposal in order to make a judgement on its ethical implications.[29]

These requirements may discourage the conduct of empirical social science research—it is time-consuming to ensure that all participants have given their informed consent to be interviewed, etc—and therefore impoverish society as a whole.[30] Academics whose work is dependent on public funding and so on the approval of a university ethics committee will in this respect find it more difficult to conduct research than, say, journalists whose work is funded independently.[31] Might the decision of a NHS or university ethics committee to refuse ethical approval for a social science research proposal be challenged for infringing academic freedom? The decisions of an ethics committee may be subject to judicial review,[32] and as a 'public authority' it would be bound to act compatibly with human rights.[33] But it is unlikely that an academic freedom argument would be upheld in the courts. In the first place, academic freedom in the United Kingdom, unlike the comparable scientific freedom in Germany, is not a constitutional right, let alone a Convention right under the European Convention. Rather, it is a limited statutory right. Moreover, academic freedom in the United Kingdom has never been understood to confer positive rights to

---

[28] ESRC Framework for Research Ethics 2010, paras 1.3.1–1.9.6. (The Framework has modified a little the stricter requirements set out in the Research Ethics Framework issued in 2005.)

[29] Ibid, para 1.9.2.

[30] R Dingwall, 'The Ethical Case against Ethical Regulation in Humanities and Social Science Research' (2008) 3 *Twenty-First Century Society* 1.

[31] G Pearson, 'The Researcher as Hooligan: Where "Participant" Observation Means Breaking the Law' (2009) 12 *International Journal of Social Research Methodology* 243 argues that researchers enjoy greater academic freedom when they are not bound by ethical guidance and procedures governing covert participant observation.

[32] Decisions of ethics committees may be subject to judicial review: *R v Ethical Committee of St Mary's Hospital, ex parte Harriott* [1998] 1 FLR 512.

[33] HRA 1998, s 6(1).

funding for research or to conduct interviews with, say, health service staff and patients.[34]

In contrast to the position in the United Kingdom, serious doubts have been raised in the United States about the constitutionality of Institutional Review Boards (IRBs), which perform similar though much broader functions to those discharged in European jurisdictions by ethics committees. In two major law review articles, Philip Hamburger has argued that they constitute a system of licensing incompatible with the First Amendment guarantee of freedom of speech; the licensing of research, in his view, amounts to a prior restraint on speech.[35] Under federal law, any university or other institution applying for federal grants to support research must establish an IRB to review research involving human subjects. IRBs license human subjects research on the basis of what is known as the Common Rule, a set of principles adopted by seventeen federal agencies and departments to set general ethical standards for government financed research.[36] Among these standards is a requirement that IRBs assess the reasonableness of the risks undertaken by the participants in the research in relation to its likely benefits and to the importance of the knowledge gained from its conduct.[37] These requirements apply to all research involving the participation of human subjects, subject to a handful of exceptions; they apply therefore not only to biomedical research but to social science and humanities research involving interviews and surveys. An IRB must have at least five members, one of whom is unaffiliated to the institution applying for the grant; in practice university IRBs are largely composed of academics, though this feature does not, Hamburger argues, make the overall scheme less vulnerable to constitutional challenge.[38]

---

[34] See above ch 4, s IV.

[35] P Hamburger, 'The New Censorship: Institutional Review Boards' (2004) *Supreme Court Review* 271; and P Hamburger, 'Getting Permission' (2007) 101 *Northwestern University Law Review* 405.

[36] Title 45 CFR (Code of Federal Regulations) part 46.

[37] Hamburger, 'Getting Permission' (above n 35) 421–27 sets out the principal requirements of the Common Rule. There is a good overview of the system in DA Hyman, 'Institutional Review Boards: Is This the Least Worst We Can Do?' (2007) 101 *North Western Law Review* 749, 750–52.

[38] Hamburger, 'Getting Permission' (above n 35) 448–52.

In Hamburger's view, it is irrelevant both that these provisions were framed to protect the safety of human participants in medical research and that much of that research involves conduct rather more than verbal and written communication. His point is that the scheme requires licensing for research that does consist of interviews and surveys (which might include, say, that of epidemiologists). What is important is the target of the law, even if it also regulates conduct. The requirement of IRB approval therefore, in his view, amounts to a prior restraint on speech. Further, it is immaterial that approval is a condition for federal funding rather than a general legal requirement imposed on all research involving the participation of human subjects, irrespective of how it is financed. The condition has been used to require licensing by IRBs of all university research, whether or not it is federally funded.[39] The government is therefore using its spending powers indirectly to regulate research; as a result, the scheme is subject to strict scrutiny under the First Amendment.[40]

James Weinstein, however, argues persuasively that as most scientific and medical research involves conduct rather than speech, IRB regulations simply do not engage the First Amendment freedom of speech.[41] The fact that such research leads eventually to academic publication does not affect this conclusion. At most the application of these regulations to stop, say, the use of interviews on subjects that are disapproved of—for example, a study of sexual preferences or practices—might be challengeable under the First Amendment. But in the absence of any indication that the IRB regulations are used to suppress this type of research, there can be no constitutional objection to the requirement of ethical approval by IRBs as a condition for the receipt of federal funding. It would also be possible to defend the requirement that all researchers at a university follow basic ethical principles, whether or not their research is federally funded; the conduct of unconstrained

---

[39] Ibid, 441.

[40] The government is entitled to impose conditions on the use of funds it makes available to family planning agencies, but it cannot use this power to justify the imposition of restrictions on the free speech of university students and academics (*Rust v Sullivan* 500 US 173, 220 (1991)).

[41] Weinstein (above n 9).

research might well weaken compliance by colleagues with the standards imposed by an IRB on the latter's federally funded research.[42]

Weinstein is also unpersuaded that IRB regulations could be challenged on the basis of any independent constitutional right of research that might be based either on the First Amendment free speech guarantee or on the due process clause, if that provision is interpreted to protect a few unspecified fundamental rights or interests.[43] Even if a research right could be established, it is unlikely to be given sufficient weight to lead to the invalidation of the regulations.

It is noteworthy that little or no importance has been attached in this context to academic freedom arguments. If academic freedom is a discrete First Amendment right, whether it is held by individual professors or by the universities that employ them,[44] it could surely be invoked to challenge restrictions on research such as those imposed by the IRB regulations. It would be immaterial then whether the restrictions amount to a limit on speech or on conduct; academic freedom arguments can be used to challenge either type of limit. Of course, it does not follow that such challenges should succeed. There are powerful arguments for requiring ethical approval, at least in the context of biomedical research, where the health and safety of human participants may be placed at risk. Moreover, it is surely important that IRB approval is necessary as a condition of federal funding rather than as a requirement for the conduct of research, even that which is privately funded; academic freedom does not entail in the United States, any more than it does in the United Kingdom, positive rights to the funding of research, free from non-discriminatory conditions imposed by the funding body.[45]

---

[42] Ibid, 555–57. See also RA Epstein, 'Defanging IRBs: Replacing Coercion with Information' (2007) 101 *Northwestern University Law Review* 735, 736 sharing Weinstein's view that there can be no general constitutional objections to the Boards.

[43] Weinstein (above n 9) 544–45, commenting on arguments raised by DR Irwin, 'Freedom of Thought: The First Amendment and the Scientific Method' (2005) *Wisconsin Law Review* 1479. Hamburger does not consider it necessary to invoke a separate constitutional right to research: 'Getting Permission' (above n 35) 409.

[44] See above ch 6, s III for discussion of the constitutional right to academic freedom in the United States.

[45] In the United States public funding decisions that are clearly made to distort public debate might be open to challenge under the First Amendment: see E Barendt, *Freedom of Speech* (Oxford, Oxford University Press, 2007) 112–16.

## III. ACADEMIC FREEDOM AND
## INTELLECTUAL PROPERTY LAWS

### A. General Principles

The impact of intellectual property (IP) laws on academic freedom and its traditional values of openness and publicity has been much discussed in the last few decades. Governments have increasingly encouraged universities to acquire and exploit patents and other IP rights (IPRs), so they reap some financial reward from their medical and scientific research. In the United States, amendments to the Patent and Trade Mark Law made in 1980, known as the Bayh-Dole Act, permit universities and other non-profit organisations to hold title to patentable inventions made in the course of government-funded research;[46] previously the government claimed the title to these inventions, which might then be available for public exploitation through non-exclusive licensing.[47] As a result American universities have set up technology transfer offices for filing and managing patents arising from inventions made by their academic staff. Comparable developments have been promoted by UK governments, particularly during the 1990s.[48] As the UK National Academies Policy Advisory Group put it, 'IPRs form a complement to the direct subvention of research by government, charitable foundations and industry, acting as an incentive to investment and effort at the stage of commercialisation.'[49] Collaboration between universities and industry has grown appreciably; universities in the United Kingdom now enjoy revenue from licences granted to industrial partners for the use of patented inventions, though this income is relatively small compared to that generated by consultancy, collaborative

---

[46] Discussed in A Monotti with S Ricketson, *Universities and Intellectual Property* (Oxford, Oxford University Press, 2003) paras 6.39–6.55. This part of the chapter is much indebted to this comprehensive study of intellectual property laws and universities in Australia, the United Kingdom and the United States. For the Bayh-Dole Act, see also Eisenberg (above n 15) 196–97.

[47] Monotti (ibid) paras 6.37–6.38.

[48] For example, see Office of Science and Technology, 'Realising Our Potential' (White Paper) (Cm 2250, 1993).

[49] UK National Academies Policy Advisory Group, 'Intellectual Property and the Academic Community' (1995) para 1.4.

and contract research with business.[50] With the pressure to reduce the dependence of universities on public funding, this source of income will become appreciably more important.

These developments are perhaps hard to reconcile with the traditional norms of scientific research identified by Merton.[51] It is second nature for academic researchers to disclose their findings as soon as possible, whether formally in writing or informally at conferences, where their coherence can be discussed with other scientists. But the publication of research findings jeopardises the chance of patenting a resulting invention, for it is a fundamental requirement of patent laws that the invention is novel; in the United Kingdom novelty is determined at the date the application for a patent is filed, so the earlier publication of details concerning the invention is commonly precluded by contract until the university or sponsoring company has filed a patent application.[52] It has been argued that IPRs are incompatible with the principles of academic freedom and the values of openness, publicity and collegiality, which it promotes. Moreover, IP law, by putting a premium on applied research, which leads to patentable inventions, might also discourage scientists from engaging in pure research concerned with theories and discoveries that cannot be patented.[53]

These arguments, however, do not do justice to the point of intellectual property laws, which are themselves designed to encourage and reward scholarly and scientific research and inventiveness. This

---

[50] See Gowers Review of Intellectual Property (HM Treasury Report, 2007) para 2.27; P Wellings, 'Intellectual Property and Research Benefits', Report for the Secretary of State for Innovation, Universities and Skills (September 2008); and the Higher Education–Business and Community Interaction Survey for 2007–08, which reports total intellectual property income for UK universities of £66 million, compared with £835 million for contract research and £3335 million for consultancy. See the Higher Education Funding Council for England (HEFCE) website, http://www.hefce.ac.uk/econsoc/buscom/hebci/ (accessed 10 August 2010).

[51] Above n 14.

[52] UK Patents Act 1977, s 2. In US patent law novelty is assessed at the time of invention rather than at the time when the patent application is filed, and an applicant is allowed a 'grace period' of 12 months before the date of filing during which they are free to disclose details of the invention. See Monotti (above n 46) paras 6.75–6.111; and Eisenberg (above n 15) 216–17.

[53] For these arguments, see P Loughlan, 'Of Patents and Professors: Intellectual Property, Research Workers and Universities' (1996) 6 *European Intellectual Property Review* 345.

fundamental point is reflected in the provision of the US Constitution, authorising Congress to 'promote the Progress of Science and useful Arts, by securing for limited Times to Authors and Inventors the exclusive Right to their respective Writings and Discoveries'.[54] IP laws are based on the assumption that without them we would have less scholarly writing and fewer inventions of value to society. Copyright and patent laws therefore serve the same ends and values as academic freedom, so it would be wrong to conclude without closer argument that they are necessarily incompatible with it. Moreover, these laws themselves strike a balance between the interests of the writer or inventor on the one hand and those of the general public on the other. Patent law requires publication of the details of an invention for which a patent is claimed, and gives the inventor exclusive rights to exploit the invention for only 20 years. After that period the invention enters the public domain, and everyone is free to exploit it. The same principle applies to copyright law, under which the right holder enjoys rights for the author's life plus 70 years, after which anyone is free to copy, publish or translate it for profit.

IP laws also provide a range of defences to infringement actions, some of which are particularly valuable to universities and their academic staff. They accommodate in this way the interests of the IP rights holders and of persons who wish to copy or conduct research on the work protected by copyright or patents law. Of course, hard questions can be asked regarding whether the balance struck by existing copyright and patent laws does justice to the values of academic and research freedom. But before these issues are discussed, something should be said about the ownership of intellectual property rights; this topic raises interesting questions concerning the scope of *individual* rights or interests of university professors in academic freedom in relation to the IP claims that may be made by universities themselves.

## B. Ownership of IPRs

In United Kingdom law, an employer owns the copyright in works made by his or her employees in the course of their employment, unless

---

[54] US Constitution, Art 1, s 8, cl 8.

there is an agreement to the contrary.[55] Academics are expected by their university employers to research and to write books and articles and to discharge these requirements in the course of normal working hours, albeit mostly during vacations, when there are no teaching or administrative duties. So one might expect universities to hold the copyright in academic work. But the traditional understanding, at least among the academic profession itself, is that copyright is held by individual professors, lecturers and other employed researchers.[56] Two court decisions support this position. In *Stephenson Jordan & Harrison v MacDonald & Evans* the Court of Appeal held that an accountant rather than his employer was entitled to the copyright in his published lectures, which set out the principles of management engineering, even though these lectures concerned work for which he was employed and the employer had provided some assistance in their preparation.[57] The crucial point is that the accountant had not been engaged to write lectures. Lord Evershed, MR, said that any lecturer, especially an academic professor, was entitled to the copyright in his or her lectures; it would have been inconceivable in his view for the University of Cambridge to have claimed copyright in the lectures given by the eminent legal historian Professor Maitland.[58] This decision was followed in *Noah v Shuba*, where Mummery J held that a consultant epidemiologist was the owner of copyright in a medical guide, although it had been published and distributed by his employer, the Public Health Laboratory.[59]

These decisions are perhaps distinguishable, for academics, unlike accountants and medical consultants, are required by the terms of their employment to give lectures and to write textbooks and scholarly articles. But academic employment never obliges a professor to write on a particular topic or to publish in a particular form; academic freedom means that these are matters for the professor to determine. It would be incompatible with individual academic freedom to allow the university

---

[55]  UK Copyright, Designs and Patents Act 1988, s 11(2).

[56]  One authoritative work on copyright law is, however, sceptical whether the traditional understanding is correct: H Laddie, P Prescott and M Vitoria, *The Modern Law of Copyright and Designs*, 3rd edn (London, Butterworths, 2000) para 21.30.

[57]  [1951] 69 RPC 10.

[58]  Ibid, 18.

[59]  [1991] FSR 14. See also the decision in Hong Kong recognising individual academic ownership of copyright: *Linda Chih Ling Koo v Lam Tai-hing* [1992] 2 HKLR 314, 325–27.

to claim copyright, for that would give it the right to determine when and where academic work is published, or indeed to prevent publication altogether.[60] Individual academics are also better placed than their employers to decide when it is appropriate, say, to allow their work to be translated and by whom, or whether to allow extracts from it to be reproduced in another work. These principles are generally recognised by universities in the United Kingdom.[61] On the other hand, universities have a stronger case to claim copyright in Internet-based materials that are prepared for distance learning courses; in these circumstances, the materials are typically commissioned by a university itself, and it is probably in a better position than an individual academic to exploit IPRs by licensing use of distance learning packages.[62]

Similar principles have traditionally been applied in the United States.[63] While under the 'work for hire' doctrine an employer is normally considered the author of works prepared by employees within the scope of their employment,[64] an 'academic exception' principle has been recognised;[65] the 'work for hire' doctrine does not apply to university professors and other academics. Academic freedom is responsible for this exception, for the freedom means that universities do not supervise the work of their academic staff. It would therefore be anomalous to regard this work as within the scope of the 'work for hire' doctrine. Moreover, to give university employers copyright would also

[60] WR Cornish, 'Rights in University Innovations: The Herchel Smith Lecture for 1991' (1992) 1 *European Intellectual Property Review* 13.

[61] See Oxford University Statutes, Statute XVI, cl 7 providing that the University does not claim copyright in books, articles and lectures, apart from those specifically commissioned by the University; Ordinance of Cambridge University Council of 27 July 2005, Intellectual Property Rights, reg 7; UCL Staff IPR Policy, para 2. See also evidence of University of Warwick to the Gowers Review (above n 50) acknowledging that for textbooks and journal articles, the 'University is content for academic creators to retain ownership of copyright … in the best traditions of academic freedom.'

[62] Royal Society, 'Keeping Science Open: The Effects of Intellectual Property Policy on the Conduct of Science' (2003) para 4.12. UCL claims copyright in teaching material of this kind: see its Financial Regulations, July 2007, reg 40.

[63] For a critical discussion of this area of law in the United States, see C McSherry, *Who Owns Academic Work?* (Cambridge, MA, Harvard University Press, 2001).

[64] See now the Copyright Act of 1976, s 201(b). 'Works for hire' are defined by s 101.

[65] Some authority was provided for this position by *Williams v Weisser* 273 Cal App 2d 726 (Cal App 1969).

inhibit professors' freedom to move from one job to another, keeping control over use of their reading lists, lectures notes and scholarly publications.[66] The 'academic exception' may have survived the reform of the copyright laws in 1976. Although the exception is not explicitly stated in the 1976 legislation, two subsequent Circuit Court decisions have upheld the copyright claims of individual academics and teachers.[67] In the second of these decisions, Circuit Judge Posner pointed out that there was no indication that Congress had intended to do away with the 'academic exception', and further it could be argued that academic articles and teaching guides were not necessarily 'prepared *for* the employer' (emphasis added) as stipulated in section 201(b) of the Copyright Act of 1976, which provides that the employer is the author of 'work for hire'.[68]

German law also recognises the individual claims of university professors to copyright in their lecture notes and their academic publications. The teaching and research freedom covered by Article 5(3) of the Grundgesetz gives them freedom to determine whether, when and how they publish these materials, and it would be incompatible with these entitlements to treat them as materials that they are required to produce in fulfilment of their employment obligations. For copyright purposes academic works are regarded as 'free works', over which the individual author holds copyright, rather than as works that employees are contractually obliged to make for their employers.[69] The force of academic freedom is therefore widely recognised in this context. Academics prize their individual copyright highly, even if often the journals in which they publish require them to assign it.[70] Further, there are sound practical

---

[66] RC Dreyfuss, 'The Creative Employee and the Copyright Act of 1976' (1987) 54 *University of Chicago Law Review* 590, 597.

[67] *Weinstein v University of Illinois* 811 F 2d 1091 (7th Cir 1987). The University only claimed copyright in a narrow range of circumstances; its policy otherwise was to allow it to be retained by individual professors. See also *Hays v Sony Corporation of America* 847 F2d 412 (7th Cir 1988).

[68] *Hays v Sony* (ibid) 416.

[69] G Schricker in M Hartmer and H Detmer (eds), *Hochschulrecht* (Heidelberg, Müller, 2004) ch 9, I, paras 55–81, commenting on Urheberrechtsgesetz (Copyright law statute) of 1965, as amended, s 43.

[70] Universities, if not individual authors, resent this practice, as it compels them to pay for a licence from the publisher to reproduce copyright material for teaching and other purposes: see Royal Society, 'Keeping Science Open' (above n 62) paras 4.4–4.8.

reasons for rejecting any claim universities might make to copyright in the books and articles produced by their academic staff; it would be very difficult for them in practice to control the exercise of the copyright in potentially several thousand copyright works.[71]

In contrast, academic freedom arguments seem often to have played relatively little part in determining the ownership of inventions that may be patented.[72] The UK Patents Act 1977 confers ownership of an employee invention on the employer, if 'it was made in the course of normal duties' or in the course of 'specifically assigned duties', and the circumstances in either event were 'such that an invention might reasonably be expected to result from the carrying out of [the employee's] duties';[73] an invention also belongs to an employer if it is made in the course of the employee's duties and, at the time of making the invention, the employee had a special obligation to further the employer's interests. Otherwise, an invention belongs to the employee rather than the employer.[74] These rules allow plenty of room for argument in disputes between a university and its academic staff over the right to apply for a patent in respect of an invention made by a researcher in the course of his or her work.[75]

In practice today UK universities usually claim the ownership of patentable inventions made by academic staff in the course of their employment (and also sometimes to inventions made by students in the course of, or incidentally to, their studies).[76] Their claims may be enforceable, as against individual members of academic staff, by

[71] For a comprehensive discussion of the practical arguments, see Monotti (above n 46) paras 7.100–7.119.

[72] But see the speech of Professor S Deakin in the Senate-House on 15 October 2002 opposing the proposal to give the University of Cambridge the right to apply for patents in inventions made by its academic staff: *Cambridge University Reporter*, 30 October 2002.

[73] S 39(1)(a). For a leading modern case on interpretation of Patents Act 1977, s 39, see *LIFFE Administration and Management v Pinkava* [2007] 4 All ER 981, CA.

[74] S 39(2).

[75] In *Greater Glasgow Health Board's Application* [1996] RPC 207, Jacob J upholding the individual claim of a Registrar in an Opthalmology Department to ownership of an invention for an optical device, conceived at home and not during clinical work, applied the copyright principles in *Stephenson Jordan & Harrison* (above n 57).

[76] Eg, Oxford University Statute XVI, cls 5 and 6; Cambridge University Ordinance of 27 July 2005, reg 6. For a discussion of UK university provisions, see Monotti (above n 46) paras 7.80–7.85.

virtue of provisions in Staff Regulations that are incorporated into the terms of the contracts of employment;[77] these provisions may require researchers to notify the university of patentable inventions and recognise university ownership of inventions made during the course of their research. Interestingly, the Cambridge University Ordinance governing intellectual property rights explicitly recognises the freedom of university staff to disseminate the results of their research 'as they wish in accordance with normal academic practice',[78] although the University will lose any right to patent any invention made in the course of it; as a result of the publication the invention cannot satisfy the requirement of novelty. The provision meets any objection that university ownership of a patent abridges the freedom of speech and academic freedom of individual researchers.

There are practical arguments for recognising university rights to ownership of patentable inventions. Unlike copyright, patents require a formal application process, which requires considerable expertise and financial commitment beyond the scope of almost all research scientists. Secondly, it is right that universities should be able to exploit the monopoly rights conferred by patents when they have provided the laboratories, equipment and other facilities used in the course of making the invention. The employee inventor's interests may sometimes be safeguarded by statutory rights to 'compensation', a fair share of outstanding benefits derived by the university from its exploitation of the patented invention.[79] In practice, university regulations frequently make provision for the distribution of profits between the inventor, the department in which he or she works and the university itself.[80]

A similar position exists in the United States. Whatever the strict legal position with regard to the ownership of inventions made by academic staff,[81] universities almost invariably claim ownership of patentable inventions.[82] The Bayh-Dole Act of 1980, which enables universities

---

[77] Eg, UCL Staff IPR Policy, para 4.
[78] Ordinance of 27 July 2005, reg 4.
[79] Patents Act 1977, ss 40–43.
[80] Eg, Oxford Regulations for the Administration of the University's Intellectual Property Policy: Council Regulations 7 of 2002, as amended, reg 7(4); UCL Staff IPR policy, Annex 2.
[81] Monotti (above n 46) para 5.63.
[82] Ibid, paras 7.86–7.97.

to exploit intellectual property rights arising from federally funded research, encourages them to make these claims. A university often requires academic staff under employment contract to assign to it any patent rights to inventions made with the use of university equipment.[83] But academic freedom is recognised by provisions acknowledging the freedom of university professors and researchers to place their inventions in the public domain, provided this course does not violate any contract with a sponsor funding the research.[84]

In an important decision,[85] the Federal Court of Australia has held recently that it would be incompatible with academic freedom and the special circumstances of academic employment to imply a term into a medical research professor's contract, under which the ownership of patentable inventions made during the course of his work belonged to the university. The Court emphasised that the defendant had no duty under his contract of employment to invent anything, that he was free to publish the results of his research at conferences and in academic literature, even though that would destroy the patentability of an invention, and that he was expected with his collaborators to solicit funding for his research outside the university. In the absence of any clear statutory provisions or express terms in a contract of employment, a science or medical professor may therefore still be entitled to claim the ownership of patented inventions made during the course of his or her work.

In this area the development of German law is particularly striking. Under the former Employee Inventors' Law (Arbeitnehmer Erfinder Gesetz (ArbEG)), inventions made by academic staff were considered 'free' inventions, owned by the individual professor or researcher, in derogation from the usual rule that inventions made by an employee as a result of discharging his or her duties belong to the employer.[86] This professorial privilege could be regarded as stemming from the scientific freedom, or freedom of research, guaranteed by Article 5(3) of the Basic

---

[83] RC Dreyfuss, 'Collaborative Research: Conflicts on Authorship, Ownership, and Accountability' (2000) 53 *Vanderbilt Law Review* 1161, 1184–85.

[84] Stanford University Research Policy Handbook, Document 5.1, Patent Policy, A 3.

[85] *University of Western Australia v Gray* (above n 1), Full Court decision upholding the decision of French J (2008) 246 ALR 603, [2008] FCA 498.

[86] ArbEG, s 4.

Law, though the usual view is that this freedom does not cover the economic exploitation of research findings. As a result of an amendment to this Law in 2002, this privilege has been abrogated.[87] Like other employees, university staff must report inventions to the university, which can itself file for a patent.[88] The amendment was intended to stimulate the exploitation of patents by universities, thereby providing them with another source of income.

However, university staff do retain some special rights. Under section 42 of the revised Employee Inventors' Law, an individual inventor is entitled to disclose his or her invention in the course of teaching and research work, provided he or she has given the university due notice, usually two months before the disclosure.[89] On the basis of constitutional rights, an inventor is free not to publicise the invention and then has no obligation to report it to the university.[90] The inventor also has a non-exclusive licence to use the invention in the course of teaching and research work—a wider freedom than that conferred by the Patents Law itself for further research on patented inventions.[91] All these privileges can be attributed to the constitutional right to freedom of research and represent a compromise between this right and the interests of university employers.[92]

The Director of a Department for Bone Surgery has challenged the requirement to notify the university of his intention to disclose his invention—a device for knee surgery—to his students, on the ground that it inhibited his freedom to discuss his research spontaneously. The requirement in his view infringed his rights under Article 5(3). The Bundesgerichtshof (Supreme Civil Court), however, rejected this argument, holding that Section 42(1) struck an appropriate balance between his freedom of research on the one hand and, on the other hand, the

---

[87] A von Falck and C Schmalz, 'University Inventions: Classification and Remuneration in Germany, the Netherlands, France, the United Kingdom, the United States and Japan' (2005) 36 *International Review of Intellectual Property and Competition Law* 912, 912–19.

[88] ArbEG, s 5.

[89] ArbEG, s 42(1). For commentary on the provision, see R Krasser in Hartmer and Detmer (eds) (above n 69) ch 9, II, paras 52–87.

[90] ArbEG, s 42(2).

[91] ArbEG, s 42(3). See below s III(C) for discussion of the provisions of the Patents Law concerning research.

[92] Von Falck and Schmalz (above n 87) 916–17.

university's own institutional guarantee under Article 5(3) and its freedom to exploit its patent rights, now vital to its economic prosperity.[93]
The decision has been criticised on the ground that the university's
ability to take out a patent depends on the scientist's right to disclose
his or her research findings. The scientist's freedom to discuss them
spontaneously should be protected, even when it is exercised without
regard to any impact on their commercial exploitation. Further, the
Bundesgerichtshof was arguably wrong to conclude that reliance on
patent rights enhanced the institutional autonomy of universities.[94]

## C. Defences to Infringement Actions

The terms of some defences to actions for infringement of copyright or
of a patent are clearly influenced by the values associated with academic
and research freedom, and these freedoms can be invoked in their
interpretation. Most obviously this is the case with the defence provided
by the UK Copyright, Designs, and Patents Act 1988 of 'fair dealing
with a literary, dramatic, musical or artistic work for the purposes of
research for a non-commercial purpose'[95] or for private study.[96] These
provisions protect the freedom of an academic to copy substantial
extracts from another's work to further his or her own work, but not to
market these extracts as an examination or study guide for students.[97]
Confining the 'fair dealing' defence to non-commercial research is on
one view odd, given that academics are now encouraged to exploit their
work commercially;[98] but the academic freedom argument for permit-
ting a scholar to use another's work for commercial research purposes
is thin. A number of other statutory defences concern permitted acts

---

[93] Decision of September 18, 2007, GRUR 2008, 140.

[94] A Reetz, 'Die Regelung des S 42, Nr 1 ArbEG auf dem "verfassungsrechtli-
chen Prufstand"' (2008) 41 *Wissenschaftsrecht* 206, esp 218 and 224.

[95] S 29(1) as amended by the Copyright and Related Rights Regulations 2003,
SI 2003/2498.

[96] S 29(1C).

[97] *University of London Press Ltd v University Tutorial Press Ltd* [1916] 2 Ch 601, 613
(Peterson J); *Sillito v McGraw Hill* [1983] FSR 545, 558 (Judge Mervyn Davies, QC).

[98] The Supreme Court of Canada has ruled that the equivalent defence in
Canadian law is not confined to non-commercial research: *CCH Canadian Ltd v Law
Society of Upper Canada* [2004] 1SCR 339.

for the purpose of instruction or examinations; for anthologies of short passages from works intended for educational use; and the recording of broadcasts by educational establishments for their educational purposes.[99] But these provisions are concerned more with general educational purposes rather than with teaching and research at universities and academic freedom.

The US 'fair use' defence, now provided by section 107 of the Copyright Act of 1976, can be invoked when there is fair use of a work for the purposes of, among others, teaching, scholarship or research. Among the factors specified in this section to be considered when determining fair use is whether it was commercial or for a non-profit educational purpose. Applying these criteria, it has been held that the copying of journal articles for the use of researchers working for Texaco did not constitute 'fair use', although a comparable quantity of copying by a university professor might well be covered by the defence.[100] Insofar as academic freedom is covered by the First Amendment free speech guarantee,[101] the fair use defence should be interpreted in conformity with the freedom and its underlying values.[102] Academic freedom requires a generous understanding of the scope of the defence, even when it entails some restriction on the economic interests of the IPR holder.

UK and German patent laws allow a defence for an action for infringement in some circumstances, notably when an otherwise infringing act is 'done privately and for purposes which are not commercial' or is 'done for experimental purposes relating to the subject matter of the invention'.[103] Both these defences promote the values of academic study and research. The second of them enables further research on a patented drug or other medicinal device to improve its efficacy and eventually make and market a better product.[104] It is not confined to university or academic research but can be invoked by

[99] Copyright, Designs, and Patents Act 1988, ss 32–35.

[100] *American Geophysical Union v Texaco, Inc* 60 F3d 913, 916 (2nd Cir 1994).

[101] See the discussion above in ch 6, s III.

[102] M Ryan, 'Fair Use and Academic Expression: Rhetoric, Reality, and Restriction on Academic Freedom' (1998) 8 *Cornell Journal of Law and Public Policy* 541.

[103] UK Patents Act 1977, s 60(5)(a) and (b); German Patent Law of 1980, BGBl 1981 1 S 1, s 11.

[104] See the Gowers Review (above n 50) para 4.4.

industrial researchers who might want eventually to patent a superior product.[105] In its leading decision in the Clinical Experiments (*Klinische Versuche*) case, the German Federal Supreme Court ruled that the Patent Act provision allowing experimental trials should be construed in accordance with the freedom of research guaranteed by Article 5(3) of the Grundgesetz; it would be wrong in view of this freedom and the social obligations imposed on property owners to allow unlimited protection for patent rights when that would impede further technical development.[106] Experimental clinical trials might therefore be conducted to see whether a licensed drug could be used for a wider range of conditions than that for which it had originally been marketed.

In comparison, US courts have interpreted the common law 'experimental use' defence very narrowly.[107] In the leading case, *Madey v Duke University*,[108] the Federal Circuit Court of Appeals ruled it should be construed to cover only tests conducted purely to satisfy idle curiosity or for abstract inquiry. It would be wrong to allow a university the benefit of the defence, when it conducted research on a patented product to further its business objectives, which included the education of students. It was wrong to attach any weight to the educational, non-profit character of Duke University. In effect, as Duke argued when it unsuccessfully petitioned the Supreme Court,[109] the ruling stopped any use of the defence by research universities and inhibited further research on patented inventions. Property rights were given priority over academic freedom. In the United Kingdom there is little relevant authority on the scope of the patent research exception; the Gowers Review of Intellectual Property suggested that the lack of clarity inhibited further research on patented products and recommended that the scope of the exception should be clarified.[110]

---

[105] For a full discussion of European jurisprudence on these points, see WR Cornish, 'Experimental Use of Patented Inventions in European Community States' (1998) *International Review of Intellectual Property and Competition Law* 735.

[106] (1995) BGHZ 130, 259, 273 (in English [1997] RPC 623, 642–43). The ruling was upheld by the Constitutional Court, NJW 2001, 1784, though that Court did not explicitly refer to the guarantee of research freedom under Art 5(3).

[107] For discussion of the principles underlying the exception, see Eisenberg (above n 15) 220–26.

[108] 307 F3d 1351 (Fed Cir 2002).

[109] Certiorari denied by the Supreme Court, 539 US 958 (2003).

[110] Above n 50, para 4.6.

IV. RESEARCH CONTRACTS

## A. The Dangers of University–Industry Collaboration

In November 1988 the University of California at Berkeley signed a contract with Novartis, a Swiss pharmaceutical company and producer of genetically modified crops, under which Novartis agreed to provide $25 million to fund basic research in Berkeley's Department of Plant and Microbial Biology.[111] In return the University granted Novartis first rights to negotiate licences for the exploitation of up to a third of the Department's discoveries—including those arising from publicly funded research—and allocated the company two of the five seats on the Department's research committee, which allocated research funds for the faculty. More than half the faculty thought the deal would have an adverse impact on academic freedom. One issue of particular concern to them was that Novartis could require the postponement of publication of any research it funded for up to four months; normally, commercial sponsors of research insist on a short delay in the publication of its results of one or two months, in order for the sponsor (or the university) to take out a patent on an invention made in the course of research. Other members of the Faculty defended the deal, as did the Chancellor of Berkeley, Robert Berdahl, who pointed out the increasing dependence of universities on corporate rather than state funding.

The Berkeley–Novartis deal is often considered emblematic of the dangers, as well as the advantages, of collaboration between universities and industry— the 'Academic-Industrial Complex', as it was termed by Eyal Press and Jennifer Washburn in their classic article, 'The Kept University'.[112] This section of the chapter is concerned with the impact of this collaboration on academic freedom and whether legal challenges can be made to the restraints imposed by provisions in research contracts. Commercial sponsors of research—particularly, but not only pharmaceutical companies—may impose significant constraints on the

[111] For a full account, see J Washburn, *University Inc: The Corporate Corruption of Higher Education* (New York, Basic Books, 2006) 3–17.

[112] E Press and J Washburn, 'The Kept University' (2000) 285 *The Atlantic Monthly* 3, 39–54. For general discussion of these issues, see D Bok, *Universities in the Marketplace* (Princeton, Princeton University Press, 2005) esp chs 4 and 8; and M Robertson, 'Research and Academic Freedom' in J Dawson and N Peart (eds), *The Law of Research* (Dunedin, Otago University Press, 2003) 27.

freedom of university researchers to publish their findings. This is not just a matter of requiring publication to be delayed for a few months while the sponsor files for a patent but can sometimes extend to a permanent suppression of research findings, the disclosure of which might damage the sponsor's commercial reputation.[113]

Researchers may also claim that they are denied access by a sponsoring company to the full data necessary for them to do their research properly and to substantiate the claims that the company has made or would like to make for the effectiveness of a drug or other product.[114] In this context, it is important to point out the phenomenon of the 'ghost-writing' of scientific articles; articles bearing the names of distinguished medical researchers may be drafted by company scientists and do not therefore necessarily represent the apparent authors' own conclusions. The names of university scientists are added to give the article scientific credibility.[115] While some academics protest against these practices, others may tolerate them, perhaps because they have a financial interest in a sponsoring company or more generally because they want to keep on good terms with it. These links give rise to conflicts of interest with potentially damaging implications for the integrity of research.[116] To meet the dangers to academic freedom posed by these practices, the International Committee of Medical Journal Editors has from 2001 required all authors and participants in the peer review process to disclose any relationship, for example, with a pharmaceutical company,

[113] DG Nathan and DJ Weatherall, 'Academic Freedom in Clinical Research' (2002) 347 *New England Journal of Medicine* 1368; R Steinbrook, 'Gag Clauses in Clinical-Trial Agreements' (2005) 352 *New England Journal of Medicine* 2160.

[114] For a general discussion of this and other restrictions, see S Krimsky, 'Publication Bias, Data Ownership, and the Funding Effect in Science: Threats to the Integrity of Biomedical Research' in W Wagner and R Steinzor (eds), *Rescuing Science from Politics* (New York, Cambridge University Press, 2006) 61. See also the discussion of the Blumsohn affair, below s IV(D).

[115] The House of Commons Health Committee has drawn attention to the influence of pharmaceutical companies on medical journals: Fourth Report, 'The Influence of the Pharmaceutical Industry' HC (2004–05) 42-1 [196]–[201]. See also G Edmond, 'Judging the Scientific and Medical Literature: Some Legal Implications of Changes to Biomedical Research and Publication' (2008) 28 *Oxford Journal of Legal Studies* 523, 542–43.

[116] Washburn, *University Inc* (above n 111) esp chs 4 and 5; Edmond (ibid) 534–39.

that could be regarded as raising a conflict of interest;[117] editors may require authors to declare that they had unfettered access to the data and that they controlled the decision to publish the research.[118]

In the view of some distinguished scientists and medical researchers, collaboration between universities and industry poses significant risks for academic freedom.[119] Publication constraints clearly infringe the academic freedom to publish when an individual researcher or a science team decides this is most appropriate, though these constraints may be acceptable if they require a short delay to enable a patent to be taken out. But there are other, less obvious dangers. Commercial sponsors might influence the trial design and research methodology or, as already mentioned, assert control over research data.[120] They are also more inclined to finance applied research that may lead to patentable inventions than they are to support basic scientific research, which is less likely to pay commercial dividends. As a result research priorities may become distorted, as scientists come under pressure from their universities to engage in research from which their employers, as well as the sponsors, benefit financially.

On the other hand, some commentators support growing links between the academy and industry,[121] and these links are encouraged by governments. Further, it is understandable that sponsors want to stop the publication of papers or articles that might undermine, perhaps wrongly, public confidence in their products and discourage investment by them in research and development. Their interest in commercial confidentiality is recognised and well protected in law. Industries that cannot rely on university partners to honour confidentiality will

---

[117] R Smith, 'Maintaining the Integrity of the Scientific Record: Editors Make a Move' (2001) 323 *British Medical Journal* 588; and R Smith, 'Medical Journals and Pharmaceutical Companies: Uneasy Bedfellows' (2003) 326 *British Medical Journal* 1202. Richard Smith was Editor of the *BMJ* for a number of years. See also Edmond (above n 115) 546–49.

[118] See ICMJE Guidelines on conflicts of interest: http://www.icmje.org/ethical_4conflicts.html (accessed 10 August 2010).

[119] T Bodenheimer, 'Uneasy Alliance: Clinical Investigators and the Pharmaceutical Industry' (2000) 342 *New England Journal of Medicine* 1539; D Healy, 'In the Grip of the Python: Conflicts at the University–Industry Interface' (2002) 9 *Science and Engineering Ethics* 59; and Nathan and Weatherall (above n 113).

[120] Bodenheimer (ibid).

[121] TP Stossel, 'Regulating Academic–Industrial Research Relationships: Solving Problems or Stifling Progress?' (2005) 353 *New England Journal of Medicine* 1060.

increasingly conduct their research in-house or through contract research organisations, to which the principles of academic freedom are inapplicable.[122] But scientific freedom, as understood in Germany, may cover to some extent such research.[123]

While the impact of contractual restraints on academic freedom and freedom of research is clear, it is much less obvious how they can be challenged. These legal questions are explored after discussion of three well-known affairs in which academic freedom was imperilled as a result of commercial pressure, or at least of its threat. There have been many more cases, some of them fully discussed in the literature.[124] In the view of Sir David Weatherall, former Regius Professor of Medicine at Oxford University, they represent the 'tip of an iceberg',[125] not occasional, atypical episodes.

## B. The Nancy Olivieri Case[126]

Dr Nancy Olivieri, a clinical researcher at the University of Toronto and specialist at the Hospital for Sick Children (HSC), undertook clinical trials of the drug deferiprone, manufactured by Apotex for the treatment of thalassemia, a blood disease. Two contracts agreed in 1993 and 1995 between Apotex and Dr Olivieri and her collaborators contained confidentiality clauses, under which the company had a right to control communication of the trial data for either a year or three years after the conclusion of the agreement, though it appears that this clause was not incorporated in another contract for continuation of the pilot study. After initially favourable results, Dr Olivieri noted some adverse reactions to the drug and wanted to notify volunteers for the clinical trials. The Research Ethics Board advised her to alter the information

---

[122] For the growth of contract research organisations, see Bodenheimer (above n 119); Steinbrook (above n 113) 1261; and Edmond (above n 115) 532–33.
[123] See above ch 5, s VII.
[124] For a short account of some of these cases, see Robertson (above n 112) 38–41. For a fuller treatment, see Washburn, *University Inc* (above n 111) esp chs 1 and 4.
[125] Communication to the author, 24 June 2009.
[126] See Washburn, *University Inc* (above n 111) 123–24; Nathan and Weatherall (above n 113); and A Schafer, 'Biomedical Conflicts of Interest: Learning from the Cases of Nancy Olivieri and David Healy' (2004) 30 *Journal of Medical Ethics* 8.

given them. Apotex then terminated the contract in 1996 and warned Dr Olivieri that she remained bound by the confidentiality provision and should not present her findings at conferences. Despite these warnings, she did present them at conferences and published them in *The New England Journal of Medicine.*

A disturbing feature of this affair was that Dr Olivieri did not receive support from HSC or the University of Toronto. Indeed, she was dismissed from her position as Director of the hemoglobinopathy programme at HSC. It emerged subsequently that the University and HSC were expecting a donation of $20 million from Apotex, and there was a possibility of a further, larger donation later. After protests from a number of medical professors and researchers, eventually a settlement was negotiated between HSC and Dr Olivieri, and she was reinstated as Director of the programme. The Ontario College of Physicians and Surgeons eventually vindicated her at the end of 2001, finding that none of the allegations had any substance.

The Canadian Association of University Teachers (CAUT) commissioned an independent inquiry into the affair. Its report, published in October 2001, found that the confidentiality clause was inappropriate, for it could be used by sponsors to suppress information about the risks to participants in clinical trials; further, the threats by Apotex to enforce it infringed Dr Olivieri's academic freedom.[127] That freedom is connected to the ethical duty of researchers to alert doctors around the world to the risks of taking a drug. The Report concluded that the case 'demonstrated the importance to the public interest of ensuring that in hospitals affiliated with universities, … staff who hold academic appointments have the right to academic freedom and its protection'.[128] That view was shared by David Nathan and David Weatherall in their article on the implications of the episode: institutions should support the right of faculty to publish their research, particularly if they reveal doubts about the safety of a drug.[129]

---

[127]   CAUT, *The Olivieri Report* (Toronto, Lorimer, 2001) s C, paras 13 and 35.
[128]   Ibid, para 73. For CAUT comments on further litigation by Apotex against Dr Olivieri, see the CAUT website, http://www.caut.ca/news_details.asp?nid=1197&page=490 (accessed 21 April 2010).
[129]   Above n 113, 1370–71.

## C. The David Healy Case[130]

Coincidentally, the University of Toronto also featured in the second case. David Healy accepted its offer of a post as a Clinical Director at its Centre for Addiction and Mental Health (CAMH) together with a Professorship in the Department of Psychiatry. Healy had become a strong critic of the Prozac class of antidepressants, the use of which had, in his view, caused some of their takers to kill or commit suicide.[131] In November 2000, less than a year before he was due to take up his new post in Toronto, he gave a lecture at CAMH, which was apparently generally well received. But barely a week later, he received an email from its Director, Dr Goldbloom, to the effect that the job offer had been withdrawn; there was not a 'good fit' between Healy and CAMH. Healy suspected that an influential pharmacologist, Professor Charles Nemeroff, with strong links to pharmaceutical companies, had reminded CAMH of the financial support they provided the Centre.

Healy took proceedings against both CAMH and the University for breach of contract—apparently not an absolutely straightforward claim as no contracts had been signed[132]—and for defamation. He also sued for interference with his right to academic freedom, in this way seeking to establish a novel common law tort.[133] A number of scientists petitioned in support, defending Healy's academic freedom. The university on the other hand denied its decision had anything to do with academic freedom; it suggested that Healy had expressed extreme views—though they were no different from those he had held when he was appointed—and he would not have enjoyed the support of his new colleagues. It is unlikely that Healy would have won on this point had the case gone to court, for courts are reluctant to establish new torts, particularly if their contours are far from clear. The claim was eventually settled in 2002. Healy was given a visiting professorship for three years, and the university acknowledged its support for the free expression of

[130] Washburn, *University Inc* (above n 111) 122; and David Healy's own account, 'Conflicting Interests in Toronto' (2002) 45 *Perspectives in Biology and Medicine* 250.
[131] Healy gave evidence in a number of civil actions brought in respect of deaths following the taking of antidepressants: Healy (ibid) 252, 255–56.
[132] Communication from Healy's legal adviser, Peter Rosenthal, 10 July 2009.
[133] No reliance was placed on the Canadian Charter of Rights and Freedoms, which does not explicitly recognise academic freedom.

critical views. In return Healy accepted assurances by the university that pharmaceutical companies had not put direct pressure on it to rescind his appointment,[134] though he is sure that this decision was taken after they had expressed unease with his views.


## D. The Aubrey Blumsohn Case[135]

In 2002 Dr Aubrey Blumsohn, a senior lecturer and honorary consultant in bone metabolism, and Professor Richard Eastell of Sheffield University (the 'investigators') were engaged by Procter & Gamble to work on a study of its drug Actonel, used in the treatment of osteoporosis by increasing bone density and reducing fractures. Eastell had been involved in earlier studies of the drug; he was also chair of the Procter & Gamble UK scientific advisory board. The parties to the contract were Procter & Gamble and Sheffield University, but its terms were accepted by the two investigators. Blumsohn and his colleagues reviewed blood and urine samples, 'blinded' from knowing which patients had taken Actonel and which were on a placebo; they compiled laboratory data, which were sent to Procter & Gamble for statistical analysis and would show how monitoring tests could be used to assess the drug's effectiveness. Using such monitoring tests, other researchers had found that the Procter & Gamble drug was less effective than other drugs on the market.

Blumsohn asked Procter & Gamble for data access codes so he could independently check the analysis of the raw data he had supplied the company. In his view the contract, as well as basic principles of medical ethics, entitled him to this information: under the contract the investigators were required to include data, as well as their interpretation, in their final report. Procter & Gamble initially refused access but subsequently granted access to partial data analyses, which Blumsohn

[134] For the settlement, see (2002) 324 (7347) *British Medical Journal* 1177.

[135] This account is based on articles by J Revill in *The Observer*, 4 and 11 December 2005; J Washburn, 'Rent-a-Researcher: Did a British University Sell Out to Procter & Gamble?', available at http://www.slate.com/id/2133061/ (accessed 10 August 2010); and Blumsohn's own account, 'Authorship, Ghost-Science Access to Data and Control of the Pharmaceutical Literature: Who Stands Behind the Word?', available at http://www.aaas.org/spp/sfrl/per/per46.htm (accessed 12 August 2010).

considered misleading. His doubts about the effectiveness of Actonel in reducing bone fractures were reinforced. In the meantime Procter & Gamble drafted 'ghost-written' research papers and statistical reports for Blumsohn to present to medical conferences; he was named as the principal author. The company insisted throughout this time that it was entitled to keep its full databases confidential and indeed that this was standard industry practice.

Throughout 2003 and 2004 Blumsohn repeatedly raised his concerns with Professor Eastell. This did not help matters. Eastell told him that the University had to watch its relationship with Procter & Gamble because the firm provided substantial support for the Sheffield Medical Centre. Nor were representations to other university officers, including the Vice-Chancellor, at this time Professor Robert Boucher, any more productive. But when in the summer of 2005 Blumsohn announced his intention to discuss the affair with medical journalists, the University threatened disciplinary action. He was suspended from his duties in September, on the grounds that he had refused to comply with management instructions by briefing journalists and that his conduct over the preceding months had been incompatible with the duties of office. The dispute between Sheffield University and Dr Blumsohn was eventually settled at the end of March 2006. He left the university for an undisclosed sum as part of a confidential settlement; but a gagging clause in an earlier offer, which would have prevented him from discussing the affair at all, was removed.

One or two other elements of the episode should be mentioned. In December 2005, reference was made to it in the course of a debate in the House of Commons on the increasing influence of the pharmaceutical industry on medical research and publications.[136] Early the following year, Procter & Gamble revised its policy and guaranteed medical researchers full access to research data.[137] It also allowed investigators access to data codes, which enabled them to see that the analysis did not support the conclusions in the 'ghost-written' research papers. Professor Eastell himself subsequently admitted that he had not had full access to data in earlier research projects.[138]

---

[136]  Hansard HC vol 440 col 1028 (8 December 2005).
[137]  J Revill, *The Observer*, 26 February 2006.
[138]  *Times Higher Education*, 12 October 2007, 4.

In this case the issue was the compatibility with academic freedom of restrictions on researchers' access to full data under the control of the drug company that financed their research. Even if the data are the property of the company and their disclosure to the public might infringe commercial confidentiality, access restrictions mean that academic researchers cannot properly vouch for the accuracy of their published conclusions or be held responsible for them. The practice of ghost-writing is objectionable for similar reasons. Such a publication lacks the fundamental requirement of authenticity; it is not the work of the scientist whose name it bears. Academic freedom is abused in these circumstances. The freedom is valuable only insofar as it is exercised to discover truth,[139] and that requirement is not met when 'ghost-written' articles are published on the basis of incomplete research.

### E. Legal Discussion

There are a number of obstacles to a successful challenge to any contractual restraints imposed by drugs companies and other sponsors of research on the exercise of academic freedom. In the United States constitutional academic freedom cannot be asserted against private persons and institutions because of the 'state action' doctrine; only public bodies are bound to respect constitutional rights.[140] The principles of professional academic freedom have been accepted by universities but not by corporations financing research, so it could hardly be argued that they are incorporated into the terms of research contracts. Further, if academic researchers become parties to or acknowledge as binding the terms of onerous research contracts, it may be argued that they have waived or surrendered any right to academic freedom they might otherwise have claimed.

Comparable difficulties arise in the United Kingdom. Even if strictly only a university and a commercial organisation are the parties to a research contract, say, a Material Transfer Agreement (MTA),[141]

---

[139] See above ch 3, s III.

[140] Above ch 6, s I.

[141] Under MTAs samples are transferred either by a university or by a commercial drugs or other company, to university researchers for them to use in their research.

individual researchers or investigators generally sign their acceptance of its terms. Typically, an MTA contains provisions about confidentiality that require the university and the investigators not to disclose to others technical and business information given to them during the course of the contract. This obligation may subsist for a number of years after termination of the research contract.[142] Further, the university is normally required by the MTA to provide the sponsoring company with a manuscript of any proposed presentation or publication for a period—perhaps as long as 60 days—before submission, to give the company time to secure patent protection, though in the course of negotiating the contract the university may try to reduce that period, say, to 30 or 45 days. The company also normally claims the right to review any manuscript and to insist on changes to protect its confidential information.[143]

Investigators could not easily challenge provisions of this kind. Even if they are not formally party to an agreement, by acknowledging its terms they would be taken to have waived their academic freedom. English courts would almost certainly enforce the contract rather than accept that academic freedom justified a breach of its terms. It is unlikely that they would be persuaded to accept a new head of public policy, under which terms incompatible with freedom of research and publication would not be enforced. In this context, the academic freedom claim would be a moral argument but not one of legal force.[144] On the other hand, a third party, for example, a journalist, to whom an academic researcher had disclosed confidential information or sent a copy of their proposed publication, might be able to take advantage of a public interest defence if he or she were sued for breach of confidence. That defence could almost certainly be invoked when, say, confidential information was disclosed in order to warn members of the public that

---

[142] For example, Blumsohn was required under the Procter & Gamble contract to keep such information confidential for ten years beyond the term of the agreement.

[143] Universities may try to reduce the severity of these terms, but some companies, such as GlaxoSmithKline, may treat them as nonnegotiable: communication from Alex Weedon, Legal Affairs and IP Manager of UCL Business, 9 July 2009.

[144] Cf Schafer (above n 126) 11.

a drug whose properties had been researched was unreliable or had harmful side-effects.[145]

It might be easier to invoke scientific freedom arguments in this context in Germany. *Wissenschaftsfreiheit*, like all the rights guaranteed by the Basic Law, not only is a defensive right protected against infringement by the state but is a fundamental constitutional value.[146] That means that the state, including the courts, must ensure its observance in all legal relations, including those governed by contract. Courts could, and probably should, interpret the terms of research contracts in a way that respects the central values of scientific freedom and freedom of research. A researcher should be free to communicate his or her finding that, say, a drug is dangerous, even though that is prohibited by the terms of his or her agreement with the company financing the work and supplying the research material. That is not because the contract directly infringes the individual right guaranteed by Article 5(3) of the Basic Law but because its enforcement would violate the central values of scientific freedom, which are of importance to everyone—and in this context of particular significance to the health and safety of patients and participants in clinical trials.[147]

Quite apart from these legal difficulties, individual medical researchers and scientists may be quite unconcerned by the terms of research contracts; their primary interest is in obtaining financial support for their research. Alternatively, they may be reluctant to challenge such terms because they have a financial interest in the company: they may sit on the company board. In that event there is a conflict of interest, which may weaken any resolve researchers may have to assert academic freedom. They may therefore be happy to accept contractual restraints that university lawyers would like to renegotiate.[148] What is imperative therefore is that university lawyers and administrators ensure as far as

---

[145] In *Lion Laboratories v Evans* [1985] 2 QB 526, the Court of Appeal held that the defendant had an arguable public interest defence to publish confidential information that showed the unreliability of a device used by the police to detect excessive drinking.

[146] Above ch 5, s III(D).

[147] See E Schmidt-Assmann, 'Free Access to Research Findings and Its Limitations' in Nowotny et al (eds) (above n 15) 109, 118–21.

[148] Communications from US university lawyers at UK/US Higher Education Roundtable held at New College, Oxford, 30 June 2009; and from Alex Weedon, Legal Affairs and IP manager for UCL Business, 9 July 2009.

possible that academic freedom is safeguarded when they negotiate the terms of research contracts with outside sponsors. But universities themselves, as the three cases discussed earlier in this section illustrate, have sometimes been unwilling to assert the values of academic freedom, for they too are dependent on the financial support of drugs companies. They may be reluctant to challenge the terms offered by powerful commercial companies because they fear that the latter will take their business to other universities or make increasing use of contract research organisations, which do not even claim to defend academic freedom.[149]

## V. GOVERNMENT RESEARCH CONTRACTS AND ADVICE

Similar issues to those discussed in the previous section may arise when academics conduct research for a government department or other public authority. Under the terms of a typical agreement in the United Kingdom,[150] the government has first option to publish the report of research it has commissioned if, after independent peer review, it is found to be of good enough quality. If it does not meet this standard, then researchers are generally free to publish it elsewhere. But the government can veto publication if it considers that would be against the national interest or infringe commercial confidentiality.[151] Permission is normally granted to publish an article or book based on research work, or short extracts from a report.[152] Researchers are required not to make any public communication about their research without the consent of the government,[153] and they are not free to use personal data acquired during the course of their research in other publications, unless permission is granted and other conditions are met.[154]

[149] See Schafer (above n 126) 22–23.
[150] For example, the Standard Conditions for Social Research Commissioned by the Home Office, cl 19.
[151] Evidence of Professor P Wiles CB to the Science and Technology Committee, HC (2006) 900-II, Evid 61-2.
[152] Standard Home Office Conditions (above n 150) cl 19.2.
[153] Ibid, cl 17.
[154] Ibid, cl 20; and Communication with Professor Tim Hope, Keele University, 14 July 2009.

Academics, particularly criminologists, have sometimes expressed considerable anxiety about the implications of these provisions for academic freedom. Governments, they allege, may refuse to publish any research findings that they find politically embarrassing and may further try to prevent researchers publishing 'suppressed' conclusions independently.[155] In the United Kingdom, the House of Commons Science and Technology Committee has expressed concern about allegations of this kind, though it did not think it could assess their veracity. It urged the government's Chief Scientific Adviser to investigate them. Research commissioned by a government department should be published without inappropriate interference.[156]

In principle, a government committed to evidence-based policymaking should either itself publish research it has commissioned or permit academic researchers to publish it elsewhere, subject only to minimal constraints to safeguard national security, public health or safety. There is of course a danger that it will use its contractual powers to prevent the disclosure of evidence that its policies are flawed. It will not do to argue that academic freedom is wholly irrelevant to research commissioned by government, in contrast to research on topics chosen independently by university scholars and scientists. For the same argument for academic freedom applies to both types of research: universities are established and their scholars and scientists employed to conduct and publish disinterested research. It makes no sense for a society to set up universities and then to suppress the research findings of their academic staff, whether they are made in the course of their independent research or made as a result of direct employment by the government.[157] Government remains free, of course, to discredit research that comes up with uncomfortable conclusions, as it did in the United Kingdom when researchers at the London School of Economics concluded the government had underestimated the costs and other difficulties of

---

[155] Centre for Crime and Justice Studies, King's College London, 'Critical Thinking about the Uses of Research', paper by T Hope and R Walters, available at http://www.crimeandjustice.org.uk (accessed 10 August 2010); and M Presdee and R Walters, 'The Perils and Politics of Criminological Research and the Threat to Academic Freedom' (1998) 10 *Current Issues in Criminal Justice* 156 for these allegations in an Australian context.

[156] Science and Technology Committee, 'Scientific Advice, Risk and Evidence Based Policy Making' HC (2005–06) 900-I [94]–[98].

[157] See above ch 3, s III regarding this persuasive argument for academic freedom.

introducing a national identity card.[158] Alternatively, it is free not to commission university research but to conduct it within its departments; civil servants and other public employees do not enjoy academic freedom. Further, government is perfectly free not to employ 'troublesome' academics again, when they publish conclusions it dislikes; a failure to reemploy them does not infringe their academic freedom.

The legal question is more difficult. The question is whether university researchers could challenge the application of these contractual restraints as infringing freedom of expression or academic freedom. Human rights arguments might be made in this context, as the limits are imposed by public authorities[159]—not, as in the case of comparable restrictions by a drugs company, by a private person. But it is very unlikely that a challenge on the basis of academic freedom would succeed. Academic freedom in the United Kingdom is a statutory right but not a Convention right, which the courts are required to protect under the Human Rights Act 1998.[160] Freedom of expression could, however, be invoked. But a court would probably hold that a researcher had freely agreed to waive or surrender full freedom of expression when he or she entered into an agreement imposing confidentiality restrictions and allowing the government first option to determine whether research findings should be published. The argument of principle for upholding academic freedom set out in the previous paragraph would probably not be accepted by a court.

But a successful legal challenge might be made in the United States, where courts are unwilling to enforce prior restraints on publication, except in situations of grave national emergency.[161] In *Board of Trustees of Leland Stanford University v Sullivan*[162] a federal District Court judge, Harold Greene, upheld Stanford University's challenge to a broad

---

[158] For the disagreement between the government and the LSE researchers, see Science and Technology Committee, 'Sixth Report' HC (2005–06) HC 1032 [62]–[67]. It was reported that the government attempted to stop publication of the LSE research: *The Times*, 3 July 2005.

[159] HRA 1998, s 6(1).

[160] A different position obtains in Germany, where intellectual or scientific freedom may be claimed by everyone: see above ch 5, s I.

[161] For the US courts' hostility to prior restraints on speech, see Barendt (above n 45) ch 4.

[162] 773 F Supp 472 (DDC 1991), discussed by R O'Neil, *Academic Freedom in the Wired World* (Cambridge, MA, Harvard University Press, 2008) 127–28.

confidentiality clause attached to a grant by the National Heart, Lung, and Blood Institute; under the clause researchers had to obtain government approval before publishing or discussing preliminary research results. The government conceded it could not impose this obligation as a general requirement but argued that it could do this as a condition of a grant. The judge rejected that argument. The clause appeared to apply to all research, whether or not it was funded by the National Institute. It was incompatible with the First Amendment freedom of speech to 'subject to government censorship the publications of institutions of higher learning and others engaged in legitimate research'.[163] It is striking that the US government did not appeal against this important ruling; it accepted that it could not impose restrictions on the right to publish research findings.

Another question is whether government interferes with academic freedom if it dismisses an adviser from his or her position for publishing views it regards as damaging. This question was raised in October 2009 when Sir David Nutt was asked by the Home Secretary, Alan Johnson, MP, to consider his position as chairman of the Advisory Committee on the Misuse of Drugs (ACMD) after he gave a lecture at King's College London criticising the government for reclassifying cannabis from Class C to Class B against the advice of the ACMD.[164] Scientists criticised the government for interfering with academic and scientific freedom;[165] in their view an academic member of a government advisory committee enjoys full freedom to communicate his or her views publicly, whether in an academic lecture (as in Sir David Nutt's case) or through the media, provided it is made clear that he or she does not speak for the government and does not disclose confidential information.

The question, however, is whether government wrongly interferes with academic freedom if it decides to terminate the adviser's appointment in these circumstances; it can argue that it is entitled to choose its advisers and to work with people who are not openly critical of its policies. The decision to sack Sir David Nutt was probably misconceived

---

[163] *Stanford University v Sullivan* (ibid) 478.

[164] *The Guardian,* 31 October 2009, 6.

[165] Statement of Principles for the Treatment of Independent Scientific Advice, issued on 6 November 2009, supported by 28 senior scientists, available at http://www.senseaboutscience.org.uk/index.php/site/project/421 (accessed 10 August 2010).

and might have the effect of discouraging scientists and others from the acceptance of appointments to advise or work with government. But scientific advisers who take official appointments can no longer claim unlimited academic freedom when they speak about government policy, for that freedom must be balanced against the reasonable concern of government to have full trust and confidence in its advisers. The government was not suppressing the publication of views it disliked—a clear interference with academic freedom and freedom of expression; rather it was indicating its lack of confidence in the continued appointment of the speaker in his position as chair of an advisory committee. Even though the ACMD is a statutory body, its members and its chair are appointed by the Home Secretary;[166] they are perfectly entitled to express their views freely and exercise academic freedom, but they cannot expect to keep their appointments if government loses confidence in them.

## VI. FREEDOM OF RESEARCH AND DATA PROTECTION

Member states of the European Union are required to enact data protection laws to protect the fundamental rights of individuals, in particular their privacy with respect to the processing of personal data.[167] But the achievement of this object has an impact on freedom of research. By imposing limits and conditions on the processing of personal data, particularly sensitive personal data, laws such as the UK Data Protection Act 1998 (DPA) may inhibit the freedom of medical and other researchers to use such data in their research and incorporate them in their published work. Epidemiological research, for example, may be curtailed by the requirements that data be processed 'fairly and lawfully' and the other data protection principles,[168] as well as by the additional requirements for the processing of 'sensitive personal data', which includes information relating to the data subject's health and sexual life.[169] It would be more difficult, if not impossible, to conduct research into contemporary politics and social affairs, if researchers

---

[166] Misuse of Drugs Act 1971, s 1 and Sch 1.
[167] Directive 95/46/EC, Official Journal, L 281, 31.
[168] DPA, Sch 1 sets out the data protection principles for the processing of personal data.
[169] DPA, s 2.

were required to obtain the explicit consent of all persons identified in consequent publications for the disclosure of information about, say, their political and religious beliefs,[170] and to allow them access to the data that the researchers have compiled.[171] This section discusses briefly the impact of the DPA on academic research—a subject that has had little treatment in the literature on the statute.[172] The discussion is primarily concerned with the specific provisions allowing exemption from the data processing requirements when processing is for research purposes, and exemption from these requirements when data are processed for the purposes of journalism or artistic or literary purposes.

One point of fundamental importance is that 'data controllers' must notify the Information Commissioner, so that they are included in the register maintained by him.[173] Notification, which must be made annually, must be given of various particulars, including a description of the data and categories of data subject to which they relate, and the purposes for which data are to be processed.[174] A fee is payable with notification: £35 for small bodies with fewer than 250 employees; £500 for larger bodies with more than 250 employees *and* an annual turnover of more than £25.9 million. It is an offence for a data controller to fail to notify the Commission. It matters therefore who is a 'data controller', defined in the legislation as 'a person who determines ... the purposes for which and the manner in which any personal data are ... processed'.[175] It is assumed that normally an academic institution rather than a particular research insti-

---

[170] These beliefs are 'sensitive personal data' for the processing of which stringent conditions are imposed to satisfy the requirement that data are processed fairly and lawfully: see DPA, s 4(3) and Sch 3.

[171] Under DPA, s 7 an individual has rights of access to personal data, including a right to have communicated to him information constituted by the data of which he is the subject and information about the source of that information.

[172] The leading book is R Jay, *Data Protection: Law and Practice*, 3rd edn (London, Sweet and Maxwell, 2007). See also P Carey, *Data Protection: A Practical Guide to UK and EU Law*, 3rd edn (Oxford, Oxford University Press, 2009). A much fuller treatment is provided by D Erdos, 'The European Convention Turned on its Head? Academic Social Inquiry, Freedom of Expression and the UK's Data Protection Act 1998', paper presented on 6 May 2010 at Oxford University Faculty of Law Public Law Discussion Group. I am indebted to David Erdos for sending me a copy of his paper.

[173] DPA, ss 18–19.

[174] Ibid, s 17(1).

[175] Ibid, s 1(1).

tute within it, let alone an individual researcher, is the data controller.[176] Now that makes sense for the processing of, say, student records, faculty and other employee information, as well as for other university records compiled for statistical purposes. But a university does not determine the purposes for which individual scholars and scientists accumulate personal data in the course of their research or the manner in which it is processed. Indeed, it would be incompatible with the fundamental principles of their academic freedom to ascribe that authority to the university, or even to the Deans or Heads of Department within it. However, if the university is not treated as the data controller in this context, it follows that the individual academic, or at least the lead researcher in a departmental team or laboratory, must be treated as the data controller and satisfy the notification requirements. On either interpretation, the data protection legislation inhibits the exercise of academic research freedom.

A second fundamental point is that the legislation restricts only the processing of 'personal data', that is, data relating to a living individual who can be identified from the data or from those data and other information likely to be possessed by the data controller.[177] Fully anonymised data can therefore be used for, say, medical or statistical research, without any need to rely on the specific exemption for processing for research purposes conferred by the legislation. Published historical research, however, generally refers to particular individuals (or small communities from which individuals can be identified) to give it credibility and colour, and will therefore be caught by the legislation; it would need to claim one of the exemptions provided in the DPA to escape its inhibiting impact.

Headed 'Research, History and Statistics', section 33 of the DPA confers a few limited exemptions for processing for research purposes. 'Research purposes' explicitly include research for historical and statistical purposes, but there can be no doubt that they also cover medical and all forms of academic or commercial research.[178] The exemptions are very limited. In departure from the second data protection principle,[179]

[176] Jay (above n 172) para 18.20.
[177] The leading case on the meaning of 'personal data' is *Durant v Financial Services Authority* [2004] FSR 28, CA.
[178] Jay (above n 172) para 18.21.
[179] The second principle requires that data shall be processed only for specified purposes and are not to be processed further in any way incompatible with those purposes: DPA, Sch 1, Part 1.

the further processing of data only for research purposes is not to be treated as incompatible with the purposes for which they were originally processed. Data processed only for research may be kept indefinitely, in derogation from the fifth principle requiring personal data to be kept for no longer than necessary for the purpose for which they are processed. Finally, data processed only for research are exempt from the right of access to personal data conferred by section 7. But this third exemption applies only if the results of the research do not identify the data subject. It is therefore of no use for historians whose work identifies the people about whom they write. Moreover, none of these exemptions applies unless the processing satisfies two conditions:[180] the data are not processed to support measures respecting individuals; and they are not processed in such a way that substantial damage or distress is caused to any data subject. These requirements deprive the provision of much of its utility. It would not help, for instance, a social science researcher whose work led to published criticism of or disciplinary sanctions against a public official.

The research provisions provide no exemption from the important first data protection principle, which requires fair and lawful processing. That requirement means that one of a number of conditions must be met, among them the consent of the data subject to the processing, or that processing is necessary for the purposes of the legitimate interests of the data controller or of third parties to whom the data are disclosed, except where that processing unwarrantably prejudices the data subject.[181] Academic researchers could surely take advantage of the second alternative, since the disclosure of information obtained by research is a legitimate interest, which normally does not prejudice any freedom or interest of the data subject. On the other hand, they will find it difficult, or at least very irksome, to satisfy the complex notification requirements set out in Schedule 1 of the DPA, under which a data controller must ensure 'so far as practicable' that data subjects are informed of his or her identity and the purposes for which it is intended to process the data, for processing to be treated as fair.[182]

The processing of sensitive personal data for research purposes must additionally comply with one of the conditions set out in Schedule 3 of

---

[180]  DPA, s 33(1).
[181]  Ibid, Sch 2, paras 1 and 6.
[182]  Ibid, Sch 1, Part II, para 2.

the DPA. They are satisfied if *explicit* consent is given or, amongst other conditions, the processing is for medical research purposes and is undertaken by a health professional.[183] Sensitive personal data may also be processed if this is in the substantial public interest and is necessary for research purposes; but the usefulness of this provision is significantly reduced by the requirements that the processing does not support measures or decisions with respect to any data subject, and does not cause, nor is likely to cause, substantial damage or distress to a data subject or any other person.[184] The provision may therefore benefit archivists but would not assist, say, political scientists investigating the health or political opinions of a prominent figure, if the disclosure or other processing of this sensitive data would cause him or her substantial damage. The consent of the data subject is therefore under the DPA not a *necessary* condition for the processing of personal data or even sensitive personal data: it is one of a number of alternative grounds on which processing can satisfy the data protection principles. It should be added that information acquired by a doctor from a patient is governed by the law of confidentiality, so any processing of that information for research would be illegal, unless it can be justified in the public interest or becomes lawful under statute.[185]

A much broader exemption is provided by DPA, section 32. Processing undertaken with a view to the publication by any person of any journalistic, artistic or literary material is exempt from most of the requirements of the legislation, including all the data protection principles except the seventh[186] and the access rights conferred by section 7. But there are two conditions: the data controller must reasonably believe that, having regard to freedom of expression, publication is in the public interest and also that, in all the circumstances, compliance with the relevant requirement of the legislation is incompatible with one of the 'special purposes': journalism, artistic or literary purposes.[187]

---

[183] Sch 3, para 8.

[184] Data Protection (Processing of Sensitive Personal Data) Order, SI 2000/417, reg 9, made under DPA, Sch 3, para 10.

[185] See Health Service (Control of Patient Information) Regulations 2002, SI 2002/1438, made under Health and Social Care Act 2001, s 60; and NHS Confidentiality Code of Practice (November, 2003).

[186] The seventh principle requires the data to be kept secure against unauthorised use, accidental loss, etc.

[187] DPA, s 32(1). The leading authority on the interpretation of this provision is the decision of the Court of Appeal in *Campbell v MGN* [2003] QB 633.

There is no reason why this provision should not in principle grant university academic staff exemption for the processing of personal data, provided this is done with a view to publication. It would be wrong to hold it covered only the press, book and other literary publishers.[188]

On the other hand, there are some difficulties. First, the exemption depends on the reasonable beliefs of the data controller—almost certainly the academic institution in which the researcher works, unless he or she has notified the Commissioner to be registered as a data controller. It should not be difficult for a researcher to persuade the university that publication of the work is in the public interest, but it might be harder to persuade it to take the view that compliance with the relevant data protection provision would be incompatible with, say, literary purposes. In particular, it may be difficult to argue that compliance with a data access request made *subsequent to* publication would be incompatible with the special purpose, since that purpose would then have already been realised.[189] The best argument for exemption in these circumstances is that academic research would be inhibited if a scholar feared that eventually he or she would have to disclose all the information compiled about a data subject if the latter made an access request for its supply.[190] Unless that argument is accepted, data protection laws might have a chilling effect on the exercise of academic freedom by social scientists. This exceptionally complex legislation should certainly be construed to respect freedom of expression, which academics exercise when they publish their research.[191]

[188] The Supreme Court of Sweden has decided that the comparable exemption in Swedish law is not confined to formal journalism but covers any publication designed to provoke public discussion: Decision of 12 June 2001, noted in Jay (above n 172) para 3.14.

[189] Ibid, para 17.17.

[190] A subject access request has been made in respect of data processed by Sean Matthews in connection with S Matthews, *Academic Freedom and the University of Nottingham* (York, Zoilus Press, 2009). See below ch 8, s II(D). The prospects of such requests might well discourage the writing of studies reporting and analysing contemporary events, and so inhibit the exercise of academic freedom.

[191] The Data Protection Act should be interpreted, so far as possible, in conformity with the right to freedom of expression: Human Rights Act 1998, s 3.

# 8

# *Academic Freedom in the Age of Terrorism*

## I. INTRODUCTION

GOVERNMENTS IN THE United Kingdom, the United States of America and many other countries have been faced in the last decade with the growing threat of international terrorism, in particular what the UK government has identified as the 'real, current and sustained threat … from al-Qa'ida influenced terrorism'.[1] They have introduced legislation to meet this threat. For example, in the United States, agencies have been given greater powers to access documents and records, including library records, to see what material has been read by those suspected of supporting al-Qa'ida and other terrorist organisations,[2] while the UK Parliament in 2006 made it an offence to encourage or glorify terrorism and to distribute terrorist publications.[3] Provisions in earlier UK legislation, the Terrorism Act 2000, which penalise the possession of articles for the purpose of terrorism or of documents useful to persons committing or preparing such acts, have been applied to deal with the increasing threats posed by al-Qa'ida.[4] The UK government has also taken steps to alert universities to the dangers arising from the activities of extremist groups on their campuses, in particular through the recruitment of new members from impressionable and vulnerable students.[5]

---

[1] 'Promoting Good Campus Relations, Fostering Shared Values and Preventing Violent Extremism in Universities and Higher Education Colleges', Department of Innovation, Universities and Skills (2006 and 2008) Annex A, 18.

[2] USA PATRIOT Act, discussed below in s III.

[3] Terrorism Act 2006, ss 1–2, discussed below in s II(B).

[4] See further below s II(A).

[5] See 'Promoting Good Campus Relations' (above n 1).

Some academics in the United Kingdom and in the United States have argued that the strict enforcement of these laws make it difficult, even illegal, to teach courses examining the origins and ideology of terrorism or to conduct research in this area. It might, say, be against the law for a university library to have on its shelves material that, on one interpretation, supports terrorism in some situations—in the Gaza strip, for instance—even though professors and their students would use it only in seminar discussion to help them understand the factors motivating potential terrorists in this context. These laws and their application by universities anxious to help the police and security services might significantly inhibit teaching and research, even if it is unlikely that professors, or their universities, would be prosecuted in these circumstances. The argument is that the mere existence of broad terrorism laws has a chilling effect or impact on academic work.

These anxieties are not confined to the United Kingdom and the United States. Australian scholars have expressed considerable disquiet regarding recent legislation enacted by the Howard government and its application to inhibit teaching and research in that country.[6] On the other hand, Canadian anti-terrorism legislation has not given rise to the same problems.[7] Further, it does not appear that terrorism and other comparable criminal laws have had a significant impact on the exercise of scientific freedom in Germany. So this chapter is concerned only with the repercussions of recent terrorism legislation for academic freedom in the United Kingdom and the United States.

In this context the recent period after the events of 11 September 2001 and the London bombings of 7 July 2005 is perhaps not unique. Academic freedom in the United States came under similar threats during the McCarthy period in the early 1950s and again during the Vietnam War. Indeed, the early rulings of the US Supreme Court on academic freedom arose from challenges to the application of laws requiring university professors (and other public employees) to take

[6] E MacDonald and G Williams, 'Banned Books and Seditious Speech: Anti-terrorism Laws and Other Threats to Academic Freedom' (2007) 12 *Australia and New Zealand Journal of Law and Education* 29; J-C Tham, 'Australian Terror Laws and Academic Freedom' in JL Turk and A Manson (eds), *Free Speech in Fearful Times: After 9/11 in Canada, the US, Australia, and Europe* (Toronto, Lorimer and Co, 2007) 234.

[7] See K Roach, 'Freedom and Security in Post-9/11 Canada' in Turk and Manson (eds) (ibid) 121.

loyalty oaths, disclaiming membership of the Communist party and other subversive organisations.[8] It is more difficult to point to a comparable period in the United Kingdom, when serious concerns were expressed regarding the impact on academic freedom resulting from legislation enacted to meet threats to national security and public safety—although radical lecturers sometimes felt under pressure during both the 1930s and the immediate post-war period.[9] Further, according to one specialist in this field, the recent legislation has only intensified the difficulties faced by academics when they attempted to investigate terrorism in Northern Ireland during the 1970s and 1980s.[10]

One object of this chapter is to examine the scope of recent terrorism legislation, particularly in the United Kingdom, and to see how far it might have an impact on the exercise of academic freedom. It has sometimes been argued that universities have intervened too readily to apply legislation and ensure that their staff are not using material that could be understood to support or promote terrorism. Two recent episodes at Nottingham University are discussed to see how far the anxieties expressed by some academics are justified or whether, as others have contended, these fears have been exaggerated. Section II deals with these topics, while section III looks more briefly at the position in the United States after 9/11. Despite the political tensions and anxiety about national security in the United States in recent years, and despite occasional threats to the exercise of academic freedom, the horrors of the McCarthy period have not been repeated—perhaps because the American Association of University Professors (AAUP) and other educational and libertarian bodies have defended the freedom effectively. These organisations have, it has been said, learned much from the failure to stand up for academic freedom during the 1950s, when Senator McCarthy persecuted liberals and intellectuals.[11]

---

[8] Eg, *Sweezy v New Hampshire* 354 US 234 (1957); and *Keyishian v Board of Regents* 385 US 589 (1967). Both cases are discussed above in ch 6, s III(A).

[9] See above ch 4, s II(C).

[10] Interview with Professor David Miller, Strathclyde University, 8 October 2009.

[11] R O'Neil, *Academic Freedom in the Wired World* (Cambridge, MA, Harvard University Press, 2008) ch 4; and R O'Neil, 'Academic Freedom in the Post-September 11 Era: An Old Game with New Rules' in E Gerstmann and MJ Streb (eds), *Academic Freedom at the Dawn of a New Century* (Stanford, Stanford University Press, 2006) 43.

## II. UK TERRORISM LAWS

This section examines the impact on academic freedom of two major enactments: the Terrorism Act (TA) 2000 and the Terrorism Act (TA) 2006. But the potential impact of this legislation can only be properly assessed in the context of the European Convention on Human Rights and Fundamental Freedoms (ECHR), incorporated into UK law by the Human Rights Act 1998 (HRA), which is discussed below in section II(C). Finally, this section looks at two recent episodes when claims have been made that university authorities have taken decisions with potentially disturbing implications for academic freedom.

### A. Terrorism Act 2000

This significant statute placed on a permanent footing measures in terrorism legislation that had been enacted during the 1970s and 1980s to deal with the troubles in Northern Ireland.[12] Section 1 of the TA 2000 contains a very broad definition of 'terrorism', so that it includes the use or threat of violence or of serious damage to property, designed to influence the government of any country and made for the purpose of advancing any cause, whether political, religious or ideological.[13] It is immaterial whether the targeted government is democratic or totalitarian,[14] so incitement to cause serious damage to property in, say, Libya or Zimbabwe would be caught by the legislation, even if it was intended to help bring about democratic government in those countries.

Two criminal offences in the TA 2000 might implicate university teachers and researchers. Under section 57 it is an offence to possess an article in circumstances that give rise to a reasonable suspicion that the possession is for the purposes of the commission or instigation of an act of terrorism. Documents and records such as notebooks with instructions on how to denote an explosive can be 'articles' for the

---

[12] For the background to the terrorism legislation, see C Walker, *Blackstone's Guide to the Anti-Terrorism Legislation*, 2nd edn (Oxford, Oxford University Press, 2009) ch 1.

[13] See ibid, ch 1(C); and C Walker, 'The Legal Definition of "Terrorism" in United Kingdom Legislation and Beyond' (2007) *Public Law* 331.

[14] *R v F (Terrorism)* [2007] QB 960, CA.

purpose of section 57.[15] With some hesitation, the Court of Appeal in *R v Zafar* ruled that possessing a document for the purpose of *inciting* others to commit acts of terrorism falls within the provision,[16] so a researcher who keeps propaganda with this purpose could be convicted under the section. But the Court of Appeal held that there must be a direct link between the object or document possessed and the terrorist act;[17] it would not be enough to show that the defendants possessed, for example, ideological or religious material that would be used to stiffen their resolve to instigate terrorist acts. More importantly in this context, it is a defence to show that the articles, including documents, were not possessed for the purposes of terrorism,[18] so an academic who kept this material, say, for discussion at university seminars on the causes of terrorism could not be convicted of this offence.

It is perhaps more likely that an academic could be prosecuted under TA 2000, s 58(1).[19] That section makes it an offence for a person to collect or make a record of information of a kind likely to be useful to someone committing or preparing a terrorist act, or to possess a document or record with information of that kind. But the defendant has a defence if he or she can show that there was a 'reasonable excuse' for the conduct or possession.[20] Clearly section 58(1) would cover academics and others, such as journalists, who collect, say, terrorist training manuals containing practical advice about detonating explosives, even if they do this to illustrate points made at seminars or to provide support for their arguments in research publications.[21] The Crown must show that the defendant knew of the kind of information in the records or documents, though it need not prove that he or she was aware of its

[15] *R v Rowe* [2007] QB 975, CA.

[16] *R v Zafar* [2008] QB 810, para 31.

[17] Ibid, para 29.

[18] TA 2000, s 57(2). Under s 118 if a defendant adduces evidence that raises an issue whether the possession was for terrorist purposes, the burden of proof shifts to the prosecution to prove beyond reasonable doubt that the possession was for such purposes.

[19] It is possible that an academic could be prosecuted under both ss 57 and 58, as was the student in the Scottish case *R v Mohammed Atif Siddique*: see [2010] HCJAC 7, reporting his successful appeal to the Appeal Court of the High Court of Justiciary.

[20] TA s 57(3). S 118 shifting the burden of proof to the prosecution applies also to this offence.

[21] See Walker, *Blackstone's Guide* (above n 12) para 6.45.

precise contents.[22] An academic would of course rely on the 'reasonable excuse' defence afforded by the provision. The House of Lords discussed its scope at length in *R v G*:[23] the defendant must show that he or she had a good reason for accumulating the information, not merely, as in the case of the section 57 offence, that it was not acquired for terrorist purposes. Whether there was a reasonable excuse would depend on all the circumstances; Lord Rodger declined to rule in abstract whether it would be a defence to show that information had been downloaded 'out of curiosity', the archetypal academic motive.[24]

In the absence of any specific defence for them, scholars are clearly liable to be prosecuted for the offence under s 58 of the TA 2000, but they should have little difficulty in showing that they had 'reasonable excuse' for collecting such information. That does not, however, dispose of the academic freedom argument. Scholars researching terrorism might understandably hesitate to collect information of this type, even if they have been advised that if prosecuted, they would have a good defence to the charge. No academic wants to face arrest or criminal charges, with the implications these events carry for their professional standing and promotion prospects. The law may well have a 'chilling effect' on terrorism research.

## B. Terrorism Act 2006

In the wake of the bombings of the London transport system in July 2005, the government introduced further measures to meet the terrorist threat. The TA 2006 introduced the offence of encouragement of terrorism, defined as 'a statement ... likely to be understood by some or all of the members of the public ... as a direct or indirect encouragement ... to them' to commit, prepare or instigate terrorist acts.[25]

---

[22] *R v G* [2009] 2 All ER 409, paras 47–50 per Lord Rodger. This decision of the House of Lords provides an authoritative discussion of the scope of both ss 57 and 58 of the TA 2000.

[23] Ibid, paras 71–85.

[24] Ibid, para 83.

[25] TA 2006, s 1(1). For commentary on this and other provisions of the TA 2006, see T Choudhury, 'The Terrorism Act 2006; Discouraging Terrorism' in I Hare and J Weinstein (eds), *Extremist Speech and Democracy* (Oxford, Oxford University Press, 2009) ch 23.

Statements that glorify the commission, etc of these acts, whether in the past, the future or generally, are to be treated as indirectly encouraging them, provided they are statements from which 'members of the public could reasonably be expected to infer that what is being glorified is being glorified as conduct that should be emulated by them in existing circumstances.'[26] Under section 2 it is an offence to disseminate 'terrorist publications',[27] an activity that includes not only its distribution or electronic transmission but also its possession with a view to its dissemination. Further, the TA 2006 proscribes training in the skills of terrorism, including instruction in the making, handling or use of noxious substances and instruction in the use of any technique for doing anything else capable of being done for terrorist purposes.[28]

The Association of University Teachers (AUT) raised serious concerns about the implications of earlier drafts of these provisions for the exercise of academic freedom.[29] The teaching of history and current international affairs would in its view be inhibited by the new offences of encouragement and glorification of terrorism, as a lecturer might not want to take the risk of a charge of indirect encouragement of terrorism by discussing with understanding in a university seminar the motives of suicide bombers; further, a lecturer might be guilty of the offence under section 2 if he or she failed to appreciate that a student was likely to understand, say, terrorist propaganda distributed in an international affairs class, as encouraging (or glorifying) terrorist acts. Moreover, in the view of the AUT, the provision on training for terrorism would hamper the teaching of chemistry.

Accepting these concerns, the Joint Parliamentary Committee on Human Rights urged that the Bill should include specific defences to the offences created by sections 1 and 2 to allow for freedom of expression. A 'reasonable excuse' or 'public interest' defence should be included in the measure to protect the legitimate activities of the media

---

[26] TA 2006, s 1(3).

[27] Defined in s 2(3) as publications containing material likely to be understood as directly or indirectly encouraging terrorist acts, or material likely to be useful in the commission or preparation of such acts.

[28] TA 2006, s 6. The skills that it is an offence to provide training for are defined in s 6(3).

[29] Evidence to the Joint Parliamentary Committee on Human Rights, 'Third Report' HL (2005–06) 75(II) HC 561(II) 91–93.

and academics.[30] During the debates in the House of Lords, Baroness Williams of Crosby moved amendments to provide specific exemptions from clauses 1 and 2 for statements made solely for the purpose of academic teaching and research, and from clause 6 for professional chemists engaged in teaching and publishing their research.[31] The amendments were supported by the then chief executive of Universities UK, Baroness Warwick, and by other speakers. The purpose of the amendments was to put beyond doubt that academics and librarians would not be caught by the legislation when they engage in the normal course of their teaching and research. The government resisted the incorporation of these amendments, but the clauses were modified to ensure that in the absence of any specific intent to encourage terrorism, persons making statements or disseminating publications would have a defence, if they could show they did not endorse the views in the statements or publications and it was clear from the circumstances that they did not endorse them.[32] The clause on training for terrorism was amended to provide that it would be an offence only if the lecturer, at the time of providing the instruction or training, knew that a person receiving it intended to use the relevant skills for terrorism. In the government's view, these changes to the Bill ensured the provisions would protect 'all legitimate academic interests'.[33]

Should the Bill have been amended to give greater protection to university teachers and researchers, and to their exercise of academic freedom? The argument is that the TA 2006 will have a 'chilling effect' on academic freedom of teaching and research because university staff will be inhibited by the fear of investigation or prosecution if, for example, they publish an analysis of terrorist propaganda or discuss it in class. Only a specific exemption for any statements made in the course of academic teaching or research would remove this chilling effect.[34] Baroness Williams pointed to the provision in the Obscene Publications

---

[30] Third Report of the Joint Committee on Human Rights, 'Counter-Terrorism Policy and Human Rights: Terrorism Bill and Related matters' HL (2005–06) 75(i) HC 561(i) [35] and [45]–[48].

[31] Hansard HL vol 512 cols 620–25 (7 December 2005).

[32] See TA 2006, ss 1(6) and 2(9).

[33] Hansard HL vol 512 cols 625–29 (7 December 2005) (Baroness Scotland of Asthal).

[34] That would go further than Baroness Williams' amendment, which would have provided exemption only for statements made *solely* for academic purposes.

Act 1959 that a publisher does not commit the obscenity offence if he or she shows that publication is for the public good on the grounds of its scientific, literary or artistic merit.[35] The literary or other merits of a novel such as *Lady Chatterley's Lover* trump any tendency it may have to corrupt its readers. But it would be difficult to make a comparable argument in the context of statements encouraging terrorism; if they do make more likely the commission of terrorist atrocities, that harm is hardly outweighed by the concerns of academic freedom. Moreover, it is not clear that the understandable anxieties of scholars and scientists are any more pressing in this context than, say, the concerns of journalists and other writers and publishers who might be understood to encourage terrorism in the course of their work.

That is not to deny that academic work might be inhibited by an apprehension that teaching or research in this area will lead to police investigation or even prosecution under the TA 2006. It is not enough for the authorities to point out that bona fide scholars have nothing to fear because they will have a good defence to any charge (for instance, the defence in section 2(9) of the Act that 'the publication neither expressed his views nor had his endorsement'). The offences should have been more restrictively drafted so the prosecution has to prove that the defendant intended to encourage to commit acts of terrorism. Academics, however, are not the only people who can properly complain that their work and their freedom of speech is improperly fettered by these provisions.[36]

## C. The Impact of the ECHR

The Joint Committee on Human Rights was unsure whether the provisions in the draft Terrorism Bill of 2005–06 would survive a legal challenge on the grounds of their incompatibility with the ECHR guarantee of the right to freedom of expression.[37] English courts must

---

[35] HL Debates (above n 31) col 622, referring to the Obscene Publications Act 1959, s 4.
[36] For the argument that the encouragement provisions would not survive constitutional challenge in the United States, see E Barendt, 'Incitement to, and Glorification of, Terrorism' in Hare and Weinstein (eds) (above n 25).
[37] Third Report of the JCHR (above n 30) paras 21–41.

now interpret the terrorism legislation, so far as they can, in conformity with this and other Convention rights.[38] If that cannot be done, they may declare a provision incompatible with the Convention.[39] Further, account must be taken of relevant jurisprudence of the European Court of Human Rights in Strasbourg, though UK courts are not bound to follow the Strasbourg Court decisions.[40] So it is worth briefly examining this jurisprudence to see if academic scholars could claim that the TA 2006 infringes their right to freedom of expression (or conceivably another Convention right).

Terrorism legislation clearly impinges on a number of Convention rights: freedom of expression and association; personal liberty and privacy; and the right to a fair trial.[41] Academic freedom is engaged by the Convention, at least insofar as it overlaps with freedom of expression. So academics could certainly claim that their freedom to publish research findings and their freedom to discuss contemporary political issues freely in or outside the classroom are covered by the right to freedom of expression, which is guaranteed by Article 10 of the ECHR.[42] (The freedom to discuss issues in the classroom or a seminar is of course limited by strong professional constraints; for example, the discussion must be relevant to the subject matter of the lecture or seminar course and syllabus, so in this context lecturers do not enjoy full freedom of expression to say what they like.[43]) But insofar as Article 10 of the ECHR is engaged, the UK government would argue in this context that the restriction on exercise of the freedom of expression is necessary in order to safeguard national security and to prevent crime and disorder.

The Strasbourg Court has considered this argument in a number of cases from Turkey, where the government has frequently prosecuted editors, journalists and writers for inciting the Kurdish community to violence in its campaign for a separate state. Two decisions holding the application of Turkish laws incompatible with the Article 10 guarantee

---

[38]   HRA 1998, s 3.

[39]   Ibid, s 4.

[40]   Ibid, s 2.

[41]   For a thorough examination of this question see S Sottiaux, *Terrorism and the Limitation of Rights: The ECHR and the US Constitution* (Oxford, Hart, 2008).

[42]   This issue is further discussed in the context of extramural expression below in ch 9, s III(A).

[43]   See above ch 2, s II.

are particularly striking. In *Öztürk v Turkey*,[44] the Court held that there had been a violation of Article 10 when the National Security Court convicted the publisher of a biography of a founder member of the Turkish Communist Party: the national court had accepted the prosecution argument that poems in the book sought to undermine the state and to stir up hatred. The European Court emphasised the sincerity of the publisher's aim to circulate a biography of an important national figure who had died in controversial circumstances after his arrest[45] and itself assessed the likely impact of its publication. It was not persuaded that the book would have any harmful effect on the prevention of disorder in Turkey.[46]

Similar principles had been applied in *Erdoğdu and İnce v Turkey*, in which the Court upheld a challenge to the conviction of a journalist and editor of a review who had published an interview with a Turkish sociologist concerning the formation of political attitudes in the Kurdish community and the reactions to them of the Turkish state.[47] There was no good reason to treat the interview as an incitement to violence.[48] Further, the Court rejected the argument that as the penalties on the applicants had been deferred, there was no effective restriction on freedom of expression; the journalist and the editor were still faced with the future prospect of heavy penalties. The ruling amounts perhaps to an acknowledgement of the 'chilling effect' of restrictions on freedom of expression and of the press.[49]

Though neither Turkish case involved a university professor or lecturer, it seems clear in the light of these decisions that the prosecution of bona fide academic publications would be incompatible with the Convention right to freedom of expression. Nor could a university professor or lecturer be charged under the terrorism legislation in respect of a newspaper article or interview in which, for example, he or she argued for greater understanding of the origins of terrorism and the motives of its supporters; academic staff, like other citizens, enjoy

---

[44] Application no 22479/93, decision of 28 September 1999.
[45] Ibid, paras 65–68.
[46] Ibid, para 69.
[47] Application nos 25067/94 and 2068/94, Decision of 8 July 1999.
[48] Ibid, paras 51–52.
[49] Ibid, para 53.

full freedom of political expression.[50] That does not mean, of course, that the controversial provisions of the TA 2006, let alone the terms of the earlier legislation of 2000, as such infringe the right to freedom of expression or academic freedom; but the European jurisprudence does require courts in England to interpret these provisions compatibly with the exercise of these rights.

## D. Two Episodes at Nottingham University

Two recent episodes at Nottingham University should be mentioned, if only to highlight the impact of the terrorism legislation on academic life in the United Kingdom. But it is less clear how far either of them shows that academic freedom is now seriously at risk as a result of university authorities' response to this legislation. In May 2008 Rizwaan Sabir, a Nottingham Master of Arts student, and Hicham Yezza, personal assistant to the Head of the School of Modern Languages and Cultures, were arrested and detained for a few days after the latter downloaded on his computer an edited version of the al-Qa'ida training manual at Sabir's request, in order to assist him in research for his dissertation.[51] The manual is accessible from the US Department of Justice and other respectable websites, and the full manual is available for purchase from Amazon;[52] it is also available from the university library.[53] The police had been informed by the university after members of the staff at the Modern Languages School had noticed the document on Yezza's computer while he was absent from work. Dr Rod Thornton, Sabir's dissertation supervisor in the School of Politics and International Relations, had seen him previously on two or three occasions and had discussed his bibliography. Apparently, attempts by Dr Thornton to

---

[50] See below ch 9, s II regarding extramural expression.

[51] This account is drawn from a number of sources, notably the discussion of the episode by M Daly and S Matthews, *Academic Freedom and the University of Nottingham* (York, Zoilus Press, 2009); as well as accounts and opinion pieces in *Times Higher Education* (see below nn 55 and 60).

[52] Telephone interview with Dr Rod Thornton, Lecturer at the School of Politics and International Relations, October 13 2009. See his discussion of the manual (11 July 2009), available at the Teaching Terrorism website, http://www.teachingter-rorism.net (accessed 7 August 2010).

[53] Email from Dr Thornton, 14 April 2010.

discuss the arrests with the University Registrar were unsuccessful.[54] The University's response to the arrests was fully discussed at meetings of its authorities, which endorsed its actions.[55]

Both Sabir and Yezza were released without charge after a few days, so no prosecution was brought under the terrorism legislation.[56] Indeed, Sabir completed his MA and subsequently enrolled as a doctoral student at the university.[57] But it would be wrong to conclude that the episode may not have worrying implications for the exercise of academic freedom. Admittedly, students themselves are not entitled to claim the right to academic freedom conferred by the Education Reform Act 1988.[58] Nor are members of university administrative staff. So neither Sabir nor Yezza enjoyed academic freedom in law. In principle, however, students, particularly research students, should enjoy the same intellectual freedom as members of the academic staff. In Germany they would be covered by the right to scientific freedom (*Wissenschaftsfreiheit*), which can be claimed by anyone engaged in serious scholarly research.[59] Moreover, Dr Thornton would have had academic freedom to download the training manual for his own research and to discuss its contents with his research students, so it makes little sense to deny the latter the same freedom. This point is, however, of only theoretical interest for this episode; the difficulties arose because Sabir had sent the training manual to Yezza, an administrative assistant who was not himself engaged in research work.

What perhaps the episode does show is that university authorities should whenever possible consult academic supervisors and Heads of Department before calling in the police in a case of this kind. That step might in some circumstances assure them that it would be inappropriate and unnecessary to refer the matter to the police, a course that is likely, as it did in the Nottingham episode, to attract bad publicity for the university. On the other hand, it is understandable in these anxious times that university authorities will err on the side of caution and

[54] Telephone interview with Dr Thornton (above n 52).

[55] *Times Higher Education*, 17 July 2008, 8.

[56] However, Yezza was rearrested for breach of immigration rules and later sentenced to nine months' imprisonment for deception of the immigration authorities.

[57] In 2009 he transferred to the University of Strathclyde.

[58] See above ch 4, s III(C).

[59] See above ch 5, s II.

260 Academic Freedom in the Age of Terrorism

want to participate actively in the application of terrorism laws. In this particular episode, it is relevant that at the time of the discovery of the al-Qa'ida training manual Yezza was absent from the office and so could not explain why he had downloaded it or discuss its contents. Therefore there was no reason for the authorities at Nottingham University to make any link between the manual and research student work in the Politics School, so it would be wrong to blame them for trespassing on academic freedom.

But equally one can understand why a few academics in the Politics School thought the university had been overzealous in ensuring the enforcement of the terrorism laws to the cost of academic and intellectual freedom.[60] The then Vice-Chancellor, Sir Colin Campbell, issued a notice to all university staff, stating that there is no 'right' to access terrorist materials and that those who do this for research purposes are likely to have a good defence after perhaps some period in detention while charges under the terrorist legislation are investigated.[61] Although legally correct, the notice could be read as expressing indifference to the values of academic freedom and research. Universities should be primarily concerned to defend the research freedom of their staff and students, when, as soon became clear in this case, there was no chance of a successful prosecution for possession of a terrorist publication.[62]

The second episode raises perhaps more complex academic freedom issues. In the wake of the arrests in 2008, the School of Politics and International Relations revised its system for the review of reading lists (Module Review); course syllabi and reading lists are now examined by a teaching group to ensure they meet certain standards.[63] The revised system of Module Review applies to all courses in the School and was approved by its governing body, on which academic staff have a large majority. Dr Thornton objected to the revision of the system, which,

---

[60] See the views of AG Nilsen, V Pupavac and B Renz, all Nottingham University academics, in *Times Higher Education*, 5 June 2008, 26–27.

[61] Reported in *Times Higher Education*, 17 July 2008, 8.

[62] Even if the elements of the offence of dissemination of a terrorist publication had been made out, Shabir and Yezza would have had the defence that the publication did not express their views nor had their endorsement: TA 2006, s 2(9), discussed above in s II(B).

[63] *Times Higher Education*, 25 June 2009, 9; and telephone interview with Professor Paul Heywood, Head of the School of Politics and International Relations, Nottingham University, 24 November 2009.

he has argued, was originally designed to apply only to his reading lists.[64] Some academic staff in the School, however, have defended the process, as have other academics at Nottingham.[65] In favour of this step, it has been argued that the revised Module Review ensures that a syllabus is covered comprehensively; that overlap problems with the syllabi of other courses are minimised; and that assessment methods are fair, etc. These principles could be formulated and applied to any university course, and there could be little or no objection to them. In the context of the earlier events, the Review was designed, at least in part, to advise lecturers whether material on their reading list might be illegal or regarded as encouraging violence or terrorism.[66] Module Review was intended in this way to help academic staff and students, who would be assured that any material on the lists had been reviewed and endorsed by the School; it could therefore be seen as protecting their academic freedom.[67] Nevertheless, though the reviewing committee does not have authority to 'censor' reading lists, a few members of the School have regarded its institution as an attack on their academic freedom to teach courses as they think appropriate.[68]

Resolution of this conflict of views depends to some extent on whether academic freedom should be ascribed to individual teachers on the one hand or to an academic institution or one of its Schools or Departments on the other. Clearly some systems of course review might inhibit, if not altogether curtail, the freedom of an individual lecturer to teach a course as he or she thinks appropriate. Lecturers might be required, in an extreme form of this process, to teach from prescribed reading lists and be forbidden to add further materials. The Nottingham Module Review has been defended with the argument that teaching freedom is an *institutional* right of the university under the Higher Education Act (HEA) 2004[69] and that it is a reasonable exercise of that freedom for university departments to monitor the reading lists

[64] Telephone interview, 13 October 2009.
[65] See P Eadie and M Humphrey, 'Nottingham "Censorship": A Defence' (3 August 2009), available on the Teaching Terrorism website (above n 52).
[66] Telephone interview with Professor Heywood (above n 63).
[67] Comment of Professor Heywood on earlier draft of this section.
[68] See the expression of views on 'Nottingham: Reading Lists Inspected for Capacity to Incite Violence' (15 July 2009) on the Teaching Terrorism website (above n 52).
[69] Discussed above in ch 4, s V(A).

provided by their members.[70] However, it would be wrong to infer anything from the HEA 2004. The institutional freedom of universities to determine the content of their courses and how they are taught was recognised to protect their autonomy against the Director of Fair Access; the legislation was not designed to formulate prerogatives of university authorities or Heads of Department by which they could circumscribe the teaching freedoms of individual academics.

There is no simple answer to the question how far departmental committees or Heads of School or Department are entitled to monitor, or even regulate, the contents of individual academics' reading lists. By convention and general practice, at least among older universities, it is for individual academics to determine how exactly they teach their courses, though for good reasons basic syllabi and reading lists may be prescribed in university regulations; faculty or departmental control is only exercised in extreme cases where, for instance, there is a serious allegation that a lecturer has been teaching material unrelated to the prescribed syllabus or to the course description, or that he or she is introducing, say, pornographic material into class discussion when this is wholly irrelevant to the theme of the lecture or seminar.

Reading lists have usually been exchanged as a matter of courtesy or when a lecturer wants the advice of a colleague teaching a related course; on the other hand, there is evidence that schemes like the Nottingham Module Review are becoming more common.[71] David Miller, convenor of the *Teaching Terrrorism* group, has said that he is unaware of any other university that has instituted a formal system for the review of reading lists.[72] In his view, Nottingham's policy amounts to a 'fundamental attack on academic freedom'.[73] Indeed it would do so, if the Module Review were imposed by university administrators and enabled the reviewing committee to censor or to prescribe the contents of individual academics' reading lists. However, the Nottingham system does not have these objectionable features, so it is surely acceptable. But in the context of the events that preceded it, when the university arguably displayed some indifference to the values (though not the law)

---

[70] Eadie and Humphrey (above n 65).
[71] Telephone interview with Professor Heywood (above n 63).
[72] *Times Higher Education*, 25 June 2009.
[73] Ibid, 9.

of academic freedom, it is hardly surprising that members of the School have found its introduction disturbing.

### III. ACADEMIC FREEDOM IN THE UNITED STATES AFTER 9/11

The destruction of the Twin Towers on 9/11 has had a significant impact on academic freedom in American universities,[74] as it has had on the exercise of general civil liberties in the United States. The enactment of the Uniting and Strengthening America by Providing Appropriate Tools Required to Intercept and Obstruct Terrorism Act[75]—understandably and invariably referred to as the USA PATRIOT Act—gives the executive, among other powers, greater authority to investigate the use of libraries and to exclude visitors to the United States on the basis of their expression of views sympathetic to terrorist causes. These provisions have implications for research by scholars in the United States and for the freedom of universities to invite academics from other countries to take up visiting professorships.[76] Quite apart from these new legal provisions, there is widespread public anxiety about further terrorist atrocities, which sometimes has led to pressure on universities to discipline or even remove from their staff professors considered sympathetic to terrorist organisations or even those who have expressed unpopular views on the Middle East, in particular the continuing tension between Israel and Palestinians.

### A. The **PATRIOT** Act

The PATRIOT Act was passed within a few weeks of 9/11 with little dissent in Congress. It amends earlier legislation, notably the Foreign Intelligence Surveillance Act[77] so the Director of the Federal Bureau

---

[74] For general discussion, see O'Neil, *Academic Freedom in the Wired World* (above n 11) ch 4; B Doumani (ed), *Academic Freedom after September 11* (New York, Zone Books, 2006) esp the Introduction; and Gerstmann and Streb (eds) (above n 11) esp chs 3–5.

[75] Public Law 107-56 (26 October 2001).

[76] WG Tierney and VM Lechuga, 'Academic Freedom in the 21st Century' (2005) *Thought and Action* 7, 12–14.

[77] 50 USC, ss 1801 ff.

of Investigations (FBI) may now apply for court orders requiring the production of 'any tangible things (including books, papers, documents, and other items) for an investigation to protect against international terrorism or clandestine intelligence activities', as long as any investigation of a US person is not conducted solely in respect of activities protected by the First Amendment.[78] (The proviso is unlikely to provide much of a safeguard for academic freedom. Quite apart from doubts whether there is an individual First Amendment right to academic freedom or freedom of research,[79] the proviso only precludes investigations relating *solely* to activities protected by the Amendment.) Such a court order must not disclose that it has been issued for the purpose of such an investigation; moreover, any disclosure of the investigation or court order is forbidden, except to the persons required to produce the documents or other records.[80] This extreme 'gag order' means that it is illegal for a librarian to inform, say, a university professor or researcher that records of his or her borrowings and use of a library computer have been taken by the FBI for investigation. The implications for freedom of research are clear; any scholar investigating the origins, motives and methodologies of terrorist organisations does so at risk of a clandestine FBI investigation. In particular, research cannot lawfully be conducted at all into the impact of the PATRIOT Act itself on the work of library staff or on the use of libraries, for they cannot talk about it.[81]

The other provision of the legislation that has caused difficulties for universities is section 411, which provides a broader definition of the grounds of inadmissibility, on the basis of which visas for visitors to the United States may be refused or revoked.[82] For example, anyone who is a representative of any political, social or other group whose public endorsement of terrorism, in the view of the Secretary of State, undermines US efforts to eliminate it, is caught by the definition, as is anyone who has used a position of prominence with any organisation to endorse or support terrorist activity or a terrorist organisation. A visitor

---

[78]   PATRIOT Act, s 215.
[79]   See above ch 6, esp s IV.
[80]   PATRIOT ACT, s 215(d).
[81]   PT Jaeger, CR McClure, JC Bertot and JT Snead, 'The USA PATRIOT Act, The Foreign Intelligence Surveillance Act, and Information Policy Research in Libraries' (2004) 74 *Library Quarterly* 99, 107–9.
[82]   S 411 amends the Immigration and Nationality Act: 8 USC 1182(a)(3).

may be considered to 'engage in terrorist activity' if either individually or as a member of an organisation, he or she commits, incites or solicits funds for such activity, or if he or she funds or provides any material support for it or for a terrorist organisation.

There is perhaps nothing wrong with these provisions, as long as they are implemented strictly and fairly; the difficulty is that a decision may be taken in respect of a visiting academic without the supply of adequate reasons or without any effective opportunity for the scholar to meet the cause for concern. This may well have occurred in the case of the Swiss-born academic, Tariq Ramadan, a prominent Islamic theologian and advocate of the effective participation of Muslims in European society.[83] In 2004 he accepted an endowed professorship at Notre Dame University and took steps to move there. In the summer of that year his visa was revoked by the State Department without clear explanation; Ramadan resigned his position from Notre Dame at the end of 2004, taking up a Visiting Fellowship at Oxford in the following academic year. Subsequently, the US State Department stated that Ramadan had provided material support for terrorist organisations; it is alleged that he had given donations to charitable organisations that, in the authorities' view, were linked to Hamas, regarded in the United States as a terrorist organisation.

The American Civil Liberties Union (ACLU) and New York Civil Liberties Union have challenged the visa revocation on behalf of a number of organisations, including the AAUP. One of their arguments has been that the State Department decision infringed the First Amendment free speech rights of both Ramadan and those scholars in the United States who wanted to hear him speak. The challenge failed in the District Court, but the Court of Appeals for the Second Circuit upheld the appeal in July 2009. The record did not show whether the consular official taking the decision had allowed Ramadan an opportunity to show that he did not know and had no reasonable cause to believe that the recipients of his donations were terrorist organisations. The statute required visa applicants to have a fair opportunity to contest allegations against them, so the case was sent back to the District Court

---

[83] In addition to Ramadan, other visiting scholars have been denied visas under the anti-terrorism legislation. See 'I'm a Scholar Not a Terrorist', *Times Higher Education*, 25 March 2005, discussing the refusal of a visa to a professor of history in Nicaragua.

for it to determine whether Ramadan had been given that opportunity. The important point for academic freedom is that the Court of Appeals followed a Supreme Court ruling that there is a First Amendment right to hear the views of visa applicants.[84] Universities or individual academics may therefore challenge decisions to refuse or revoke visas for visiting scholars.

## B. University Decisions after 9/11

The impact of 9/11 on academic freedom has also been felt as a result of the change in the general cultural and political climate. As during the McCarthy period, the patriotism and loyalty of scholars who question the wisdom of US foreign policy, particularly in the Middle East, or who express support for Palestinians and other militant Arabs is questioned. The budget of the University of North Carolina at Chapel Hill was threatened by the state legislature because in 2002 it included a book on the Koran in the reading list for new freshmen.[85] The University of Colorado was denounced by the state Governor and members of the legislature when it invited Hanan Ashrawi, a Palestinian spokesperson and distinguished intellectual, to speak on its campuses.[86] Attempts were made to secure by subpoena the records of a conference at Drake University, Texas, held to discuss terrorism and US Middle East policy. But the University President resisted, and eventually the subpoenas were withdrawn.[87] These are only a few of the episodes in which universities have come under pressure from the public and state politicians when they have held conferences or invited speakers to discuss the causes of terrorism, Middle East politics or related topics. These cases

---

[84] *Kleindienst v Mandel* 408 US 753 (1972).

[85] See DA Downs, 'Political Mobilization and Resistance to Censorship' in Gerstmann and Streb (eds) (above n 11) 61, 74; and J Moeser', 'Unchallengeable Orthodoxies: A Presidential Perspective', conference paper delivered at Phoenix, AZ, 20 March 2009. In 2002, James Moeser was Chancellor of the University of North Carolina at Chapel Hill.

[86] O'Neil, 'Academic Freedom in the Post-September 11 Era' (above n 11) 49.

[87] Ibid, 46–47.

have caused considerable concern and led to the publication of a special AAUP report, *Academic Freedom and National Security in a Time of Crisis*.[88]

In one episode, identified as warranting 'deep concern',[89] a tenured professor of computer science, Sami Al-Arian, was suspended from his duties at the University of South Florida (USF) and then dismissed eighteen months later. Shortly after September 11th, Al-Arian appeared on a Fox News programme, *The O'Reilly Factor*, in the course of which he admitted that he had previously made very strong anti-Israel statements—'Death to Israel'—and that he headed a pro-Palestinian organisation. Within hours, the university was flooded with telephone calls from alumni, parents and members of the public, many of them calling for immediate action to be taken. USF initially placed Al-Arian on paid leave and required him to stay away from campus, pending an investigation into whether his personal safety was in danger. Attitudes hardened, however, in the following two or three months, and at the end of the year, the USF Board of Trustees suspended him and gave notice of its intention to dismiss him. The charges were that he had not taken adequate steps on *The O'Reilly Factor* to indicate that he was speaking personally rather than as a university representative, and further that his extramural speech on this programme and in later media interviews significantly disrupted the ability of the university to function effectively. These charges were rightly found by the AAUP investigating committee to lack any credible foundation.[90] Al-Arian had not claimed to be speaking for the university when he made his anti-Israel remarks, and the disruption, if that is the right word, should be attributed to the reactions of parents and other members of the public. Al-Arian was suspended and threatened with dismissal for exercising his constitutional right to freedom of speech, or on another view for exercising an aspect of academic freedom—the freedom of extramural expression.[91]

[88] AAUP Report, 'Academic Freedom and National Security in a Time of Crisis' (2003) 89(6) *Academe* 34–59, available at http://www.aaup.org (accessed 7 August 2010).

[89] O'Neil, 'Academic Freedom in the Post-September 11 Era' (above n 11) 47.

[90] 'Academic Freedom and Tenure: University of South Florida', Report of AAUP Investigating Committee (2003) 89(3) *Academe* 59–73, available at the AAUP website (above n 88).

[91] See below ch 9, s II for discussion regarding whether it is appropriate to categorise extramural expression as an aspect of academic freedom.

In fact, subsequent developments mean that the conflict of views between the university authorities and the AAUP has ceased to have practical importance. Early in 2003, Al-Arian was charged with the offences of raising money and providing support for terrorist organisations; he was immediately dismissed by the University without ever being given a chance to defend himself. He was eventually acquitted of the most serious charges but then pleaded guilty in 2006 to a lesser offence rather than face a retrial. He accepted deportation, so ending his dispute with USF.[92] Nevertheless, the episode shows very clearly the pressure on universities to discipline awkward members of academic staff for the expression of radical or unpopular views. They are particularly vulnerable to this pressure during periods of anxiety brought about by terrorist atrocities.

## IV. CONCLUSIONS

Terrorism laws do therefore have an impact on the exercise of academic freedom, as they do of course on the civil liberties exercised by every member of the public. In the United States this is reflected in the special report of the AAUP published at the end of 2003, which expressed general anxiety on the matter,[93] while in the United Kingdom a group of academics specialising in terrorism studies have formed a group to discuss the implications of recent legislation for the teaching of their subject.[94] To some extent these consequences are inevitable, given the broad terms in which legislation is typically drafted to meet every conceivable contingency and to counter terrorist plots before they come to fruition.

Moreover, university academic staff should not be immune from the application of terrorism laws. But it would be much better if these laws were drafted more narrowly, so that academics who have no intention at all to promote or encourage acts of terrorism would be at less risk of prosecution when they, say, acquire or access terrorist propaganda or other material for the purposes of their teaching or research.

---

[92]  O'Neil, *Academic Freedom in the Wired World* (above n 11) 88.

[93]  Above n 88.

[94]  See the Teaching Terrorism website (above n 52), to which frequent references have been made in this chapter.

Further, the broad terms of UK terrorism legislation and its failure to incorporate any specific defence for teaching and research are not the only reasons for the vulnerability of academics. Universities may themselves fail to support academic freedom in this area. This is particularly likely to happen when they themselves face pressure from the public to support the government in the war against terrorism and to show that support by disciplining those who adopt a different, perhaps more nuanced, perspective.

# 9

# *Freedom of Extramural Speech*

## I. THE PROBLEM OF EXTRAMURAL SPEECH

EXTRAMURAL SPEECH (OR expression) raises some troublesome questions about the scope of academic freedom law. In particular, it is unclear whether academic freedom applies at all to this speech: the expression by academics of their views on general political topics. This type of speech should be distinguished from other kinds of academic expression that are clearly covered and largely protected by academic freedom:[1] lectures and seminars; scholarly and scientific publications; and the criticism of academic administration termed 'intramural expression'. Publication freedom is an aspect of freedom of research; issues in this context were treated above in chapter seven, as well as in the chapters discussing the general principles of academic freedom law in the United Kingdom (chapter four), in Germany (chapter five) and in the United States (chapter six). Intramural expression concerns the speech of academics about their universities' policies and practices or about education standards. It is generally recognised that professors and lecturers should be free to disseminate their concerns on such topics, for these matters are closely linked to the organisation of teaching and research and to university governance.[2]

The freedom of extramural speech relates to the right often claimed by professors and other academic staff to communicate their views on

---

[1] The distinction between coverage and protection is familiar in free speech jurisprudence. See E Barendt, *Freedom of Speech* (Oxford, Oxford University Press, 2007) 75–76. In the context of academic freedom, the distinction refers to the difference between a statement that, say, a type of research activity engages academic freedom, and a statement that the university cannot restrict the activity because it is protected by academic freedom.

[2] See above ch 2, s III(C).

general political and social affairs. It should be noted that it is immaterial where the speech is made. A professor may make a political speech on his or her university campus, while conversely intramural expression can be disseminated at a public meeting miles from the university; the distinction between extramural and intramural speech relates to its overall content, not the place where it was delivered. Matthew Finkin and Robert Post define extramural expression as 'speech made by faculty in their capacity as citizens, speech that is typically about matters of public concern and that is unrelated to either scholarly expertise or institutional affiliation'.[3] As will be seen later in this chapter, a definition along these lines is not free of difficulties; it suggests, perhaps rather paradoxically, that academics have greater freedom to speak their minds on matters wholly unconnected to their expertise than they have on matters on which they are expert.

Leaving aside that point for the moment, the definition is good enough to bring out the essential problem of extramural expression: why should academics have *academic freedom* to speak freely about issues of general concern that have little or nothing to do with their academic work? Certainly, university professors and researchers should be as free as other citizens to communicate their views about these issues. They are equally entitled to blog, to write letters to newspapers and to speak at political meetings. But these rights might more plausibly be regarded as covered by the freedom of speech that all citizens enjoy, rather than as aspects of academic freedom.

Nevertheless, freedom of extramural expression is often treated as an important aspect of academic freedom. For example, in its 1940 Statement, the American Association of University Professors (AAUP) said that college and university teachers 'should be free from institutional censorship or discipline' when they speak or write as citizens; the AAUP, however, emphasised that the freedom should be exercised with restraint and that academics 'should show respect for the opinions of others and should make every effort to indicate that they are not speaking for the institution'.[4] Investigations into disputes concerning the scope of extramural freedom of expression form a significant part

---

[3] M Finkin and R Post, *For the Common Good: Principles of American Academic Freedom* (New Haven, Yale University Press, 2009) 127.

[4] For the complete text of this part of the 1940 Statement, see above ch 6, s II(B).

of the AAUP Committee A case work.[5] Chapter four made reference to two well-known academic freedom disputes in the United Kingdom involving Arnold Toynbee and Harold Laski. Both concerned extramural speeches and writing to which prominent members of the public and eventually the university authorities took exception.[6] Freedom of extramural expression has also been an issue in a few recent episodes in the United Kingdom in which academics have been disciplined or subject to criticism for disseminating controversial political views in non-academic publications.[7]

So the questions whether and why academic freedom covers the right of academics to engage in extramural speech must be canvassed. That is the subject of section II of this chapter. On balance, the case for extending academic freedom to cover the right is unpersuasive; it is better to treat this right, as it is in Germany, as an aspect of freedom of expression (section II(C)). Section III is concerned with the law in the United Kingdom and discusses the most important statutory provisions relevant to freedom of extramural expression, as well as a few recent episodes in which this freedom has been claimed, generally without success. The final section of the chapter looks at constitutional principles and court decisions concerning freedom of extramural speech in the United States. Professors' free speech interests are also recognised by the AAUP, but that may not always give them legal protection if their university employers consider, say, extremist or racist speech seriously damaging to good community relations on campus (section IV(B)).

## II. SHOULD ACADEMIC FREEDOM COVER EXTRAMURAL SPEECH?

### A. The Arguments for Coverage

A number of arguments can be made for extending the coverage of academic freedom to extramural speech. The most obvious is that it may be difficult to distinguish such speech from the scholarly discourse and publication that clearly falls under freedom of research and academic

---

[5] Finkin and Post (above n 3) 140–48.
[6] See above ch 4, s II(C).
[7] See below s III(B).

freedom. Academic historians, for example, may write book reviews for newspapers and appear on popular radio and television programmes; in these circumstances, it is hard to draw a sharp line between their academic freedom to publish, say, a review in a scholarly or serious journal on the one hand and more ephemeral writing for a Sunday paper on the other. It is perhaps even harder to determine when they are speaking outside their area of expertise; does an historian exceed his or her competence if he or she draws parallels between the dangers to British independence posed by Napoleon and the erosion of national sovereignty resulting from UK membership in the European Union? Some scholars develop expertise on matters well outside their original academic speciality. For example, Noam Chomsky, a linguistics scholar, has become a (controversial) expert on US foreign policy,[8] while the biologist Richard Dawkins is often considered expert on theological or philosophical questions about the existence of God. Their writing in these areas certainly draws on their scholarly skills, if not their initial professional competence.

But the argument from the difficulty of line-drawing is a poor one. For there are many cases in which it would be easy to see that a scholar or scientist is writing or speaking entirely outside his or her field of competence, for example, if a physicist or engineer denies the Holocaust, or if a historian or literary scholar challenges evolution theory. We need to find an argument other than the alleged difficulty of line-drawing for extending the coverage of academic freedom to these cases of extramural speech and publication. Even in the case of Chomsky, the argument for coverage is really that his writings on US foreign policy are seriously researched and therefore fall under his freedom of research and publication—not under a separate freedom of extramural speech.[9]

Finkin and Post resort to two stronger arguments for holding extramural expression covered by academic freedom. First, they contend that it is better for universities not to intervene when a member of academic staff makes a controversial extramural pronouncement on a matter of political or social concern. Otherwise they will come under constant pressure to step in when alumni, students or other members of the public take a strong dislike to the speech of academic staff.

---

[8] Finkin and Post (above n 3) 134.
[9] Ibid, 135.

Universities should be free to disclaim all responsibility for what their staff say and write, just as they are not considered responsible for the contents of the books and other material in their university libraries.[10] Further, if they succumb to this sort of pressure, they may become more vulnerable to pressure to intervene to regulate the research and academic writing of their staff. As Finkin and Post concede, this argument is concerned with protecting universities and other higher education institutions.[11] It does not really explain why universities should not regulate controversial extramural speech when they are confident that this is the right thing to do, let alone does it establish a right or freedom for academic staff to engage in it.

A third, though related, argument is without doubt the strongest: the intervention of university authorities, or its threat, in these circumstances creates an atmosphere of distrust between university administrators and academic staff, which makes it harder for the latter to teach and research freely. Freedom of extramural speech is therefore a 'prophylactic protection for freedom of research and freedom of teaching',[12] perhaps in much the same way as a broad constitutional privilege for defamatory publications is required to protect freedom of political speech.[13] But this argument, like the first, rests on the questionable assumption that universities cannot be trusted to distinguish between the regulation of freedom of research or teaching on the one hand and the regulation of extramural speech on the other.[14] Moreover, it implies that professors do not enjoy rights as citizens to speak freely about matters of public concern; on the contrary, it assumes that without the extension of academic freedom to cover these rights, they would have no legal liberty to speak freely.

[10]   Ibid, 136–39.
[11]   Ibid, 139: the freedom 'finds its justification in counsels of institutional expedience and prudence'.
[12]   Ibid, 140.
[13]   In *New York Times v Sullivan* 376 US 254 (1964) the Supreme Court formulated the requirement that a libel claimant had to prove the defendant knew the defamatory allegations were untrue, etc, as such a rule was necessary to safeguard the freedom of political speech, including the publication of true defamatory allegations.
[14]   The *New York Times* privilege (ibid) is justified with the similar argument that juries cannot be relied on to distinguish true from false defamatory allegations, so a wide privilege was necessary to provide a defence for all allegations published without knowledge of their falsity, etc.

## B. The Arguments against Coverage

The strongest argument against treating extramural expression as an aspect of academic freedom is that it would give academics a privileged position to communicate their views on matters of public concern. Professors and other academic staff should enjoy the same free speech rights as other citizens, not a greater freedom to speak about matters of general public controversy. Academic freedom is a professional freedom, protecting the core functions of research and teaching; it should be distinguished from freedom of speech and other general civil liberties. Professors can put forward convincing arguments for allowing them greater freedom than other employees to determine how they do their work—free from the direction of Heads of Department and university administrators.[15] But the claim that they should enjoy greater freedom to comment on matters of public concern is understandably regarded as elitist.

This argument has been put persuasively in a classic article by William van Alstyne, a distinguished American writer on both freedom of speech law and academic freedom.[16] He pointed to two other disadvantages in the conflation of academic freedom and freedom of speech. First, bringing inflated claims to wide free speech rights as an aspect of academic freedom makes less likely the general acceptance of genuine academic freedom claims.[17] The case for academic freedom—rarely a popular argument—is politically weakened when it is extended to cover, say, a wide right to disseminate racist or other extreme views. Secondly, this extension might actually reduce the strength of a free speech claim. The point is that professors, like other citizens, have free speech rights to say what they like, subject only to the limits imposed by the general laws of incitement, libel and so on. But academic freedom confers a right to teach and publish on the basis of the standards that have been accepted by the profession and are applied through the processes of peer review and quality assessment. Van Alstyne pointed out that if extramural expression were regarded as an aspect of academic

---

[15] See the arguments above in ch 3.

[16] W van Alstyne, 'The Specific Theory of Academic Freedom and the General Issue of Civil Liberty' in E Pincoffs (ed), *The Concept of Academic Freedom* (Austin, University of Texas Press, 1975) 59.

[17] Ibid, 64–65.

276 Freedom of Extramural Speech

freedom, its dissemination might be held to the same standards. An eccentric nuclear scientist would not be as free as other citizens in newspaper letters or on a blog, say, to deny the Holocaust or to argue that the US government was responsible for the destruction of the Twin Towers, because those views are wholly unacceptable by the standards of historical scholarship and would be an abuse of academic freedom.[18] Assimilating academic freedom and freedom of speech would therefore lead to diminishing the scope of professors' free speech rights.

Whatever the merits of these arguments, the key point is that in principle professors and other academics should enjoy the same free speech rights as other citizens, and it would be wrong for academic freedom to confer on them wider free speech rights. That conclusion might mean that universities, like other employers, could discipline their (academic) staff for seriously disruptive extramural speech, for example, the circulation of a racist publication that made it impossible for the particular employee to work in harmony with colleagues from minority racial or ethnic groups. For freedom of speech may be curtailed in the context of the employment relationship. Employers may discipline or even dismiss employees for speech that is lawful and not proscribed by the general law.[19] Moreover, freedom of speech may not be strongly protected against the decisions of *private* employers; in the United States, the state action principle means constitutional rights can only be invoked directly against the decisions of public authorities and employers. It is for these reasons that Finkin and Post do not find van Alstyne's argument persuasive. In their view, ordinary civil liberties principles, including constitutional free speech rights, do not afford professors adequate protection when they engage in extramural expression.[20] In particular, professors at, say, Harvard or Stanford—private universities—cannot assert freedom of speech rights against their universities. Finkin and Post conclude that professors should be able to invoke academic freedom to cover their extramural expression.

---

[18] Ibid, 69–70. For an argument that Holocaust denial need not be regarded as covered by academic freedom, see S Fish, 'Holocaust Denial and Academic Freedom' (2000) 35 *Valparaiso Law Review* 499.

[19] See Barendt, *Freedom of Speech* (above n 1) ch 14, s III; and also below s IV for further treatment of this area of law in the United States.

[20] Finkin and Post (above n 3) 132–33.

This perspective is understandable in the context of US constitutional law, insofar as that law gives professors at public universities wider free speech rights than those enjoyed by their peers at private colleges. Moreover, Finkin and Post are arguing for an understanding of the *professional* academic freedom, formulated by the AAUP and generally recognised by universities in the United States.[21] They are not arguing that academic freedom gives academic staff wider *constitutional* free speech rights than those held by other employees. But their theoretical arguments could be deployed to make that case. That step would be wrong. A clear line can be drawn in principle between academic freedom on the one hand and freedom of speech on the other. Freedom of extramural expression belongs to the second. It is wrong to extend academic freedom to cover it.

## C. The Separate Treatment of Political Speech in German Law

German constitutional law draws a distinction between the freedom of expression of opinion, guaranteed by Article 5(1) of the Grundgesetz, and the artistic and scientific freedom guaranteed by Article 5(3). As explained in chapter five, it matters how a speech or interview is characterised: the expression of a political opinion may be limited by general laws, while the exercise of scientific freedom (*Wissenschaftsfreiheit*) can be restricted only by laws protecting other constitutional rights and values, notably human dignity. *Wissenschaftsfreiheit* can be asserted by anyone— not only academics—whose publication or communication indicates a serious intention to express the truth.[22] Extramural political speeches and activity are covered by freedom of expression rather than scientific freedom, for they are not disseminated to further knowledge or state new truths.[23] In accordance with this principle, an Administrative Court in Kassel held that a medical student could not claim academic freedom (*akademische Freiheit*) when in infringement of the state university law he distributed party political leaflets and displayed placards in the medical school clinic.[24] There was no authority for extending the rights in

---

[21]  See above ch 6, s II for the professional understanding of academic freedom.
[22]  BVerfGE 90, 1 (1994), discussed above in ch 5, s III(B).
[23]  Decision of the Berlin Administrative Court, *JZ* 1973, 209, 210.
[24]  *NJW* 1980, 661, 662.

Article 5(3) to cover this sort of speech. Nor was this political activity protected by freedom of expression, since that did not confer any right to distribute leaflets, etc in any place the speaker chose; regulations could limit this form of expression as incompatible with the purpose of a university.

On the other hand, another Administrative Court decision has taken a broad view of the scope of *Wissenschaftsfreiheit*.[25] A university professor was entitled to claim the protection of that freedom for the terms of an interview conducted at his home and later broadcast. In the course of the interview, the professor protested strongly against the introduction of new security laws, which, he thought, should be challenged in the courts. If these challenges failed, then citizens might have to exercise their right of resistance to opponents of the constitutional order.[26] The political content of the interview did not take it outside the scope of scientific or academic freedom, for the professor had been interviewed as a legal expert on data protection laws. Equally importantly, the court held that it was immaterial that his views were disseminated through the mass media rather than in an academic journal or at a conference. It was through the mass media that the general public had access to the important findings of academic research on matters of contemporary interest, such as environmental protection and healthy living.[27] But if the same views had been expressed by, say, a linguistics professor without expertise in constitutional and data protection law, they might have been treated as an exercise of freedom of expression. In those circumstances, it would have been easier to regard them as extramural expression rather than as an aspect of scientific freedom.

Drawing a line between academic (or scientific) freedom and the general liberty of freedom of speech may therefore not be straightforward. In the United Kingdom and the United States, the coverage of extramural speech by academic freedom is problematic because it seems to give academics wide free speech rights that are not enjoyed by other citizens. In contrast, German law might allow for a more generous interpretation of the scope of scientific freedom, since it is a right that belongs to everyone, not only to academics working in universities. In that jurisdiction it may be right to bring within the scope of scientific

---

[25] *NJW* 1989, 1688.
[26] GG, art 20, IV.
[27] *NJW* 1989, 1689.

freedom blogs, broadcast interviews and press and magazine articles that lack academic form, provided their content is based on serious research.[28] But even in Germany, purely political expression, unrelated to the pursuit of knowledge, is not covered by scientific freedom. The German jurisprudence supports the conclusion that a line can and should be drawn between academic freedom and freedom of extramural expression.

### III. UK LAW

This section of the chapter discusses the statutory provisions that might be involved in disputes concerning the scope and protection of extramural expression in the United Kingdom. The second part is concerned with some recent episodes in the United Kingdom involving extramural expression; in particular it examines, in the context of the Frank Ellis affair at Leeds University, how the balance between the freedom of speech of academics and good race or community relations might be struck. The dismissal of Chris Brand from Edinburgh University is also mentioned, but as that case involved broader issues it is examined in full below in chapter ten.

### A. Statutory Provisions and General Principles

Freedom of expression, including the extramural expression of academics, is protected in English (and Scots) law under the Human Rights Act 1998 (HRA) as one of the rights guaranteed by the European Convention on Human Rights (ECHR). The legal position is, however, far from straightforward. If universities are treated as 'public authorities', they are directly bound to comply with the Convention rights; it would then be unlawful for a university to act incompatibly with the right by, for example, sacking an academic simply because it disapproved of his or her political views.[29] Universities are, however, probably only to be treated as 'public authorities' because some of their

---

[28] See the discussion above in ch 5, s III(C).
[29] HRA s 6(1)(a).

functions are 'of a public nature'.[30] In that event, they are not so treated in relation to their private acts and decisions. That would mean that they are not directly constrained by the right to freedom of expression (and other Convention rights) when they discipline members of their staff; that would be regarded as private acts taken under the employment contract. However, a court or tribunal considering an action for breach of contract or unfair dismissal is bound to uphold Convention rights,[31] so in that indirect way freedom of (extramural) expression might be invoked by academics if they are disciplined for what they have said or written.

The HRA requires legislation to be interpreted and applied, so far as possible, to give effect to Convention rights.[32] That means that when two interpretations can be given to a statutory provision, say, in public order legislation, a court must choose the interpretation that allows for the exercise of freedom of expression (and related Convention rights such as freedom of assembly) rather than the one that inhibits the exercise of these freedoms. But the right to freedom of expression guaranteed by Article 10 of the ECHR is far from absolute. Its exercise may be limited when 'necessary in a democratic society', among other things, to prevent disorder and to protect the rights of other people.[33] The European Court and Commission of Human Rights have upheld restrictions on freedom of expression to protect the rights of racial, ethnic and religious groups insulted or seriously offended by hate speech or by profane films;[34] indeed, in some cases it has been held that racist speech, including denial of the Holocaust, does not even engage Article 10.[35] It falls altogether outside the terms of the freedom of expression guarantee.

Quite apart from these points, it is unclear how fully the right to freedom of expression is protected within the context of the employment

---

[30]  Ibid, s 6(3)(b).

[31]  Ibid, s 6(3)(a), providing that courts and tribunals are 'public authorities'.

[32]  Ibid, s 3.

[33]  ECHR, art 10(2), incorporated into UK law by Sch 1 of the HRA.

[34]  For example, see 9235/81, *X v Germany* 29 D & R 194; and *Otto-Preminger-Institut v Austria* (1994) 19 EHRR 34.

[35]  8348/78, *Glimmerveen v Netherlands*, 18 D & R 187; and 250596/94, *Remer v Germany*, 82 D & R 117.

relationship.[36] Any employer may argue that speech which is perfectly lawful under the general criminal and civil law might nevertheless disrupt relations between members of staff and hinder the effective discharge of their responsibilities. In the academic context universities have a legitimate interest in ensuring that colleagues speak civilly to one another and do not insult or seriously offend students by, say, making racist remarks either in class or outside the campus. If they do not intervene, departments may become demoralised and will attract fewer student applicants. Equally, it would be wrong to conclude that employees, particularly academic staff, surrender or waive their rights to speak freely and associate with others in political parties and pressure groups when they start work. In its leading decision in this area, the European Court held that Germany infringed the Convention when a school teacher was dismissed because she was a member of the Communist party.[37] Balancing the right to freedom of expression against a state's interest in ensuring that its schools work effectively, the Court held that dismissal of the teacher was a disproportionate interference with her exercise of the right; there was no evidence that she had made an attempt to indoctrinate her students or even adopt a position hostile to the German Constitution, outside her work. Although there is no clear authority on the point, it is uncertain whether the European Court, or the English courts, would uphold claims by lecturers that their Convention rights to freedom of expression had been infringed if universities took disciplinary measures for, say, extremist speech (whether on or outside the university premises) that had insulted or seriously offended colleagues or students on racial or religious grounds.

In practice, statutory provisions other than the HRA are much more likely to determine disputes in the United Kingdom arising from extramural speech. One set of provisions is strongly protective of freedom of speech. The Education (No 2) Act 1986 requires university authorities to take 'reasonably practicable' steps 'to ensure that freedom of speech within the law is secured for members, students and employees of the establishment and for visiting speakers'.[38] The use of university premises must not be denied to any individual or organisation on the

---

[36] Barendt, *Freedom of Speech* (above n 1) 486–96; and L Vickers, *Freedom of Speech and Employment* (Oxford, Oxford University Press, 2002) ch 7.

[37] *Vogt v Germany* (1995) 21 EHRR 205.

[38] Education Act (No 2) Act 1986, s 43(1).

ground of the views held by the individual or by any member of the organisation, or of any of its objectives or policies.[39] Universities have been required to draw up codes of practice to ensure that these duties are complied with.[40] The background to these unusual provisions was the student disruption of meetings addressed by Conservative ministers and right-wing speakers in the 1970s and early 1980s.[41] Although intended largely to protect the free speech of visiting speakers, they also protect the freedom of speech of academic staff and indeed all university employees. They are concerned with speech on university campuses, but that would cover some extramural speech—though not of course, say, meetings elsewhere or letters to a newspaper.

These provisions only require university authorities to safeguard freedom of speech 'within the law'. They can forbid a meeting if it is clear that the speaker is going to incite crime, infringe public order legislation, use threatening (or other) language intended or likely to cause racial or religious hatred, or in some other way to break the law. Of course, this will rarely be clear. Extremist speakers, keen to provoke controversy and perhaps disorder, typically do not circulate advance copies of their text; even if they did, they might depart from it and use inflammatory language. So a Working Group for the Committee of Vice-Chancellors and Principals in 1998 concluded that universities are entitled to act on their reasonable belief or suspicion that a speaker will infringe the law; in that event the university authorities may prevent or stop the meeting.[42]

Another provision strongly protective of free speech is of course the academic freedom clause in the Education Reform Act 1988. It requires universities to ensure that their academic staff have 'freedom within the law to question and test received wisdom, and to put forward new ideas and controversial or unpopular opinions' without putting their jobs at risk.[43] On a broad interpretation, this language would give strong protection to the extramural speech of university professors,

---

[39]   Ibid, s. 43(2).
[40]   For example, see Oxford University Code of Practice approved by University Council on 13 July 2009, *Oxford University Gazette*, 29 July 2009, 1382–83.
[41]   E Barendt, 'Free Speech in the Universities' (1987) *Public Law* 344.
[42]   Committee of Vice-Chancellors and Principals of the Universities of the UK (CVCP), 'Extremism and Intolerance on Campus' (1998) paras 5.2–5.3 and 7.0–7.2.
[43]   ERA 1988, s 202(2)(a), set out in full above in ch 4, s III(C).

lecturers and other academic staff; they could say what they like on any political topic or other subject of public concern, as long as they did not infringe the general law. Universities would not be free to discipline let alone dismiss a member of academic staff for, say, circulating a leaflet—on or outside campus—that disparages the intellectual ability of a particular ethnic group, unless its terms brought it within the offence of incitement to racial hatred or some other criminal offence. Academic freedom would on this broad understanding trump a university's right to discipline a lecturer for extramural speech, however disruptive that is of relationships within a department or between the lecturer and his or her students.

For two reasons the academic freedom clause should be understood more narrowly. First, some of the language ('freedom . . . to question and test received wisdom') strongly suggests that the right is concerned with the traditional academic freedoms of research and teaching, rather than a general freedom of speech on matters of public concern. The freedom to disseminate unpopular views would then cover an academic's freedom to challenge established orthodoxies at conferences, seminars and through scholarly publications, but not a right, say, to communicate extreme political views at public meetings or on a personal blog. The second reason is one of principle. The broader interpretation would give academic staff wider free speech rights than the administrative and support staff in universities or other employees, for example, those working for hospitals or banks, who might want to claim a freedom to disseminate their views on matters of public policy, particularly those affecting their work. For the reasons given earlier in this chapter, it would be wrong to conflate academic freedom and general freedom of speech, although admittedly it may sometimes be difficult to draw a sharp line between them.[44] The academic freedom clause has been understood to cover the right of academics to voice their concerns about matters of university governance[45]—freedom of intramural expression—but there is no strong reason why it should be interpreted to confer special rights for academics to speak more freely than other citizens on matters of general public concern.

---

[44] See above s II.
[45] Above ch 4, s IV(A) and (C).

Even if the broader view of the academic freedom clause were correct, it would not give professors absolute freedom of speech. It only confers 'freedom within the law'. Academic staff do not enjoy academic freedom rights to infringe the restrictions imposed by the laws against criminal incitement, incitement to hatred on the grounds of race, religion or sexual orientation, public order laws or the laws penalising the publication of obscene or indecent material. Moreover, the phrase 'within the law' means that they have no academic freedom rights to commit civil wrongs, notably the torts of defamation, breach of confidence or misuse of personal information.

To these myriad restrictions on freedom of extramural expression should be added the laws concerning harassment of individuals on the grounds of race, gender, ethnicity, religion or belief, sexual orientation or disability.[46] Under these laws, employers may be liable for acts of harassment by their employees,[47] so universities have a real interest in preventing one member of staff from engaging in, say, racist or sexist conduct that creates a hostile environment for colleagues. These laws are relatively unproblematic in this context. For the most part they are concerned with conduct in the workplace, which certainly includes intimidating and hostile racist, etc remarks and expressive conduct. They impinge on speech and conduct that is targeted at individuals, rather than on speech that raises issues of public concern. For that reason, there are serious doubts whether such speech is even covered by freedom of expression, let alone by an academic freedom clause such as that in the Education Reform Act 1988.

A more complex argument is whether universities are now entitled to regulate speech that, in their view, makes it more difficult for them to fulfil their positive obligations under race relations and other legislation. The Race Relations (Amendment) Act 2000 (RRAA) requires all public authorities—including for this purpose universities, further and higher education institutions—in carrying out their functions, to show due regard to the need to eliminate racial discrimination and to promote equality of opportunity and good relations between different racial

---

[46] Race Relations Act 1976 (RRA), s 3A; Sex Discrimination Act 1975, s 4A; Employment Equality (Religion or Belief) Regulations, SI 2003/1660, reg 5; Employment Equality (Sexual Orientation) Regulations, SI 2003/1661, reg 5; Disability Discrimination Act 1995, ss 3B and 28SA.

[47] For example, see RRA, s 32.

groups.[48] Specific duties—for example, to prepare a written statement of their policies for promoting race equality and to assess and monitor the impact of their policies on the pupils, staff and parents of different racial groups—have been imposed on educational bodies to supplement the general duties under the RRAA.[49] There are similar duties to eliminate discrimination against disabled people,[50] while the Equality Act 2006 requires public authorities to have due regard to the need to promote equality of opportunity for women.[51]

On one view universities should therefore intervene when a member of their academic staff expresses racist views (or other extreme remarks), even if that expression does not contravene the criminal law or amount to harassment of another member of staff or a student. Otherwise, the university would be in breach of its own obligations under the RRAA. As will be seen, that view was taken by Leeds University when a lecturer on its staff expressed extreme racist opinions in an article in a student newspaper.[52] On that analysis, the pursuit of equal opportunity and good race relations on campus would trump freedom of expression. Against that, it can be argued that a line should be drawn between freedom of *speech* on the one hand and racially discriminatory *conduct* on the other. Universities and other public bodies should take steps to ensure that their staff do not engage in discriminatory conduct, but there is no good reason to interpret the RRAA as requiring them to regulate the extramural expression of their employees, whether academic, administrative or support staff. In this context, it will be recalled that the HRA requires courts to interpret legislation, so far as possible, compatibly with freedom of expression and other Convention rights.[53]

The imposition of these new statutory obligations has been partly responsible for a clear shift in attitude towards the balance between freedom of (extramural) speech and the promotion of tolerance and good race relations on campus. This shift is shown by the different emphases in two studies the universities commissioned. In 1998

---

[48] S 2 (substituting Race Relations Act 1976, s 71).
[49] Race Relations Act 1976 (Statutory Duties) Order 2001, SI 2001/3458.
[50] Disability Discrimination Act 1995, s 49A, inserted by Disability Discrimination Act 2003, s 3.
[51] Sex Discrimination Act 1975, s 76A, inserted by Equality Act 2006, s 84.
[52] See below s III(B).
[53] See text at above n 32.

a working group set up by the Committee of Vice-Chancellors and Principals emphasised that vigorous debate is perfectly proper and that universities should tolerate a wide range of views, even those that are uncomfortable and provocative.[54] They should not use their disciplinary procedures to promote policies in favour of institutional harmony if that entails the suppression of views about matters of sexual orientation, race or sex.[55] In the Working Group's view, such use was precluded by the free speech provisions of the Education (No 2) Act 1986.

The general perspective of the group, chaired by Professor Les Ebdon, Vice-Chancellor at the University of Bedfordshire, in providing new guidance for Universities UK in 2005 on these matters could not have been more different. For this group, the primary concern was to deal with hate crimes and intolerance and 'thus ensure that academic freedom cannot be exploited to damage the legitimate freedoms of others'.[56] Its report drew attention to the growing diversity in the ethnic backgrounds of students attending universities and the greater demands of equalities legislation.[57] Reasonable and proportionate preventive action should be taken to reduce the incidence of hate crimes. One guideline suggested by the group for dealing with episodes of hate crime or intolerance is particularly striking: if an expression of opinion is highly offensive, with the potential to develop into harassment, 'the balance is likely to lie in favour of restricting that activity.'[58] In short, freedom of speech is only one factor to be considered by university authorities and may be outweighed by the need to prevent the growth of intolerance or the commission of hate crimes.

This second perspective does not do justice to the importance of protecting freedom of expression, which should only be limited when its exercise gives rise to a clear likelihood of an imminent crime or harassment; restrictions on speech on the ground that it is offensive, with the potential for harmful consequences, infringes the guarantee provided by the Education (No 2) Act 1986 and by the HRA.

---

[54] 'Extremism and Intolerance on Campus' (above n 42) para 2.1.

[55] Ibid, para 4.7.

[56] Universities UK, 'Promoting Good Campus Relations: Dealing with Hate Crimes and Intolerance', Executive Summary (2005).

[57] Ibid, paras 1.4–1.5.

[58] Ibid, para 3.4.

## B. Extramural Expression Cases in the United Kingdom

Freedom of extramural expression has been an issue in a handful of recent episodes, though none of them have reached the courts or employment tribunals. They raise the difficult question whether a university is entitled to discipline a member of academic staff in respect of his or her speech on general political or social issues that the university considers inimical to its legitimate interests in, for example, good staff–student relations or harmonious working relationships within departments.

The best known of these episodes involved the dismissal of Chris Brand, a lecturer in the Psychology Department, by Edinburgh University in 1997. The case raises a number of complex academic freedom issues and is fully examined below in chapter ten. The point to mention here is that the principal charge against Brand related to his sending of an email that condoned or sought understanding for paedophilia in certain circumstances. The Tribunal that examined the charges against the Brand, as well as the appeal decision, concluded that Brand could not claim academic freedom.[59] That is correct: Brand was not publishing the results of his research or giving his opinion on a matter on which he was an acknowledged expert. It was a case of extramural expression. Brand was exercising freedom of speech, a right to which all citizens are entitled. There could have been no legal objection if, say, a retired university academic or other employee had sent an email in identical terms. But Edinburgh University took the view that Brand had deliberately courted controversy when he sent this email, in circumstances when he had been advised to be careful, and must have known that he would be wrecking his already damaged relations with his departmental colleagues; in that context it concluded that there was 'good cause' to dismiss him.[60]

The other major episode concerns the suspension in 2006 of Dr Frank Ellis, a lecturer in the Russian and Slavonic Studies Department at Leeds University. He held extreme right-wing views, which he had outlined some years earlier at a conference in the United States and earlier in 2006 in an interview with the Leeds University student

[59] See below ch 10, ss II and III.
[60] See below ch 10, ss II and V.

newspaper, the *Leeds Student*. What triggered his suspension was an article in this paper, in which, among other things, he described findings that the average IQ in sub-Saharan Africa was significantly lower than that accepted for recruitment in the US armed forces, stating that '[e]verywhere one looks [in that part of Africa] there is unbelievable corruption and stupidity, superstition and savagery' and sexual incontinence. Ellis also wrote that multiculturalism was doomed and further expressed support for the British National Party.[61]

Ellis was suspended because Leeds University took the view that he had infringed its equality and diversity policy, had jeopardised the fulfilment of its statutory obligations under the RRAA and had failed to comply with management requests to apologise for the distress that his remarks had caused many people.[62] In this context it should be noted that the University had several thousand students from overseas and that there had been student protests and a petition calling for Ellis to be sacked. These factors played a part in the University's decision but were not decisive. Nor was the University greatly concerned by any threat to staff relations within the small Russian Department or the larger Modern Languages School, of which it was a part.[63] Rather, the decision was motivated by the desire for Leeds University to stand as 'a civilised community', where students would be free from the fear of racial harassment; further, the University was keen to honour its statutory obligations to promote good relations between different racial groups.[64] Legal advice suggested that it might be lawful to dismiss Ellis; whether it would be depended on how the facts were assessed, ultimately by an employment tribunal. At any rate the first steps towards the start of disciplinary procedures were taken, though no final decision had been made whether to initiate them. Ellis then applied to take early

---

[61] The text of the full article by Ellis from which *Leeds Student* published its edited version is available at http://www.amren.com/mtnews/archives/2006/03/campus_storm_ov.php (accessed 8 August 2010).

[62] Statement of issues by Roger Gair, University Secretary, reported on BBC News Report on 23 March 2006 and confirmed to the current author in a telephone interview on 5 August 2009.

[63] In this respect the Ellis case is quite different from the dismissal of Brand by Edinburgh, where the impact of the paedophilia email on departmental relations was crucial: see below ch 10.

[64] Telephone interview with Roger Gair, University Secretary, 5 August 2009.

retirement, and this was accepted; Leeds agreed to pay a year's salary and contributed to his legal costs.[65]

Did Leeds University have a strong case for disciplining Dr Ellis? It is clear that he was not exercising academic freedom; he was employed in the Russian Department, and his views did not relate at all to his expertise. The question is whether Leeds University could discipline him for expressing views that it regarded as abhorrent. Understandably, it wanted to distance itself from the terms of the article. But it is far from clear that Ellis had committed any criminal offence in repeating and supporting the views taken, for example, by Herrnstein and Murray in *The Bell Curve*, repulsive though those views are to most people, whether on or outside the university campus. He was entitled to freedom of speech, even if his exercise of that right offended many people.

The crucial question is whether the University's obligations under the RRAA made a significant difference: is a university entitled to discipline a member of its staff for exercising freedom of speech or extramural expression, because the particular publication makes more difficult or jeopardises the achievement of the university's duty to promote good race relations? Leeds University took the view that it was entitled to do this. But another view can be taken. A member of staff is certainly not free to jeopardise the fulfilment of the university's obligations by personally discriminating against minority students or by taking steps that clearly inhibit their achievement, for example, by refusing to complete necessary forms or to take any staff training required by the university in discharging its specific obligations under the race relations legislation.[66] In these circumstances the academic's *conduct* (not speech) would imperil achievement of the university's obligations. But statutes must be interpreted in conformity with Convention rights,[67] and it was perfectly possible to construe the RRAA so that it did not interfere with Ellis's freedom of expression. Leeds University would have been on stronger ground if it had made an argument that, after publication of the article, it was impossible for his colleagues to work with Ellis or for students to be expected to attend his classes. But that does not appear to have been part of its case.

---

[65] Report in *Times Higher Education Supplement*, 21 July 2006.

[66] See above s III(A) for the requirements imposed by SI 2001/3458.

[67] HRA, s 3, discussed above in s III(A).

Another episode concerned David Coleman, Professor of Demography at Oxford University. He is a fellow of the Galton Institute, formerly the Eugenics Society, and was a founding member of Migration Watch, an organisation that campaigns for a reduction in the number of immigrants to the United Kingdom. After a meeting in London in January 2007, when Coleman had spoken in a personal capacity in support of this cause, a few students signed a petition calling on him to stop using his University title when speaking on immigration matters and urging Oxford University to consider the suitability of his tenure as a professor. In effect it was a call for Coleman to be sacked. In Coleman's view, the petition, launched by Oxford Student Action for Refugees, was 'a shameful attempt of the most intolerant and totalitarian kind, to suppress the freedom of analysis and informed comment that it is the function of universities to cherish'.[68] That is right. Coleman's freedom of speech was plainly under attack. Indeed, on a broad view of it, Coleman's academic freedom was involved, for there was a relationship between his expertise as a demographer and his views on immigration. Academic freedom would clearly have been engaged had he published them in a scholarly journal. At any rate the affair fizzled out. Coleman received some support from Oxford University,[69] though he was also advised not to comment further by the University authorities.[70]

Recently, an anthropology professor at the University of East London was dismissed following an internal disciplinary hearing, which upheld various charges of gross misconduct.[71] Professor Chris Knight, it was found, had advocated in media interviews violence against officers responsible for policing the G20 economic summit on 2 April 2009. He had also visited the University campus in breach of an order to keep away from it on 1 April, when he had organised an Alternative G20 conference. The University had banned this conference on the ground that speeches at it would incite violence and disorder, and had suspended Knight for inciting violence. The disciplinary panel convicted him of serious insubordination in refusing to comply with

---

[68]  *Times Higher Education*, 2 March 2007, 2. Coleman defended his views in a front-page article in the *Daily Telegraph*, 8 March 2007.

[69]  In a telephone interview on 4 August 2009 Coleman described it as 'a little cool'. The University in his view wanted to keep out of trouble.

[70]  *Times Higher Education* (above n 68).

[71]  *Times Higher Education*, 30 July 2009, 11.

the order to keep off the campus. Of course, the University had been entitled to stop the conference, if it considered that violence would be incited there; in that event, the meeting would fall outside the scope of the freedom of speech and meeting recognised by the Education (No 2) Act 1986.[72] It is also understandable that a university would not want to keep on its payroll someone who had incited imminent violence on a specific occasion—a serious criminal offence. There is no reason why an academic should be treated more generously in this respect than other employees, for academic freedom does not cover a right to incite disorder or violence. It might be different if a university were to discipline, say, a politics professor who argued from Marxist principles that insurrection is inevitable if bankers do not change their ways.[73] The making of that argument—particularly in a university seminar—would be covered by academic freedom, insofar as the professor's views were derived from his or her Marxist perspective, though it would not give immunity from discipline if he or she provoked immediate violence and disorder.[74] It would not matter in that event if the incitement was made in a politics or sociology seminar or at a meeting held on or outside the campus.

## IV. US LAW

### A. Constitutional Principles

The legal position of academic extramural speech in the United States is governed by principles developed by the Supreme Court over the last four decades. As explained in chapter six, the Court has drawn a distinction between the speech of public employees as citizens on matters of public concern on the one hand and speech on a matter of personal interest or made pursuant to official duties on the other. The former is covered by the First Amendment and is protected unless the employer can show under a balancing test that the interest in promoting

[72] See above s III(A).
[73] See the Laski affair discussed above in ch 4, s II(C).
[74] In Germany, abstract teaching of the inevitability of revolution is covered by *Wissenschaftsfreiheit*, but not direct incitement to violence and disorder: Decision of the Berlin Administrative Court, reported in *JZ* 1973, 209. See above ch 5, s IV(C).

efficiency in the workplace outweighs the employee's free speech interest. The distinction may be difficult to apply to classroom teaching or to public comments made by academic staff about their universities' administrations (intramural expression), which can be regarded as both speech about matters of public concern *and* as speech made under official duties.[75] But there is no problem at all in applying it to academic extramural expression, when that is defined as a professor's speech on a matter of public concern on which he or she is not claiming to be expert. Academics' extramural expression is protected by the First Amendment, unless a university can show that it has the potential seriously to disrupt working relations on campus and that this risk outweighs the value of the speech.[76]

Two features of this position should be noted. First, under the state action doctrine it applies only to the extramural expression of professors at public or state universities. Professors at private universities cannot claim First Amendment rights against their employers if they are disciplined, say, for writing controversial newspaper articles or for using racist language on their blogs.[77] Secondly, the position might mean that professors have freedom of speech to say what they like, if they are speaking completely outside their fields of expertise, but do not have the same freedom if they say something highly controversial within their specialities, for example, if a twentieth-century historian were to deny the Holocaust in a television interview. In that particular case, the historian could not claim extramural freedom of expression on the usual definition of that term.[78] Moreover, he or she might be regarded as speaking pursuant to official duties, particularly if the university encouraged its staff to communicate with the general public about their research, and so be unable to claim freedom of speech under the First Amendment.[79] A university would have a stronger claim to discipline

---

[75] See above ch 6, s IV(B).

[76] *Jeffries v Harleston* 52 F 3d 9 (2nd Cir 1995), applying the principles formulated by the Supreme Court in *Waters v Churchill* 511 US 661 (1994).

[77] In *Rendell-Baker v Kohn* 457 US 830 (1982) the Court held that a private school could dismiss teachers for their public support of student criticism of its policies, as it was not bound by the First Amendment.

[78] See the Finkin and Post definition, set out above at n 3.

[79] However, in *Garcetti v Ceballos* 547 US 410 (2006) the Court indicated that the 'official duties' qualification to freedom of speech by public employees might not apply to academics. See above ch 6, s IV(A).

an historian whose views on the Holocaust are regarded as seriously aberrant by professional standards of scholarship than they would, say, a nuclear scientist or engineer who took the same public position. In short, academic freedom in some contexts confers less freedom than the general freedom of speech. American scholars have drawn attention to this apparent paradox.[80] This distinction, however, makes sense once it is appreciated that there is a real difference between academic freedom and freedom of speech. Exercise of the former may be limited in accordance with professional academic standards, but academics, like other people, should be free to say what they like, subject to the general law, when they speak outside their disciplines.

## B. Case Law

Freedom of extramural expression has been at issue in only a handful of cases. A leading decision is that of the Second Circuit Court of Appeals in *Levin v Harleston*.[81] A tenured philosophy professor wrote three pieces—a letter to the *New York Times*, a book review and a contribution to an American philosophy journal—in which he made denigrating remarks about the intelligence and social skills of African Americans. The President of his university, the City University of New York (CUNY), a public university, set up an inquiry to determine when speech, whether inside or outside the classroom, went beyond academic freedom and amounts to unbecoming conduct. The Court held that this step, as well as the decision to set up an alternative class for Levin's students, inhibited his First Amendment rights. President Harleston had said that Levin's views were offensive to the basic values of equality and decency, so the Court inferred that the inquiry was intended to regulate his speech. Certainly, it could not be said that it had disrupted relations on campus, for apparently no students had complained of discriminatory treatment on the basis of their race. Faculty at CUNY and

---

[80] Van Alstyne (above n 16) 76–77; and R O'Neil, *Academic Freedom in the Wired World* (Cambridge, MA, Harvard University Press, 2008) 7, discussing the position of Professor Butz, an engineering professor at Northwestern University, who may freely deny the Holocaust.

[81] *Levin v Harleston* 966 F 2d 85 (2nd Cir 1992).

other universities had criticised the President for infringing academic freedom, but the Court decided the case on free speech grounds.

In contrast, the same Court did not uphold the First Amendment claim when CUNY shortened the term of a professor as Chair of the Black Studies Department because of a controversial off-campus speech in which he severely criticised the anti-minority bias of its curriculum and made several anti-Semitic remarks.[82] In the Court's view the Trustees of CUNY were entitled to consider the speech potentially disruptive to work at the university. It added that there was no infringement to the professor's academic freedom; his administrative position had been curtailed, but he remained free to teach and speak as he liked. Further, the professor's free speech rights were no greater than those of other public employees.[83]

The fate of US campus speech codes suggests that restrictions on faculty speech will rarely be held compatible with the First Amendment. These codes were introduced in many American universities to counter the victimisation and harassment on university campuses and other premises of individuals on the basis of their race, ethnicity, religion, sex, sexual orientation and a number of other specific grounds. For the most part they were directed at the victimisation of students by other students, though some universities also formulated faculty speech or harassment codes.[84] District Court decisions have ruled campus codes overbroad and so incompatible with the First Amendment.[85] They were targeted at certain types of speech on the basis of their content and could be applied to many types of offensive speech that were certainly protected by freedom of speech. In *Doe* a graduate psychology student assistant successfully challenged broad provisions in the University of Michigan anti-discrimination and harassment code, which might have precluded him discussing in class controversial ideas about the biological basis for differences in the educational attainment of racial groups, men and women. The courts were not persuaded the codes

---

[82] *Jeffries v Harleston* 52 F 3d 9 (2nd Cir 1995). See O'Neil (above n 80) 65–67 for commentary.

[83] *Jeffries v Harleston* (ibid) 14.

[84] For a general study of campus speech codes, see DA Downs, *Restoring Free Speech and Liberty on Campus* (Cambridge, Cambridge University Press, 2005).

[85] *Doe v University of Michigan* 721 F Supp 852 (ED Mich 1989); *UWM Post, Inc v Board of Regents of University of Wisconsin System* 774 F Supp 1163 (ED Wis 1991).

should be upheld, on the grounds that they were intended to promote
diversity and equal educational opportunities. Rather, they hurt intellectual diversity by limiting the variety of ideas that could legitimately
be expressed. The pursuit of equality could not justify restrictions on
speech.[86] Though concerning restrictions on student speech, these decisions would clearly apply to comparable restrictions on faculty speech,
whether on or outside the campus. The arguments that persuaded
Leeds University in England to contemplate disciplinary proceedings
against a lecturer for racist speech would have attracted little or no support in the United States.[87]

## C. AAUP Jurisprudence on Extramural Expression

As mentioned above in section I, the 1940 Statement of the AAUP treats
extramural expression as an aspect of academic freedom, although it
urges professors to exercise restraint and show respect for the opinions
of others when they make pronouncements as citizens.[88] One central
issue considered in a number of AAUP investigations has been whether
universities can discipline, even dismiss, professors because they regard
their extramural speech as irresponsible and as damaging to university
reputation or standing in the community. The AAUP position is that
the speech must show that the professor is incompetent to teach and
conduct objective research; that would be the case if his or her extramural expression contained clearly false statements of fact. It was wrong to
dismiss a professor because he or she has condoned extramarital sexual
relations, even though expression of that opinion was regarded in 1960
in Illinois as prejudicial to the standing of the university.[89]

One implication of the principle that extreme extramural speech must
show an academic's unfitness to teach and research is that the faculty, or
at least university authorities with strong academic representation, should

---

[86] See in particular *UWM Post* (ibid) 1176, per Warren, Senior District Judge.
[87] See above s III(B).
[88] For the text of the 1940 Statement, see above ch 6, s II(B).
[89] Dismissal of Leo Koch, biology professor, by University of Illinois for
expressing this view condemned by Committee A of AAUP: Finkin and Post
(above n 3) 144–46; and see TI Emerson and D Haber, 'Academic Freedom of the
Faculty Member as Citizen' (1963) 28 *Law and Contemporary Problems* 525, 540–41.

decide whether it is appropriate to discipline the academic. It is wrong for a university council or board of trustees to take the substantive decision. For that reason, the decision of the Board of Regents of the University of California itself not to reappoint Angela Davis, a militant Marxist, as an assistant philosophy professor, rather than leave the matter to be determined by the University President may have been wrong.[90] In 2007 Professor Ward Churchill was dismissed by the Board of Regents of the University of Colorado, although a majority of the faculty committee had recommended only his suspension for serious research misconduct; the Board might have been influenced by Churchill's essay in which he blamed US foreign policy for 9/11 and referred to the workers in the World Trade Center as 'little Eichmanns'.[91] A body such as a Board of Regents appointed by politicians is ill-equipped to determine whether a member of academic staff should be dismissed because his or her extramural speeches demonstrate a lack of academic integrity; in particular, it may be unduly influenced by public feelings about their content. This point is valid, whether extramural speech is treated, as it is by the AAUP, as an aspect of academic freedom or, as it should be, as an aspect of the general right to freedom of speech.

---

[90]  Finkin and Post (above n 3) 147.

[91]  In April 2009 a jury awarded Churchill nominal damages for wrongful dismissal, taking the view that the University had not proved that he would have been dismissed even if he had not published these extreme views. This verdict was vacated by the District Court on 7 July 2009.

# 10

# *The Chris Brand Case*

T HE DISMISSAL OF Chris Brand from his Lectureship at
Edinburgh University in 1997 was one of the most controversial and unhappy episodes in the history of British universities in the post-war period. It involved a number of academic
freedom issues and, because of its complexity, deserves a chapter of
its own. The account that follows is based on a number of sources.
Edinburgh University provided several papers following a request
for documents and information under freedom of information legislation.[1] However, the University does not keep records relating to
an employee's termination of employment for longer than six years,
so it was unable to provide a number of important documents,
including the reports of two inquiries, which were conducted in
1996 before the institution of the Tribunal to consider the charges
against Brand. Chris Brand himself supplied me with a copy of the
University Tribunal decision, which, by a majority, recommended his
dismissal; and also a copy of the appeal decision of Gordon Coutts,
QC, which upheld the Principal's decision to dismiss him. I also
interviewed some of Brand's colleagues and a former student, as
well as Brand himself and Professor Hector MacQueen, a member
of the Tribunal.[2] Finally, some reference is made to contemporary
accounts of the events in *The Scotsman*, the *Guardian* and the *Times
Higher Education Supplement*.

---

[1] Freedom of Information (Scotland) Act 2002.
[2] It should be noted that some colleagues of Mr Brand were unwilling to discuss the episode with me; I would have liked to discuss it with Professor Neil
MacCormick, but after a long illness he died in 2009. However, we did exchange
emails in June 2008 (see below n 64).

I. EVENTS BEFORE THE TRIBUNAL HEARINGS

## A. The General Background

It is important to sketch the background to the events of 1996, if only because much of the evidence given at the Tribunal hearing related to Brand's general career at Edinburgh University rather than to the specific events that led to the Tribunal's institution. Chris Brand was appointed in 1970 to a lectureship in the Department of Psychology; he had previously worked at Grendon open prison on prisoner rehabilitation. He never applied for promotion, so remained protected by the system of academic tenure that applied to all members of academic staff who were neither appointed nor promoted after November 1987.[3] Difficulties began to surface in March 1986 when fourth-year students requested a meeting with Dr Halla Beloff, then the Acting Head of the Department. Many of them found that Brand's lectures laid undue emphasis on genetic explanations for cognitive differences between members of different racial groups and the genders. Some women students found his manner patronising and offensive, both in class and during personal meetings. One told me that they felt 'toyed with'.[4] But other students had no problem with Brand's teaching and considered the objections to it stemmed from 'political correctness'.[5] Following a meeting with the Head of the Department, Brand resigned from his post as Director of Studies, so he no longer had general responsibility for advising students on their academic work and career prospects. He himself considered the accusations made against him to be unsubstantiated or based on extreme feminism.

The situation did not improve over the next ten years. Dr Beloff told me that Brand's manner at departmental academic seminars became increasingly confrontational, while his relationships with other members of the Department became more distant. Many colleagues were, she thought, frightened of him.[6] But another Departmental colleague

---

[3]  See above ch 4, s III(C).

[4]  Telephone interview with anonymous student, 15 June 2009.

[5]  Letter of Helen Guldberg to *Guardian*, 1 May 1996; and communication from Professor Vincent Egan, a PhD student at Edinburgh under Chris Brand's supervision 1984–87, 10 September 2009.

[6]  Personal Interview with Dr Beloff, 5 June 2009.

'got on with him alright' and had respect for him.[7] He shared, however, Dr Beloff's anxiety that students, particularly women students, felt they were disparaged, even bullied; according to this colleague, Brand would revel in upsetting people. But it is accepted that Brand never received any warning during this period, whether formal or informal, to the effect that his conduct was unacceptable and that it might lead to disciplinary proceedings.[8]

At this stage it is important to say something about the character of Brand's academic views. Brand is, in his own words, a 'racial realist', though the term 'scientific racist' is more frequently used to describe adherents to his views; he argues that there are differences between the IQ of different racial groups and that genes, not environmental factors, are responsible for these differences. Similarly, genes often explain the circumstances of poor, single mothers. He is a fellow of the Galton Institute, the successor to the Eugenics Society, which favours racial improvement through selective breeding. Indeed, Brand himself encouraged women students to look for intelligent husbands as a step towards this improvement; but he has never supported forced state eugenics as practised by the Nazis.[9] Brand therefore shares the controversial views maintained by Richard Herrnstein and Charles Murray in their famous book *The Bell Curve*[10] and also those of Arthur Jensen, a former professor of educational psychology at the University of California in Berkeley.[11] For some academics expert in this area, the view that genetic rather than environmental factors explain IQ differences between different ethnic groups and between men and women is misconceived, lacking any serious scientific basis. But it is held by a number of well-known international scholars,[12] including some from

[7] Telephone interview with an anonymous colleague of Mr Brand, 22 August 2008.

[8] The possible significance of the absence of warnings is discussed below in s IV.

[9] See *Scotsman on Sunday*, 21 April 1996; and G Younge, 'The Gene Genies', *Guardian, G2,* 1 May 1996, 2.

[10] *The Bell Curve* was first published in 1994 (New York, Simon Schuster).

[11] See in particular A Jensen, *The g Factor: The Science of Mental Ability* (Westport, CT, Greenwood, 1998).

[12] In 1994 the *Wall Street Journal* published 'Mainstream Science on Intelligence', a statement supporting this view drafted by Professor Linda Gottfredson and signed by 51 other university professors specialising in race and intelligence; the statement is published in (1997) 24 *Intelligence* 13.

the United Kingdom, for example, Richard Lynn, a former psychology professor at the University of Ulster, Coleraine.[13]

Brand outlined his arguments in a book, *The g Factor: General Intelligence and its Implications*, which was due to be published in the spring of 1996. But the publisher, Wiley and Sons, withdrew Brand's book from circulation a week after its publication was announced, largely, it seems, because its managers were horrified by remarks of Brand to the press that black people are less intelligent than whites.[14] One of Brand's colleagues told me that the book was a good one and deplored the publisher's decision to withdraw it.[15] Many people, including the Principal of the University, Sir Stewart Sutherland, also regretted the publisher's decision. One can only speculate now whether the events later that year would have occurred had that decision not been taken. Professor Neil MacCormick, then Provost and Dean of the Faculty for Law and Social Sciences (which included the Psychology Department) attempted to help Brand find another publisher but without success. However, perhaps prompted by the controversy arising from the withdrawal of Brand's book, there was a student boycott of his lectures, and some students wrote a letter to *The Scotsman* calling for a 'decent standard of lecture, free from the inflammatory personal comments that have been endured by psychology students at Edinburgh University for the past 20 years'.[16]

The Principal immediately asked Professor MacCormick to conduct an enquiry into Brand's teaching style and relationship with his students; its findings were to be examined to see whether there was a basis for disciplinary action. At the same time, the Principal stated that institution of the enquiry did not compromise Brand's academic freedom. But he expressed concern at the manner in which Brand had reportedly expressed his views; it was unacceptable to express views in a manner that indicated the absence of an open mind.[17] Professor MacCormick's report was never published, but it appears from a University news

[13] J Hinde, 'Branded an Outcast', *Times Higher Education Supplement*, 15 August 1997. Lynn, like Jensen, is a prominent defender of *The Bell Curve*. For a recent statement of his views, see *The Global Bell Curve: Race, IQ, and Inequality Worldwide* (Augusta, GA, Washington Summit Publishers, 2008).

[14] News report in *Guardian*, 18 April 1996, 4.

[15] Telephone interview, 22 August 2008.

[16] Letter to *The Scotsman* of Kirstine Mullin and three others, 25 April 1996.

[17] *The Scotsman*, 25 April 1996, 3.

release that it stressed the importance of the responsible exercise of academic freedom in the context of relations between lecturer and students. Brand was encouraged to present his ideas in a more balanced way, while the Department would be asked to consider redistributing teaching loads so students had access to other views on the controversial topics covered in Brand's lectures. Professor MacCormick's recommendations did not propose disciplinary measures, but they contemplated that if Brand did not change his teaching style, disciplinary action might follow.[18] However, there is no indication from the news release that Professor MacCormick or the Principal formally warned Brand at this stage to avoid talking to the press and to keep a low profile. In an interview with me, Brand denied making any undertaking of this sort.[19] The point may be an important one, since it seems to have been assumed subsequently that at some time in the course of this year, Brand was advised to keep out of the public eye.

Rather bizarrely, in October 1996 Brand was appointed Convenor of the Psychology Department's Ethics Committee.[20] This step led to immediate student protests; a petition calling for his removal from the position was signed by over 500 students. Brand stepped down from this position a few days later.[21] On 31 October, a demonstration by the Anti-Nazi League prevented him from taking a departmental seminar. That prompted the Principal to write a letter to *The Scotsman* supporting the principle of the open exploration of ideas at universities and implicitly defending Brand's freedom to disseminate his views. Sir Stewart Sutherland regretted the publisher's decision to withdraw Brand's book, even though personally he found the views attributed to Brand 'false and obnoxious'.[22]

[18] Edinburgh University News Release, 'Academic Freedom, Teaching Responsibilities and Mr Chris Brand', 31 May 1996.

[19] Personal interview, 4 June 2009.

[20] The decision appears to have been an aberration on the part of the Head of Department, who was perhaps keen to give Brand some administrative work.

[21] *The Scotsman*, 22 October 1996.

[22] Letter to the *The Scotsman*, 4 November 1996. Sir Stewart had not read *The g factor*, so was careful to say he was expressing an opinion on the views attributed to Brand in media reports. In communicating this opinion, the Principal was exercising freedom of speech, not making an academic judgement.

## B. The Paedophilia Email

Matters came to a head when Brand sent an email on 16 October to an American friend who had set up a website on his behalf to campaign for the publication of his book, *The g Factor*. She did not put the email on the website,[23] but Brand had also sent it to a number of contacts, most of them supporters of the publishing campaign. The email expressed shock at the arrest of an elderly Nobel prize winner, Daniel Gajdusek, on charges of paedophilia. Brand's email stated, 'academic studies and my own experience suggest that nonviolent paedophilia with a consenting partner over age 12 does no harm so long as the paedophiles and their partners are of above average intelligence and educational level.' It mentioned that as a 13-year-old choirboy, he had given sexual favours for money. One of the email's recipients forwarded it to the *Daily Record*, a leading tabloid newspaper in Scotland, which broke the story on 8 November. At that point, Brand put the email on his own Edinburgh University website, in order to ensure that its exact terms were available to the public; he did not want it to get an exaggerated impression of the terms of the email.

At the request of the Provost, Neil MacCormick, Brand was immediately suspended. Professor MacCormick also made a formal complaint that Brand's conduct was bringing the University into disrepute and might be seriously disrupting the work of the Department of Psychology. Petitions from members of the Anti-Nazi League were sent, celebrating Brand's suspension and urging the University to remove him 'permanently (sic) from all positions he holds at our university'. A Vice-Principal, Richard Field, was invited by the Principal to investigate whether there was a case for convening an internal disciplinary tribunal. It was on the basis of his report (unfortunately not now available), submitted at the end of January 1997, that the Tribunal was set up to consider three charges and to make appropriate recommendations to the Principal.

## II. THE TRIBUNAL HEARINGS AND REPORT

The Tribunal consisted of three members: the convener (or chair), Professor Ian Cunningham, a retired Professor of Agriculture; Dr

---

[23] Apparently, she was unsure whether it was wise to do so—a sensible view in light of its repercussions!

Brian Oakley, a computer scientist with industrial experience (both members of and nominated by the Edinburgh University Court); and Professor Hector MacQueen, Professor of Private Law, nominated by the University Senate. The case for the University was made by its Secretary, Dr Martin Lowe; for the most part Brand conducted his own defence, assisted by a former lecturer, Geoffrey Sharps. No longer a member of the Association of University Teachers, Brand did not get any help from that body; nor did he try to enlist support from Liberty, the Council for Academic Freedom and Academic Standards or other organisations that defend free speech and academic freedom.

The Tribunal met over three full days, spread out over several weeks, in which it heard from a number of witnesses, who had been invited to give evidence by Martin Lowe.[24] Among those giving oral evidence were Professor Robert Grieve, Head of the Psychology Department from about 1987 to 1997; Professor Robert Morris; Dr Halla Beloff; at least two other Departmental colleagues; and a few present and former students. Their testimony supplemented a body of written evidence, for example, minutes of staff–student liaison committee meetings at which student dissatisfaction with the use of racist and sexist examples in Brand's lectures and offensive language had been noted. Chris Brand did not himself call any witnesses—surely a mistake if he were correct in his belief that some colleagues would have been supportive. On the other hand, he invited the Tribunal to call Professor MacCormick and Sir Stewart Sutherland to give evidence, but it refused to take this step.

Under the provisions of the Staff Administrative Manual (SAM) the role of the Tribunal was to hear the charges against the member of staff and to determine whether they constituted 'good cause' for dismissal.[25] It was to make findings of fact and recommendations to the Principal. As will be seen in the following paragraphs, the Tribunal was far from unanimous on a number of points, so it decided that each view would be fully represented in its report, though it did not disclose which member held it. 'Good cause' was defined in SAM in the alternative as *either* conviction for an offence, deemed such as to render the person unfit for the execution of duties *or* 'conduct of an immoral, scandalous or disgraceful nature incompatible with the duties of … office' *or*

---

[24] Telephone interview with anonymous colleague of Mr Brand, 22 August 2008.
[25] SAM of 1993, paras 4.1 and 5.1.

finally conduct amounting to failure or persistent refusal or neglect to perform the employee's duties. The Tribunal rejected Brand's argument that only a single act equivalent in gravity to a criminal offence could be sufficiently serious to amount to good cause for dismissal; on this point it accepted the University argument that behaviour by an academic that destroyed the necessary bonds of mutual trust between university and its staff could amount to good cause.[26]

Three charges of 'gross misconduct' amounting to good cause for dismissal were made against Brand.[27] The first was that his conduct, in particular the email commenting on paedophilia, were of a disgraceful nature incompatible with his duties. Secondly, it was charged that his conduct, as set out in Professor Field's report, amounted to a failure or a persistent refusal or neglect to perform his duties. The third charge concerned satirical remarks made earlier in 1996 by Brand about Edinburgh University, his Department, Sir Stewart Sutherland and Professor MacCormick and published on his Internet blog, *The g Factor Newsletter*, which, it was alleged, were damaging to the reputation of the University and its departments. There is no need to discuss this third charge at length. The Tribunal did not consider the remarks amounted to gross misconduct, and two of them did not uphold the charge at all, for they did not find any evidence that the 'rather puerile remarks' had damaged the University's reputation. Moreover, the Tribunal was aware of the university tradition of tolerating the criticism by academic staff of its administration.[28] (Brand's Internet commentary in this respect would be regarded as intramural expression rather than extramural comments on matters of general public concern.[29]) On the other hand, two members of the Tribunal considered these remarks, considered in conjunction with the paedophile email, could not simply be condoned as an exercise of free speech; that would ignore the responsibility expected of academics.[30]

[26] Tribunal report, s 2: Gross Misconduct.

[27] The Manual in some places used the term 'gross misconduct', and it was also used by the Tribunal. In his appeal ruling, Gordon Coutts, QC, pointed out that this might have caused some confusion, though the terms 'good cause' and 'gross misconduct' were synonymous.

[28] Tribunal Report, paras. 4.3.2–4.3.3.

[29] For this distinction, see above ch 9, s I.

[30] Tribunal Report, para 4.3.4.

The first two charges were considered at length by the Tribunal. In its view, the first charge was the most powerful part of the case against Brand. It concluded that by seeking to give maximum publicity for the terms of the paedophile email through press interviews and releases,[31] Brand had 'courted further controversy and showed a desire to pursue his own goals at the expense of others'.[32] It accepted that his primary aim in communicating his views on the arrest of the Nobel prize winner might have been to promote his campaign for publication of his book but found it was irresponsible for him not to have appreciated the damage their publication might do to the University and his already fragile relations with his colleagues in the Department. In that context, it was relevant that the Psychology Department ran a nursery for small children, whose parents might well become anxious that one member of the Department considered the general public horror of paedophilia unjustified.[33] Though there was little evidence of actual damage to the Department, the Tribunal had no doubt of the potential damage stemming from publication of the email. Moreover, it was clear there was 'calamitous damage … to Mr Brand's relationship with other members of his Department'.[34]

In a particularly striking paragraph,[35] the Tribunal indicated that it was not the *content* of the October email that was decisive. Moreover, there was no requirement for academics to communicate their views on public controversies only in footnoted texts; that requirement would intrude on their freedom of speech, not just their academic freedom. But any citizen, particularly an academic, should communicate his or her views responsibly and be aware of the manner in which they are expressed and the impact on their audience. In an earlier paragraph it pointed out that Brand had not attempted to present balanced views on a matter on which he was not an expert.[36] The Tribunal's conclusion on the first charge was that Brand had behaved with poor judgement; he should have been aware of the outcry likely to result from the manner in

---

[31]  Ibid, paras 4.1.5–4.1.7.

[32]  Ibid, para 4.1.15.

[33]  For Dr Beloff, this factor put Brand's email 'beyond the pale' of acceptability: Personal Interview, 5 June 2009.

[34]  Tribunal Report, para 4.1.13.

[35]  Ibid, para 4.1.14.

[36]  Ibid, para 4.1.8.

which he published his views. As a result, any remaining trust and confidence that Departmental colleagues held in Brand had been destroyed. It upheld unanimously the first charge of gross misconduct.

The Tribunal devoted even more space to the second charge of persistent refusal or neglect to perform duties and clearly found its resolution more difficult. It was on this charge that it had to consider substantial written and oral evidence relating to Brand's lecturing style, his treatment of postgraduate students and the breakdown of his relations with other members of the Psychology Department. The evidence left the Tribunal in no doubt that Brand's 'personal style is aggressive, confrontational, loquacious and argumentative'.[37] It did not shrink from characterising his teaching style as 'unacceptable'. In the Tribunal's view, academic freedom does not give university lecturers complete liberty to teach in any manner they like. Lecturers have a responsibility to respect the sensitivities of their students and to communicate with them effectively.[38]

With regard to the breakdown in Brand's relations with his colleagues, the Tribunal said that this fact alone could not justify dismissal. Otherwise, it would be too easy for groups in a university department to declare that they could no longer work with an 'awkward' colleague and so secure his or her dismissal.[39] Another difficulty was that no formal warning, oral or written, seems to have been given to Brand, let alone any disciplinary proceeding initiated against him.[40] Each incident had been dealt with informally by the Head of Department or Dean at the time. For that reason, one member of the Tribunal concluded that it was wrong to revisit previous episodes that had not been thought in the past to merit more than informal treatment.[41] In his view the material was spent for disciplinary purposes.

The majority, however, thought that Brand's previous conduct should be considered in conjunction with the paedophilia email; this conduct over many years explained why so many colleagues had been willing to give evidence in the proceedings, though they clearly found it

---

[37] Para 4.2.14.
[38] Para 4.2.15. The Tribunal cited a paper by M Billig, *Giving Academic Freedom a Brand Name*, later published in (1997) 7 *Feminism and Psychology* 283.
[39] Tribunal Report, para 4.2.25.
[40] Ibid, para 4.2.1.
[41] Ibid, para 4.2.27.

disagreeable to do so.[42] The email would not have had the same impact had it not been for the earlier conduct, towards both colleagues and students. While the individual events in earlier years did not themselves merit dismissal, the majority considered that cumulatively they had led to a total breakdown in collegiality, which justified a finding of misconduct. One member of the Tribunal found that the evidence justified a finding of gross misconduct, which would merit dismissal, but another thought it supported only a finding upholding the lesser charge of misconduct.

So the Tribunal upheld the first charge unanimously, the second by a majority (but with only one member concluding that Brand's conducted amounted to gross misconduct) and dismissed the third.[43] By a majority it recommended that the Principal should consider the dismissal of Brand from his post at Edinburgh University, while the third member recommended that he should be given a formal warning with regard to his publication of material and public pronouncements; but any further public pronouncements on Brand's part should be vetted. The Tribunal, it appears unanimously, were of the view that if the Principal did not dismiss Brand, it would be wrong for him to remain a member of the Psychology Department.[44]

### III. THE PRINCIPAL'S DECISION AND THE APPEAL

The Tribunal submitted its Report and recommendations on 31 July 1997. Under the Universities Commissioners' Ordinance[45] and the Edinburgh SAM, the Principal had a number of options. He could dismiss the member of staff or impose a lesser sanction: advice about future conduct; a formal warning; suspension for up to three months on full pay; or a combination of these penalties. Sir Stewart Sutherland dismissed Brand on 8 August. His decision concluded that terminating the employment was the most appropriate course; there was 'no case for continuing to employ such a member of staff … effectively at the

---

[42] Confirmed in a telephone interview with an anonymous colleague, 22 August 2008.

[43] Paras 5.1–5.4 summarise the Tribunal's Conclusions.

[44] See Tribunal Report, paras 6.1–6.3.

[45] SI 2700/1992.

expense of others carrying out their duties and at a continuing cost
to what is, ultimately, the public purse'.[46] The most interesting paragraph of the decision stated that it had been made clear to Brand well
before the paedophilia email that 'he ... had responsibilities to act with
care, whether in a departmental, teaching or wider situation; advice he
apparently chose to ignore.' The inference may be drawn that at some
stage in 1996—most probably after Neil MacCormick's report on his
teaching—Brand had been told to avoid controversy. Sir Stewart's
statement also made it plain that his decision did not inhibit the proper
exercise of academic freedom, under which academic staff can undertake their own research and speak about their conclusions. He implied
that Brand's conduct fell outside the scope of this freedom.

Reaction to the Principal's decision was mixed. Dr Beloff was agree-
ably surprised that the University 'bit the bullet',[47] for any decision of
this kind was difficult for a university to take. Another departmental
colleague, however, told me that some people were surprised how
'harsh' the decision had been; in his view, even if Brand had remained
a member of the Department, 'we would have got on with him'[48]—
perhaps a surprising sentiment in view of the evidence given by many
colleagues at the Tribunal. Professor MacQueen, the member of the
Tribunal who had recommended a lesser sanction, was also surprised at
the decision to dismiss.[49] Brand himself thought he had an even chance
of 'getting off', as he put it.[50]

Brand exercised his right of appeal. It was heard on 10 and 11 February
1998 by T Gordon Coutts, QC, a senior advocate at the Edinburgh Bar,
with both the appellant and University being represented by advocates.
The appeal was robustly dismissed on 24 March.[51] Coutts held that
the Tribunal's conclusions on the first charge were fully supported by
its findings of fact. The appellant had shown a 'total disregard for his

[46] Edinburgh University News Release, 'Chris Brand Dismissed Following
Disciplinary Tribunal', 8 August 1997.

[47] Personal interview, 5 June 2009.

[48] Telephone interview, 22 August 2008.

[49] Personal interview, 4 June 2009. The Tribunal members expressed their views
and recommendations anonymously, but Professor MacQueen told me that he
favoured a lesser sanction than dismissal.

[50] Personal interview, 4 June 2009.

[51] Gordon Coutts, QC's ruling is summarised in an Edinburgh University News
Release of that day. Mr Brand himself sent me a copy of the entire ruling.

position as a responsible member of the University' by the manner in which he had expressed his views on paedophilia and the timing of their expression, 'when he was effectively on probation'. Coutts therefore accepted the University argument that Brand was on probation after Professor MacCormick's investigation earlier in 1996. With regard to the second charge, he accepted the Tribunal majority view that it was right to consider Brand's overall employment record when determining the appropriate course to be taken in respect to the first charge. He disagreed sharply with the view of the third member of the Tribunal, who had considered that previous episodes were spent and should not have been taken into account. In his view the appeal did not raise any issue of academic freedom. The appellant had not been dismissed for his views but 'because it was established that his behaviour made it impossible for him to work within a university Department'. That constituted 'good cause' for dismissal.

The appeal decision did not really add much to the lengthy consideration of the case by the internal University Tribunal. If anything, it appears rather less sympathetic to Brand's arguments. The most interesting point in the ruling was its adoption of the idea that Brand was 'on probation' from some time in 1996, with the implication that he had been warned or least strongly advised to refrain from all controversy. This phrase had not been used by the Tribunal, which instead had stated very clearly that Brand had not been given any formal warning.[52]

## IV. THE UNFAIR DISMISSAL CLAIM

Brand took proceedings for unfair dismissal, with some assurances from an American Internet entrepreneur, Jim Woodhill, that his costs would be met if his proceedings were unsuccessful.[53] But they were settled in October 1999 before the case came to the Edinburgh Employment Tribunal. The University agreed to pay Brand £12,000 in return for the abandonment of his claim. No 'gag' clause was included in the settlement, so Brand has been at complete liberty to discuss the affair since then.

---

[52] See para 4.2.1.

[53] Email communication to me on 2 September 2008. It is in fact very rare for costs to be awarded against an unsuccessful applicant to an employment tribunal.

310 The Chris Brand Case

In a news release disclosing the terms of the agreement,[54] the University denied that it had proposed the settlement. It decided to make an offer rather than contest the proceedings, largely to avoid imposing any further strain on the witnesses from the Department of Psychology who had given evidence at the internal Tribunal. Employment Tribunal proceedings would have required them to repeat this experience and would also have given Brand further publicity; media reports of the proceedings might not have been to the University's advantage.[55] The settlement also saved the University the financial costs of the proceedings, which would have amounted to several thousand pounds. Brand did not obtain the total maximum sum that the employment tribunal could have awarded; at that time this was in the region of £17,000,[56] so the settlement was almost certainly reasonable from the University's point of view. Brand was probably less satisfied; in the year or so after his dismissal he took on work as a waiter in hotels and restaurants in the Edinburgh area, though he was subsequently engaged to do research for Jim Woodhill.

If the case had come to the employment tribunal, one issue might have been whether the failure to give Brand any formal warning about his teaching style and general manner to students meant that his dismissal was unfair. Certainly, it would have been much better if he had been formally warned; in the absence of such a warning, he might well have concluded that there was no serious dissatisfaction with his teaching and that he had complied with any informal admonitions given by the Heads of Department with whom he had worked. But though desirable, a formal warning was not necessary if the employer could have shown that there was serious misconduct justifying dismissal.[57] Edinburgh University would have argued that the paedophilia email in the overall context justified that step.

---

[54] Edinburg University News Release, 'Statement on Chris Brand Case', 28 October 1999.

[55] Court Minutes for 8 November 1999, 50.

[56] Employment tribunals could award both a sum by way of compensation for an unfair dismissal (at that time the maximum for such an award was £12,000) and make a basic award calculated by reference to a claimant's age, length of service and salary at the time of dismissal: see S Deakin and GS Morris, *Labour Law*, 2nd edn (London, Butterworths, 1998) 495–97.

[57] Ibid, 484–85.

## V. ASSESSMENT OF ACADEMIC FREEDOM ASPECTS

It is difficult for a commentator at this distance from the events to pronounce a critical verdict on this case, unless there was an obvious and significant mistake in its disposition. I do not think there was any mistake of that kind, though it is possible to take issue with some of the finer points in the reasoning of the Tribunal. In particular, its handling of the second charge ('persistent refusal or neglect to perform duties') was unsatisfactory; the majority appears to have upheld this charge because the earlier incidents were assessed in the light of the paedophilia email.[58] But it seems wrong to have brought the email into consideration in determining the second charge. Rather, the earlier incidents—which had been dealt with informally—explained why the publication of the email had such a serious impact on Brand's relations with his colleagues. They were relevant to the disposition of the first charge, but not a good ground for upholding the second.

It is more helpful to bring out the academic freedom aspects of the affair and to examine its resolution from the perspective of that freedom. First, there is the significance of the content of Brand's lectures: was it material that Brand is a 'scientific racist' and that his lectures reflected that controversial and, to some people, offensive perspective? Academic freedom means that a university lecturer is entitled to choose how a course is taught and to select the materials for discussion. So I do not think it mattered that Brand lectured from the perspective of a 'scientific racist', nor it seems, did anyone think it mattered. But that does not mean that he was free to use the classroom to indoctrinate students or compel them to take a particular line if they were to pass their examinations. There is in fact no evidence that Brand did use his lectures in this way; indeed, a former student told me that it would be wrong to use the word 'indoctrination' in relation to his classes. Rather, it was a matter of 'balance'; controversial perspectives were, I was told, put forward as if only an idiot would take a different view.[59] Any lecturer, particularly one aware that his or her views are generally regarded as heterodox, should, for example, give students a balanced reading list, so they can form their own views, and should not silence

---

[58]  Tribunal Report, paras 4.2.28–4.2.29.
[59]  Telephone interview, 15 June 2009.

them if they adopt in classroom discussion a perspective other than his or her own.[60]

More concern was expressed at the Tribunal hearing about Brand's teaching style: the use of racist and sexist examples, offensive language and inappropriate references to sexuality.[61] Clearly, teaching freedom does not give an academic the right to use such language gratuitously or excessively, though equally it would be silly to expect a lecturer to avoid all four-letter words when teaching a course, say, on Erotic Literature.[62] All general statements of the rights and responsibilities of university teachers, for example, the 1940 Statement and Guidelines of the American Association of University Professors, emphasise that they should exercise their freedom responsibly, should be aware of the sensitivities of their students and should avoid giving gratuitous offence.[63] There is a difference between the appropriate academic challenge of students on the one hand and unnecessary provocation on the other. It is difficult to take issue with the Tribunal's treatment of this question. Perhaps the most perplexing aspect of this part of the affair was that Brand had never been given a formal warning about his teaching style.

The treatment of the email was the central issue in the case, for it was on the charge of publishing comments on paedophilia that Brand was 'convicted' of gross misconduct warranting his dismissal. The first point is that publication of the email should not be regarded as an exercise of academic freedom. It was not in any sense an academic publication issued only after scientific research. Further, its subject matter, as the Tribunal pointed out, was not one on which Brand claimed or had any particular expertise. But the arrest of an elderly physicist on charges of paedophilia was an event on which Brand, like everyone else, had a right to express his views; it was a matter of general public concern. Nor, as Brand has correctly argued, did the email encourage or incite paedophilia: it was never alleged that Brand had committed an incitement to crime. At most, the email could be regarded as condoning

---

[60] A former PhD student of Brand told me that he did provide balanced reading lists and allowed students to put forward different views: communication from Vincent Egan, 10 September 2009.

[61] Tribunal Report, paras 4.2.2–4.2.4.

[62] These questions have often arisen in US cases: see the discussion above in ch 6, s IV.

[63] See above ch 6, s II(B) and (C).

paedophilia. Brand was therefore exercising his right to freedom of speech or expression, a right enjoyed by all citizens, whether they are academics or not. That happens also to have been the view of Professor Neil MacCormick, albeit one expressed nearly twelve years after the events.[64]

If the paedophilia email had been sent by, say, a Professor of Greek with no track record in provoking controversy, pointing out that sexual relations with young boys were common from the sixth century BC in Ancient Greece,[65] it is hard to imagine that the authorities in Edinburgh would have taken any exception to it. But of course Brand had provoked controversy earlier in the year when he attempted to have his book published, and he had offended many students and colleagues for a number of years. Further, it seems likely that he had been strongly advised, if not formally warned, to avoid further controversy, following the inquiry into his teaching. On that footing the Tribunal's unanimous conclusion is understandable: Brand was recklessly or, on a stronger view, deliberately courting further controversy in a way that would destroy whatever chance there might have been of restoring good relations with his academic colleagues.

This leads to the final point: how far may a university take into account considerations of collegiality—the value of harmonious relations within a department, faculty or college—in determining whether a member of its staff may be disciplined for exercising his or her right to freedom of speech? It was pointed out in the previous chapter that extramural freedom of expression is far from absolute. Its exercise may be limited in the United Kingdom to protect good relations on campus between academic staff and students drawn from different racial or religious communities, at least when there is any serious danger of harassment or disorder.[66] University employers have legitimate interests, for example, in ensuring that a department works smoothly and that students from different backgrounds feel encouraged to apply for places and, once admitted to the university, are able to work there without hindrance.

---

[64] Email of Professor Neil MacCormick, 24 June 2008.
[65] The subject of the book KJ Dover, *Greek Homosexuality* (London, Duckworth, 1978).
[66] See above ch 9, s III.

Brand's exercise of his freedom of extramural expression should be seen in that context. That, of course, does not give departmental colleagues a right of veto. It would never be right to discipline an academic simply because a group of his or her colleagues disliked the unconventional views of that academic, whether on issues of university government or on a matter of general public concern.[67] Equally, a university is surely entitled in considering disciplinary charges against an academic to take account of persistent rudeness, provocation and offensive behaviour or language, if that leads to a total breakdown of relations within a department. Indeed, in the last analysis academic freedom itself may justify recourse to such considerations. For academic freedom rests on professional standards, formulated and applied within an academic community, and those standards require at least a minimal level of civility in dealing with colleagues and with students and respect for their dignity.

[67] The Tribunal explicitly rejected conceding such a 'right' to secure the dismissal of an awkward colleague: Report, para 4.2.25.

# Select Bibliography

THIS IS A select rather than comprehensive bibliography. It refers primarily to monographs and collections of essays or articles on academic freedom. A few leading law review and other journal articles are also referred to, while other references to helpful literature can be found in the notes to each chapter.

### GENERAL WORKS ON ACADEMIC FREEDOM AND ITS JUSTIFICATIONS

Two collections of essays explore the character of academic freedom and its justifications. *The Concept of Academic Freedom* (EL Pincoffs (ed), Austin, University of Texas, 1975) contains essays by leading American philosophers, including John Searle, Thomas Scanlon, Rolf Sartorius and Judith Thomson, examining the arguments for academic freedom and freedom of research and for academic tenure, which is regarded by many scholars in the United States as a necessary condition for the effective protection of these freedoms. The collection also includes a classic essay by William van Alstyne, 'The Specific Theory of Academic Freedom and the General Issue of Civil Liberty', in which the author distinguishes academic freedom from the general right to freedom of speech to which everyone is entitled. The second collection, *The Future of Academic Freedom* (L Menand (ed), Chicago, University of Chicago Press, 1996) looks at academic freedom from historical and cultural perspectives, as well as from that of philosophical principle. Ronald Dworkin's 'We Need a New Interpretation of Academic Freedom', discussed in chapter three of this book, is particularly rewarding.

Similar general issues have been explored in the UK context by Lord Robbins in his British Academy lecture 'Of Academic Freedom' (Oxford, Oxford University Press, 1966) and in chapter sixteen of the

Report of the Committee that he chaired, 'Higher Education' (Cm 2154, 1963). Graeme Moodie's 'On Justifying the Different Claims to Academic Freedom' (1996) 34 *Minerva* 129 provides an excellent discussion of leading questions of principle: what claims may be made to academic freedom and how may they best be justified? In *Academic Freedom* (London, Routledge, 1993) Conrad Russell, a distinguished historian, reviewed rather pessimistically the increasing limits on university autonomy that were imposed by the Conservative government in the 1980s and early 1990s. Gordon Graham's essays in *The Institution of Intellectual Values* (Exeter, Imprint Academic, 2005) share many of Russell's concerns; he calls on universities to defend the values of a liberal education, which had been given their classic statement by John Henry Newman in *The Idea of a University* (edited with an introduction by IT Ker, Oxford, Clarendon Press, 1976).

The tensions in Germany between academic (or scientific) freedom and the increasing political demands on universities are discussed by Dieter Grimm, formerly a judge of the German Constitutional Court, in *Wissenschaftsfreiheit vor neuen Grenzen?* (Göttingen, Wallstein, 2007). *Academic Freedom and the Inclusive University* (SE Kahn and D Pavlich (eds), Vancouver, University of British Columbia Press, 2000) examines, largely from a Canadian perspective, the tensions between academic freedom and the modern mass university.

## ACADEMIC FREEDOM IN THE UNITED KINGDOM

The evolution of the modern British university is explored in a number of books. Among the most illuminating are R Berdahl, *British Universities and the State* (Cambridge, Cambridge University Press, 1959); M Shattock, *The UGC and the Management of British Universities* (London, Society for Research into Higher Education and Open University Press, 1994); and for more recent developments, R Stevens, *University to Uni* (2nd edn, London, Politico's, 2005). All of these accounts shed light on the reasons for the decline of institutional academic freedom since the 1950s and 1960s. An optimistic view of the state of academic freedom in the immediate post-war period was taken by Lord Chorley in 'Academic Freedom in the United Kingdom' (1963) 28 *Law and Contemporary Problems* 647. But his view was probably much too complacent (see chapter four, note 2). Malcolm Tight edited a valuable collection of essays, written and published as the Education Reform Act 1988 was proceeding through Parliament: *Academic Freedom and Responsibility* (London, Society for Research into Higher Education and Open University Press, 1988).

There are very few specifically legal treatments of academic freedom in the United Kingdom. However, K McGuinness, *The Concept of Academic Freedom* (Lampeter, Edwin Mellen Press, 2002) must be mentioned: it canvasses many legal issues and discusses leading cases in a number of jurisdictions. Written when the author was at Bournemouth University, the book adopts a comparative approach with an extensive treatment of US decisions as well as of the much thinner English legal material. Regrettably, there is no Table of Cases. The most authoritative work on the law concerning UK universities is D Farrington and D Palfreyman, *The Law of Higher Education* (Oxford, Oxford University Press, 2006); chapter sixteen covers academic freedom and the autonomy of higher education institutions.

Three other sources should be mentioned. The journal *Education and the Law*, published from 1989, from time to time carries articles and notes on academic freedom and related issues concerning universities and their staff. Secondly, the Annual Reports of and other documents relating to the Council for Academic Freedom and Democracy (see chapter four, section II(D)) provide much information on the state of academic freedom during the 1970s and 1980s; they can be found in the Hull University Archives. A third useful source of information is the *Times Higher Education Supplement*, now simply *Times Higher Education* (*THE*).

ACADEMIC FREEDOM IN GERMANY

Analyses of the guarantee of *Wissenschaftsfreiheit* in Article 5(3) are to be found in the many commentaries on the Basic Law (*Grundgesetz*). A full treatment, published in 2004, is by Michael Fehling in the *Bonner Kommentar zum Grundgesetz* (now edited by R Dolzer, C Waldhoff and K Graßhof, Heidelberg, CF Müller), a loose-leaf publication updated every year. Also valuable is the discussion by Christian Starck in H von Mangoldt, F Klein and C Starck (eds), *Kommentar zum Grundgesetz* (5th edn by C Starck, Munich, Franz Vahlen, 2005). A shorter account is given by Hans Jarass and Bodo Pieroth in *Grundgesetz für die Bundesrepublik Deutschland* (9th edn, Munich, CH Beck, 2007) on pages 212–20. Two comprehensive books on higher education law should be mentioned.

The more academic is Werner Thieme's *Deutsches Hochschulrecht* (3rd edn, Cologne, Carl Heymanns, 2004), while *Hochschulrecht: Ein Handbuch für die Praxis* (M Hartmer and H Detmer (eds), Heidelberg, CF Müller, 2004) provides a detailed account of all aspects of the law affecting universities and their staff.

Three monographs should be mentioned: P Freundlich, *Wissenschaftsfreiheit und Bundesverfassungsgericht* (Göttingen University Dissertation, 1984) provides a stimulating examination of the constitutional background to the drafting of Article 5(3) and of the early decisions of the Constitutional Court on its interpretation. The books by Claus Dieter Classen, *Wissenschaftsfreiheit außerhalb der Hochschule* (Tübingen, JCB Mohr, 1994) and by Hans-Heinrich Trute, *Die Forschung zwischen grundrechtlicher Freiheit and staatlicher Institutionalisierung* (Tübingen, JCB Mohr, 1994) both emphasise that the freedom can be claimed outside universities, for example, by scientists working in research institutes. Trute also brings out the institutional and organisational dimensions to the freedom; it should not be seen simply as an individual right but requires the state to finance and organise research in accordance with the values underlying scientific freedom.

It is difficult to highlight periodical literature. In comparison with comparable American writing, articles in German legal journals are usually very short and concentrate on particular arguments. However, the essays by Martin Schulte, 'Grund and Grenzen der Wissenschaftsfreiheit', and Reinhard Hendler, 'Die Universität im Zeichen der Ökonomisierung and Internationalisierung', published in (2006) 65 *Veröffentlichungen der Vereinigung der Deutschen Staatsrechtlehrer* at pages 110 and 238 respectively are particularly worth reading; both raise a wide range of academic freedom issues of particular relevance in the age of the managed university.

## ACADEMIC FREEDOM IN THE UNITED STATES

A number of books published in the last few years discuss the current state of academic freedom in US universities. Robert O'Neil's *Academic Freedom in the Wired World* (Cambridge, MA, Harvard University Press, 2008) examines a number of legal questions, including the central question regarding how conflicts between the claims of universities and those of their academic staff are resolved. The implications of new technologies for academic freedom are also discussed. The book by Matthew Finkin and Robert Post, *For the Common Good* (Newhaven, Yale University Press, 2009) is concerned with professional academic freedom, the principles formulated and applied by the American Association of University Professors (AAUP). Two valuable collections of essays should be mentioned: *Academic Freedom after September 11* (B Doumani(ed), New York, Zone Books, 2006); and *Academic Freedom at the Dawn of a New Century* (E Gerstmann and M Streb (eds), Stanford, Stanford University Press, 2006). Amy Gajda, *The Trials of Academe: The New Era of Campus Litigation* (Cambridge, MA, Harvard University Press, 2009) expresses concern at the increasing volume of litigation involving academics, which in her view threatens academic freedom.

For an historical account of the development of the idea of academic freedom in the United States, reference should be made to W Metzger, *Academic Freedom in the Age of the University* (New York, Columbia University Press, 1955) and to the essay by the same author, 'Academic Freedom in Delocalized Institutions' in his collection *Dimensions of Academic Freedom* (Urbana, University of Illinois Press, 1969). Two polemical books should be mentioned. D Downs, *Restoring Free Speech and Liberty on Campus* (New York, Cambridge University Press, 2005) is very critical of university codes restricting free speech on campus. On the other hand, Stanley Fish, *Save the World On Your Own Time* (New York, Oxford University Press, 2008) argues with characteristic vigour that professors should stick to teaching and academic research and should not claim academic freedom to put the world to rights.

There is an enormous literature on the subject in US law school reviews and journals. Some articles amount in effect to monographs offering distinctive views on the scope and meaning of academic freedom. It is difficult to make a selection, but among the most valuable are the following: M Finkin, 'On "Institutional" Academic Freedom' (1983) 61 *Texas Law Review* 817; W Metzger, 'Profession and Constitution: Two Definitions of Academic Freedom in America' (1988) 66 *Texas Law Review* 1265; JP Byrne, 'Academic Freedom: A "Special Concern of the First Amendment"' (1989) 99 *Yale Law Journal* 251; D Rabban, 'A Functional Analysis of "Individual" and "Institutional" Academic Freedom under the First Amendment' (1990) 53 *Law and Contemporary Problems* 227; and J Areen, 'Government as Educator: A New Understanding of First Amendment Protection of Academic Freedom and Governance' (2009) 97 *The Georgetown Law Journal* 945.

Academic freedom is extensively discussed in the annual and special reports of the AAUP and in its journal, *Academe*, recent issues of which are accessible from the AAUP website, http://www.aaup.org.

SPECIAL TOPICS

**Academic Freedom and Intellectual Property**

An essential work is A Monotti with S Ricketson, *Universities and Intellectual Property: Ownership and Exploitation* (Oxford, Oxford University Press, 2003), which provides a comprehensive, theoretical and practical guide to the impact of intellectual property laws in the United Kingdom, the United States and Australia on academic freedom. C McSherry, *Who Owns Academic Work? Battling for Control of Intellectual Property* (Cambridge, MA, Harvard University Press, 2001) is a stimulating discussion of the conflicts between the claims of universities and of their academic staff to the ownership of copyright and patents, mostly in the context of US law.

**The Links between Universities and Business**

The impact on academic freedom of the growing links between universities and industry, in particular pharmaceutical companies, is the subject of J Washburn, *University Inc* (New York, Basic Books, 2006). As its subtitle, *The Corporate Corruption of Higher Education*, indicates, the book, written by a prominent freelance journalist, argues that universities have too often abandoned their traditional values in their pursuit of economic gain. A more measured but nevertheless critical account of university–business links is given by Derek Bok, a former President of Harvard, in *Universities in the Marketplace* (Princeton, Princeton University Press, 2003).

**Universities and Terrorism**

A short but vivid account and analysis of the first episode at Nottingham University, described in chapter eight, section II(D) of this book, is provided by Macdonald Daly and Sean Matthews (York, Zoilus Press, 2009).

# Index

visiting speakers 184, 281–282
von Humboldt, Wilhelm 11, 120, 123

warnings, formal 306–307, 309–310,
  312
Washburn, J 226–227, 229, 231–232

Weimar Constitution 121–122, 135
welfare 12, 71, 206, 208–209
*Wissenschaftsfreiheit see* scientific
  freedom

Yudof, MG 30, 54